PRIVATE LABELS, BRANDS, AND COMPETITION POLICY

The Changing Landscape of Retail Competition

PRIVATE LABELS, BRANDS, AND COMPETITION POLICY

The Changing Landscape of Retail Competition

Edited by

ARIEL EZRACHI

ULF BERNITZ

OXFORD
UNIVERSITY PRESS

OXFORD
UNIVERSITY PRESS

Great Clarendon Street, Oxford OX2 6DP

Oxford University Press is a department of the University of Oxford.
It furthers the University's objective of excellence in research, scholarship,
and education by publishing worldwide in

Oxford New York

Auckland Cape Town Dar es Salaam Hong Kong Karachi
Kuala Lumpur Madrid Melbourne Mexico City Nairobi
New Delhi Shanghai Taipei Toronto

With offices in

Argentina Austria Brazil Chile Czech Republic France Greece
Guatemala Hungary Italy Japan Poland Portugal Singapore
South Korea Switzerland Thailand Turkey Ukraine Vietnam

Oxford is a registered trade mark of Oxford University Press
in the UK and in certain other countries

Published in the United States
by Oxford University Press Inc., New York

First published 2009

British Library Cataloguing in Publication Data
Data available

Library of Congress Cataloging in Publication Data
Data available

Typeset by Cepha Imaging Private Ltd, Bangalore, India
Printed in Great Britain
on acid-free paper by
CPI Antony Rowe, Chippenham

ISBN 978-0-19-955937-4

1 3 5 7 9 10 8 6 4 2

PREFACE

Recent decades have witnessed a distinct increase in the sales and popularity of private labels. The growing market share of private labels has transformed the landscape of retail competition in developed countries. Major retailers are no longer confined to their traditional roles of purchasers and distributors of branded goods. By selling their own label products within their outlet they compete with their upstream brand suppliers on sales and shelf space.

The unique relationship and the increased role played by private labels raise fundamental questions as to their pro-, and possible anti-, competitive effects. This book sets out to explore the effects and the different variables which shape brand competition. Seventeen chapters, authored by leading academics, practitioners, and competition officials, produce a comprehensive picture of the law, policy, and economics in this area. Chapters in this book are grouped under seven sections which are described below.

The Nature of Retail Competition

The first section in this book outlines the forces which shape retail competition and the development and growth of private labels. Chapters in this section utilize empirical data and economic modelling to provide a comprehensive picture of brand competition and its effect on pricing, profit, innovation, and competition.

In Chapter 1 Richard Herbert considers the main drivers of private labels. The chapter illustrates the development of private labels and reflects on the influence of 'country' and 'consumer' factors on private labels and manufacturers' brands. The chapter also reflects on possible counter strategies which manufacturers may adopt when faced with powerful private labels.

Chapter 2 contrasts the business model of branded goods with that of own labels. In this chapter Dick Bell illustrates through case studies the relationship between retail concentration, the development of private labels, and the effect that each can have on the sales and profitability of manufacturers' brands.

In Chapter 3 Howard Smith and John Thanassoulis consider the economics of the bargaining interface between suppliers and retailers. The authors explore the economics of the branded good and private label supply chains and put forward a model for the analysis of the retailer-supplier interface for private label goods.

Market Power and the Abuse of Dominance

This second section explores the sources of market power in consumer goods industries and the way in which market power impacts on the retailers' position vis-à-vis suppliers and consumers and their ability to introduce private labels effectively.

In Chapter 4, Robert L Steiner presents a unified theoretical framework of market power in consumer goods industries. The chapter outlines the competitive process which results in horizontal and vertical market power. It reflects on the failure of traditional competition analysis to recognize the effects of non-horizontal market power on consumer goods industries.

In Chapter 5 Paul W Dobson and Ratula Chakraborty consider the possible effects generated by a growth in brands' and private labels' market power. The effects of brands and private labels on consumer welfare are illustrated using a range of scenarios including 'horrors' and 'heroes' categories.

In Chapter 6 Andrés Font Galarza reflects on the possible application of Article 82 of the EC Treaty to cases involving private labels and the relevant variables to be considered in such application. Both business-to-consumer and business-to-business scenarios are reviewed.

Vertical Restraints

The nature of private labels and brand competition is one in which horizontal, vertical, and market power issues are weaved into each other. These unique characteristics challenge the formalistic horizontal/vertical dichotomy and raise questions as to the adequate treatment of vertical agreements.

In Chapter 7 David Gilo explores the effects on competition generated by the participation of a retailer in the supplier's market via a private label and participation of a supplier in the retail market via dual distribution. The analysis is then considered in light of the European vertical block exemption.

In Chapter 8 Ioannis Lianos discusses the genealogy of the vertical/horizontal dichotomy in United States and in European Communities competition law.

The chapter reflects on the analysis of agreements concerning dual distribution and private labels.

In-store Competition, Pricing, Marketing, and Advertising

This section focuses on the way in which private labels affect in-store competition, marketing, and advertising. The discussion touches on the supply of shelf space, the choice of products and price, the retailer's access to confidential information, the use of look-alikes, and the impact private labels have on marketing and advertising.

In Chapter 9 Pieter Kuipers explores the effects of the retailers' combined customer-competitor role on the dynamics of in-store competition. The chapter reviews a range of variables which affect the nature of retail competition, among them the asymmetry of information and the control of access to consumers, shelf space, and product positioning.

In Chapter 10 Ulf Bernitz considers the practices of misleading packaging, copycats, and look-alikes. The chapter explores the functions of trademarks and brands and the application of the European Unfair Commercial Practices Directive.

In Chapter 11 Rainer Olbrich, Gundula Grewe, and Ruth Orenstrat review the development of private labels and their impact on in-store competition, price, choice, and consumer welfare. The analysis in this chapter is based on a wide ranging empirical study conducted in Germany.

In Chapter 12 Ariel Ezrachi and Jonathan Reynolds extend the debate and explore the competitive effects of advertising and promotion campaigns. The authors consider the unique characteristics of retailers' private labels and reflect on the interrelationship between advertising, brand competition, and private labels.

Retail Consolidation and the use of Remedies

This section reviews the way in which mergers, acquisitions, and buying alliances are appraised by the competition authorities. It explores the competitive effects of retail consolidation and the use of ex-ante and ex-post remedies to address concerns over increased market concentration, increased economic dependency and collusion.

In Chapter 13 John Ratliff outlines the range of considerations relevant in the review of mergers and acquisitions in the retail sector. The chapter also explores the assessment of the competitive impact of buying alliances and the application of the EC Horizontal Cooperation Guidelines.

In Chapter 14 Alastair Gorrie reviews the choice of remedies in merger cases involving the supermarkets and groceries sectors. The chapter also includes discussion of ex-ante remedies used in market investigations and the use of *ex-post* remedies in cases involving Article 81 EC and Article 82 EC.

On the control of merger and acquisitions also note Chapter 15 which explores, among others, the US merger regime.

The US Experience with Private Labels

In Chapter 15 Jeffrey Schmidt and Terry Calvani discuss the private label experience in the US. The chapter is divided into two parts. In the first part, private labels are considered in the context of the US merger regime, including a review of the US Horizontal Merger Guidelines and the definition of the market in cases surrounding private label products. The second part of the chapter considers the application of the US Robinson-Patman Act to cases involving private labels. This part focuses on the treatment of price discrimination and the interpretation of the 'like grade and quality' requirement under the Act.

On the US Horizontal Merger Guidelines also note discussion by Steiner in Chapter 4.

Consumer Welfare and Enforcement Standard

The last section focuses on the objectives of competition law and the protection of consumer welfare. It raises important questions as to the type of welfare which competition law should advance and the goals of enforcement. These policy considerations are reviewed in the area of private labels.

In Chapter 16 Philip Marsden and Peter Whelan consider the range of objectives EC competition law is set to protect. After exploring the positive and negative effects generated by private labels, the discussion focuses on the consumer welfare objective and its protection under European competition law.

In Chapter 17 Renato Nazzini reflects on the adequacy of traditional competition law in the area of private labels analysis. He considers the objectives of competition law and questions the view that competition law should seek to protect the 'competitive process' or maximise consumer welfare.

On consumer welfare also note the discussion by Dobson and Chakraborty in Chapter 5.

LIST OF CONTRIBUTORS

Dick Bell, Oxford Institute of Retail Management; Associate Fellow of Green Templeton College, Oxford.

Ulf Bernitz, Professor of European Law at Stockholm University; Director, The Wallenberg Foundation Oxford/Stockholm Association in European Law, Institute of European and Comparative Law, University of Oxford; Senior Associate Fellow, Pembroke College, Oxford.

Terry Calvani, Of Counsel, Freshfields Bruckhaus Deringer US LLP.

Ratula Chakraborty, Loughborough University Business School.

Paul W Dobson, Loughborough University Business School.

Ariel Ezrachi, Director, The University of Oxford Centre for Competition Law and Policy; Slaughter and May Lecturer in Competition Law, Oxford University; Fellow, Pembroke College, Oxford.

Andres Font Galarza, Partner, Mayer Brown LLP.

David Gilo, Associate Professor, Buchmann Faculty of Law, Tel Aviv University.

Alastair Gorrie, Partner, Orrick Herrington & Sutcliffe, London.

Gundula Grewe, University of Hagen, Germany.

Richard Herbert, Global Insight and Development Director at Europanel.

Pieter Kuipers, Deputy General Counsel Europe of Unilever.

Ioannis Lianos, City Solicitors Educational Trust Lecturer in European Union Law, UCL, Faculty of Laws; Jevons Institute of Competition Law and Economics.

Philip Marsden, Director and the Senior Research Fellow at the Competition Law Forum of the British Institute of International and Comparative Law.

Renato Nazzini, Reader in law, University of Southampton.

Rainer Olbrich, Chair of Marketing, University of Hagen, Germany.

Ruth Orenstrat, University of Hagen, Germany.

John Ratliff, Partner, Wilmer Cutler Pickering Hale and Dorr LLP ('WilmerHale'), Brussels.

Jonathan Reynolds, University Lecturer in Management Studies, Saïd Business School, University of Oxford; Fellow, Green Templeton College, Oxford; Academic Director, Oxford Institute of Retail Management.

Jeffrey Schmidt, Director, Bureau of Competition, Federal Trade Commission.

Howard Smith, Department of Economics, Oxford University.

Robert L Steiner, Economist, Senior Fellow, American Antitrust Institute (AAI), Washington, DC.

John Thanassoulis, Department of Economics, Oxford University.

Peter Whelan, Research Fellow at the Competition Law Forum of the British Institute of International and Comparative Law.

CONTENTS—SUMMARY

PART IV IN-STORE COMPETITION, PRICING, MARKETING, AND ADVERTISING

PART V RETAIL CONSOLIDATION AND THE USE OF REMEDIES

PART VI PRIVATE LABELS—THE US EXPERIENCE

PART VII CONSUMER WELFARE AND ENFORCEMENT STANDARD

CONTENTS

TABLE OF CASES

EUROPEAN UNION

European Court of Justice

Court of First Instance

Commission Decisions/Competition cases

NATIONAL CASES

FTC Review

TABLE OF LEGISLATION

EUROPEAN UNION

EC Treaty

Regulations

Directives

Commission Notices and Guidelines

NATIONAL LEGISLATION

Germany

United Kingdom

United States of America

INTERNATIONAL INSTRUMENTS

Part I

THE NATURE OF RETAIL COMPETITION

1

PRIVATE LABELS—WHAT DRIVES THEM FORWARD?

*Richard Herbert**

Private labels have existed for a long time, yet the significant development in their market shares is a relatively recent phenomenon. This chapter reviews the development of private labels, the sources for their success, and the possible counter strategies which may be adopted by branded manufacturers. The chapter builds on a study conducted in 2003 and 2004 by Europanel in partnership with Professor Jan-Benedict Steenkamp. The study set out to identify the reasons for the success of private labels to help branded manufacturers understand effective counter strategies. This study shows which country and category factors lie behind the size and development of private labels. It examines issues such as the

* Richard Herbert is the Global Insight and Development Director at Europanel.

impact of country culture, economic situation, and trade structure. It also looks at consumer perceptions at category level such as quality, value, trust, and marketing activity.

A. The Growth of Private Labels

Brands developed strongly in the 20th century. They provided a name to what were previously sold as unbranded products by local producers or farmers. These brand names and their manufacturers thereby provided quality assurance and trust to consumers.

Private labels have also existed for a very long time—in the UK, retailers like Marks & Spencer, Sainsbury's, and Tesco have sold private labels since the 1920s. But in overall market terms, these were much less developed until relatively recently.[1] Especially since the 1960s other retailers also started to introduce private labels. This development typically followed a route of 'generic' to 'quasi brand' to 'umbrella brand' to 'segmented brand'.[2] Each stage in turn developed the personality of private labels from basic low quality very low price; through middle of the road average quality and smaller price advantage; to the current segmented private labels which, in several countries, target specific sectors and can be higher quality and higher price.

This private label development is closely linked to the increased size and power of retailers. As retailers became larger, their competitive landscape required differentiation one from the other to drive footfall, loyalty, and hence profitability. This gave the retailers greater power and, in a circular way, brought even more emphasis on private labels.[3] One reason for these patterns is that private label shares are much higher within the larger retailers.[4] As these retailers themselves have grown, then so have private labels within the total market. For example, if a retailer has 50 per cent of its business in private labels and the market share of the retailer rises from 10 per cent to 30 per cent, the total country private label share itself increases by 10 percentage points.[5]

---

[1] For general background, see Europanel website: <http://www.europanel.com> accessed 2 May 2008.

[2] For further reading see: J Quelch and D Harding, 'Brands versus Private Labels: Fighting to Win' [1996] 74 *Harvard Business Review* 99; J-B E M Steenkamp and M G Dekimpe, 'The Increasing Power of Store Brands: Building Loyalty and Market Share' [1997] 30 *Long Range Planning* 917; T A Henderson and E A Mihas, 'Building Retail Brands' [2000] *McKinsey Quarterly* 110.

[3] Ibid.

[4] Source: Europanel.

[5] Source: Europanel.

The real explosion in private labels has occurred quite recently. In the UK, private labels had reached a share of 19 per cent by 1970—it is now about double that level;[6] in Germany, it was just 12 per cent in 1975 and is now nearly three times the size; in Spain, the share was just 7 per cent in 1990 and is now some 30 per cent; whilst in Eastern Europe, private labels did not exist even in the late 1990s and now have overall market shares of some 20 per cent.[7]

Naturally there are many parts of the world where this phenomenon remains under-developed such as in Italy, Russia, Asia, Latin America, and even in the USA relative to Europe. Here the power of individual retailers is far less developed due either to the strength of traditional trade outlets (small corner stores) or to the dispersed geographical nature of the market.[8] Therefore, globally private labels still represent less than 12 per cent of the packaged grocery market.

Compare this with Western Europe at 28 per cent or individual countries at over 35 per cent; this shows the scale of the continued threat to manufacturer brands. Witness the more recent trends, particularly in economies where retailers have increased their size and power, and we see private label shares catching up with those seen in Germany, France, and the UK. Figure 1.1 illustrates the particular case in Eastern Europe.

Another aspect of the private label expansion has been the significant variation between the different parts of the packaged grocery business. Size and growth has been much more pronounced in food, drink, and household categories and much lower in personal care. This is due partly to consumer perceptions regarding these categories and partly to category characteristics.[9] The technology needed to create effective personal care products is perceived to be more difficult and also personal care as a category has been underdeveloped in the large grocery retailers.

With such significant increases in market share, private labels have had a huge impact on manufacturer brands. Overall in countries like Germany and the UK, well over 30 per cent of the available category sales have been lost and are effectively no longer available to manufacturer brands.[10]

---

[6] Source: Europanel.

[7] Source: Europanel.

[8] Although Wal-Mart leads the US market, its market share is lower than the number one retailer in many other countries and, additionally, its private label shares are also lower.

[9] See: S Burton and others, 'A Scale for Measuring Attitude Toward Private Label Products and an Examination of Its Psychological and Behavioral Correlates' [1998] 26 *Journal of The Academy of Marketing Science* 293.

[10] Source: Europanel. Also see: S J Hoch, 'How Should National Brands Think about Private Labels?' [1996] 37 *Sloan Management Review* 89.

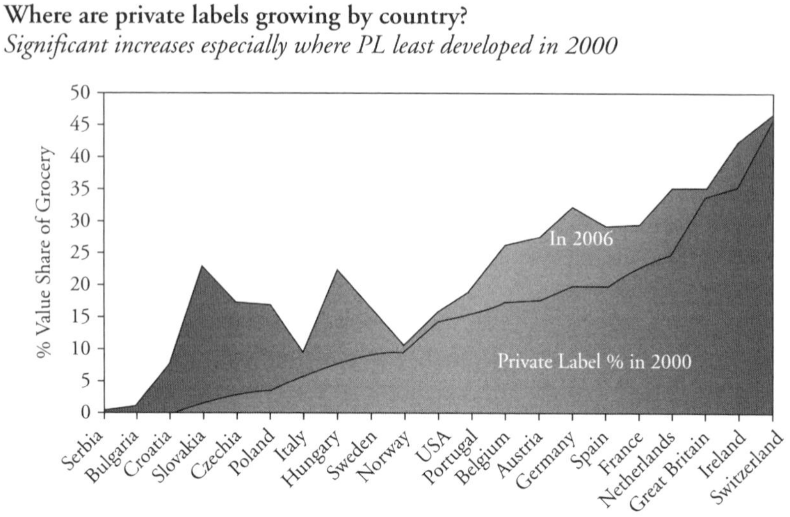

Figure 1.1: *Source*: Europanel (© Europanel)

The effect has been most devastating on those smaller brands that have had less investment and have less differentiation in the marketplace. Brand leaders have been impacted much less by the expansion of private labels, at least in market share terms, and number 2 brands less than number 3 brands, and so on. Many brands, caught in the middle in this way, have disappeared with their manufacturers turning to private label production as a way out. These effects have been consistent across countries and can be expected in any country where private label production is still to develop. The dangers remain, in these instances, most particularly for those smaller brands.[11]

Today, especially where retailers are most powerful such as in the UK, private labels act as brands in their own right. Effectively they are not private labels any more but retailer brands promoting the character and personality of the retailer itself. And, of course, within category and retailer, the private label is the number one brand!

These 'retailer brands' are segmented with low price generic offerings, middle-of-the-road standard products, and targeted high quality options. In the latter category, there are products aimed at specific consumers—children's ranges, healthy ranges, additive free, organic, and premium. This enables retailers to use their private labels to attract and cover many demographic segments, age ranges,

[11] Hoch (n 10).

and household sizes and types. And they have done this successfully. Take the case of the premium ranges, where retailers have successfully targeted high-end consumers with matching attitudes and have achieved price levels much higher than the leading manufacturer brand.[12]

B. The Study—What Drives Private Label Success?

In 2003 and 2004, Europanel in partnership with Professor Jan-Benedict Steenkamp,[13] set out to identify what lies behind and what drives private label success. The aim was to help manufacturers to understand these drivers in order to implement relevant and effective counter strategies.

The study was based on 33 countries in Western Europe, Eastern Europe, USA, Latin America, and South East Asia. It was based on a wide range of fast-moving consumer goods categories in the food, beverages, household, and personal care fields. Dependent on purchase data availability between 40 and 100 (average 60) such categories were included in each country.

The datasets were based on two sources. Firstly Europanel represents the international interests of the continuous household panels operated by GfK and TNS. These sources provided the quantitative actual purchasing information trends required by category—annual values, private label shares, manufacturer brand shares, individual retailer shares, the number of buyers, and their demographic profiles. Secondly, a separate household attitudinal study in each country was fielded. This was designed to identify attitudes to private labels in the same set of categories contained in the household panel datasets. These attitudinal surveys were based on nationally representative samples of main household purchasers and were mostly conducted via the internet. To qualify, the respondent must have been a regular buyer of products in the category.

The project framework was based on the fact that private label shares vary considerably across four dimensions—these are the four C's of Country, Category, Consumer, and Customer (retailer).[14] By correlating consumer attitudinal scores to private label shares on these four dimensions, the study identified which consumer attitudes are most closely related to private label success. Hence, this

[12] Source: Europanel. Also see: M Corstjens and R Lal, 'Building Store Loyalty Through Store Brands' [2000] 37 *Journal of Marketing Research* 281; K L Ailawadi, S A Neslin and K Gedenk, 'Pursuing the Value-Conscious Consumer: Store Brands Versus National Brand Promotions' [2001] 65 *Journal of Marketing* 71.

[13] See: N Kumar and J-B E M Steenkamp, *Private Label Strategy: How to Meet the Store Brand Challenge* (1st edn, 2007, Harvard Business School Press).

[14] Framework defined by Steenkamp (n 2).

could determine which elements drive consumer purchasing behaviour and so provide guidance on actionable counter strategies.

Although the framework was based on four C's, the focus was on two of them—Country and Category. The reasons for this lie in the results and will be discussed later.

By category

At the category level, the attitudinal questionnaire items were based on two sources: firstly previously published academic scales and, secondly, on the results of a similar project run in February 2001 for a specific client, covering France, Germany, Italy, Spain, and the UK. The study identified, from the literature, relevant constructs regarding consumer choice in a category.[15]

On price-quality perceptions, the study examined the quality gap between brands and private labels, the value gap between brands and private labels, and the extent to which consumers believe there is a relationship between price and quality. Regarding the importance of the category to the consumer, the study looked at the level of consumer involvement or interest, the perception of product performance risk and social symbolism (does the choice of product say something about you). For brand trust perceptions, this included the trust gap between brands and private labels and the trust in manufacturer brands.

The topic of consumer buying in the category was covered by the desire for variety, the importance to the overall household budget, and the extent of impulse buying. Marketing activities included the perceived advertising intensity, the perceived level of brands' innovation activity, and perceived promotional intensity. Finally the study identified consumer production perceptions including the extent of packaging similarity between brands and private labels, how difficult it is to manufacture products in the category, and the extent to which it is believed that private labels are produced by brand manufacturers.

To measure each construct the study used previously validated scales, consisting of more than one statement, to arrive at the score for each attitude. For example, two statements were used and then averaged for promotional intensity:

Q38 There is always a special offer on (XXXXX).
Q54 It is easy to find a special offer on (XXXXX).

15 For more details see: Burton and others (n 9) and P S Richardson, A K Jain, and A Dick, 'Household Store Brand Proneness: A Framework' [1996] 72 *Journal of Retailing* 159.

By country

The 'category' dimension, as described above, used a specific and tailored attitudinal questionnaire. The analysis at the country level, however, was based on the examination of many published factors and these were narrowed down to the following seven relevant factors.

Firstly on national culture,[16] this included *power distance* or the extent to which the less powerful accept and expect that power is distributed unequally (source Schwartz[17]) and *uncertainty avoidance* or society's tolerance for uncertainty and ambiguity (source Schwartz). Then on the economy, the study considered *socio-economic modernity*, a measure of a country's development based on economic, technical, and health indices (source AiMark[18]). It also considered *competitive environment* in terms of a measure of competitiveness (e.g. infrastructure, government, and business efficiency) (source IMD[19]). Lastly on retail environment, this included *concentration* measured by the market share of the top five retailers (source Europanel[20]); *international retailers* in terms of the market share of international retailers (source Europanel); and *hard discounters* via their market share (source Europanel).

C. Results and Recommendations— At Country Level

The major outcome of this part of the project concerned managing expectations. This is because many of the key reasons why private labels are more successful in one country than another are outside manufacturer control and influence.

Retail environment

Three drivers of why private labels have higher market shares in some countries and less in others relate to retail structure.

First, trade concentration supports private label development. Where there are fewer key retailers and where they have become larger, this leads to increased

16 For more details see: G Hofstede, *Culture's Consequences: Comparing Values, Behaviors, Institutions and Organizations Across Nations* (2nd edn, 2001, Sage Publications).

17 S Schwartz, 'Beyond Individualism/Collectivism: New Cultural Dimensions of Value', in *Individualism and Collectivism: Theory, Method, and Applications* (1994, Sage), 85–119).

18 A measure created by Aimark which is a cooperation between Europanel and an academic network under the leadership of Professor J-B Steenkamp.

19 IMD Yearbook—from the global business school based in Lausanne.

20 Europanel is jointly owned by GfK and TNS. Data is sourced from these companies' consumer panels.

retailer power and competition. Retailers then have the size, scale, and image to develop their own labels and this is used as one of the major ways in which they can differentiate themselves one from the other.

Second, this is taken to another level when the main retailers in a country are successful internationally. In such circumstances, retailers already have the size and scale to have developed their own label ranges. As they develop their size and image in a new country, they can introduce and build these points of difference.

The third retail trade factor that lies behind private label size and share is the development and strength of discounters. These types of retailer contribute to the development of private labels in two ways. In themselves their product range is very highly or even exclusively private label. Hence their growth as retailers plays a significant part in the overall private label share increase. Their second effect is seen at competing 'mainstream' retailers who want to deny these discounters room for growth, by competing at the value end of the market. This competitive response is largely geared at private labels and again provides more impetus to these products and the importance of price.

Economy

There is no doubt that the economic environment plays a role in the development of private labels. A long term study of the relationship between private label shares and economic swings has shown how downturns in the economy are linked to increases in private labels. In addition, the study finds that this increase is not subsequently lost.[21]

In this study (see section B above), we find two 'economic development' factors to be significant in relation to the variance in private label shares across countries. The conditions for private labels are enhanced where societies are modern and competitive. Modernity means economic, technological, and health 'well-being', whilst competitive means country and government infrastructure and efficiency.

Culture

Finally to see why private labels have developed more in some countries, the study looked at national cultural characteristics. Two of these in particular help to

[21] L Lamey and others, 'How Business Cycles Contribute to Private Label Success: Evidence from the United States and Europe' [2007] 71 *Journal of Marketing* 1.

provide an environment conducive to private labels. Firstly there is the tolerance of uncertainty. This is important because the purchase of private labels is a risk, at least initially, compared with the ingrained belief in and perceived quality of brands. Therefore, the more a society can handle risk, the higher its private label share.

Similarly private labels thrive where societies are more egalitarian. Brands can confer a 'status' on their purchaser, and where societies are more hierarchical, showing that 'status' is a much more important consideration. But in egalitarian societies 'status' has much lesser importance and so the purchasing of private labels is more acceptable.

Summary—country level

There is little a manufacturer can do directly about most of these factors that underpin the general level of private label shares in a country. They cannot influence the retail trade structure or the general economic conditions or the cultural traits of a country. However, it is important to know these drivers in order to manage expectations, to identify when pressures from private label will be at their highest, and to develop strategies to offset the retailer and economic effects.

For example, during economic downturns, a manufacturer would be advised not to reduce marketing spend and impetus. This would only serve to heighten the positive effect on private labels. Additionally, a manufacturer would be advised to work with retailers to help them provide differentiation through brands.

In addition, it is vital to understand the cultural values in a country. These can then be used to define communication strategies that help counter private labels in each country. One example would be emphasizing the risk inherent in making the wrong choice in countries which have a more conservative attitude towards taking chances. Another approach would be promoting the 'status' of buying a brand in hierarchical cultures.

D. Results and Recommendations—Category Level Globally

Whatever the underlying private label shares in a country driven by its trade structure, economic environment, and culture, there remains considerable variation in private label success within a country. This variation is most pronounced between different categories, although it is also seen between different retailers and to a degree, but less so, between different consumers.

Understanding why there is this degree of disparity between private label shares and what consumer perceptions drive these, provides manufacturers with the ammunition for counter strategies. In this case, unlike the factors at country level, the elements driving private label success by category are ones that are largely within the control and influence of brand manufacturers.

The study analysed these variants in two ways. Firstly the scores by category for each consumer perception were correlated with the private label shares by category. This identified the strength and direction of the relationship. Then categories were ranked top to bottom for each consumer perception according to their score. The private label shares for the top 50 per cent of categories were then compared against the bottom half.

Based on these analyses, the study identified six global factors which correlate most strongly with private label success. These six and combinations of them should form the basis for any brand strategy in relation to private label competition. See Figure 1.2

Advertising intensity

The survey questionnaire asked consumers to rate the amount of advertising by brands in each category. Where these (perceived) advertising intensity scores are low, private label shares are significantly higher. Looking at the bottom group of categories (with the lowest advertising intensity scores) private label shares are 77 per cent higher than in the top group. The amount of, and intensity of advertising is certainly an activity within manufacturers' direct control.

Relationship between four key factors and private label share within a category
For example: If perceived adspend is low, PL share is 77% higher

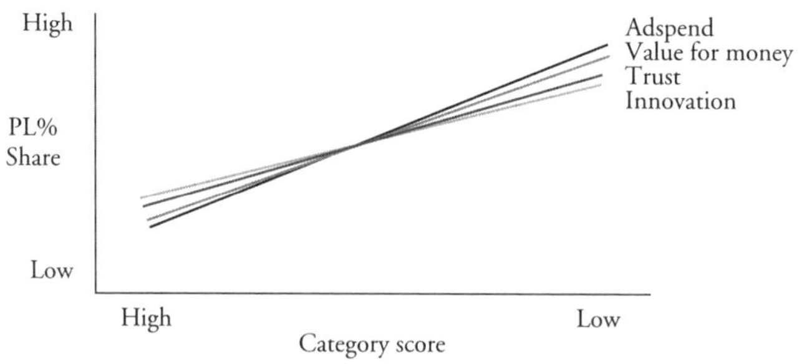

Figure 1.2: *Source*: Europanel/AiMark (© Europanel)

Value for money

Consumers were asked about their perceptions of brand value for money compared with private labels in each category. Again the analysis compared the categories in the bottom 50 per cent of scores with those in the top 50 per cent. Private label shares are 76 per cent higher where brands are not seen to offer much, if any, advantage in terms of value for money. Whilst this is a comparative measure, manufacturers can still have a significant influence on the standing of their brands here. The approach to communication, the words and visuals used, product quality, quality and extent of innovation, pricing and so on—these all have a significant bearing on the perception of relative value.[22]

Brand trust

This looked at the extent to which consumers put their trust in brands and how far brands deliver on their promises compared with private labels. This is the third most important global factor underpinning private label success within a category. In this case, the bottom scoring 50 per cent of categories on this attribute show private label shares which are 61 per cent higher than the top scoring categories. Like value for money, this is largely within manufacturers' control. It must be a key principle for any brand that consumers should be confident in their brand choice and that the product will live up to their expectations. If not, there is not much of a barrier to switching to private label.

Innovation intensity

Here the study looked at consumer perceptions of the amount of new product activity within each category. Again this proves to be a significant influencer on the size and category share of private label and is another issue fully within manufacturers' direct influence. In those categories in the bottom half where the levels of new product activity are seen to be low, private label shares are 56 per cent higher on average. The lack of activity and investment in this critical area directly leads to increased direct competition from private labels.

Packaging

Respondents in the survey were asked about how far brands and private labels within a category look the same. Therefore this examines the rather more contentious issue of look-alike packaging which in turn encourages belief that

---

[22] For further reading see: Ailawadi, Neslin, and Gedenk (n 12). V A Zeithaml, 'Consumer Perceptions of Price, Quality, and Value: A Means-End Model and Synthesis of Evidence' [1988] 52 *Journal of Marketing* 2.

private labels are made by the major brand manufacturers. This study provides clear evidence that private labels are significantly more successful where packaging is perceived to be similar. Manufacturers must defend their intellectual property in this regard and cannot allow situations where consumers can confuse brands and private labels and their provenance. Additionally brand manufacturers should ensure that consumers understand that they do not produce private labels for any retailer. Again, there are direct and specific actions that can be taken, such as statements on the product, in communications, or on delivery vehicles.[23]

Quality

This identified the degree to which consumers believe that the quality of brands was better than private labels in each category. This is the last of the top six factors, but again private labels are much more successful where consumers believe there is little to choose in quality between brands and private labels. Since their outset, the heritage of manufacturer brands is the communication and delivery of good consistent product quality. The loss of this major attribute is very worrying, especially to see that in many categories private labels are viewed as having higher product quality than brands!

To summarize at the global level, private labels are significantly more successful in categories where there is less brand advertising; less brand innovation; poor perception of brand quality and value for money; potential confusion because brands and private labels look the same; and, critically, where consumers have lost their trust in brands.

These findings may at first reading seem very obvious. But if this is the case, then why do so many categories in so many countries suffer from a situation where private labels are growing or have high share levels and outperform manufacturer brands? If the reasons are obvious, why are manufacturers allowing brands to lose their leadership and reasons for being? In all cases, as above, there are many actions and counter strategies that can be adopted which will make life that much more difficult for private labels to succeed.[24]

Among these one would recommend considering everything that is done in relation to private labels and not just branded competitors. Ensure that private labels are always part of your research and testing. Maintain marketing expenditure

---

[23] For further reading see: J-N Kapferer, 'Stealing Brand Equity: Measuring Perceptual Confusion Between National Brands and Copycat Own-Label Products' [1995] 23 *Marketing and Research Today* 96.

[24] Hoch (n 10).

by advertising and innovating more and, critically, more cleverly. Consider the elements of differentiation, quality, value, and trust in all brand communication, making sure that these messages can be seen and heard. Communicate, communicate, and communicate on the quality and value of the brand. But most importantly, deliver on the promises.[25]

E. Results and Recommendations—Category Level Locally

Having identified the most important consumer perceptions globally, the study then analysed variance by country as well as the specific performance of each category at this local level.

Country variance

As detailed above, this study into private label success examined many other consumer perceptions. Beyond the six most important global factors, the same correlation and top versus bottom analysis led to the identification of a number of other factors which, although less important across all countries, are important in individual instances. These factors include the following which enhance private labels' chance of success: *low social symbolism* or where consumers do not believe that purchasing brands in a category says something about the buyer; low *promotional intensity* in terms of the perception of the frequency of promotions in each category; where there is the belief that the major brand manufacturers make private labels; low *performance risk* such that consumers don't believe there is a real risk, performance or financial, if choosing the wrong product in a category; and low *involvement* in relation to the importance or relevance of the category to the consumer. See Figure 1.3.

Naturally every country has slightly varying ratings and importance for each of the perceptions but there are some cases where the differences are more significant. For example, in Sweden social symbolism is very important. On the other hand the belief in Spain that branded manufacturers make private labels is more significant. By contrast, performance risk is a more important driver in Poland and Brazil.

Therefore, to fine-tune counter strategies, these variations can be important, especially for the emphasis and nuances in communication.

25 P Barwise and S Meehan, *Simply Better: Winning and Keeping Customers by Delivering What Matters Most* (1st edn, 2004, Harvard Business School Press).

Drivers of PL at category level differ by country
global aggregation hides country variance

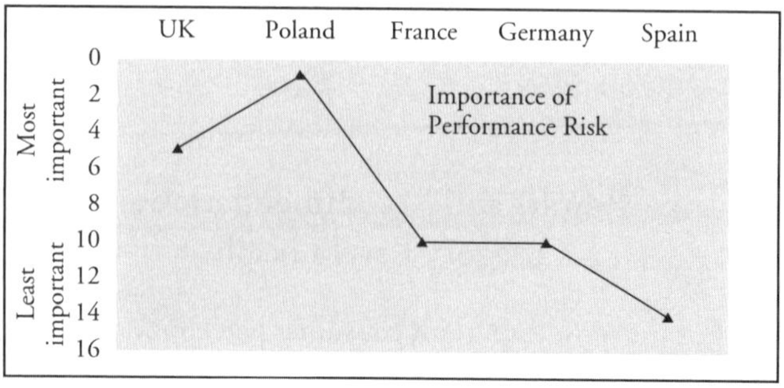

Figure 1.3: *Source*: Europanel/AiMark (© Europanel)

Category performance

For individual categories, the relative private label shares between countries also vary enormously. Using yogurt as an example may be illustrative. In the market for yogurt, private label share is 26 per cent in the UK, 39 per cent in Germany, and 46 per cent in France. Taking into account the underlying private label shares in a country, these shares index from 73 in the UK (27 per cent lower than total grocery) to 166 in France (66 per cent higher than average). Indexing the yogurt private label shares within retailers in France against the average grocery private label share for that retailer reveals variation from 72 to 108.

Hence it is very important to understand the competitive structure, the importance and role of the category, and, critically, its performance on the key perceptions that drive private label success. One size does not fit all and what and how to act will vary considerably by category, from country to country, and from retailer to retailer. Taking the yogurt and other examples further, it can be seen how important the differing perceptions are. The perception of 'value for money' for yogurt brands in France and Germany is low, whilst in the UK it is much higher. For laundry detergents, brand trust is very low in Germany and high in France (see Figure 1.4). The consequent difference in private label shares (high in Germany, low in France) is not surprising. With potato crisps, the perceived level of advertising expenditure in France is amongst the lowest whilst in the UK it is amongst the highest. The relative private label share in France is twice that of the UK.

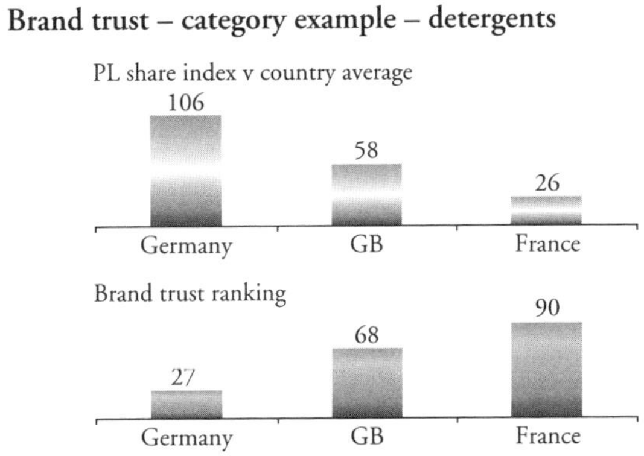

Figure 1.4: *Source:* Europanel/AiMark (© Europanel)

For each category across countries or for key categories within a country, this type of performance measurement and monitoring can help to guide strategy and priorities.

F. Counter Strategies in Action—A Case Study

Naturally, re-evaluation of strategy and a focus on private labels as a core or most important competitor, costs money. It is important to show that there are examples of well run brands in competitive categories that have withstood the pressures from private labels and even developed themselves.

One excellent example is Walkers crisps within the potato crisps category in the UK. At the time of our study, Walkers had increased their category share from 27 per cent in 2002 to 32 per cent in 2004.[26]

Looking at the scores for the potato crisps category on the main consumer perceptions in the study, this showed the category to be at the top or very close to the top compared with other categories on all the key perceptions in the UK. Walkers, as the brand leader, was doing an excellent job of communicating through advertising, innovation, quality, value, differentiation, and trust.

26 Source: Europanel.

These values are clear. They have recognizable distinctive packaging, quite different from private labels. They have a range of different products catering for different needs—in addition to standard crisps there was Salt n Shake, Lite Bites, and Crinkle Cut. They had also been extremely active in new products, especially at the premium end of the market with Sensations and with short-run seasonal flavours.

Through effective promotions and pricing, they had also remained competitive, and because of the fast throughput Walkers' reputation for freshness was maintained.

One of the most impressive aspects of Walkers at that time was their consistent advertising and communication strategy. Using footballer Gary Lineker and playing on his very clean reputation (never booked or sent off!) they had aired 25 different commercials over a ten-year period! All ads focusing on quality, desirability, and recognition.

It is clear from this case study that Walkers had marketed their brand highly effectively in relation to branded competition but also, and critically, against private labels. They had maintained a consistent high brand value approach and reaped the long-term share benefits.[27]

G. The Other Two C's—Consumer and Customer

As is clear above, the focus of this study was on country and category. The results on the other two dimensions are the reason for this concentration.

The analysis showed that all consumers across different demographic segments and types buy private labels and that there is no significant variation at the macro level. The attitudes that they hold to brands in relation to private labels by category are much more important.

This is also true at customer (or retailer) level. The consumer perceptions that lie behind the variation between categories are also true by retailer. The perceptions of value, quality, trust, and so on of the individual retailer private labels are a key determinant of success and failure.

[27] Further reading on effective brand management: J-N Kapferer, *The New Strategic Brand Management: Creating and Sustaining Brand Equity Long Term* (2nd edn, 2004, Kogan Page).

H. Conclusions and Recommendations

This global study establishes significant links in the relationship between consumer attitudes and the success of private label as measured by consumer purchasing. As a result, it also points the way for manufacturers to adopt effective counter strategies.

Private labels have developed particularly since the 1960s in the larger countries of Western Europe. But even here, the scale of this development has been especially marked from the 1990s onwards as a result of increased retailer concentration, competition, and power. The speed of development in Eastern Europe to over 20 per cent market share in less than ten years is a demonstration of the threat that private labels continue to pose to manufacturer brands globally. Bearing in mind that the worldwide private label share is still less than 12 per cent, there is a huge remaining danger to branded business and this menace cannot be ignored.

The development of discounters in more recent years in Europe amply demonstrates the key direction for manufacturers. These retailers focus on price, and in Germany the competitive reaction from other retailers has been price. As a result, price has been promoted by all as the key determinant of consumer choice and because discounters do this best, they have won. By contrast the main UK retailers, Tesco, Sainsbury's, et al., were also threatened by these low-price retailers. Their reaction was one of value and service—a counter strategy rather than a copycat strategy. In this case, the mainstream retailers won.

As described above, private labels remain a very serious force globally in relation to branded business. And private labels are becoming even more competitive by stealing traditional branded territory. They are not just competing through value but increasingly through high quality and premium products.[28]

These are excellent lessons for brand manufacturers. The message is about counter and not copycat strategies that value rather than devalue the brand. At a country level, when economic times are bad, manufacturers should not react by reducing marketing spend as this serves to support private label development. And manufacturers should utilize national cultural characteristics in the way in which their brands are communicated. Manufacturers should also understand the impact of increased retailer concentration and try to work with retailers on appropriate differentiation. There is evidence that, to maximize returns, retailers need to have a

[28] Corstjens and Lal (n 12).

balanced brand and private label strategy.[29] Consumers who spend heavily on private labels are not the most profitable or revenue generating for the retailer.

Within each country there are very clear guidelines on effective brand marketing. Activity through advertising, consistent new product introduction, and effective promotional strategies are a first pre-requisite. These activities should always be checked for content in comparison with private label competition—do they provide clear evidence of brand benefits, quality, and value? They should never be purely price driven and thereby play directly into the hands of private label. Communications must always enhance brand trust and the brand itself should always live up to its consumer promises.

There are particularly strong competitive actions that manufacturers can take to mitigate the effects of private label. This study would support a strategy where branded manufacturers do not make private label products themselves and state to consumers that this is the case. A very significant number of consumers think that private labels are made by brand manufacturers and this has a significant positive effect on the sales of private label.

In this regard, any confusion of provenance driven by packaging similarity must be vigorously pursued by brand owners. Protect the brand equity, look, and feel, and get a reputation in the industry for being prepared to take legal action if necessary.

Finally, these strategies work. The Walkers case study discussed above shows this. Another example may be found in the market for fruit juices, until recently a highly commoditized category dominated by price and private labels. Today the development of branded Smoothies and premium fruit and vegetable juices shows what can be achieved.

---

29 K Ailawadi and B Harlam, 'An Empirical Analysis of the Determinants of Retail Margins: The Role of Store Brand Share' [2004] 68 *Journal of Marketing* 147.

2

THE BUSINESS MODEL FOR MANUFACTURERS' BRANDS

*Dick Bell**

A. Introduction

Brands are unique products, differentiated from their competitors and thus not directly substitutable. Brands, through marketing, appeal directly to the consumer or purchaser and thus reach over the retail trade. The process of marketing, involving product development, advertising, and distribution, results in manufacturers' brands incurring a high level of non-variable cost. A consequence is that brand profit rises disproportionately to an increase in sales value and similarly falls by a greater percentage following a reduction in sales.

* The author is a member of the Oxford Institute of Retail Management and an Associate Fellow of Templeton College, Oxford.

The development of manufacturers' brands was in its heyday when the process of retail distribution was atomistic. Today, in the early 21st century, there is an oligopolistic structure of retailing where each chain positions itself as a retail brand and a champion of the consumer. In most countries of Europe, grocery retailing is dominated by four or five chains, and a clash of the titans now exists between large retailers such as Tesco, Carrefour, and Rewe, and multinational manufacturers such as Unilever, Nestlé, and Proctor and Gamble. Distribution of manufacturers' brands is no longer determined solely by an eager sales force, nor by high levels of consumer sale. Retail selling space is controlled with military precision by large retailers using category management techniques. The large retail chain offers alternatives to the manufacturers' brands in the form of their private label products and can refuse to stock, or de-list, components of the manufacturers' brands. Sudden changes in the range stocked by an oligopolistic retailer, particularly when unforeseen, can significantly affect the sales and consequentially the profit, of the brand of a manufacturer.

This chapter describes the nature of a manufacturer's brand and the effects on profitability of changes in volume that may result from the concentrated structure of grocery distribution. A definition is offered of a manufacturer's brand and a description provided of the key elements, and their interrelationship, that are involved in managing a brand. The business model of a manufacturer's brand is explained showing the dynamic effect of changes in volume upon profitability and the impact that innovation can have on changing the competitive balance. Finally, by way of two case studies the relationship is explored between retail concentration, the development of private label, and the effect that each can have on the sales and profitability of manufacturers' brands.

B. Definition of a Brand

The European Brands Association (AIM)[1] provides the following definition of a brand:

> A manufacturers brand is developed to meet identified consumer needs, carries an individual name and has a distinctive packaging design. The brand, and the product it embodies is unique. Consumers recognize the attributes of a successful brand and identify it by its distinctive packaging. A brand is essentially a label; but it is not just *any* label. It is the means to recognize a differentiated product, whose differentiation is valued by consumers. The brand identifies one particular product out of a population of competing products. The brand performs two communication functions for the consumer. First, it communicates the goodwill that has built up from past

[1] Association des Industries du Marque.

> performance of all products that have carried that brand name. This is the *reputation* function. Second, it enables the consumer to choose, on the strength of both past experience and the brand's reputation. This is the *recognition* function. Brand names are individual; they permit the distinction between types of the same product such as chocolate or carbonated beverages.[2]

A brand is thus a promise to the consumer, created by a unique selling proposition (USP) and supported by a 'reason why'. An example is the 1990s advertising for Pedigree Chum dog food in the UK '*Top breeders recommend it*' why? '*Because it's solid nourishment*'. The promise is solid nourishment creating an expectation by the consumer of product performance each and every time the product is presented to the dog.

In this sense a manufacturer's brand differs from a retailer's private label. The brand name of the private label is, in general, the store name of a retailer that sells many product categories. The retailer is thus bestowing their general reputation, for price, quality, and range, to a variety of many individual products. The retailer's general reputation may be unique amongst retailers offering a distinctive price, range, and level of quality; however this reputation applies to *all* of their private label products. A good example of this is the Canadian retailer Loblaws who applied the title 'Presidents Choice' to their own-label products because they were selected by the President of the corporation to be worthy of the title. Thus whilst a manufacturer's brand meets a specific consumer need, such as the need for 'a lighter taste of chocolate', the retailer's own label, though perhaps a similar product, cannot communicate as effectively the distinctive benefits of each product. It may succeed in communicating the benefits for some products but cannot achieve this for each of the products in the range. This difficulty in communicating the benefit of individual products is greater for retailers that offer a wide product range, as is the case with large supermarkets and hypermarkets.

C. Components of the Marketing Mix

A manufacturer's brand, such as Coca Cola or Persil, if it is to be successful, must retain its distinctiveness, be widely known by consumers, and be widely available to purchase. McCarthy referred to the components of the marketing mix of a brand as the four Ps: Product, Promotion, Place, and Price.[3] Each of these components guides the development and management of a brand.

---

2 The Benefits of Brands: A reference manual published by AIM (copy with author).

3 W D Perreault and E J McCarthy, *Basic Marketing* (16th rev edn, 2006).

Product

Product refers to the recipe or formulation of the product and how the product is packaged. It embraces taste of the product, its performance versus its competitors, its appearance, and the type of packaging (whether it is in a tin, a carton, a bottle, etc.). There are three aspects to Product which collectively contribute to the brand being preferred by consumers. These are design, relevance, and consistency.

Design: Successful brands are unique and therefore require a continuing programme of product development. This is necessary, not simply to ensure that the product is different, but rather continually to evaluate whether there are better formulations that improve consumer acceptance or reduce the cost without reducing the acceptability of the product. Innovation is thus at the heart of the product development of a brand. Gillette is reputed to have spent £700 million developing the Mach iii razor.

Relevance: Brands have to be continually relevant to the needs of consumers, or, more specifically, to the group of consumers at whom the brand is targeted. The Mars Bar, for example, has traditionally been targeted at younger men. Consumer needs change, often subtly, over time so manufacturers of brands invest significant sums of money in both consumer market research and product testing to ensure that the product remains relevant to its target audience.

Consistency: It is important that products that are purchased and used on a frequent basis must maintain a consistency of product performance and appearance. Frequency depends on the nature of the product and type of consumer; Coca Cola may be used daily whereas Persil Washing powder may be used weekly but in both cases the product is used many times per year. It is thus important that on each and every occasion the product tastes/looks/performs in the same way. Variation in product performance creates uncertainty in the mind of the consumer leading to a weakening of loyalty to the brand and ultimately distrust. Manufacturers thus invest large sums in order to ensure that the raw materials, production processes, and storage conditions are all consistent, thereby achieving a consistent consumer experience.

Promotion

McCarthy used promotion as a euphemism for consumer communication. In this sense promotion includes advertising, consumer promotion such as couponing and in-store promotion, and temporary price reduction. An objective of a brand owner is to communicate directly with consumers so that they provide information that relates to any change in product or packaging; to remind them of the core values of the brand; and to draw the brand to their attention when they are in the retail store. Importantly, each of these methods involves communication directly between the brand owner and the consumer rather than through the retailer as an intermediary.

Notification of change: The objective is to inform existing customers that change will occur in product design, packaging, or labelling, to describe the benefits of change, and induce non-buyers to switch to the brand. The medium employed is generally advertising through various media or direct mail, but, regardless of the medium, it is always designed and paid for by the brand owner. To this extent it is a direct cost of branding and reaches over the heads of retailers direct to consumers.

Reinforcing brand values: Brand values are both physiological and psychological. The physiological values relate to product design and performance, whilst the psychological values relate to image or style. It is important to remind consumers of these values and to put the brand to 'top of mind' prior to a shopping occasion. The consumer is thus aware of the brand and its attributes and may then translate this 'top of mind' awareness into a purchasing decision.

In-store display: The consumer must be able to identify easily the brand when in store. Easy identification by the consumer when in store is important if the manufacturer's brand is to be selected in preference to other brands. The brand owner thus seeks to obtain visibility for the brand in each and every relevant retail outlet. Routes to visibility include secondary display space such as end of gondola, visibility on shelf (generally at eye level), and a reduced price. All in-store communi cation is organized through the retailer and thus differs from advertising. The communication to the consumer is, at best, shared with the retailer and may even be between the retailer and the shopper.

Place

Place is where the consumer can expect to purchase the brand and relates to both the type of shop and the location within the store. There is a cost to the brand owner of achieving the required availability of the brand. In the case of organized retail chains, such as supermarkets, the cost is determined by the imperative to supply at a competitive price and the required level of in-store promotional activity. Where retailers are less organized, such as independent stores buying via wholesalers, the cost to the brand owner is in the form of a large sales force that can provide a support service to the retailer. The nature of the cost of achieving 'place' thus varies by retail channel and size of store.

A feature of distribution is the need to have the brand available in all relevant stores. If communication to consumers is to be successful in terms of notifying change and reinforcing brand values, it is imperative that the consumer can find the product on each visit to a retail store. Limited distribution of a brand impairs the effectiveness of advertising and leads to lost sales. This is particularly pertinent in situations of both high frequency of usage and less frequent shopping occasions which are often associated with larger stores that are located out of town. The breadth of required distribution depends upon the nature of the product use and types of stores where the consumer expects to purchase the product. Thus an impulse product such as a chocolate bar or soft drink, purchased for immediate consumption, requires distribution in a wide range of outlets (from sports stadium to supermarket), whereas a product that is a pre-planned purchase, such as cat or dog food, may be available in a restricted range of retail outlets (for example grocery stores and pet shops). Distribution costs thus vary between brands according to the nature of the consumer purchase. However, both impulse and pre-planned purchases need to be available in *all* outlets within their appropriately defined range of shops. Selective distribution of a brand diminishes volume sales and reduces the effectiveness of advertising. The objective for the brand owner is to achieve the greatest accessibility to the potential purchasers of the brand.

Price

Price is not a cost to the brand and in this sense is different from the other P's of Product, Promotion, and Place. McCarthy's reference to Price did not refer simply to the monetary value of the brand. The monetary value is an important yardstick in the purchasing decision-making process of the consumer. The consumer, however, weighs the price of the brand versus competing products within the context of the value they place on each brand. Thus Price is a measure of value and is a function of both monetary price and product quality. Since a brand also acquires psychological values, obtained via usage and advertising, then McCarthy's definition of Price embraces monetary value, product quality, and consumer perception. 'Price' as defined by McCarthy is thus influenced by the other P's, specifically Product and Promotion. This influence is, however, constrained by the competition provided by alternative products. The degree of competition is influenced by the number of available substitutes, the closeness of substitutability (similarity of product), and the price of the substitutes. In this context the presence of own label is important since retailers' private label products tend to reflect the qualities of the brand leader. They also avoid the costs associated with the other P's and, in general, have a lower monetary value. Private label thus has an important influence on the 'Price', as defined by McCarthy, of the manufacturer's brand.

The price of private label: This has to be viewed in both a relative and an absolute context. The private label product may adopt the attributes of the brand leader in

Table 2.1 Comparative cost for a manufacturer

Cost component	Brand manufacturer	Private label producer
Unit sales value[a]	100	*70*
Manufacturing variable cost		*50*[e]
Raw materials	50	
Packaging	25	
Processing	20	
	5	*20*
Gross margin[b]	50	
Advertising & promotion[c]	12	*1*[f]
Contribution to fixed cost	38	*19*
Fixed costs[d]	28	*11*
Product development	5	*1*[g]
Administration	15	*8*
Sales & distribution	8	*2*[h]
Net margin	10	*8*

Notes:
[a] This is the manufacturers' unit selling price.
[b] This is independent of changes in volume.
[c] These costs do not vary with volume. Increases or decreases, which can be made at short notice, do not automatically translate into immediately higher or lower volume sales but will be expected to do so after a time lag.
[d] Fixed costs cannot be changed in the short term. They are fixed in anticipation of an annual volume.
[e] Private label suppliers are rarely able to achieve the economies of scale of the brand manufacturer.
[f] Private label suppliers may be asked to contribute to their customers (a retailer) decision to promote the private label.
[g] Private label manufacturers will undertake some product development, but not the level of innovation of the brand owner.
[h] The private label supplier avoids the cost of a sales force required for universal distribution but incurs the cost of physical distribution to the retailers depot.

terms of packaging and product similarity. It is thus possible to appear to be similar to the brand leader yet be different in product design. In this situation the product cost may be less than the brand, and we would not then be comparing like with like between a brand and a private label product. Even when product costs are similar for the two, private label avoids the costs of product specific advertising (Promotion), distribution (Place), and primary product development (Innovation). This is illustrated in Table 2.1.

This analysis of the comparative cost structure between a manufacturer's brand and a similar private label product is verified by research undertaken by the UK Competition Commission during their investigation of supermarkets

Table 2.2 Differences in cost composition between private label and branded equivalent products

Suppliers cost saving	10.6%
Lower supplier margin	18.8%
Retailers purchase saving	29.4%
Lower retail price	19.3%
Higher retail margin	10.1%

Source: UK Competition Commission 2000

published in 2000.[4] They analysed the source of the difference in retail price between a brand and a similar private label and concluded that the retail selling price of the private label was 19.3 per cent less than the brand, even though retailers were able to buy the private label product at a 29.4 per cent lower price. The lower buying price was achieved through a lower supplier margin of 18.8 per cent and a cost saving by the private label producer of 10.6 per cent. The calculation of a 10.6 per cent cost saving is presumed to be based on similarly incurred costs of manufacturing variable cost and fixed cost. Table 2.2 summarizes the differences in retail buying and selling prices.

D. The Business Model of a Brand

The model comprises a set of interrelated elements. These elements are essentially defined in Table 2.1 above. Changing one element can be expected to have an effect on the other elements; thus an increase in expenditure on advertising and promotion will, all other things being equal, lead to an increase in sales volume. Similarly, increased sales effort can be expected to lead to improved distribution of the brand which in turn will result in an increased volume of sales. Distribution is based on the number and the quality of retail outlets that stock the brand. A supermarket and a convenience store have the same numerical value of distribution but by weighting each store by their volume of sales then the supermarket will contribute to a higher weighted distribution. A third factor which will lead to an increase volume of sales is the introduction of a more effective or distinctive product which, again all other things being equal, will lead to a higher sales volume as consumers switch from other brands. A fourth factor that will lead to an increase in sales volume is a reduction of price. This can only be

[4] UK Competition Commission, 'Supermarkets: A Report on the Supply of Groceries from Multiple Stores in the United Kingdom' (October 2000) <http://www.competition-commission.org.uk/rep_pub/reports/2000/446super.htm> accessed 25 May 2008.

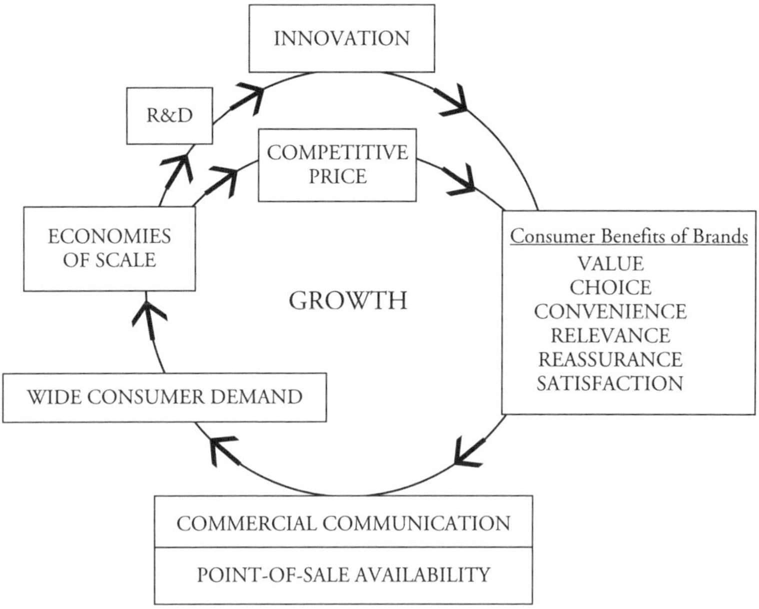

Figure 2.1

achieved, without reducing profitability, through increased efficiency leading to lower costs. Importantly, changes in sales will only occur after a time lag in response to a change of one of the aforementioned factors, and the duration of the time lag will vary between each of the factors.

The effect of increasing sales volume as a consequence of changing one of the component elements thus introduces a dynamic effect into the business model for brands. Growth is the dynamic factor. This is illustrated by Figure 2.1.

An increase in advertising (commercial communication) can be expected to lead to an increase in sales value. Should the consequent increase in value exceed the incremental investment in advertising then profit will rise. The increase in profit can then be used to fund further reinvestment into the brand, leading to more sales value and ultimately profit. This is the virtuous circle of branding. Kashani, Miller, and Clayton[5] in their research aptly described this process:

> Innovation, consumer value creation and communication are all elements of a virtuous cycle of brand building. At each turn of the cycle, innovative brands create more consumer value. Thereby earning greater consumer franchise, which, in turn,

[5] K Kashani, J Miller, and T Clayton, 'A Virtuous Cycle: Innovation, Consumer Value and Communication' (A research paper prepared for AIM 2000) <http://www.aim.be/docs/virtuous_circle.pdf> accessed 10 March 2008.

translates into growth in sales and market share, higher savings in communication expenditure, and greater returns on investment. With greater returns come the added resources for further innovation and, thus, the cycle repeats itself.

Innovation is not the exclusive preserve of any one manufacturer. The process is open to all competitors. Thus if a competitor can generate a higher level of innovation then they will embark on the virtuous cycle, leaving other brands to lose volume and enter into the vicious circle of decline, losing volume and cutting costs leading to further lower volumes. Innovation, in product, advertising, or distribution, is therefore a competitive process. Brands can never rest on their laurels.

The financial structure of brands

The financial structure of brands means that growth is particularly beneficial. Table 2.1 illustrates that manufacturer brands have a level of non-variable cost at approximately 50 per cent of sales value. These are costs that can be varied in the medium term but do not vary directly in line with changes in volume. Since direct variable costs are half of total sales value, it follows that only half of any increase in sales value is required to cover direct cost and the remaining 50 per cent flows directly through to profit. Thus profitability rises disproportionately with increases in volume. The virtuous cycle of growth is immensely profitable for manufacturers' brands, the exact extent depending on the proportion of variable cost to sales. Conversely a fall in sales value can have a hugely negative effect on profit. A 10 per cent reduction in sales value, with net margin 10 per cent of sales, will lead to a 50 per cent reduction in profit as illustrated by Table 2.3.

The sensitivity of brand profitability to a change in sales makes the brand extremely vulnerable to any unforeseen loss of sales.

The relationship between growth and distribution

Exploring the relationship of brand growth to increased weighted distribution is analogous to the question 'which came first; the chicken or the egg?' Increased

Table 2.3 The effect on profit of a change in sales

Financial structure	Predicted sales	10% fall in sales	Difference %
Sales value	100	90	–10
Variable cost	50	45	–10
Advertising	12	12	0
Fixed cost	38	38	0
Net margin	10	5	–50

Table 2.4 Number of grocery stores 1970–2000

	1970	1980	1990	2000
France	N/A	66,700	49,500	37,900
Germany	N/A	95,000	80,400	66,400
Netherlands	N/A	8,220	6,070	5,600
Spain	N/A	105,300	97,600	67,300
United Kingdom	138,000	88,900	50,300	34,000

Source: AC Nielsen grocery universe

levels of consumer use, and hence demand, will lead to more retailers stocking the product. Equally, increased availability of the brand through wider numerical distribution drives sales. The extent of increased sales is influenced by the nature of the purchase, thus an impulse purchase such as chocolate or ice cream might respond buoyantly to wider distribution. Studies suggest during the early life of a brand wider distribution drives sales, but once accepted by consumers, increased product usage drives wider distribution.

E. The Structure of Modern Retail Distribution

Distribution of fast-moving consumer goods is primarily, though not exclusively, through retail grocers, and grocers are dominated by a few large retail chains. There have been three noteworthy trends in grocery retailing in both Europe and North America. The first is towards larger stores such as supermarkets at the expense of smaller stores. Table 2.4 shows the reduction in the number of stores as small stores have closed in response to the opening of large surface retail outlets.

The second has been a trend to increased concentration of ownership leading to the emergence of large retail chains. Most countries of Europe now experience high levels of retail concentration in the grocery market. Table 2.5 shows the combined market share in each country of the five largest retailers and expresses this using the Herfindahl-Herschman Index (HHI), a measure of concentration widely used by competition authorities. In most industries a level of over 1,500 would be deemed concentrated.

The third trend has seen the integration of wholesaling and retailing within a retail chain identified by Bell in a series of articles in the European Retail Digest.[6] The effect of these changes is that increases or decreases in numerical distribution

6 D Bell, 'Food Retailing in the Nordics' [1999] 24 *European Retail Digest* 19.

Table 2.5 European grocery market concentration 2000

Country	Market share	HHI
Netherlands	95	2,394
Sweden	95	2,990
Austria	93	2,211
Denmark	84	2,502
Norway	84	2,500
Switzerland	84	2,535
France	83	1,619
Finland	83	2,529
Germany	76	1,216
Belgium	72	1,128
UK	71	1,255
Portugal	54	671
Spain	51	462
Greece	45	509
Italy	31	285
Median	**83**	**1,619**

Source: AC Nielsen

are 'lumpy'; they do not change gradually as they did when there were a large number of smaller independent retail outlets. These large step changes in distribution have a significant effect on the volume sales, and hence profitability, of a brand. Changes in shopping behaviour and retail structure have increased consumer search costs. Consumers tend to shop weekly and travel further to large, often out-of-town supermarkets. It can no longer be assumed that consumers will switch between retail outlets on the same shopping occasion to purchase their preferred brand. Retail switching has become more difficult, leading to an increased propensity to switch brands. The ease of switching between brands has further been facilitated by the development of private label products, positioned by the retailer as an alternative to the brand leaders.

Distributor power

Sales of a manufacturer's brand within a retailer are influenced by many variables. These include the extent of the brand range that is listed, the position of the brand on the shelf, the quantity of space on the fixture, the level of promotional frequency and intensity, and by additional display locations within the store. All of these factors are determined by the retail chain, so each chain has considerable influence on the sales level achieved by any brand. Consider the example of a retailer with a market share of 20 per cent. Research at OXIRM has shown that if the retailer decides to stock half of the items in the brand range by de-listing the slower selling items, then sales of the brand might decline by a third. If the brand is then relocated from the fast-selling position on the fixture to a slow-selling position then sales might decline by 15 per cent. A combination of the two would reduce the brand sales by 43 per cent. Thus the brand owner would lose 43 per cent of sales, even though the brand is still stocked, in a retailer with a 20 per cent market share. The brand would then lose 8.6 per cent of total sales. Table 2.3 has shown that a 10 per cent fall in sales can lead to a 50 per cent fall in profit. The retailer thus has significant power over the supplier simply through attempting to optimize the in-store marketing variables of range, price, and space. The consumer is hardly induced to switch stores, quite apart from the high switching costs, since half of the brand range accounting for two-thirds of sales is still available.

The emergence of monopsony retail power, however benevolently this is exercised, has created the ability to impose economic shocks on the manufacturer's brand. These shocks can rapidly turn the virtuous cycle of a brand into a vicious circle, pushing the brand into a vortex, as the following case studies show.

F. The Effect of Private Label on Manufacturer Brands: Case Studies

The growth in market share of private label products has a direct impact upon manufacturer brands whose share correspondingly decreases. The growth in market share of private label is not constant in all retailers and the effect is not uniform across all manufacturer brands. Growth in private label may result from a policy of increasing the number of private label lines. This may be, but is not necessarily, accompanied by a corresponding reduction in lines of manufacturers' brands. Growth may also arise from better marketing by a retailer of its own products or by more favourable location within their stores. The effect of these activities may differentially affect manufacturer brands. Decisions to reduce lines to accommodate private label range expansion will be based on rates of sale of each line item, and the listing fees that manufacturers are prepared to pay.

The loss of volume has a significant effect on the financial viability of manufacturer brands. In general these have large margins after variable cost but high fixed costs associated with distributing and developing their products. This results in an inability to adjust costs proportionately to changes in volume.

The complexity of the way brands are affected by private label[7] and the subtle financial structure of manufacturer brands are illustrated by two case studies. These describe the different ways in which brands are affected by the growth of private label and the different financial models by which brands operate. Both case studies show the corrosive effect on brand profitability.

G. The Case Study of Laundry Products in Spain

Laundry market trends

In 1998 the laundry market in Spain was fragmented with no brand having a dominant market share. The aggregate share of private label products at 14.2 per cent exceeded that of the brand leader, Ariel, with a market share of 13.1 per cent.

The share of private label products more than doubled in the three years following. All major brands lost market share between 1998 and 2001. The larger brands lost proportionately less than the smaller named brands. The collection of small brands retained market share. Few of these brands had universal national distribution.

The value of the total market for laundry products increased by 16 per cent between 1998 and 2001. The loss of market share of even the largest brands exceeded the market growth. The brand leader, Ariel, is estimated to have lost 10 per cent of its value over this time period. Skip, ranked fifth in 1998, lost 30 per cent of its value.

The growth of private label laundry products occurred in all retailers but was significant in two, Dia and Mercadona. In 1998 Mercadona sold no private label laundry products, by 2001 private label products accounted for 64 per cent of its laundry sales. Dia expanded its own label laundry sales from 43 per cent of total in 1998 to 75 per cent in 2001.

All retailers, with the exception of Lidl who sold only private label, increased the share of their private label products within the laundry category (see Table 2.7). Private label was significant in *all* retailers by 2001 whereas it had been significant in just four retailers in 1998. Sales of own label laundry products accounted for at least 10 per cent of category sales in all retailers in 2001 except Sabeco.

The rate of growth of private label was significant within a short period of time. The rapid growth rate cannot be explained solely by a significant additional

[7] R L Steiner, 'The Nature and Benefits of National Brand/Private Label Competition' [2004] 24 *Review of Industrial Organisation* 105.

Table 2.6 Volume market shares %: 1998–2001

Brand	1998	1999	2000	2001
Ariel	13.1	12.7	10.3	10.2
Dash	2.9	1.5	1.0	0.6
Skip	7.6	6.5	5.6	4.6
Colon	9.2	8.5	7.9	6.8
Elena	8.0	6.3	6.5	6.5
Dixan	5.7	5.3	4.7	4.1
WIPP	8.3	7.8	7.8	6.8
Bilore	2.8	2.4	2.0	2.1
Flota	3.5	2.8	1.8	1.5
Private label	**14.2**	**17.1**	**26.9**	**31.7**
Others	24.7	29.1	25.5	25.0
Market value (Index)	100	102	113	116

Source: Europanel

listing of private label lines *and* a reduction in listing of branded items as is illustrated in Table 2.8. We must therefore look for factors other than the size of range to account for the growth of private label in laundry products.

The source of private label growth

The growth of private label in general and specifically in laundry derives from the successful growth strategy of Mercadona. Mercadona grew its share of the Spanish

Table 2.7 Private label volume share by retailer

Retailer	Grocery market share 1998 %	Laundry dry own label share 1998 %	Laundry dry own label share 2001 %	Change in laundry own label share
Carrefour Hipers	14	17	26	*+9*
Dia	10	43	75	+32
Eroski	7	5	18	*+13*
Alcampo	4	2	10	*+8*
Sabeco	N/A	0	9	*+9*
Hipercor	6	17	18	*+1*
Mercadona	5	0	64	+64
Caprabo	3	14	21	*+7*
Lidl	2	100	97	*−3*
Total	100	14	32	+18

Source: Europanel

Table 2.8 Laundry: number of SKUs listed

	Private label			Brands		
	1998	2001	Change	1998	2001	Change
Carrefour	31	24	−7	253	280	+27
Dia	17	12	−5	105	99	−6
Eroski	13	23	+10	245	258	+13
Alcampo	13	12	−1	167	212	+45
Sabeco	7	10	+3	124	119	−6
Hipercor	12	11	−1	112	121	+9
Mercadona	0	36	+36	123	99	−24
Caprabo	13	9	−4	114	128	+14
Lidl	29	23	−6	5	4	−1

Source: Europanel

grocery market from 3.5 per cent in 1997 to 12.4 per cent in the second quarter of 2002 when it ranked second to Dia (12.7 per cent).

There were four elements in Mercadona's growth strategy: firstly a change from a classic promotional policy to a strict application of 'everyday low prices'; secondly a rationalized and disciplined approach to product range which included a strong commitment to developing and promoting its own brands; thirdly a strong marketing-led approach to its customers based on a projection of values as a food retailer. This involved food tastings, improved service, training and motivation of employees, and heavy advertising both in, and around, its stores; fourthly an aggressive store expansion plan.

Mercadona has obtained a great acceptance and value in the eyes of its customers. It has positioned itself as 'value for money' providing a discount proposition within a supermarket format offering the benefits of one-stop shopping. Other retailers have emulated Mercadona's strategy, specifically the development of private label. The growth in private label within Mercadona has been achieved by giving the products greater prominence on shelf and by communicating to customers, through advertising, the benefits of better value. As a consequence, private label share of total packaged groceries in Mercadona has grown from 0.7 per cent in 1997 to 34.2 per cent in 2001.

The brands' response

Brands that have a high gross margin and a high ratio of fixed costs are profit-sensitive to reductions in volume. A 10 per cent value loss, as experienced by Ariel, can be expected to result in a profit reduction of 46 per cent if fixed costs

Table 2.9 The business model for laundry brands in Spain

	Base Situation	10% volume reduction;[a] same costs	10% volume reduction; reduced advertising[b]
Manufacturer sales value	100	90	90
Manufacturing variable cost	45	40.5 (45%)	40.5
Gross margin	55	49.5 (55%)	49.5
Advertising & consumer promotion	15	15	10.7
Sales & distribution	8	8	8
Fixed costs	20	20	20
Net margin	12	6.5 (7.2%)	10.8 (12%)

Source: Author's calculations.

Notes:

[a] In this situation volume falls by 10%. The gross margin remains the same in percentage terms but the absolute reduction of 5.5 affects the net margin by the same amount. Net margin falls by 46%.

[b] In this situation the manufacturer responds by cutting advertising to preserve the net margin percent. The absolute margin has fallen by 10%, equal to the volume reduction. Advertising has been cut by 29% to absorb all of the reduced sales value.

cannot be reduced (see Table 2.9). Such a reduction is difficult to make in the short term. A 24 per cent volume loss, as experienced by Skip (Table 2.6, showing a loss of three share points (40 per cent) in a market growing by 16 per cent), would lead to a negative profit position.

The cost that can be cut most quickly to compensate for reduced volume is advertising. Advertising, however, is used to raise consumer awareness of the brand and is a driver of future volume. Cutting advertising thus cushions the *immediate* profit reduction and jeopardises *future* volume growth that would be the source of a profit recovery. Distribution costs are based on an infrastructure designed to achieve widespread product availability irrespective of volume variations. These costs, which are labour intensive, cannot be cut instantly and, like advertising, a cut to cushion profit would jeopardize future sales volume. Fixed costs reflect customer service levels and product development. These are also labour intensive and cannot vary directly with volume.

The case of WIPP

We can consider the case of the brand WIPP given the business model above and the market performance in Table 2.1. WIPP's market share fell from 8.3 per cent in 1998 to 6.8 per cent in 2001, a reduction of 18 per cent over three years. The value of the market increased by 16 per cent over the same period so the brand sales' value reduced by 5 per cent (0.82 x 1.16).

The WIPP advertising budget was high in 1998 as the brand entered the expanding liquid detergents segment of the laundry category. The brand had previously only been sold as a regular detergent. The WIPP advertising budget in 1998 peaked at EUR12.5 million.[8] Net margin was negative as a result of the heavy marketing investment required to enter a new segment.

In 1999 market share fell by 0.5 per cent and sales value by 4.3 per cent. Advertising was reduced to a level, at 25 per cent, considered to be high for the category. Annual advertising budgets are set in anticipation of market shares and there is a lag between a shortfall in anticipated share and cuts in advertising. The reduction in advertising expenditure enabled WIPP effectively to break even at the net margin level. Advertising was reduced by a further 46 per cent to below category average in 2000. Market share was maintained at the 1999 level enabling net margin to rise to 15 per cent of sales value. Net margin averaged 2.5 per cent over the three years 1998 to 2000 compared with the category business model of 12 per cent.

Table 2.10 WIPP: key financial parameters

	1998		**1999**		**2000**		**2001**	
Market share %	8.3		7.8		7.8		6.8	
	Euros Mn	%	Euros Mn	%	Euros Mn	%	Euros Mn	%
Retail value	45.0		43.0		47.8		42.9	
Manuf. value[a]	38.2	100	36.6	100	40.6	100	36.5	100
Gross margin[b]	21.0	55	20.1	55	22.3	55	20.1	55
Advertising[c]	12.5	33	9.0	25	4.9	12	6.5	18
Distribution[d]	3.25	9	3.25	9	3.25	8	3.25	9
Fixed cost[e]	8.1	21	8.1	22	8.1	20	8.1	22
Net margin[f]	(2.85)	(7.5)	(0.25)	(0.7)	6.05	15	2.25	6.2

Source: Author's calculations.

Notes:

[a] Retail margin of 15% on laundry in Spain.

[b] Based on the business model for laundry in Spain.

[c] Source GfK. Discounted by 35% of the rate card value.

[d] Business model of 8% applied to 1997 manufacturers' sales value.

[e] Business model of 20% applied to 1997 manufacturers' sales value.

[f] The residual of the manufacturer sales value less the variable and fixed costs.

[8] Advertising expenditures published by GfK and adjusted for volume discounts.

In 2001 WIPP market share fell by one share point, following the previous year's cuts in advertising and growth of private label. Advertising had been increased in response to the 2000 share performance. As a consequence, net margin fell by 63 per cent to 6.2 per cent of sales value.

In summary, WIPP had above average advertising expenditure and entered new market segments but could not prevent a declining market share in the face of own label growth; this decline in sales value led to low net margins.

H. The Case of Cat Food Products in Germany

Wet cat food market trends

Between 1993 and 2001 the market share of private label products of wet cat food in Germany doubled. In 1993 the aggregate of private label products was second only to the brand leader, Whiskas. Certain retailers such as Aldi sold only private label. Table 2.11 shows the market share for all major brands and for private label for the years 1993 and 2001. By 2001 private label products were the dominant force in the market and were three times the size of the leading proprietary brand, Whiskas.

All major brands lost market share between 1993 and 2001. The brand which lost most share was Whiskas, the brand leader in 1993. It remained the leading proprietary brand in 2001 measured in both volume and value share. The loss in Whiskas' market share increased in successive years between 1997 and 2001, culminating in a loss of three share points by value. Table 2.12 shows the change in Whiskas' market share from 1997 to 2000.

Table 2.11 Market shares % 1993–2001

	Volume share %			Value share %		
Brand	Jan/Feb 1993	Nov/Dec 2001	Change in No. of Share Points	Jan/Feb 1993	Nov/Dec 2001	Change in No. of Share Points
Sheba	4.4	3.4	−1.0	12.6	9.3	−3.3
Whiskas	31.2	16.6	−14.6	36.9	23.7	−13.2
K-E-K	20.8	15.7	−5.1	18.0	14.1	−3.9
Brekkies	7.8	4.3	−3.5	4.6	2.6	−2.0
Felix	9.4	9.8	−0.4	7.6	11.0	+3.4
Private label	24.5	**48.0**	+23.5	**18.0**	**36.1**	**+18.1**
Other	1.8	2.1	+0.3	2.3	3.2	+0.9

Table 2.12 Whiskas market share

Year	Volume %	Change on previous year	Value %	Change on previous year
1997	24.6	–	30.5	–
1998	23.2	–1.4	30.0	–0.5
1999	22.0	–1.2	29.3	–0.7
2000	20.3	–1.7	27.7	–1.6
2001	17.6	–2.7	24.7	–3.0

Reasons for the reduction in Whiskas' market share

The loss of Whiskas' sales was not uniform across all retailers. In 1997, 61 per cent of Whiskas' sales were in four grocery retailers: Tengelmann, Edeka, Rewe, and Markant. This is comparable to the share of the German grocery market held by these four retailers. By 2001 sales of Whiskas had declined by 62 per cent in Tengelmann and by 30 per cent in Rewe, whereas the sales decline by Whiskas was just 10 per cent in all other retailers. Tengelmann and Rewe accounted for 60 per cent of the Whiskas national decline.

During this time the volume share of private label wet cat foods rose from 20 per cent (1997) to 54 per cent (2001) in Tengelmann. In Rewe the share of private label cat food rose from 40 per cent to 55 per cent.

The change in sales of a brand in any individual retailer can occur for one or more of the following reasons: firstly, a reduction in sales per shop stocking the brand—this may result from higher prices, greater competitor activity, or consumer disfavour; secondly a reduction in the number of retail stores stocking the brand—this is referred to as numerical distribution; thirdly a reduction in the number of lines (SKU's) a retailer chooses to list—this may be a *consequence* of a decline in sales per shop or it may be a *cause* of lower market share.

Tengelmann reduced the number of Whiskas' items per shop from 25 in 1997 to 15 in 2001. To place this in context, a 40 per cent reduction in items listed would, *ceteris paribus*, lead to a similar reduction in sales. In practice, deletions would be concentrated on lower-selling items thus halving the loss. A 20 per cent sales reduction in a retailer with a 10 per cent market share would lead to a loss of two share points within the total wet cat food market category. Rewe reduced the weighted distribution of Whiskas by 8 per cent between 1997 and 2001. This could be expected to translate into an 8 per cent reduction in sales. Such a reduction in a retailer with a 20 per cent market share would lead to a loss of 1.6 share points within the total wet cat food market category. During this time the number of own label items of wet cat food per shop increased

Table 2.13 Whiskas: sales and distribution by retailer

Retailer	Distribution weighted		Items per shop		Sales per shop	
	1997	2001	1997	2001	1997	2001
Metro	100	100	35	54	1,411	2,171
Tengelmann	100	100	25	15	420	192
Edeka	99	98	20	24	190	210
Rewe	100	92	17	20	336	275
Markant	100	100	22	31	255	236
Spar	98	99	17	20	184	124

by 24 per cent in Tengelmann and 11 per cent in Rewe. This is shown in Table 2.13.

The spiral of decline

The initial Whiskas response to the increased threat of private label products was to maintain list price. Trade promotion was used tactically to promote the brand where the threat from private label was greatest. In 1999 the average price of Whiskas in all outlets fell by 0.5 per cent. This price reduction was effectively 2.5 per cent if it had been concentrated in retailers that were heavily promoting their private label cat food.

Fast moving consumer goods, such as Whiskas, have a high gross margin and relatively high fixed costs associated with distribution, marketing, product development, and manufacturing investment. Consequently the profitability of these brands is heavily affected by changes in volume. If gross profit (margin after

Table 2.14 Business model for pet food brands in Germany

Value of net sales (After trade promotions)	100	90[a]
Marginal costs (Materials & manufacturing)	55	49.5 (55%)
Gross profit margin	45	40.5
Advertising & consumer promotions	12	12
Distribution	8	8
Fixed costs & depreciation	20	20
Net profit	5	0.5

Notes:
[a] The reduction in net sales in this illustration derives from a 10% fall in volume. Should a reduction in net sales derive, not from lower volume but from lower prices or increased trade discounts, then the level of marginal costs would not change from that in column 2 of Table 2.14.

Table 2.15 Whiskas—the key financial parameters

	1997		1998		1999		2000		2001	
	Euros Mn	%	Euros Mn	%	Euros Mn	%	Euros Mn	%	Euros Mn	%
Manuf. Sales value[a]	176.9	**100**	178.2	**100**	175.4	**100**	166.3	**100**	151.1	**100**
Gross margin[b]	79.6	45	80.2	45	78.9	45	74.8	45	68.0	45
Advertising[c]	20.6	12	16.1	9	21.6	12	18.6	11	19.9	13
Distribution[d]	14.2	8	14.2	8	14.2	8	14.2	9	14.2	9
Fixed cost[e]	35.4	20	35.4	20	35.2	20	35.2	21	35.4	3
Net margin[f]	9.5	5	14.5	8	7.9	5	6.8	4	−1.4	(1)

Notes:
[a] Industry estimates.
[b] Based on the business model for pet food in Germany.
[c] Industry estimates. Includes consumer promotions.
[d] Business model of 8% applied to 1997 manufacturers' sales value.
[e] Business model of 20% applied to 1997 manufacturers' sales value.
[f] The residual of the manufacturers' sales value less the variable and fixed costs.

manufacturing) were 50 per cent and net profit is 5 per cent, then a 10 per cent reduction in sales would result in net profit falling to zero. Table 2.14 above shows the effect of a 10 per cent volume decline for the pet food business model in Germany.

The level of advertising on Whiskas was increased by 40 per cent in 1999, consumer promotions were maintained, and increased emphasis was given to the new single-serve format. These activities failed to prevent a fall in the value of manufacturer sales by 2 per cent in that year. The consequence of increased marketing activities and reduced sales was a fall in net margin of 46 per cent (see Table 2.15).

As a response to the situation of increased marketing expenditure and falling sales in 1999, advertising was cut in 2000 to the lowest level since 1994. In 1994 private label share was 20 share points lower. The reduction in advertising coincided with a fall in manufacturer sales value of 5.3 per cent. We cannot conclude with certainty that the reduced advertising was the primary reason for the fall in sales. The cuts in advertising were, in any event, not sufficient for net margin to be restored.

In 2001 consumer prices increased by 2 per cent, advertising remained at the low level of 2000, manufacturer sales fell by 9.1 per cent, and value market share fell by three share points. The fall in market share was higher than for any year in the previous decade. Net profit collapsed to a negative level. Brand sales and profit had entered the spiral of decline. These effects are shown in Table 2.15.

In summary Whiskas lost sales due to reduced distribution in two major retailers. Increased advertising could not drive up sales in other retailers, where distribution was already close to 100 per cent, to compensate for lost distribution in Tengelmann and Rewe. As sales fell, so expenditure on advertising, distribution, and fixed costs rose as a percentage of total revenue and net margin fell correspondingly. Whiskas was thus faced with the dilemma: it needed to cut advertising to maintain net margin as sales value fell, but cuts in advertising would have exacerbated the decline in sales. In the event the loss of distribution led to a negative net margin.

I. Conclusion

The major conclusion from the two case studies is that large retailers control the in-store marketing levers of product range, space allocation, pricing, and promotional activity. Importantly, they control these variables for both their own brands and for manufacturer brands. Changing each of these variables can directly affect the level of sales, and hence market share, for each brand within the retail chain.

The retailer not only has the power to change these variables but is now less constrained by potential adverse consumer reaction. Consumers are primarily concerned with choice across many categories and with the value of the total shopping basket; increases in the average size of a supermarket have been accompanied by a reduction in shopping frequency and an increased cost to the consumer of shopping in different stores; finally the emergence of oligopolistic retailers in Europe reduces the number of alternative retailers.

The case studies of WIPP in Spain and Whiskas in Germany illustrate the effect that a unilateral decision by a retailer can have upon the profitability of a brand. The example from Spain shows the effect of reducing the number of lines listed by one retailer for all manufacturers. The action was not specific to the range of one manufacturer. This contrasts with the example from Germany, which shows the effect upon one manufacturer of the action of one retailer in reducing the number of lines listed by 40 per cent and of another retailer reducing the number of its stores that listed that manufacturer's full range. In the Spanish example, the manufacturer compensated by reducing advertising to protect their profit margin but still suffered a reduced level of profitability. The consequence was that they failed to benefit from the heavy marketing expenditure that had been undertaken to support their entry into new market segments. The unpredictable action (to the supplier) of a retailer changing their product range increased the risk to the supplier's investment into new product development and range expansion.

In the German example the effect of selective action by two retailers led to the manufacturer's brand becoming unprofitable. In contrast to Spain, the manufacturer sought to maintain advertising in the face of decreasing sales volumes. Such a response in an atomistic retail structure, where consumers shop in several stores, can be expected to increase distribution of the brand. However, in an oligopolistic retail structure consumer sales of Whiskas did not increase and those retailers that reduced Whiskas' distribution did not suffer any loss of market share.

There is one significant difference between the cost structure of a laundry brand in Spain and a pet food brand in Germany and that is the level of gross margin. The pet food margin is 10 points lower than that for laundry, which makes the brand more vulnerable to reductions in sales volume. The combination of this increased vulnerability and the mistaken belief that maintaining advertising expenditure would drive sales thus pushed Whiskas into a loss-making situation in Germany. It is to be expected, however, that a cut in advertising would have accelerated a sales decline, but may have delayed, though not prevented, the decline in profit. The judgment the manufacturer had to make was whether the impact on gross margin of a faster reduction in sales could have been off-set by a cut in advertising expenditure.

3

BARGAINING BETWEEN RETAILERS AND THEIR SUPPLIERS

*Howard Smith and John Thanassoulis**

A. Introduction

A branded good is supplied by a single firm. A private label good can be supplied by many. So competition is more extreme and conditions more uncertain for private label suppliers.

This chapter investigates the economic consequences of these differences. We outline a bargaining theory framework which helps one to understand why profits accrue where they do in supply chains. We focus on the buyer power of large retailers and its impact on the investment incentives of suppliers. The analysis applies to the retail sector generally and to supermarkets in particular.

* Department of Economics, Oxford University. The authors would like to thank the Milk Development Council (MDC) and DEFRA for financial support for the research discussed in this chapter. In addition we are grateful to all the executives from the milk industry who kindly made themselves available for us to interview. The views in this chapter are solely ours and cannot be attributed to the MDC, DEFRA, or any other industry participant.

Part of our motivation is to understand the economic effect of retailer size. This has become an important worldwide policy issue in recent years with the emergence of large retail firms such as Wal-Mart, Carrefour, and Tesco. It is often argued that large retailers have greater buyer power, i.e. can negotiate lower prices than a small retailer. It is sometimes further argued that a large retailer can have an upwards effect on prices negotiated by smaller retailers, with adverse consequences for their viability. This is called a *waterbed* effect. Finally, it is sometimes claimed that buyer power can reduce suppliers' incentives to invest in cost-reducing innovations. These issues have all come under intense scrutiny from competition authorities. For example, they are studied in the recent Competition Commission inquiry into the UK grocery market.[1]

We begin the chapter by reviewing the literature on retailer-supplier bargaining with an upstream monopolist. This framework is applicable to the case of a branded product. Here, to stock the product the retailer must strike an agreement with the monopoly supplier. We analyse buyer power, waterbed effects, and supplier investment incentives. The shape of the suppliers' cost function drives the results: for example if the branded supplier has economies of scale then (as we will explain) it actually secures a higher price from the larger retailers (while the reverse holds if it has diseconomies of scale). The analysis provides a benchmark case: a point of comparison for the case of private label products.

The fundamental point of difference between private label and branded products is that when procuring a private label product the retailer is not restricted to source from a single supplier. Furthermore the consumer is unaware of the supplier's identity so the retailer can change suppliers without consumers noticing any change. This reduces switching costs to the retailers and allows them to alter suppliers at relatively short notice. This in turn has the potential to create output uncertainty for any given supplier of a private label good as it cannot accurately forecast its success in securing contracts with retailers.

In the marketing literature, branded goods are often subdivided into two groups, primary and secondary. Primary brands, such as Coca-Cola, enjoy a high level of brand recognition from consumers and therefore are considered must-stock items for most retailers. Secondary brands are much weaker, and retailers can substitute one brand for another without much impact on consumers. Therefore secondary brands operate under competitive conditions very similar to private label products. Hereafter for ease of presentation we will refer to branded and

[1] UK Competition Commission, 'The Supply of Groceries in the UK Market Investigation: Provisional Findings Report' [2007] <http://www.competition-commission.org.uk/inquiries/ref2006/grocery/prov_findings/prov_find _report.pdf> accessed 25 May 2008.

private label products, but we emphasize that we intend that secondary brands should be analysed using the framework we set out for private label goods.

To inform our understanding of the private label market we conducted interviews with a number of industry executives in a leading private label good market, fresh milk. We also discuss another private label goods market, the market for carbonated soft drinks (CSD). In both cases the evidence confirms the importance of output uncertainty for suppliers of private label products.

We sketch a model developed by Smith and Thanassoulis (hereafter ST) that can be used to analyse the retailer-supplier interface for private label goods.[2] The framework in ST captures the main features of private label markets that emerged from the interviews and case studies. Thus it considers a retailer-seller bargaining interface where suppliers compete to supply a product that is homogeneous to consumers and competition between suppliers creates output uncertainty for individual suppliers.

We show how this model can be used to understand the profit split between retailers and suppliers for private label goods. We find that the competition faced by private label suppliers transforms the bargaining game, compared to the branded good benchmark case. We show that the supplier output uncertainty (brought about by competition) creates a new source of buyer power for large retailers, the logic of which can be explained as follows: sellers are uncertain of their total output when negotiating with a buyer. They therefore discount contracts they might win with other buyers due to this upstream competition—the more competition, the less likely the other contracts are to be won. Hence the supplier sees the buyer she is negotiating with as incremental business from a relatively low base. If the total cost curve is non-linear this influences the expected costs of supplying the buyer, e.g. if there are economies of scale it reduces them and the large buyer can negotiate a better deal. This is the reverse of the finding (noted above) for the branded good case.

The theoretical prediction that buyer power is present in the case of private label goods but not for (primary) branded goods is supported by an empirical study of the prices paid to suppliers, recently published by the Competition Commission.[3] They use a large cross section of the prices paid by supermarket buyers of alternative sizes, with the aim of determining whether large buyers negotiate lower prices. Their results reveal a striking difference between primary-branded and non-primary-branded goods (the latter comprising private label and secondary

2 H Smith and J Thanassoulis, 'Upstream Competition and Downstream Buyer Power' [2006] Centre for Economic Policy Research Discussion Paper No 5803.

3 Competition Commission inquiry into the UK grocery market (n 1) app 8.1, paras 44 and 45.

brands). For primary brands there is no evidence of lower prices for large buyers. But for non-primary brands there is clear evidence that large buyers secure lower prices. For reasons explained in this chapter, this difference can be explained by the level of output uncertainty faced by each type of supplier.

We also explain how the uncertainty faced by private label suppliers generates waterbed effects which are not present for the branded products case; the direction of these waterbed effects depends on the shape of the suppliers' cost function but the most likely effect is to increase the price paid by smaller retailers. We also discuss the investment incentives of private label suppliers.

The outline of the chapter is as follows. We begin with a discussion of retailer-supplier bargaining in the case of branded goods. We then discuss case study evidence for two leading examples of private label goods sold in supermarkets. The rest of the chapter uses the ST bargaining framework to analyse supply chains for private label products.

B. Upstream Monopoly: The Case of a Branded Product

The conventional textbook approach to vertically related markets is to assume a *market* interface: an upstream firm, say a manufacturer, chooses a price for a product which it then sells to the next stage in the supply chain, say the retailer.[4] In the simplest case (double-marginalization) the retailer takes the supplier's price as given and in turn sets its own retail price to final customers, considering only its own profits and treating the supplier's price as a marginal cost. The retailer sets a price that is too high and hence output which is too low (in terms of maximizing the sum of the profits of the manufacturer and retailer) because the retailer does not optimize output against true industry marginal cost. This in turn suggests the manufacturer can do better by using a two-part tariff in which the retailer pays an initial fixed fee and then a per-unit price equal to true marginal cost.

An obvious weakness of this overall approach is that it ignores the power of many retailers, i.e. retailers are treated as passive price takers when in reality we know that they often bargain actively with suppliers over prices. A literature has recently emerged which rectifies this weakness, by studying the implications of a *bargaining interface* between retailers and suppliers.[5]

---

[4] J Tirole, *The Theory of Industrial Organization* (1988), ch 4.

[5] The *market interface* and *bargaining interface* terminology is drawn from R Inderst and G Shaffer (forthcoming), 'The Role of Buyer Power in Merger Control' in W Collins (ed), *Issues in Competition Law and Policy, ABA Antitrust Section Handbook*, where a comprehensive literature survey may be found. The first papers to study a *bargaining interface* were PW Dobson and

Almost all of the bargaining interface literature has considered buyer power in the context of an upstream monopolist. The assumption of an upstream monopolist is appropriate for the setting of a branded good. This is true regardless of the presence, or otherwise, of secondary and tertiary branded goods. If such goods exist, while being of lower value than the branded good, retailers will seek to bargain with the branded good supplier. The secondary branded goods may strengthen the hand of the retailer in these negotiations as they provide a fall-back option for the retailer in case of bargaining deadlock with the branded supplier. This increases the profits the retailers secure, but doesn't alter the insights we go on to describe. We present the main results from this literature to help understand the economics of branded goods supply chains.

The bargaining interface literature has identified the *shape* of the supplier's cost function as an important influence on the bargained outcome. The key insight of the literature is that a monopoly upstream supplier with economies of scale actually bargains to a higher negotiated price from larger buyers, in contrast to the concerns expressed in the introduction.[6] That is large buyers are weak buyers. We now explain the economic logic behind this result.

An upstream monopoly knows that each retailer has no desirable alternative source of supply. With efficient bargaining the supplier can therefore expect to conclude deals with all retailers for whom supplying the product is beneficial. That is, at the conclusion of all negotiations, all retailers for whom the branded good is desired will stock it. It follows that the branded supplier knows what his final output will be, i.e. the sum of the outputs agreed with each retailer. Let us call this final output Q.

Suppose that an individual retailer negotiates with the supplier over a fixed volume q, say the volume that maximizes the profits to be split in the negotiation. It is standard to assume that the two parties split the gains to be had from trade. These gains depend on the *incremental cost* Δc to the supplier of making the q units. As the supplier expects to produce Q units when all deals are agreed, the relevant incremental cost is the cost of producing Q minus the cost of producing (Q − q), i.e. $\Delta c = c(Q) - c(Q - q)$ where c(Q) denotes the supplier's total cost of supplying volumes Q.

M Waterson, 'Countervailing Power and Consumer Prices' [1997] 107 *The Economic Journal* 418, and V Ungern-Sternberg, 'Countervailing Power Revisited' [1996] 14 *International Journal of Industrial Organisation* 507.

6 T Chipty and C M Snyder, 'The Role of Firm Size in Bilateral Bargaining: A Study of the Cable Television Industry' [1999] 81 *Review of Economics and Statistics* 326.

This is true for each retailer. The monopoly supplier therefore conducts every negotiation assuming all the other negotiations go according to plan and they bargain with each buyer assuming Q to be the post-negotiation reference output.

With this insight in hand, we can now show how retailer size affects the negotiated price. Suppose the total cost curve is concave as in Figure 3.1: the case of economies of scale. The supplier's total output Q is marked at the right on the horizontal axis. Because of economies of scale the average cost of supplying the last few units of output is smaller than the average cost of supplying the last units for a larger number of units. This is illustrated by the two chords (linear segments) drawn on the diagram. Working back from Q the gradient of the small chord gives the average incremental cost $\Delta c/q$ of supplying a small buyer assuming that all other negotiations go to plan. This is flatter than the counterpart for the larger retailer. The small buyer's output thus has a lower average incremental cost than the large buyer's. As the supplier and retailer split the gains from their relationship this implies that the small buyer will be able to negotiate a lower price.[7]

Thus with upstream economies of scale large buyers are *weak*: they should get a higher price than smaller buyers. The intuition for this, perhaps surprising, result is that branded good manufacturers are able to extract a greater fraction of their infra-marginal costs from larger buyers. That is the larger buyers pay a greater proportion of costs incurred in getting to full output. If on the other hand there are diseconomies of scale the reverse conclusion holds and the large retailer has the greater buyer power (this can be seen by drawing a convex total cost curve instead of the concave one in Figure 3.1).

The presence of scale economies for the monopoly supplier results in a concave total cost function. In turn this leads to lower average incremental cost $\Delta c/q$ for small buyers than large buyers when the supplier assumes that its post-negotiation total output will be Q in both cases. Hence large buyers are weak buyers.

Whether upstream technology is characterized by economies of scale or not will depend on the particular industry. However where logistics form a substantial fraction of the cost base then the operations research literature has shown that economies of scale are to be expected.[8]

---

[7] This insight is formally shown in Chipty and Snyder (n 6).

[8] See, for example, LD Burns and others, 'Distribution Strategies that Minimize Transportation and Inventory Costs' [1985] 33 *Operations Research* 469.

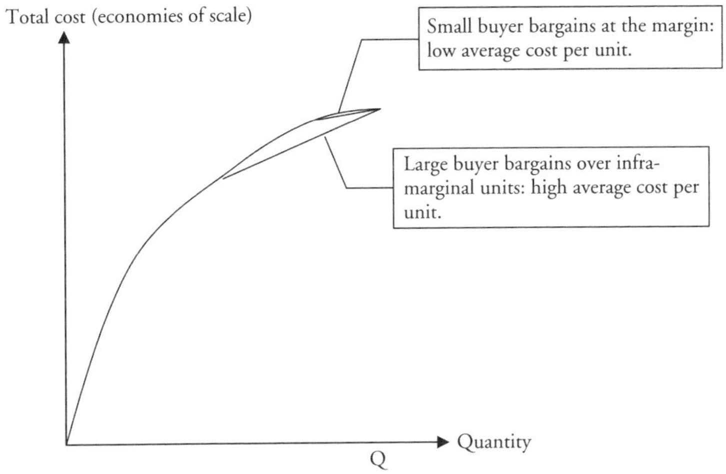

Figure 3.1: Buyer power with upstream monopoly (the branded good case)

It is important to recall that the price secured by a given retailer from their supplier will not only depend upon the general costs of production, but also upon any retailer specific costs. If, for example, many small buyers are in far away or hard to reach places then this would increase the prices they pay—not because of a weakening of their bargaining power, but because these specific costs must be covered. Likewise if large buyers can order in (cheaper to deliver) full palette quantities, or are in easier to reach places, then the specific costs will be lower. Once again the final price agreed here will reflect these lower specific costs of service as well as general buyer power.

As we noted in the introduction, in their 2007 report into the UK grocery market the Competition Commission secured commercially sensitive retailer-supplier prices and conducted an empirical analysis of the magnitude of buyer power effects.[9] They were unable to find a statistically significant relationship between buyer size and net input price paid[10] for branded good supply. This would be the expected result if any large buyer weakness effect arising from the economics of monopoly supply is counterbalanced by lower retailer specific costs of servicing a contract with a large buyer as we describe.

We now consider the effect of buyer size on supplier investment incentives. Concern is often expressed that large retailers may reduce supplier investment

9 Competition Commission inquiry into the UK grocery market (n 1) app 8.1, paras 44 and 45.
10 The net price is the per unit price for supply adjusted by any promotions or other overall reductions received at the time of invoice.

incentives. Inderst and Wey make an important counter-argument.[11] They consider the model we have just discussed. Suppose a supplier is considering an investment to reduce cost *at the margin*, i.e. to reduce the cost function at point Q on the diagram. Because a small buyer's output approximates to the seller's marginal output the small buyer is able to capture a proportion of the cost reduction in the negotiations. But for a large buyer the incremental cost is determined further from the margin so the large buyer captures proportionately less of a cost reduction at the margin. Consequently an increase in the proportion of large buyers actually increases the incentive of the supplier to lower production costs at the margin. This in turn is welfare enhancing for consumers as it increases the efficient industry output.

Finally we ask whether there are any waterbed effects in the monopoly supplier framework, i.e. does an increase in the size of one retailer have adverse consequences for another smaller retailer? The answer is very simple: the growth of a large buyer (say by merger of any two buyers) has no effect on the price negotiated by a third party provided it has no effect on Q. Thus there are no waterbed effects that arise for any third party with demand q provided Q is unaffected.

Having discussed the economics of bargaining in branded good supply chains we now turn our attention to private label supply chains. To understand the empirical reality of the competitive environment facing private label suppliers we first discuss two case studies.

C. Private Label Goods: Two Case Studies

Milk

Milk is a clear example of a private label good. Each supermarket receives its liquid milk pre-packaged with the supermarket's own branding so that consumers do not differentiate between suppliers. The supermarkets vary in size. There are four big firms that sell about 60 per cent of the liquid milk in the UK: Tesco, Wal-Mart, Morrison, and Sainsbury. But there are a number of other much smaller supermarkets such as Waitrose, Aldi, Somerfield, and so on. The inequality in the size of the buyers allows scope for buyer power effects. Three suppliers supply nearly all of the milk to the big supermarkets: Arla, Dairy Crest, and Robert Wiseman.

[11] R Inderst and C Wey, 'Buyer Power and Supplier Incentives' [2007] 51 *European Economic Review* 647.

To inform our understanding of private label supply chains we conducted interviews with milk buying managers at major UK supermarkets and sales directors at UK milk suppliers. The following description emerged from these interviews.

The standard supply contract in the industry is a rolling one in which supermarkets need offer only three months' notice of termination. The price per litre of milk is agreed in advance and is constant until renegotiation or contract termination. The executives we interviewed did not suggest that these standard features of the contracts varied by size of supermarket buyer. Renegotiation or termination of contracts does not happen at predictable times, nor in some dynamic order. Instead any or all supermarkets can seek to terminate and change suppliers at any given point in time. As a result, during a renegotiation phase a supplier may lose some of its existing contracts while gaining new ones. We do not have data as to times that renegotiation results in prices changing without a change in the supplier. However times when renegotiation resulted in one or more of the largest supermarkets terminating an existing contract were provided to us by one industry participant. These times confirm the unpredictability of renegotiation phases. Starting from October 2001, these contract terminations occurred after the following gaps: 6 months; 10 months; 10 months; 11 months; 2 months; 9 months; 6 months; 6 months.[12] Supermarkets have relative ease in switching suppliers as the milk is supplied in their own supermarket colours. Thus milk is an own label product and so final consumers would be unaware of any change in the identity of milk supplier.

The industry participants we interviewed informed us that the volumes associated with a given contract are very accurately predictable. One supermarket reported offering its supplier 15 years of data on the volumes of milk sold in any given store on any given day.[13] However as contracts can be won and lost the total volumes actually supplied by a given supplier are volatile. Industry sources provided the data contained in Table 3.1 on volume volatility to supermarket buyers as a result of competition between the three main suppliers. The table shows considerable volume variation for all processors. In fact, in the two months between November 2004 and January 2005 the three largest supermarkets (accounting for around half of all UK grocery sales) all changed their suppliers almost simultaneously.

[12] One medium sized chain store buyer was explicitly mentioned as an exception to the uncertain renegotiation phases described above. This supermarket sought to coordinate with the large supermarket buyers by following the large buyers' renegotiation phase and sourcing from suppliers who had been successful in winning the biggest contracts. This was not typical buyer behaviour in this industry.

[13] The exception is that milk sales become less predictable in the few days running up to Christmas.

Table 3.1 Volumes sold to largest four supermarkets by main UK milk processors

Date	Processor, 1 mlpa	Processor, 2 mlpa	Processor, 3 mlpa	Total
12/03	585	690	870	2,145
11/04	575	555	1020	2,150
1/05	350	835	940	2,125
10/05	430	760	920	2,110

Sources: Data from industry

Though the product is homogeneous, supply requires the inter-working of complicated supply chain arrangements and so supermarkets do engage in negotiations with a supplier: auctions or arms' length contracting are not practical. During these negotiations both parties make offers. This process was captured by the following quote: 'We [the supplier] suggest a pence per litre price X. They [the supermarket] respond by saying that is much too high, we could go to your rivals and get Y. And so it goes on.'[14]

Supermarkets either source from just one supplier, or divide their needs into two distinct geographical contracts and use one supplier for each of these contracts. The division is usually on a north-south basis in Great Britain. Thus it is not the case that supermarkets subdivide their contracts to source a bit from each of the main suppliers. In October 2006 the supermarket contracts of the largest supermarkets were given by the figures in Table 3.2 (normalized into market shares).

Failure of negotiations between buyer and supplier can be very visible and lead to unwillingness of key negotiators to work together. A well reported, if extreme, example of such a split occurred one level up in the supply chain between a given supermarket supplier, and their supplier: a farmers' cooperative. This split resulted in the parties being unable to agree to do business directly with each other until key personnel retired.

Finally the supermarkets indicated that they have a good knowledge of the suppliers' cost conditions, which stems in part from the fact that supermarket buyers have contacts across many suppliers.

This picture of the negotiations is consistent with published sources. For example, the KPMG (2003) report into the dairy supply chain notes that:

> . . . negotiations . . . seem to follow guidelines which are relatively common across most supermarket/supplier relationships. The trigger is usually an invitation to

[14] Interview conducted with supermarket supplier during January 2006.

Table 3.2 Market shares in October 2006

	Processor 1	Processor 2	Processor 3	Total
Supermarket 1	-	15.66	9.10	-
Supermarket 2	5.08	5.61	-	-
Supermarket 3	-	-	10.79	-
Supermarket 4	-	1.69	2.96	-
Supermarket 5	4.66	-	4.66	-
Supermarket 6	1.90	-	-	-
Supermarket 7	1.38	-	-	-
Other buyers	19.37	9.21	7.94	-
Total	*32.38*	*32.17*	*35.45*	*100*

Sources: Data from industry

tender by the supermarket or a periodic supplier review programme similar to the Sainsbury initiative in early 2002. The invitation to tender usually contains a demand profile using assumed quantities and container sizes. Bids are made on a per-gallon basis regardless of actual product size and a supplier is selected.[15]

A feature which emerged very strongly from the interviews and from published sources is that there is considerable output uncertainty for suppliers. In its 2003 investigation of the milk processing industry, the Competition Commission wrote:

> It is now the case that a high proportion of the sales of each processor to national multiples is concentrated in only three or four customers, such that the loss of any one of these is likely to have a serious consequence for the processor. The merger parties told us that the national multiples were fully aware of this fact and play off the major processors against each other. [The national multiples] have the ability to switch volumes easily between suppliers . . .. In contrast a processor cannot readily find another avenue to market if it loses sales to a national multiple.[16]

In sum we identified the following key features of the private label milk supply chain:

1. Supermarkets unilaterally start new procurement rounds at unpredictable points in time.

---

15 KPMG, 'Prices and Profitability in the British Dairy Chain: Report to the Milk Development Council' [2003], paras 178–180.

16 UK Competition Commission, 'Arla Foods Amba and Express Dairies plc: A Report on the Proposed Merger' [2003] para 5.97 <http://www.competition-commission.org.uk/rep_pub/reports/2003/483arlaexpress.htm#full> accessed 25 May 2008.

2. Supermarkets negotiate over a per unit transfer price taking as given the required quantities.
3. The suppliers' costs are well known to the supermarkets.
4. Although the volumes demanded by any *individual* retailer are highly predictable, suppliers are uncertain which retailers they will supply in any period and hence they are uncertain at the point of negotiation about their total output.

Carbonated soft drinks

A recent investigation by the Competition Commission investigated a merger between two of the firms that operate in the carbonated soft drinks (CSD) market: Cott Beverages Limited and McCaw (Holdings) Limited. The following information comes from their published report.[17]

The UK soft drink market is large, amounting to 230 litres per person annually. The CSD market accounts for about 50 per cent of this. The CSD market includes drinks such as colas, lemonades, mixers, energy drinks, and carbonated flavoured waters. Unlike milk there are several well known CSD branded goods including Coca-Cola, Pepsi, Fanta, 7-Up, Tango, Lucozade, and Irn Bru. However the private label part of the market remains important at 25 per cent of CSD production volumes.

The main economic features we found in the supply chain for milk also appear in the private label supply chain for CSDs. As the Competition Commission report makes clear, the market is characterized by competition between suppliers, supplier dependency on retailers for output, and frequent retendering by retailers.

The Competition Commission noted that review of contracts was done by retailers on a regular basis:

> Supply agreements for own-label CSDs are typically subject to annual review. Retailers' focus on price appears to be the main factor leading to the short duration of these supply agreements. At the end of a 12-month period, a retailer may continue the existing supply agreement at the existing price, extend it at a reduced price (often as a result of threatening to retender the business), or put the business out to tender.[18]

The private label nature of the good facilitates ease of switching on the part of supermarkets:

> Many retailers told us that switching suppliers was straightforward and inexpensive. Cott cites recent examples of Lidl, Tesco and Sainsbury's switching to Cott and being

---

[17] UK Competition Commission, 'Cott Beverages Ltd and Macaw (Holdings) Ltd Merger Inquiry' [2006] <http://www.competition-commission.org.uk/rep_pub/reports/2006/fulltext/512.pdf> accessed 25 May 2008.

[18] Ibid, para 2.28.

> supplied in as little as two to 12 weeks . . . Retailers own the brand name, packaging tends to be homogeneous and it is relatively straightforward to replicate a recipe. The only costs that a customer seems to have to bear when switching are administrative and logistical. Cott suggested that these costs were limited to tendering costs, establishing new product and supplier codes, and approving product specifications. Retailers also expressed similar views.[19]

Accordingly, retendering is a game with no advantages for the incumbent supplier:

> The ease of customer switching, and the practice of retailers periodically retendering their supply of own-label PET[20] bottled CSDs, means that there is generally limited competitive advantage to being the incumbent supplier in terms of obtaining future business when it is retendered.[21]

As with the case of milk, the supplier of private label CSDs experiences output uncertainty as a result of competition for supermarket contracts:

> The loss of an individual supply agreement with a retailer can have a significant impact on the supplier's overall financial performance. For example, in 2005 Macaw's CSD volumes decreased by just over 10 per cent as a result of losing a major supply agreement.[22]

Thus we conclude that private label procurement has a number of common features with retailers using the threat to switch suppliers to attain low prices. We have investigated the effects of such bargaining interfaces and report the insights this work has generated in the following sections.

D. Competition Upstream: The Case of Private Label Suppliers

We now discuss the economics of private label supply chains. We draw on some insights from Smith and Thanassoulis (ST): a paper that adds to the literature on retailer-supplier bargaining by introducing upstream competition.[23] The effect of the upstream competition is to generate uncertainty for suppliers, a feature that is highlighted in our case studies of private label suppliers.[24] In the rest of the

---

19 Ibid, para 5.21.

20 Polyethylene Terephthalate, i.e. plastic used for soft drink bottles.

21 Competition Commission (n 17) para 5.22.

22 Ibid, para 5.30.

23 Smith and Thanassoulis (n 2).

24 Supplier competition where uncertainty is *absent* has been studied in R Inderst and C Wey, 'Bargaining Mergers and Technology Choice in Bilaterally Oligopolistic Industries' [2003] 34 *RAND Journal of Economics* 1, and C de Fontenay and J Gans, 'Vertical Integration in the Presence of Upstream Competition' [2005] 36 *RAND Journal of Economics* 544. In both these models

chapter we discuss buyer power, waterbed effects, and investment incentives in the private label supply chain.

We formalize our consideration of the private label procurement bargaining interface. We here borrow from ST and consider a number U of suppliers of a homogeneous good. By homogeneous we mean that the consumer is unaware of which supplier supplied the good, as is the case for own-label products.

The U upstream suppliers compete to supply D downstream retailers. Each retailer has a known demand q which may vary across retailers, i.e. we allow for retailers of different size. The U suppliers are symmetric in the sense that they have access to the same technology and so share the same total cost function c(Q). We assume that each retailer seeks only one supplier, perhaps because of the costs of contracting for example. In some real-world examples supermarkets have more than one supplier, but even in such cases negotiations are likely to be over relatively lumpy units.

Except in the special case where the supplier's cost function c(Q) is linear, the incremental cost Δc of serving a retailer with given demand q depends on the total overall output Q of the supplier. For example, with economies of scale the incremental cost Δc declines as Q increases. We saw this in Figure 3.1. However in the case of upstream competition the seller is likely to be uncertain of its overall output Q at the time of negotiation with any retailer. So it must form an *expectation* of incremental cost Δc.[25]

We can now determine natural upper and lower bounds to the negotiated price. The upper bound is determined by the supermarkets' ultimate outside option. If a supermarket fails to agree with any of the U suppliers then we assume it can source the private label product from outside the domestic market (or from a less desirable substitute supplier) at a high exogenous cost of κ per unit. This serves as an upper bound to the price agreed with the U suppliers: a retailer would not pay more to domestic suppliers than she would have to pay to other possible suppliers

(as in ours) competing suppliers bargain with downstream firms in a manner that splits the gains from the relationship. However, the models imply that no supplier is a loser. This implication may be realistic in cases where the upstream firms are all highly differentiated, so that all downstream firms would like to source input separately from each of the upstream firms. However, it is unrealistic if upstream firms are substitutable, as in the case of private label supply, because it requires payments to the firms that fail to supply any product.

[25] We do not allow the buyers to coordinate their purchases on one supplier in the case of economies of scale. This would not be optimal in a repeated setting as the victorious supplier would then wield monopoly power. We note that such coordination on one supplier does not happen in any case in the UK milk or CSD supply chains.

from outside the domestic market for the good, inclusive of all transport costs to get it to the retailer.

No supplier will agree to an overall price per unit of less than the expected per unit incremental cost $\Delta c/q$, as this would be loss making on average. Thus, expected per unit incremental cost $\Delta c/q$ acts as the lower bound for any bargaining agreement.

But how is the expectation of $\Delta c/q$ formed? As there are several competing suppliers, no individual supplier can assume that it will win orders from all the retailers. This is therefore a different situation from the monopoly (branded good) case. It is reasonable to assume that the supplier will condition on the size of the retailer that approaches it for negotiation and that the size of the retailer is a positive signal about the supplier's ultimate output. For example, if the supplier has economies of scale and a large buyer approaches it for supply, it can increase its forecast of its overall output Q; this in turn will reduce its forecast of incremental costs Δc for any given q.

To determine where the negotiated price will fall between these bounds, imagine a more specific modelling framework as follows:

1. Each supplier makes a separate agent available to deal bilaterally with each retailer.
2. Each retailer selects a supplier at random for negotiation.
3. Each supplier's agents negotiate simultaneously and separately. This implies uncertainty for each of the supplier's agents as to his firm's ultimate total supply.
4. If a negotiation should break down then a retailer can commence bargaining with another supplier. Ultimately, if the retailer fails to agree terms with all U suppliers then the good can be sourced from an external market at higher cost κ.

This bargaining form captures the following implicit buyer threat: 'You are only one of U suppliers. If we fail to strike a deal then I will still have U – 1 suppliers I can source product from. Thus to get the business you must make it worth my while.' However, as there are now fewer competing suppliers the retailer is a little disadvantaged at this point.

The retailer must therefore be able to get at least the profit it secures if only U – 1 suppliers are left. But note that *if* there are only U – 1 suppliers left the retailer's threat is weakened, because there are now even fewer suppliers left to threaten to move to. This means that there is an advantage (to both the Uth supplier and the retailer) of striking a deal (rather than moving to the next supplier). The monetary size of this advantage is the *incremental pie*. Thus the bargaining problem between Uth supplier and retailer is how to split the incremental pie. The exact way this is split is determined by the bargaining power of the supplier. We use the parameter λ to refer to the retailer's bargaining power; this is defined such that the incremental pie is split λ parts to the retailer and $1 - \lambda$ parts to the supplier. λ is between 0 and 1.

The extent to which the supermarkets can negotiate price towards the lower bound (the supplier's expected per unit incremental cost $\Delta c/q$) is determined by two factors:

(i) The number of suppliers U: the more suppliers there are the more options the supermarket has to turn to before the ultimate outside option of sourcing abroad at κ.
(ii) The supermarket bargaining power parameter λ: the greater the bargaining power of supermarkets the greater their ability to bargain in any one-to-one negotiation with an individual supplier.

The total payment per unit by the retailer will depend on four industry parameters: κ (cost of sourcing abroad); $\Delta c/q$ (expected per unit cost of supply); λ (supermarket bargaining power); and U (number of upstream competitors). This is depicted in Figure 3.2. κ and $\Delta c/q$ give the upper and lower bound to the agreed per unit payment. The position of the agreed price between these limits is determined by the supermarkets' bargaining power λ and the number of competing processors U. An increase in either λ or U has a downward effect on the price negotiated with the supplier.

κ and $\Delta c/q$ give the upper and lower bound to the agreed per unit payment. The position between these limits is determined by the supermarket's bargaining

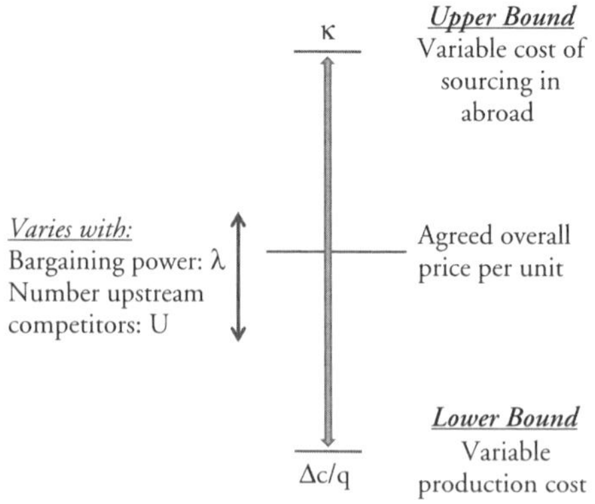

Figure 3.2: The four parameters determining the supermarket-supplier split

power λ and the number of competing suppliers of private label goods. An increase in either λ or U has a downward effect on the price negotiated with the supplier.

The model delivers a simple expression for the actual per unit price paid by the supermarkets to the suppliers. This is done by working backwards through the U potential suppliers, i.e. we first compute the price that would be agreed with the last remaining supplier using κ as the outside option; this price then is in turn the outside option used when negotiating with the U - 1th supplier, and so on. As shown in ST the agreed per unit price which results is given as follows:

$$[\text{Overall per unit payment by retailers}] = \Delta c/q + (1 - \lambda)^U(\kappa - \Delta c/q)$$

where Δc is expected incremental cost. This equation gives the price (ie payment per unit) paid by supermarkets to suppliers. This price is decreasing in both λ and U.

The term $(1 - \lambda)^U$ is of key importance. It may take values in the range zero to one. It represents the bargaining position of the supplier. Thus the price paid by the retailer to the processor is pushed to its lower bound $\Delta c/q$ as $(1 - \lambda)^U$ goes to zero and is pushed in the other direction to its upper bound κ as $(1 - \lambda)^U$ increases to one. $(1 - \lambda)^U$ is the share of the *available* surplus $(\kappa - \Delta c/q)$ that the supplier captures in the negotiations. Thus, private label manufacturers will be able to extract a higher share of the profit if they combine into fewer firms.

Our model highlights that there is an upper bound on the price the suppliers can extract in negotiations with supermarkets. This upper bound is determined by the cost κ to the supermarkets of going outside the immediate market for the input. As depicted in Figure 3.3, the per unit *bargained over surplus* is just $(\kappa - \Delta c/q)$. It is of this that suppliers are in a position to receive a share of $(1 - \lambda)^U$. Even though the supermarkets may be able to raise retail prices well above κ and enjoy additional surplus (depending on competitive retail market conditions) this additional surplus is *beyond the reach* of the suppliers via negotiations, as it is still available to the retailers if they dropped local suppliers and sourced from abroad.[26]

Figure 3.3 highlights the irrelevance of retailers' margins above κ. The supermarkets may be able to raise retail prices well above κ and enjoy additional surplus (depending on competitive retail market conditions). But this additional surplus is beyond the reach of the suppliers via negotiations, as it is still available to the retailers if they dropped local suppliers and sourced from further afield.

[26] Or alternatively from an inferior substitute supplier.

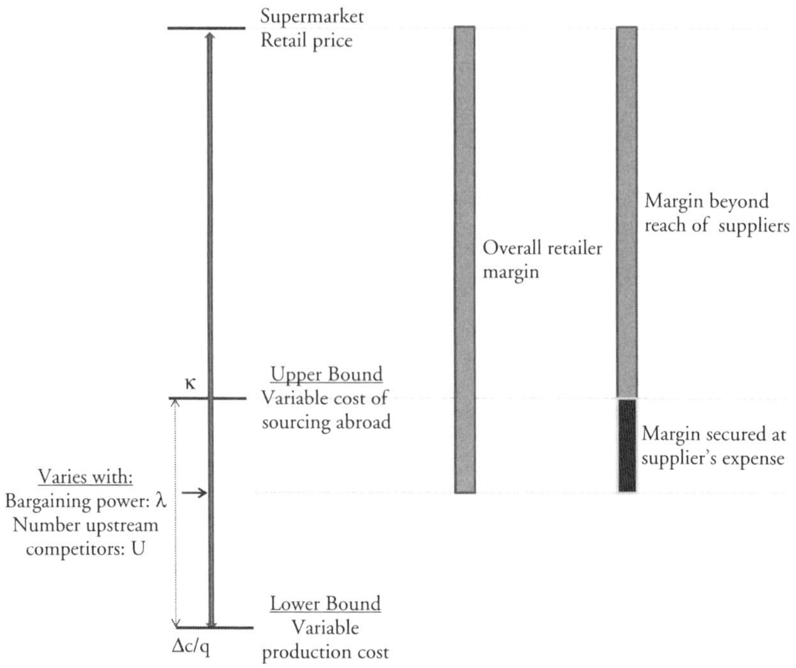

Figure 3.3: What the supplier can and can't bargain over

Example: application to the milk market

The model can be used empirically to explore the implications of changes to costs and changes to market structure (e.g. via merger).[27] In the case of the milk market the option of going abroad to source milk is widely discussed and provides a natural figure for the upper bound κ.[28] As a benchmark figure we have computed that the bargained-over surplus ($\kappa - \Delta c/q$) is approximately five pence per litre, predominantly driven by the cost of transport between Northern Europe and Great Britain. Note that five ppl is much lower than the overall difference between marginal costs and retail prices in the milk market: i.e. much of the supermarkets' surplus is out of reach to milk suppliers.

27 In H Smith and J Thanassoulis, 'Estimating Bargaining Power in the Supply Chain', contained in The Milk Development Council, 'The Milk Supply Chain Project', [2008], ch 1, we use data on supermarket-supplier payments to estimate a value for λ and hence provide an empirical analysis of bargaining power in the UK milk market. See: <http://www.mdcdatum.org.uk/PDF/Oxford%20 Milk%20Supply%20Chain%20Project%20FINAL%20Jan%202008.pdf> accessed 25 May 2008.

28 See: DEFRA, 'The Potential for GB-European Trade in Liquid Milk' [2007] <http://www.defra.gov.uk/foodrin/milk/documents/gb-eu-trade-liquidmilk.pdf> accessed 25 May 2008.

The best that suppliers can hope to do is to extract more of the bargained over surplus. Suppose, hypothetically, $\lambda = 0.5$. As the number of milk processors U is 3, this would imply that the proportion of the bargained-over surplus extracted by processors in the negotiations is given by $(1 - 0.5)^3 = 0.125$. However a merger of the processors would increase this to $(1 - 0.5)^2 = 0.25$.

E. Buyer Power

We now turn to buyer power in the private label goods market. Buyer power effects are determined by the shape of the supplier's total cost curve c(Q). We noted in the last section that the negotiated price is a function of the *expected* per unit incremental cost $\Delta c/q$. When forming this expectation, the buyer conditions on the observed size of the retailer with which it is negotiating. Therefore if the supplier is approached by a relatively large retailer, this is a positive signal about the supplier's expected total output and this changes the expected incremental cost. In the case of economies of scale it reduces the expected incremental cost Δc of supplying a given quantity q of output. This suggests that with economies of scale and private label goods it is the large buyers that wield the greatest power.

For a visual depiction of the result, consider Figure 3.4. Here we compare the expected incremental cost of serving two alternative retailers, one large and one small. The large retailer has volume q_1 and the small retailer has volume q_2. The figure depicts the expected per unit incremental costs $\Delta c/q$ for the seller conditioning on any realization of supplier volumes won from all other (D – 2) possible retailers. If negotiating with the large buyer therefore there are two possibilities to form expectations over: the contract with the smaller retailer is (i) won or (ii) lost. The per unit incremental costs $\Delta c/q$ for each of these possibilities are given by the gradients of the two chords shown in the left hand panel of the figure. If negotiating with the small buyer the corresponding diagram is on the right.

The presence of scale economies results in a concave total cost function. This leads to lower expected per unit incremental cost $\Delta c/q$ when negotiating with the large buyer provided the seller does not attach a high probability to winning other contracts.

Suppose that the total number of suppliers U is larger than 2. In this case, as a result of upstream competition, each supplier is more likely to lose rather than win any other given contract. Thus more weight is put on the steeper of the two chords. In this sense competition causes suppliers to discount other contracts. The gradients of the chords drawn equal the per-unit incremental cost of delivering the required volumes. As the steeper of the two chords is flatter for the large

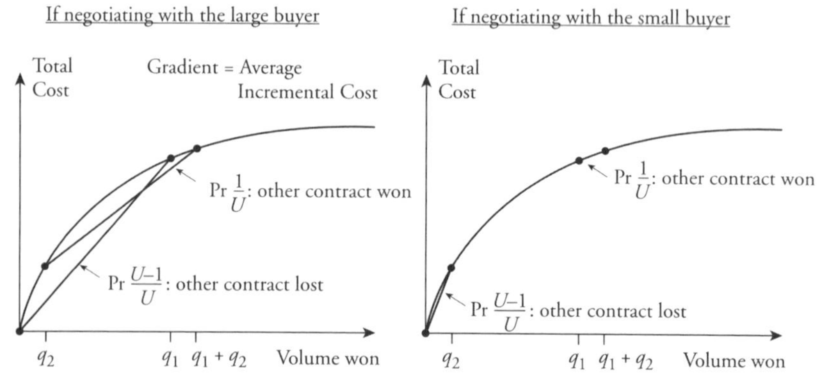

Figure 3.4: Buyer power with upstream competition (the private label case)

buyer (left diagram) than for the small buyer (right diagram) the large buyer gets a better deal. In short, securing a large buyer is better news as to final volumes as other possible contracts are subject to competition and so only won with some probability. Thus a deal with a large buyer is more likely to help steer the supplier into profit. Therefore the supplier is willing to negotiate a lower price to such a buyer.

Thus we have identified that for private label goods and economies of scale there is a new source of buyer power, and large buyers enjoy more of it than small buyers. The result contrasts with our discussion in Section B for a branded good supplier where (with economies of scale) the small buyer had the buyer power. Clearly, private label suppliers operate under very different conditions from branded suppliers.

We have focused on the case of economies of scale. We have previously noted in the operations research literature that delivery and logistics naturally give rise to economies of scale as more customers often means a greater population density among customers, and with greater customer density more efficient routing algorithms are possible.[29] Thus, economies of scale is perhaps the most natural assumption for products delivered to supermarkets. If, however, diseconomies of scale are assumed, the model generates the opposite result: small buyers exert buyer power (to see why, imagine Figure 3.4 with convex total cost functions).

To the extent that the large buyers also have lower specific costs of being serviced (due, for example, to ordering in multiples of full palettes and being in

29 Discussed further in Burns and others (n 8).

easy-to-reach places with better infrastructure) we would predict a clear direction for buyer power: large retailers should have it in the case of private label goods (and secondary brands). This is indeed what the Competition Commission study into supplier prices found (as we noted in the introduction).[30] We have already noted that there was no such evidence of buyer power in the case of branded goods.

F. Waterbed Effects

What happens to suppliers of private label goods when there are changes in concentration among retailers? We focus on the effects on small retailers when large retailers get bigger, i.e. waterbed effects.

Suppose that buyers become more asymmetric while holding their combined purchase volumes constant. For example, two retailers might merge or a large retailer may buy up stores from a small retailer. Then our model provides clear waterbed effect results for the other firms. The direction of these depends on the shape of *per-unit incremental costs*. Before we explain the intuition for this result we discuss what it means for the per-unit incremental cost to be convex or concave.

The per-unit incremental cost of serving a given client with demand q is the per unit cost for these q units from the existing volume base. Thus the per unit incremental cost is plotted as a function of the volumes already being supplied to others. With economies of scale this incremental cost per unit will be declining in volumes already won as each successive unit is a little cheaper to produce. If these incremental costs decline at a declining rate then these are convex.

When incremental costs are convex in this sense the increase in retailer asymmetry raises the transfer prices for all other downstream firms (ie there is a standard waterbed effect). The result is a simple consequence of (i) the fact that the bargained price obtained by any retailer is a function of expected per unit incremental costs $\Delta c/q$, and (ii) the fact that when a cost function is convex then the expected cost increases when the distribution of the seller's output undergoes a mean preserving spread.[31]

Hence our research identifies a mechanism by which downstream mergers or partial acquisitions can have adverse consequences for the supply terms of other retailers. Note that this effect is not present in the case with upstream monopoly,

30 Competition Commission inquiry into the UK grocery market (n 1) app 8.1, paras 44 and 45.
31 This is a familiar result from risk theory.

e.g. the case of a branded good, because the monopolist is certain of its final output. Note also that the effect we identify works on all retailers as the increased volatility in final volumes is felt by all suppliers. Hence even small buyers not in direct competition with the large merging retailer still see a deterioration in the deal they can secure from their suppliers.

Whether a given cost structure has a convex average incremental cost is an empirical question. However there are reasons to believe that with economies of scale the case of convex average incremental costs is likely to be the most relevant.[32] Thus one would typically expect a standard waterbed effect to operate.

In their investigation into the UK grocery market, the Competition Commission (2007) considered whether waterbed effects might operate in the UK. The model they used assumed an upstream monopolist and they noted that it was unclear how relaxing this assumption to upstream competition could generate waterbed effects.[33] The discussion in this section, and in ST more generally, highlights one mechanism through which this may happen.

G. Investment Incentives

We now ask how the presence of large buyers wielding buyer power alters the incentives of private label suppliers to invest in new technology. In many homogeneous good industries, such as liquid milk supply, a production innovation is unlikely to be covered by patents. For example, if cost reduction is due to better practice or larger plants using well understood technology then this is easily replicable. We therefore make use of the concept of *anticipatory equilibrium*: does a supplier wish to invest after internalizing that its rivals will react by matching the investment? In support of our contention that this reciprocal investment is the relevant case note that in the current Competition Commission report into the UK grocery industry, 60 per cent of suppliers responding to the Competition Commission's survey claim that they conduct innovation to 'keep up with the market'.[34]

We consider at what level of production a supplier would choose to deploy a small cost-reducing innovation which lowers the cost of producing one unit by a small amount. The thought experiment here is whether incentives to invest are

[32] With economies of scale, convex average incremental costs are implied by convex decreasing marginal costs: marginal costs falling increasingly gradually to some constant level as volumes increase. In contrast for the marginal cost function to be concave one would require the unnatural condition that marginal costs collapse at an ever increasing rate.

[33] See: Competition Commission (n 1) app 5.4.

[34] Competition Commission (n 1) app 8.2, para 34.

strongest 'at the margin'—that is at high levels of production; or perhaps incentives are strongest at low levels of production. This question is of interest for consumer welfare as innovations at the margin could be expected to filter down into lower retail prices and higher output.

We find that with competition upstream, suppliers facing the bargaining interface described would rather lower costs well inside their expected production levels. There are two reasons. Firstly when bargaining with buyers the supplier will be at pains to share as little of the cost reduction with the buyer as possible. A buyer can claim a fraction of the cost saving if its volume turns out to be pivotal in getting the supplier to access the lower cost unit. A cost reduction at high levels of production is more likely to be dependent on signing up any given buyer and so the buyers extract more of the rents. Secondly, after the input prices are agreed, the cost reduction is only triggered if volumes are sufficiently large. Thus, in the context of upstream competition, a cost reduction at high volume levels is less likely to be achieved. Combining therefore, if the cost reduction is deployed for a unit produced when volumes are low then costs are more certainly lowered but negotiated prices stay high. Thus the output uncertainty experienced by private label suppliers focuses their cost-reducing incentives towards the infra-marginal units rather than the marginal units of output (the latter being the more beneficial to consumers).

An example of this result at work is the practice of suppliers focusing small cost improvements on peak load facilities rather than those production facilities used at the margin. Our case study interviews in milk confirmed that such practices are widespread.

Endogenous technology choice

If a sufficiently large downstream buyer emerges then one can ask how the upstream firms would seek to alter their entire production technology. Here ST identify a new effect: the presence of large buyers ensures that suppliers, if choosing between technologies yielding the same costs at expected volumes, prefer technologies with increasing returns to scale as opposed to decreasing returns to scale. These in turn favour large buyers over small ones who become relatively disadvantaged.

This might be thought of as surprising because if a large downstream buyer is created then, as a result of competition, only one supplier will be victorious in winning her business. On the other hand a technology exhibiting increasing returns to scale would result in small buyers (who are likely to be won) being more expensive to serve on their own. Nevertheless, even though suppliers realize that if they move to a technology of economies of scale their rivals will copy, the industry would still rather move to a technology from which they can charge the large buyer less.

The reason why this happens lies in the changes to the expected costs. By moving to a technology exhibiting economies of scale the expected costs of production for each supplier fall as volumes won have undergone a mean preserving spread. On the other hand the price reduction to the large buyer cannot be too great as the cost of sourcing from outside the domestic market remains high and constrains the bargaining agreement. Thus on balance the suppliers are happy to take their chances in competition with economies of scale as the expected cost reductions outweigh the lower input prices secured.

Of course a move to a technology exhibiting economies of scale disadvantages the smaller buyers, as we have already established. A manifestation of this move to technology exhibiting economies of scale in the UK liquid milk industry is the continued move to ever larger dairies (super-dairies) at which substantial economies of scale can be realized. This move to super-dairies was initiated by one of the processors, but quickly emulated by the rival processors.

H. Strategic Interaction between Branded Goods and Private Labels

In this final section we note that when private label goods are in competition with a branded product our two models interact. By having a private label good the retailer can erode the monopoly status of her branded good supplier. The private label good improves the outside option of the retailer and so allows her to extract a greater share of the surplus from the branded good supplier. We noted the link between the retailer's outside option and her bargaining split in Section B. This effect increases the value of the private label good to the retailer. However, as Section D noted, this is unlikely to filter back to the private label suppliers if competition to supply the private label good from without the immediate domestic market exists.

The ability to lower the bargained returns to the branded good manufacturer will create an incentive to design the private label good to be as close a substitute as possible for the branded good. The economics literature has found evidence suggestive of this effect. Morton and Zettelmeyer[35] note that retailers in their data sample of a number of grocery categories from some US supermarkets are more

[35] F Morton and F Zettelmeyer, 'The Strategic Positioning of Store Brands in Retailer–Manufacturer Negotiations' [2004] 24 *Review of Industrial Organization* 161.

likely to carry a private label good if the share of the leading national brand is higher. Thus, assuming that higher market shares imply a brand is more of a 'must have' to a retailer, the authors conclude that retailers may be using private labels to try to create greater within store competition—and hence extract more of the surplus from branded good suppliers.

I. Conclusions

We discussed the economics of the bargaining interface between suppliers and retailers. We initially considered the case of a branded good supplier, which by definition enjoys a monopoly position and relative certainty regarding the total output supplied to retailers. If a branded good supplier enjoys economies of scale then we showed that the small buyer enjoys buyer power. We considered the effect of retailer size on supplier incentives: an increase in the average size of retailers will increase the supplier's investment incentives at the margin as the bargaining takes place further away from the marginal units and retailers are able to capture a lower fraction of the cost reduction.

After considering some case study evidence, which highlighted the importance of output uncertainty for suppliers of private label goods, we outlined a bargaining theoretic framework applicable for private label supply chains. We found results that contrasted with the branded good case, showing that the suppliers of private label goods are in a very different bargaining environment. We emphasized the point that negotiations with suppliers occur only over the *available* surplus between incremental cost and the retailer's outside option; this may be considerably less than the difference between incremental cost and retail price. We then showed how retailer size can affect the share of the available surplus appropriated by the retailer. Specifically, we showed that if the upstream technology exhibits economies of scale then large buyers wield buyer power (the opposite of the result for the branded good case). This buyer power is generated by the positive effect on expected output that results when a supplier is approached by a large buyer. The analysis also identifies a mechanism by which downstream mergers can result in waterbed effects that harm the interests of smaller retailers.

Next we showed that the output uncertainty experienced by private label suppliers focuses their cost-reducing incentives on infra-marginal rather marginal units of output, and innovations at the margin are of greater benefit to consumers. However, when considering suppliers' choices of the entire production technology a different insight surfaces. When choosing amongst technologies which maintained the costs of expected volumes, suppliers facing a large enough buyer would rather choose increasing as opposed to decreasing returns to scale. Thus the creation of large buyers for private label goods creates a pressure for upstream suppliers to move to overall technologies exhibiting increasing returns to scale. Such a production technology creates buyer power for the large buyer and hence smaller buyers will have to pay relatively higher prices.

Finally we note that having a private label product improves the outside option for a retailer dealing with a branded good supplier. The better the private label good, the greater the share of the surplus a retailer can extract from the branded good supplier. This creates an incentive to design the private label good to be a closer substitute for the branded good. This will raise the value of the private label good itself to the retailer. However, this is not likely to filter back to private label suppliers as the prices they receive are kept in check by the competition to supply—both within and without the domestic market.

Part II

MARKET POWER AND THE ABUSE OF DOMINANCE

4

MARKET POWER IN CONSUMER GOODS INDUSTRIES

*Robert L Steiner**

A. Overview

This chapter presents a unified theoretical framework to estimate market power in consumer goods industries with differentiated products. In the industry to be described, consumer goods manufacturers buy from upstream suppliers and resell to downstream retailers who resell to household consumers. Horizontal competition takes place between firms at the same stage and vertical competition between firms at successive stages. The consumer goods manufacturer's horizontal market share is the firm's share of category sales denominated in manufacturer's (factory) prices and typically represented by the Herfindahl-Hirschman

* Economist, Washington D.C., Senior Fellow American Antitrust Institute (AAI). The views expressed are my own and do not necessarily represent those of AAI.

Index (HHI). The manufacturer's vertical downstream market share equals 1 – retailers' percentage gross margins, which determines the manufacturer's share of his brand's retail price. The manufacturer's vertical upstream market share equals 1 – its suppliers' percentage gross margins, which determines the manufacturer's share of its suppliers selling price and is the manufacturer's invoice cost.[1] Under this definition firms have both horizontal and vertical market shares and compete both horizontally and vertically.

Three forces largely determine market power-horizontal competition, vertical competition, and the internal capabilities of firms. In antitrust law and economics individual firms are typically treated as automatons and the very existence of vertical competition is systematically denied. Former Chairman of the US Federal Trade Commission (FTC), Timothy Muris states 'Market power, of course, exists only at the horizontal level'.[2] Even Supreme Court justices agree that '. . . all competitive effects are by definition horizontal effects'.[3] So in the reigning paradigm, horizontal competition is the sole determinant of market power.

However, a highly qualified industry participant disagrees. Wal-Mart Chairman Rob Walton asserts that 'The manufacturer's price is something that's determined largely by negotiating power of retailers that carry his merchandise', i.e. by vertical upstream competition.[4]

This paradigm also holds that if firms at adjacent stages have an economic relationship, it is strictly complementary in nature. Per Robert Bork, although buyers and sellers are at different vertical stages '. . . their relationship is the same in economic reality as that of partners'.[5] Had antitrust scholars interviewed individuals with hands-on operating experience, as Alfred Marshall invariably did, they would have had to reckon with the belief of industry participants that they had both a complementary and a strong competitive relationship with firms from whom they bought and to whom they sold.

---

[1] I have greatly benefited over the years from discussions with Michael P Lynch. This chapter would have been much poorer without his insightful suggestions. Any remaining errors are mine.

Throughout the chapter gross margins, unless otherwise stated, refer to percentage gross margins, e.g. (selling price – invoice cost) divided by selling price. Retailers' gross margins are abbreviated as RGMs.

[2] T Muris, 'More than Law Enforcement: The FTC's Many Tools—A Conversation with Tim Muris and Bob Pitofsky' [2005] 72 *Antitrust Law Journal* 773, 841.

[3] *Business Electronics Corp v Sharp Electronics Corp* 485 US 717 (1988) Dissent fn 4, p 11.

[4] S R Walton, 'Antitrust, RPM and the Big Brands: Discounting in Small-Town America' [1983] 11 *Antitrust Law and Economics Review* 16.

[5] R Bork, 'The Rule of Reason and the Per Se Concept: Price Fixing and Market Division' [1966] 75 *Yale Law Journal* 377, 404.

In vertical upstream competition in a consumer goods industry a manufacturer strives to beat down the margins and the selling prices of its suppliers and thereby lower its invoice costs at its supplier's expense. In vertical downstream competition, the manufacturer strives to beat down the margins and selling prices of its retailers and thereby capture a larger share of its brands' consumer prices at the retailers' expense. The reward for the manufacturer that becomes a more successful vertical upstream and downstream competitor than its horizontal rivals is that it will be buying for less and selling for more than they are. This accomplishment not only raises the firm's profits and market power in the short run but has longer term competitive effects that have gone unrecognized in antitrust analysis due in part to its denial of the existence of vertical competition. The result is to erect mobility and entry barriers that buffer the manufacturer's market power against erosion. For it is a daunting challenge to compete against a firm that can buy cheaper and sell dearer than its incumbent rivals can and that prospective entrants figure they would be able to do.

Vertical competition is positively and inexorably intertwined with horizontal competition in a chicken-egg relationship. However, vertical competition is an independent force that continues to operate and that can add market power even after a merger to monopoly, in which state there is by definition no remaining horizontal market share or market power to capture.

Organization of the chapter

The following Section B describes when and how the competitive process produces market power. It then spotlights the work of some scholars who recognized that competition has a vertical dimension. In Section C, our theoretical framework is used to critique the US Horizontal Merger Guidelines[6] whose failure to recognize and properly incorporate the competitive relationships between firms at successive stages has led to erroneous welfare conclusions.

Section D identifies the data sources for measurements of vertical and horizontal market power for individual firms and for the category (the relevant product market). A work in progress is the method the competition agencies might use to combine the traditional horizontal metrics for market power with the vertical benchmarks to obtain a better estimate of overall market power. A remaining question is how the competition agencies can take the third source of market power, a firm's internal strengths, into account.

[6] US Department of Justice and The Federal Trade Commission, '1992 Horizontal Merger Guidelines' [Revised 8 April 1997] <http://www.ftc.gov/bc/docs/horizmer.shtm> accessed 8 March 2008.

Section E analyses the competition between leading advertised brands and private labels, also called store brands. It concludes with a discussion of the British grocery industry. The final section presents the Lynch model that yielded extremely accurate predictions of private label prices given national brand prices and confirmed the inverse relationships between margins in manufacturing and retailing.

B. The Competitive Process and Market Power

How do we tell whether firms are competitors? The conventional answer is that competitors are firms that produce substitutes. This definition works nicely when firms are in a horizontal relationship but is difficult to apply to firms in a vertical relationship and hence has acted to restrict the process of competition to the rivalry among firms at the same stage. The economist F A Hayek concluded that the accepted theory of competition was so far removed from real-world competition among firms as to be of little use in policy formulation. He therefore offered a definition that he attributes to Dr Samuel Johnson, 'the action of endeavoring to gain what another endeavors to gain at the same time'.[7] In this spirit I have proposed that firms are competitors when they can take sales, margins and market shares from each other.[8] By this definition, firms in both a horizontal and vertical relationship can be competitors.

By becoming a stronger horizontal competitor, the manufacturer also becomes a stronger vertical upstream competitor, for this empowers the firm's purchasing department in its negotiations with its upstream suppliers in two ways. Larger orders typically reduce a supplier's cost due to scale economies and its markup over cost due to the stronger clout that large buyers can exert. Moreover, a highly skilled purchasing agent will strike a better deal with suppliers than a less skilled one with the same size order to place. These factors combine to raise the manufacturer's vertical upstream market share and lower his invoice cost.

A lower than category-average invoice cost means that at equal factory margins the brand's factory and retail price are lower than competing brands, so it will gain horizontal market share from them; or that at higher factory margins and equal factory and retail prices the manufacturer will be more profitable than rival producers, again making the firm a more formidable horizontal competitor and enabling it to further strengthen its internal capabilities—or some of each.

---

7 F A Hayek, *Individualism and Economic Order* (1st edn, 1947), 96. I am indebted to Michael Lynch for calling this excellent work to my attention.

8 Specifically, take from each other gross margins, $ sales or share of $ category sales.

The positive relationship between vertical and horizontal market power can also be illustrated by starting with an increase in vertical downstream market power. Through the partnership of the firm's research and development (R&D) and marketing department, the manufacturer introduces a new product concept and backs it with strong advertising. Successful advertising of an attractive item generates product identity, the ability of a consumer to recognize quickly that famous Brand X on sale at retailers A and B is the same item. Intrabrand competition is intensified and retailers' gross margins (RGMs) are beaten down, for retailers fear to place a higher price than other stores on what consumers will recognize as the same item. Thereby the manufacturer captures vertical downstream market share from his retailers. If the brand's RGM has been reduced further than those of rival makers, it also gains market power from them. At the same factory price its retail price will be lower than theirs, and it will gain horizontal market share. And at equal retail prices the manufacturer's selling price and profits will be higher than theirs—or probably some of each. Thereby the manufacturer becomes a stronger horizontal competitor who can afford to further strengthen his internal capabilities, place larger orders with his suppliers, and obtain a lower invoice price than his horizontal rivals, etc.

Should the manufacturer become a monopolist by the above process or by merger, the firm can continue to use its size and bargaining clout to enlarge its vertical upstream and downstream market shares and market power until it has driven down the margins of its suppliers and retailers to the competitive level. As a monopolist, the manufacturer is now the only source of merchandise in the category for retailers and the only customer in the category for suppliers. No longer can retailers play off rival producers against each other in search of a lower price and more advantageous non-price terms. In their bargaining with the monopolist manufacturer retailers cannot carry out a threat to switch to a rival brand if they want to continue offering an entry in the relevant product category. This provides the monopolist manufacturer with a less elastic demand curve and a higher optimal selling price and profit. Likewise, if upstream firms want to continue as suppliers to the industry, they will have to make greater price concessions than when the manufacturing sector was more competitive.

These dynamics enable the manufacturer to buy still cheaper and sell still dearer, again making entry more difficult than it would be if the manufacturer could gain no more market power once it became a monopolist.[9]

[9] Of course, a roughly similar outcome could ensue if the manufacturer became a dominant firm rather than a monopolist. The purpose of assuming the firm becomes a monopolist is to demonstrate the reality of vertical competition and market power by positing an environment in which there is no remaining source of horizontal market power to exploit.

Some earlier work that recognized vertical competition's role in market power

The contributions of important dissenters have unfortunately not seriously undermined the existing paradigm's assumption that competition is a process that only occurs among firms at the same horizontal level. For example, it has ignored the earlier cited statement by Rob Walton, Chairman of America's largest retailer, that it was vertical upstream competition through the negotiating power of retailers that largely determined the prices charged by consumer goods manufacturers.[10] And already in 1951, J K Galbraith's concept of countervailing power described how, by exerting upstream vertical clout, oligopolistic buyers constrained the prices of oligopolistic sellers.[11] Indeed, the same vertical contest takes place among less powerful firms so long as the buyer and seller are not price takers.

In 1955 the political scientist, Joseph Palamountain, jr had identified three kinds of conflict: traditional horizontal competition among retailers, 'intertype competition' among different types of retailers, and 'the one most neglected by economic theoreticians' he dubbed 'vertical conflict'.[12] He illustrated the consequences of vertical upstream and downstream market power by observing that a manufacturer whose brand enjoyed a strong preference with consumers had a bargaining advantage in dealing with its wholesaler suppliers, as did a retailer with a desirable location. Palamountain pointed out that the classical assumption that retailing is perfectly competitive explained why economists had overlooked vertical conflict, since in this environment 'power is completely absent'.[13]

In the classical economics texts, the wheat farmer was used to illustrate perfect competition. His output was too small to affect total supply or demand, so he bought and sold as a price taker. In this environment there could be no vertical competition. In agreement with Palamountain, the economist Richard Hefflebower observed that: 'In the development of price and output theory, economists have dealt primarily with manufacturing industries . . . and have treated these as though manufacturers sold finished products to consumers, or alternatively, as if the distributive trades were *analytically neutral*' (emphasis added). But, of course, some form of imperfect competition exists in all consumer goods industries, so firms are seldom price takers as buyers or sellers.

10 See: Walton (n 4), 2. In this author's experience similar views are held by many participants in consumer goods industries.

11 J K Galbraith, *American Capitalism: The Concept of Countervailing Power* (1st edn, 1952).

12 J Palamountain, jr, *The Politics of Distribution* (1955, First Greenwood Reprinting 1968), 48.

13 Ibid, 50.

The economist Michael Porter got it right in identifying the five competitive forces that determine industry profitability and competitive advantage, a term virtually synonymous with market power. Two of the five are the vertical bargaining power of suppliers and of buyers. Despite its acceptance in business schools, Porter's work has had surprisingly little influence with the competition agencies.[14]

Finally, the literature on the economic effects of advertising has helped illuminate the interplay between vertical and horizontal competition in a 'dual-stage' world where consumer goods manufacturers sell to retailers who resell to household consumers. Contributors to this literature include Emily Fogg-Meade, Alfred Marshall, Neil Borden, Mark Albion, Paul Farris, Michael Lynch, and the present author.[15] The first regularity is the tendency of advertised brands to have lower retail gross margins despite their higher retail prices. The second regularity, first implied by Marshall, is the existence of an inverse relationship between the margins of manufacturers and retailers when manufacturers' brands are strong (have a powerful consumer franchise) or are weak (lack a loyal following with consumers).

With weak brands consumers are disposed to switch brands within store rather than stores within brand. Here the feeble intrabrand competition leads to wide RGMs. The ability freely to substitute among rival manufacturers' brands gives retailers the bargaining edge in their vertical upstream negotiations and depresses manufacturer's margins. With leading advertised brands, many consumers will switch stores within brand should a retailer fail to stock a favourite brand or to price it competitively. The intensive intrabrand competition depresses retailers' margins while their inability to substitute for the manufacturer's brand provides the manufacturer with a less elastic demand curve and a higher optimal margin and price. Increasing the popularity of an existing brand not only directly raises its horizontal market share, but by the process earlier explained also increases its

---

14 M E Porter, *Competitive Advantage: Creating and Sustaining Superior Performance* (1st edn, 1985, Free Press), 5. The five competitive forces are illustrated in Figure 1-1, p 5.

15 E Fogg-Meade, 'The Place of Advertising in Modern Business' [1901] 9 *Journal of Political Economy*, 218; A Marshall, *Industry and Trade* (1920), 301–302; N H Borden, *The Economic Effects of Advertising* (1942); P W Farris and M S Albion, 'The Impact of Advertising on the Price of Consumer Products' [1980] 44 *Journal of Marketing* 17; M S Albion, *Advertising's Hidden Effects: Manufacturers' Advertising and Retail Pricing* (1983); M P Lynch, 'Why Economists Are Wrong to Neglect Retailing and How Steiner's Theory Provides an Explanation of Important Regularities' [2004] 49 *Antitrust Bulletin* 911. The contributions of the present author on this topic include R L Steiner, 'Does Advertising Lower Consumer Prices?' [1973] 37 *Journal of Marketing* 19; R L Steiner, 'The Inverse Association Between the Margins of Manufacturers and Retailers' [1993] 8 *Review of Industrial Organization* 717; and R L Steiner, 'The Evolution and Applications of Dual-Stage Thinking' [2004] 49 *Antitrust Bulletin* 877.

market power indirectly if its RGM falls further than those of competing makers.

C. The US Horizontal Merger Guidelines

The Merger Guidelines reflect the state of economic thinking in the US and its limitations. Competition is envisaged almost exclusively as a horizontal process and the firms are automatons that do not differ in internal cultures and strengths.

> The unifying theme of the Guidelines is that mergers should not be permitted to create or enhance market power or to facilitate its exercise. Market power to a seller is the ability profitably to maintain prices above competitive levels for a significant period of time.[16]

Sellers gain supracompetitive profits and market power through horizontal concentration. Unless a potential merger significantly increases concentration or occurs in an already highly concentrated market it will not increase market power and is therefore highly unlikely to be challenged by the competition agencies. Market concentration is a matter of the number of firms in the market and their respective horizontal market shares and is to be measured by the HHI.

In a prospective merger prices are to be measured at the stage at which the merger is taking place.[17] Hence, in a merger among consumer goods manufacturers, prices will be denominated in manufacturers' (factory) prices. In keeping with the unstated assumption that the retail stage is perfectly competitive, the Guidelines presume that changes in factory prices are a reliable proxy for the resultant changes in retail prices. This is to make the erroneous prediction that the RGM (the percentage retail gross margin) would not be changed by a merger that increases concentration and market power at the manufacturing stage.

The Guidelines have little to say about vertical relations but do specify one vertical way that a powerful buyer can gain market power to the detriment of society. If the buying firm is a monopsonist or possesses substantial monopsony power, it can force the upstream supplier to sell a reduced supply at prices below the competitive level.[18] How can the supplier do that and stay in business? The firm must

---

[16] Horizontal Merger Guidelines (n 6) s 0.1.

[17] Horizontal Merger Guidelines (n 6) s 1.11.

[18] On the buying side, the Guidelines define market power as '. . . the ability of a single buyer ("a monopsonist"), a coordinating group of buyers or a single buyer, not a monopsonist, to depress the price paid for a product to a level that is below the competitive price and thereby depress output'. Horizontal Merger Guidelines (n 6) s 0.1.

have a rising average cost curve, so that at a reduced output its costs are lower. However, the exercise of output-reducing monopsony power by retailers or consumer goods manufacturers is extremely rare, although there are examples of it in labour markets and in some markets further upstream including in agriculture.[19]

Studies of the typical production cost curve find that it first drops sharply and then remains essentially horizontal.[20] As a consumer goods manufacturer in several industries with access to our costs, I found our production costs generally fit that description, but that our non-production costs exhibited returns to scale over the relevant range of output including freight-in and out and salesmen's compensation that were largely variable costs. Other important non-production costs included the purchase of advertising media, rent, outside legal and accounting services, and the salaries of key personnel in all departments. These are recurrent fixed costs that do not vary much with output over the course of a year or two and become a smaller portion of total cost as output increases. Thus across the relevant output range our overall-firm cost curves reflected positive returns to scale, rather than the negative ones that are a necessary condition for the Guidelines' monopsony scenario.

Moreover, a dominant buyer, such as Wal-Mart, will bargain hard to drive down the manufacturer's price but not consciously so far as to create a supply problem. For after the bargaining has been completed, powerful retailers want to sell as much of the item as possible and characteristically will add only a small markup to the bargained-down invoice price. Thus output is expanded rather than contracted. In sum, the Guideline's assumption that vertical upstream market power arises solely from output-reducing monopsony power is clearly wrong. The Guidelines' definition leads to the ridiculous conclusion that a dominant retailer has no market power when it forces the manufacturer to reduce its price, but not below the competitive level, and without reducing (and typically increasing) output.

More broadly, a major casualty of the US Guidelines is its failure to look vertically due to its 'single-stage' blinders. Changes in elasticities and costs at one stage have important effects at other stages. For example, increases in productivity at one

19 D W Carlton and J M Perloff, *Modern Industrial Organization* (1st edn, 1990). They conclude that 'In markets other than labor, monopsony is also considered to be rare; it is likely only when resources are specialized' in the long run', p. 117. F M Scherer and D Ross, *Industrial Structure and Economic Performance* (3rd edn, 1990), 528, show that if the monopolist producer operates at constant unit costs and resells in a competitive market, there will be no supply reduction and consumers will benefit.

20 See: Scherer and Ross, ibid 47 Figure 3.5, that illustrates the L-shaped manufacturing cost curves in Johnston's research.

stage typically generate increases at adjacent stages. This dynamic occurred in the US toy industry following the 'marketing revolution' that commenced with the virtually simultaneous advent of TV advertising to children and the rapid growth of Kmart-type discount stores.[21] It also has been documented in the Mexican detergent industry following the purchase by Wal-Mart of a Mexican retailer.[22] In the long-term it is rising productivity that generates increases in productive and distributive efficiencies and is primarily responsible for boosting the standard of living.

In contrast to the thinking in American antitrust circles, the EU must be commended for daring to apply the word competition to vertical relations in its 2004 Guidelines: 'The competitive pressure on a supplier is not only exercised by competitors but can also come from its customers.'[23]

D. Measuring the Three Sources of Market Power

A firm's market power derives from its horizontal and vertical market shares and its internal strengths and culture.

Competition agencies use the HHI to measure horizontal market power. Elsewhere, I have identified the US data sources for upstream and downstream vertical market shares for the firm(s) of interest and for the category.[24] To summarize, the lower are suppliers' margins and the resultant manufacturer's invoice costs, the greater is the manufacturer's vertical upstream market share and market power relative to its suppliers and to rival makers who pay higher invoice costs. The invoice costs of individual firms are best obtained from the contribution margin programmes of virtually all major firms. These detail the purchases of its divisions and product categories as part of the calculation of their contribution to the company's overhead and profit. The prime source for invoice costs for the category is the Bureau of Economic Analysis' Benchmark Input/Output Accounts, although it is only published every five years. The Annual Survey

21 Steiner Dual-Stage Thinking (n 15) 883–885, and other articles cited in that note.

22 B Javorcik, W Keller and J Tybout, 'Openness and Industrial Response in a Wal-Mart World: A Case Study of Mexican Soaps, Detergents and Surfactant Producers' [2006] World Bank Policy Research Working Paper No. 3999.

23 Guidelines on the Assessment of Horizontal Mergers under the Council Regulation on the Control of Concentration between Undertakings [2004] OJ C31/5, s V. 'Countervailing Buyer Power'.

24 For a more thorough treatment see: R L Steiner, 'Vertical Competition, Horizontal Competition and Market Power' (forthcoming 2008) in *Antitrust Bulletin*.

of Manufacturers also provides cost of materials for product categories but includes few purchases of services. For services the investigator must turn to non-governmental sources, such as TNS Media Intelligence, for advertising outlays.

The manufacturer's vertical downstream market share is 1 – RGM. The lower the RGM the greater the manufacturer's market power. Manufacturers know their average selling price for each stock keeping unit (SKU) and usually also its RGM. Marketing research firms in most major industries are commissioned by the industry trade association to collect and publish average retail prices and quantities sold of each SKU annually or quarterly. RGMs can be computed using these retail prices and the manufacturer's selling prices. Other helpful sources are the IRS Corporation Income Tax Returns and the annual Census of Retail Trade which publish RGMs for around 50 classes of retail stores.

Having obtained an estimate of vertical market power, the question becomes how to weight and combine the measures of horizontal and vertical market power so as to devise an index of overall market power. I suggest that this should become an urgent research topic.

It may well be impossible to devise a metric to measure the third source of market power, the firm's internal strengths and its culture. Yet it is essential that economists and attorneys in the competition agencies take these into account rather than viewing firms as lifeless automatons. Suppose two manufacturers, A and B, with similar vertical and horizontal market shares are vying to acquire a sizeable competitor in the relevant market. If Firm A makes the acquisition, the agency can predict based on its culture, internal strengths, and track record that it will introduce new items whose performance attributes incorporate the results of extensive consumer research. Through skilled sourcing, it will reduce costs and ensure quality. Firm A will promote the line extensively, driving down retailers' margins. It will add a large markup to its costs so that its products will have the highest consumer prices in the category and typically the best quality. Sales will increase, and its market share will become first or second in the category (sounds like Procter and Gamble). If Manufacturer B, a rather poorly managed conglomerate, makes the acquisition, the outcome will almost certainly be quite different.

E. The Competition between Leading National Brands and Private Labels

The rivalry between the leading national brands (LNBs) of manufacturers, which typically are strongly advertised, and the private labels (PLs) or store brands (SBs) of retailers involves vertical and horizontal relationships that are not present in categories composed entirely of manufacturers' brands. Retailers have discretionary powers that cannot be exercised in the contest between the branded goods of rival manufacturers. Virtually all of these relationships were discovered in the first large-scale empirical investigation of LNB/PL relationships by the Harvard Business School research team headed by Professor Neil Borden and reported in Borden's monumental work, *The Economic Effects of Advertising* (1942). Along with Alfred Marshall's *Industry and Trade*, it remains one of the most authoritative, easily understandable descriptions of the consumer goods economy.[25] Credit also is due to the English economist, Dorothea Braithwaite, whose 1928 article was perhaps the first to identify the crucial role of brand reputation in consumer goods markets.[26]

The insights of Braithwaite and the remarkable scope of Borden's contributions

Braithwaite attributed the ability of the early advertised brands to sell for more than unadvertised manufacturers brands and private labels to their superior reputation, noting that the retail price of an intensively advertised brand of soap flakes was higher than that of unadvertised brands, although 'chemically there is absolutely no difference'. While conceding that sometimes the advertised brand was of superior quality, the advertising 'induces consumers to bear a difference in price out of all proportion to the difference in quality'.[27] Braithwaite also reported that the excellent reputation of certain large shops had enabled them successfully to introduce reputable store brands which she hoped would provide greater competition to the leading advertised brands than unadvertised manufacturers' brands had.

As part of their research programme, Borden's team interviewed 36 chain store executives and numerous consumer goods manufacturers. Borden concluded that the chains had to price their PLs below the price of the counterpart LNB because a popular advertised brand has a reputation value that 'permits it to obtain from consumers a price somewhat above that obtained by merchandise which has comparable objective characteristics but which has not had the advantage of being made well known'.[28]

Subsequent research has shown that the power of reputation does not disappear even when consumers view the quality of the LNB and PL to be identical. The contemporary marketing researcher, Raj Sethuraman, found that consumers in 20 grocery product categories were willing to pay a 28.1 per cent price premium

25 Borden (n 15); Marshall (n 15).
26 D Braithwaite, 'The Economic Effects of Advertising' [1928] 38 *Economics Journal* 16.
27 Ibid, 30.
28 Borden (n 15) 603.

for the national brand when they rated its quality as identical to that of the PL counterpart. He concluded that just because PLs were able to close the quality gap with LNBs did not mean they could close the price gap.[29]

In LNB/PL competition a reputation premium arises when the brands of the upstream national brand makers are stronger horizontal competitors than the rival brands of downstream retailers—with the result that the national brand will retail for more than the store brand with comparable physical characteristics. As earlier shown, this creates an entry and mobility barrier for the private label. The height of the barrier is elevated by the reality that the LNB virtually always turns over faster than the store brand. Therefore, unless the retailer can make a higher percentage and $ RGM on his PL than on the LNB, the LNB will be more profitable. So there is little reason, at least in the short run, for the retailer to introduce a PL. The twin requirements that the PL must sell below the retail price of the LNB due to its reputation disadvantage and yet have a higher $ and percentage RGM than the LNB to be more profitable, requires the retailer to obtain a far lower invoice cost from his suppliers than the national brand's factory price. Borden recognized this reality and reported that when advertised brands were too strong (his list for 1939 mentions soap, soap flakes, canned soup, baking soda, and corn flakes) retailers could not achieve a sufficient sales volume to obtain a low cost purchasing contract. This condition was a principal reason given by the chains interviewed by Borden's team for not introducing a store brand.[30] It illustrates one way that the popular advertised brand's larger horizontal market share makes it a stronger vertical upstream competitor.

In describing the 'struggle for brand control' Borden noted that in categories where leading advertised brands were densely distributed, price competition drove down retailers' margins, yet the brands had become so popular that wholesalers and retailers were obliged to carry them irrespective of the manufacturer's price and their own razor-thin margins. It was retailers 'desire to be free from direct price comparisons upon merchandise that consumers know to be identical'—what today we would say from intensive intrabrand competition—that produced the thin RGMs and provided the original incentive for retailers to introduce private labels. Borden understood that retailers could obtain higher gross margins on their private labels because 'exact comparisons of price have

29 R Sethuranam, 'What Makes Consumers Pay More for National Brands than for Store Brands: Image or Quality?' [2000] Harvard Science Institute Working Paper No 00-110; R Sethuranam, 'Measuring National Brands' Equity over Store Brands' [2003] 1 *Review of Marketing Science* 1.

30 Borden (n 15) 594, 595. Subsequent researchers have found that advertising intensity and private label market shares are negatively correlated. R L Steiner, 'The Nature and Benefits of National Brand/Private Label Competition' [2004] 24 *Review of Industrial Organization* 105, 118–119, provides a summary of these studies.

been avoidable' due to the fact that the PLs of different retailers were not identical.[31]

Creating a strong private label programme offered the chains a strategic path to building good will for their stores and raising profits by wresting control over the merchandise they sell from branded manufacturers. Borden discovered that retailers could often purchase manufacturers' brands on an exclusive territorial basis just as cheaply as a store brand. But he warned that this strategy was not as viable as building a strong consumer acceptance for the retailer's own brands, for should the retailer's efforts succeed in increasing the sales of the national brand, its manufacturer would be sorely tempted to terminate the exclusive and sell the brand to competing stores. Therefore, this strategy involved greater 'uncertainty and risk'.[32]

Some recent developments

The longer term prospects of achieving a large and profitable volume of PL business began to encourage chains to subsidize their store brand programmes. There proved to be many benefits flowing from a large PL market share in a product category. These included:

1. 'An umbrella effect.' A large PL market share in a category enhanced the chain's reputation with consumers and so made it easier to make successful PL introductions in other categories.
2. The ability to buy their store brands cheaper—not only from independent suppliers but also from 'dual-manufacturers', firms that made their own branded items and also supplied private labels.
3. As an added bonus, the exercise of vertical upstream bargaining power by a chain with a large PL market share not infrequently has persuaded manufacturers to sell their own LNBs to the chain at a discounted price. This practice is one of the two major developments not foreseen by Borden, although it is certainly not inconsistent with his thinking.[33]

A development that I expect would have been more surprising to Borden is the growth, especially in Britain, of the market shares of high quality private labels which has led to dynamic changes in their relationships with competing national brands. In the US the growing market shares of store brands has hastened the demise of the national and regional brands of secondary manufacturers.

[31] Borden (n 15) 592.
[32] Ibid, 39.
[33] F S Morton and F Zettelmeyer, 'The Strategic Positioning of Store Brands in Retailer-Manufacturer Bargaining' [2004] 24 *Review of Industrial Organization* 105.

Echoing a prediction that has often been heard in the trade, a Wal-Mart executive stated, '. . . in time I believe you will see only two offerings per category on the shelf—the national brand leader and the store brand. There will be no space for the second or third brand player in the category.'[34]

Three industry structures in which leading national brands and private labels compete

Retail prices would almost certainly be higher if secondary manufacturers' brands were the only rivals to the LNB's than if the latter were opposed by popular PLs. Retailers receive far greater rewards and, as Borden observed, take fewer risks by harnessing their internal strengths to build a strong PL line than devoting their efforts to establish secondary manufacturers' lines. Internal strengths are exercised in the retailer's decisions on everyday and promotional pricing, placement of brands on store shelves, end caps and island displays, and through other marketing decisions. Retailers are far freer to exercise these strengths when they can make all decisions themselves and do not need to engage in constant consultations and receive approvals from a branded manufacturer.

I have identified three characteristic industry structures involving LNBs and PLs. In 'manufacturers brand domination', a handful of powerful advertised brands dominate the relevant market. Private labels and secondary manufacturers' brands have very small market shares. The result is high levels of concentration and supra-competitive profits in manufacturing. The towering factory prices produce inflated consumer prices despite the razor-thin RGMs. However, the resultant welfare losses may be mitigated by efficiency gains in the production and distribution of LNBs and by the exercise of countervailing power by dominant retailers.

Social welfare is highest in the consumer goods industry when total surplus is maximized, there is a lively pace of innovation, quality levels are rising, and consumers can easily and intelligently choose from among items with different product attributes. This combination of conditions is most likely to occur in a structure that I have labelled the 'mixed regimen'[35] in which a handful of powerful national brands vie with high market share store brands of large retailers. The two kinds of brands 'keep each other honest' and consumers benefit due to interactions that do not occur when all items are manufacturers' brands.

---

[34] Cited by P Berlinski, 'Wal-Mart Sets New Paradigm for Private Label Success' [1997] *Private Label* 15, 19.

[35] Steiner (n 30).

With sizeable market shares PLs have sufficient popular acceptance to cause the LNBs to lose sales if priced too far above them, as Borden reported. The exercise of vertical upstream bargaining pressure by large retailers limits the LNBs' price/cost margins and constrains their factory prices, the more so when faced with inexpensive PL retail prices enabled by low invoice costs from suppliers with substantial scale economies. The intensive horizontal intrabrand competition among retailers on LNBs produces very thin RGMs. The combination of only mildly inflated LNB factory prices and slim RGMs yields a reasonable level of national brand retail prices that establish a ceiling below which the PLs must be retailed by the amount of their reputation disadvantage. Therefore, average category retail prices are quite reasonable. Moreover, in the mixed regimen product innovation by LNB manufacturers is stimulated, for it is by introducing attractive new products with superior attributes that LNB makers most effectively shield their market shares against private labels that do not yet contain these new features.[36]

The welfare-enhancing mixed regimen structure rests on a relatively equal balance of power between LNBs and PLs. If the power of the store brands is substantially eroded, the structure will be replaced by manufacturers' brand domination and average retail prices will rise.

If the power of the LNBs is emasculated, the structure will be replaced by private label domination. Concentration in the retailing sector will increase. Retailers need no longer stock popular advertised brands whose reputation premium formerly depressed the prices of PLs. Without them there will now be a smaller spread between LNB and PL prices, yet average retail prices will climb, for different stores of the same chain do not compete by price on the chain's own-label brands. Thus intrabrand competition, the chief force disciplining RGMs, is eliminated. Interbrand competition within stores, the other important force restraining RGMs, is also absent. Retailers do not carry the store brands of rival chains.

Finally, consumers will largely have lost the ability to make side-by-side price and quality comparisons within store of competing brands. This elevates the cost of search and degrades its quality. Consumers must now visit a larger number of retail outlets to view a reasonable assortment of competing LNBs and PLs whose relative prices, qualities, and performance attributes cannot be as accurately judged as when easily recognized manufacturers' brands and retailers' store brands are arrayed side by side.

---

36 Steiner (n 30). Examples are cited at 118.

The British grocery industry

Developments in the UK will be fascinating and instructive to follow. Overall, the Competition Commission has given the industry good grades.[37] However, concentration levels are far higher than in the US and there are entry barriers and various other anti-competitive forces.[38] Still, real retail food prices relative to the prices of all items fell by about 8 per cent from 2000 to 2006.[39] Innovation by branded manufacturers and by leading multiples (chains) on behalf of their store brands has been rising. Paul Dobson suggests that economies of scale at both stages help account for this outcome and that high concentration in retailing enables major supermarkets to place the huge orders that enable their PL suppliers to invest in product innovation.[40]

Private label market shares have reached around 43 per cent and are the highest in Europe and almost three times those in the US.[41] As in the US, PL quality has increased. To a far greater extent than elsewhere, British supermarkets offer multi-tier ranges from low cost through a high cost 'premium range' with quality equal to the LNBs.[42] But what distinguishes the British consumer from her US and European counterparts, is her stronger perception that store brands are 'close and credible substitutes to branded goods . . . and not seen as distinctly inferior products'.[43] Moreover, British shoppers 'have an exceptional degree of store loyalty and tend not to shop around for grocery products, but instead consistently rely on one store for most or all of their needs'.[44] For the above reasons, it would seem that private labels in Britain would have to be sold at a slimmer discount from the national brand's price than elsewhere, because the reputation premium should be lower. I am not aware of any studies that deal with this conjecture. Since retail grocery prices have declined, these conditions have not penalized the British consumer, so far.

---

37 UK Competition Commission 'Working Paper on Retail Competition' [2007] <http://www.competition-commission.org.uk/inquiries/ref2006/grocery/pdf/working_paper_retail_competi tion.pdf> accessed 25 May 2008, reports that the various adverse competitive effects 'are not at present causing a national-level deterioration in prices, product range or levels of innovation' as compared to 2000 levels (see: p 1–2).

38 UK Competition Commission, 'The Supply of Groceries in the UK Market Investigation: Provisional Findings Report' [2007] <http://www.competition-commission.org.uk/inquiries/ref2006/grocery/prov _findings/prov_find_report.pdf> accessed 25 May 2008. Figure 3-1 shows Tesco with a 26% market share and the top four grocery retailers with a 60.8% share in 2006.

39 Ibid, Figure 3.5.

40 P W Dobson, 'Exploiting Buyer Power: Lessons from the British Grocery Trade' [2005] 72 *Antitrust Law Journal* 529, 551–552.

41 Ibid, 551, Table 6.

42 Ibid, 545.

43 Ibid, 551.

44 Ibid, 535.

It appears that something like the mixed regimen presently characterizes the British food industry. However, one should watch for a trend toward private label domination in which retail concentration and PL market shares continue to grow, the unwillingness and increasing difficulty of making good price and quality comparisons among stores and among brands raises retail grocery prices (despite the narrowing of the reputation premium) and diminishes consumers' ability to make informed choices.

F. The Lynch Model

Michael Lynch has produced a formal model of the Steiner dual-stage theory. It contains a remarkably simple formula for finding the profit-maximizing retail price of the store brand (SB): (SB = PL) given the retail price of the leading brand (LB) and the factory selling prices of both brands.[45] The simplicity derives from the assumption that with a LB consumers are more disposed to switch stores within brand than brands within store. In Lynch's model consumers chose stores solely by comparing prices of the LB. The different SBs do not compete directly with each other but only with the LB within the same store.

Given these simplifying assumptions, the formula for the profit maximizing SB retail price is that it should be equal to the retail price of the LB less the difference between the LB's and SB's manufacturers' selling prices divided by two. An equivalent statement is that the difference between the LBs and the SB's $ RGMs should be equal to the difference between the manufacturers' prices divided by two. The model implies that it is the difference between the leading brand and store brand factory prices that determines whether the retailer offers a store brand and if so at what margin.

To test the predictions of his model, Lynch made use of the extensive publicly available data base from Dominick's—a Chicago area supermarket chain. This is a unique source that has been extensively mined by researchers It records the retail price and the invoice cost of all SKUs in 29 different categories stocked by the chain from which percentage and $ RGMs can be computed. In their pioneering paper Barsky, Dutta, and Levy propose that store brand manufacturers must sell at a competitive price which just covers production cost and is a decent

45 Lynch was formerly acting Director of the FTC's Bureau of Economics and served at the Federal Energy Regulatory Commission as economist in charge of Natural Gas and Pipeline policy. It is obviously impossible to do justice to Lynch's model and the empirical evidence for it in this brief summary. For a printed version see: Lynch (n 15). A revised and more complete version of this article can be accessed online at <http://www.antitrustinstitute.org/archives/files/489.pdf> accessed 25 May 2008–'Lynch revised (online) version'.

approximation of the production cost of the leading brand, assuming that the two brands are of approximately equal quality. In fact, the authors believe that the LB manufacturer's production costs are probably overstated relative to the SB's due to greater scale economies. Because the LB's manufacturer probably also enjoys a larger gross margin, the difference between the two brands' factory prices is a somewhat understated estimate of the gross margin of the LB's manufacturer.[46]

Lynch's work opens with a rich discussion in which he adds structure to the model of imperfect competition and decries the default assumptions in economics that retailing is a perfectly competitive industry. He stresses that economics has ignored the reality and importance of scale economies in retailing, production, and transportation and has made the erroneous assumption that retailers never pass through more than 100 per cent of upstream price increases.

The important variables in the Lynch model include a 'visibility' parameter that represents the propensity of consumers to switch stores within brand and determines the intensity of intrabrand competition and the RGM; a parameter for the maximum reputation premium any consumer is willing to pay for the LB and the assumption that reputation premia are uniformly distributed between zero and this maximum premium; and an optimal advertising variable that helps determine the number of consumers in the market and the reputation premium.

Roughly the second half of the presentation is devoted to using the Barsky et al data to test the three predictions of the Steiner dual-stage model.

1. the SB's retail price will be below the LB's;
2. the percentage and $ RGMs of store brands are higher than the leading brands;
3. there is an inverse association between percentage gross margins at the manufacturing and the retailing stages.

To date the empirical evidence for the third proposition is considerably more limited than for the first two. In the tables all prices are scaled by taking the factory price of the store brands to be $1.[47]

Table 4.1 displays manufacturers' and retailers' prices and both percentage and $ RGMs for the 14 soft drink brands for which there were over 300 observations.

46 R Barsky and others, 'What Can the Price Gap Between Branded and Private Label Products Tell US About Markups?' [2001] NBER Working Paper No W8426.

47 As indicated (n 45), Lynch authored both a printed version in the *Antitrust Bulletin* and a later revised and more complete version, available online. Subsequent footnotes will indicate which version is referred to. The three tables in the revised version (labelled Tables 1, 2 and 3) match those tables shown below, but the earlier *Antitrust Bulletin* version did not contain Table 4.2 below but only Tables 4.1 and 4.3 (labelled Table 2 in the *Antitrust Bulletin* version).

The table shows that the LB retail prices are always higher and that $ and percentage RGMs are always lower than SBs. Although we do not have actual margins of SB manufacturers, the data strongly suggest that they are lower than those of LB makers.[48] The combination of high manufacturers' margins and low retailers' margins is especially characteristic of the best selling brands, Classic Coke and Pepsi.

Table 4.2 shows parameters on the category level, and 'the same three regularities appear in 17 of 18 categories analyzed by Barsky et al . . . Except for frozen entrees, both percentage RGMs and $ RGMs are higher on SBs than on LBs as Steiner's first inverse association suggests'.[49] (In fact, $ RGMS are higher in all 18 categories).

The Lynch model does more than furnish qualitative results. It specifies the exact amount that the store brand's retail price will be discounted from the leading brand's price due to the reputation premium. Table 4.3 compares the predicted and actual store brand prices for the 14 soft drink brands shown in Table 4.1. In Lynch's understated words, 'The predicted prices are surprisingly close to the actual prices . . .'[50] The model also predicts that the pass-through from a uniform upstream price increase will always exceed 100 per cent and implies that 'category percentage margins will stay nearly constant through uniform upstream cost increases'.[51]

Lynch has also observed that in a UK Competition Commission report, one of the very few places where both the retail and manufacturing margins are known, retail prices of store brands are uniformly below those of the national brand, retailers have a higher percentage and $ margin on the store brand, and the retail and manufacturing margins are inversely related—again confirming the three regularities.[52] Applying his simple formula, Lynch calculated that the predicted retail price of the store brand was $5.47, about 7.5 per cent above the actual price of $5.16.

Finally, Lynch has authored a later version of his model available on the Antitrust Institute Website. He encourages further research to test whether the predictions of his theoretical models can be replicated.[53]

---

48 Lynch *Antitrust Bulletin* version (n 15) 930.

49 Lynch revised (online) version (n 45) 23.

50 Lynch revised (online) version (n 45) 29.

51 Lynch *Antitrust Bulletin* version (n 15) 939. This finding has great relevance for calculating the welfare loss in cartel cases, since it predicts that consumer prices must rise by more than the increased prices charged by the cartel to its direct purchasers.

52 UK Competition Commission, 'Supermarkets: A Report on the Supply of Groceries from Multiple Stores in the United Kingdom' [October 2000] <http://www.competition-commission.org.uk/rep_pub/reports/2000/446super.htm> accessed 25 May 2008, Chapter 8, 178–180.

53 For Lynch's latest model see: M P Lynch, 'Toward a Formal Model of Steiner's Dual-Stage Theory of Manufacturing and Retailing' [2004]. <http://www.antitrustinstitute.org>—Click on

G. Conclusion

A consumer goods manufacturer's market power flows from three sources. In the American competition agencies only the firm's horizontal market share, as represented by its HHI, is normally considered. But manufacturers bargain with firms from whom they buy and to whom they sell. In this process they obtain vertical upstream and downstream market shares which determine the manufacturer's share of his suppliers' selling prices (the manufacturer's invoice costs) and his share of his brand's retail price, respectively. The vertical and horizontal sources of market power are closely and positively related. For example, should the manufacturer capture larger vertical market shares than rival makers, he will be buying for less and selling for more than they can which will increase his horizontal market share at their expense and erect mobility and entry barriers that buffer his position against future challenges. Section D suggests how vertical market shares can be estimated. A firm's internal strength and culture are the third source of its market power.

In tracing the history of the rivalry between leading national brands and private labels, it appears that in the welfare-maximizing structure both types of brands are strong enough to 'keep each other honest'. Although this seems to have been the situation in the UK grocery industry, there is a danger that if private label shares and retailer concentration continue, the private label domination structure may come to prevail in which retail prices will rise and consumers will find it more difficult to make informed decisions as to relative brand prices and to judge their relative quality and performance features.

Based on the extensive data from the Chicago-area Dominick's supermarket chain, the innovative Lynch model is shown to be a remarkable predictor of the price of the private label (store brand), given the price of the competing national brand. The data also support the three regularities predicted in my 'dual-stage' model. The retail price of the private label is lower but its dollar and percentage retail gross margins are higher than the national brand and there is an inverse association between the margins of manufacturers and retailers. Of special interest in cartel cases is the Lynch model's prediction that the pass-through from a uniform upstream price increase will exceed 100 per cent. Hence, consumer prices will rise by more than the cartel's price increase.

Archives, type 'Michael Lynch' in 'Have this text' box, click on Search, click on '7/2/2004 Commentary—Michael Lynch: Toward a Formal Model of Steiner's Dual-Stage Theory of Manufacturing and Retailing'.

Michael Lynch would welcome any comments and can be contacted at Lynchmp@yahoo.com.

Table 4.1 (Lynch) Manufacturer and Retail Prices and Margins for Soft Drinks—Dominick's Data Base 1987–1997

Leading Brand	Ratio LB Mfr Price to SB Mfr Price	Leading Brand Retail Price*	Store Brand Retail Price*	% Discount from LB Price	Dollar Gross Margin on Leading Brand	% Gross Margin on LB	Dollar Gross Margin on SB	% Gross Margin on SB	Dollar LB Mfr Margin	% LB Mfr Margin
	1	2	3	4	5	6	7	8	9	10
Coke Classic	2.35	$2.70	$1.96	27.5%	$0.35	13.0%	$0.96	48.9%	$1.35	57.4%
Schwepps Ginger Ale	2.17	$2.50	$1.92	23.1%	$0.33	13.0%	$0.92	47.9%	$1.17	53.9%
Pepsi Cola N/R	2.23	$2.63	$1.91	27.5%	$0.40	15.3%	$0.91	47.6%	$1.23	55.2%
Pepsi Cola Diet N/R	2.25	$2.57	$1.82	29.1%	$0.32	12.3%	$0.82	45.0%	$1.25	55.6%
Barq's Root Beer	2.00	$2.52	$1.81	28.1%	$0.52	20.6%	$0.81	44.8%	$1.00	50.0%
Schweppes Tonic N/R	2.28	$3.12	$2.30	26.5%	$0.84	27.0%	$1.30	56.5%	$1.28	56.1%
Schweppes Diet Tonic N/R	2.29	$3.14	$2.32	25.9%	$0.85	27.0%	$1.32	57.0%	$1.29	56.3%

R.C. Cola	1.88	$2.48	$2.09	16.0%	$0.60	24.2%	$1.09	52.0%	$0.88	46.8%
A&W Rootbeer Reg	1.78	$2.03	$1.75	13.8%	$0.25	12.3%	$0.75	42.8%	$0.78	43.8%
Sunkist Orange	1.46	$2.39	$2.18	9.1%	$0.93	39.0%	$1.18	54.1%	$0.46	31.5%
Schwepps Ginger Ale	2.06	$3.07	$2.34	23.7%	$1.01	32.9%	$1.34	57.3%	$1.06	51.5%
Canada Dry Ginger Ale	2.36	$3.47	$2.34	32.4%	$1.11	32.0%	$1.34	57.3%	$1.36	57.6%
A&W Rootbeer SF	1.72	$2.05	$1.73	15.3%	$0.33	16.0%	$0.73	42.3%	$0.72	41.9%
Diet Coke	2.25	$2.57	$1.81	29.6%	$0.32	12.3%	$0.81	44.6%	$1.25	55.6%
Column Medians	2.20	$2.57	$1.94	26.2%	$0.46	18.3%	$0.94	48.4%	$1.20	54.5%
Column Minimum	1.46	$2.03	$1.73	9.1%	$0.25	12.3%	$0.73	42.3%	$0.46	31.5%
Column Maximum	2.36	$3.47	$2.34	32.4%	$1.11	39.0%	$1.34	57.3%	$1.36	57.6%

* Assumes all SB mfr prices equal to $1.

Source: Barsky, Robert, Mark Bergen, Shantanu Dutta, Daniel Levy, "What Can the Price Gap between Branded and Private Label Products Tell Us about Markups?" Presented at the NBER Conference on Research in Income and Wealth:Scanner Data and Price Indexes, 15–16 September, 2000 [Revised: 13 September, 2001], Table A-2, Only those brands with 300 or more observations were used. Available at: <http://papers.nber.org/papers/W8426>.

Table 4.2 (Lynch) Manufacturer and Retail Prices for Leading National Brands and Store Brands for Eighteen Categories from Dominick's Supermarkets, 1989–1997: Store Brand Shares for 17 Categories, 1992–1996, Nationwide

	Ratio LB to SB Manuf. Prices	LB Retail Price	SB Retail Price	% Discount from LB Retail Price	LB Dollar Gross Margin	LB % Gross Margin	SB Dollar Gross Margin	SB % Gross Margin	SB $ Share of Category	SB Unit Share of Category	Category %Gross Margin
	1	2	3	4	5	6	7	8	9	10	11
Category											
Laundry Detergents	1.23	$1.27	$1.07	15.3%	$0.0369	2.9%	$0.07	6.9%	3.6%	5.8%	3.1%
Canned Tuna	1.23	$1.41	$1.24	12.3%	$0.18	13.0%	$0.24	19.4%	9.8%	12.8%	13.9%
Frozen Entrees	1.27	$1.49	$1.14	23.1%	$0.22	14.5%	$0.14	12.5%	0.8%	0.9%	14.5%
Bottled Juice	1.38	$1.57	$1.25	20.6%	$0.19	12.3%	$0.25	19.9%	15.0%	16.7%	13.6%
Cheese	1.38	$1.59	$1.27	20.0%	$0.21	13.0%	$0.27	21.2%	27.4%	32.5%	15.7%
Dish Detergents	1.42	$1.52	$1.13	25.4%	$0.10	6.5%	$0.13	11.8%	5.7%	7.4%	6.9%
Cereals	1.43	$1.53	$1.21	20.6%	$0.10	6.5%	$0.21	17.7%	6.2%	9.0%	7.5%
Frozen Juice	1.44	$1.89	$1.60	15.3%	$0.45	23.7%	$0.60	37.4%	31.5%	38.1%	28.9%

Oatmeal	1.52	$1.69	$1.41	16.7%	$0.17	9.9%	$0.41	28.9%	13.7%	19.1%	13.5%
Canned Soup	1.61	$2.35	$1.75	25.4%	$0.74	31.5%	$0.75	43.0%	5.8%	9.2%	32.6%
Tooth Paste	1.61	$1.77	$1.30	26.5%	$0.16	9.1%	$0.30	23.2%	1.5%	2.3%	9.4%
Snack Crackers	1.68	$1.88	$1.38	26.5%	$0.20	10.7%	$0.38	27.7%	N.A.	N.A.	N.A.
Fabric Softeners	1.73	$1.83	$1.21	34.2%	$0.10	5.7%	$0.21	17.1%	16.2%	21.7%	8.1%
Cookies	1.77	$2.00	$1.34	32.9%	$0.23	11.5%	$0.34	25.5%	11.5%	13.8%	13.4%
Analgesics	2.01	$2.09	$1.28	38.7%	$0.08	3.8%	$0.28	22.0%	17.9%	24.6%	8.3%
Soft Drinks	2.09	$2.47	$1.79	27.5%	$0.38	15.3%	$0.79	44.0%	7.7%	18.1%	20.5%
Grooming (Razors)	2.17	$2.32	$1.33	42.9%	$0.15	6.5%	$0.33	24.6%	6.5%	10.8%	8.5%
Crackers	2.57	$2.96	$1.48	50.0%	$0.39	13.0%	$0.48	32.3%	8.0%	12.4%	15.4%
Col. Min	1.23	$1.27	$1.07	12.3%	$0.04	2.91%	$0.07	6.86%	0.8%	0.9%	3.1%
Col. Max	2.57	$2.96	$1.79	50.0%	$0.74	31.51%	$0.79	44.04%	31.5%	38.1%	32.6%
Col. Median	1.57	$1.80	$1.29	25.4%	$0.19	11.11%	$0.29	22.62%	8.0%	12.8%	13.5%
Col. Average	1.64	$1.87	$1.34	26.3%	$0.23	11.65%	$0.34	24.18%	11.1%	15.0%	13.8%

Source: Barsky, Robert, Mark Bergen, Shantanu Dutta, Daniel Levy, "What Can the Price Gap between Branded and Private Label Products Tell Us about Markups?" Presented at the NBER Conference on Research in Income and Wealth:Scanner Data and Price Indexes, 15–16 September, 2000 [Revised: 13 September, 2001], Available at: <http://papers.nber.org/papers/W8426>. Store Brand Shares from PLMA and IRI Data, courtesy of PLMA. Prices in columns 2 & 3 have been scaled from ratios by assuming that the manufacturer price for the store brand is $1 per unit in each category. Columns 9 & 10 from the Private Label Manufacturers Association. Available at: <http://papers.nber.org/papers/W8426>.

Table 4.3 (Lynch) Predicted versus Actual Store Brand Soft Drink Prices, Dominick's Data, 1987–1997

Leading Brand	Predicted	Actual	Pred. less Actual	%Error
Coke Classic	$2.03	$1.96	$0.07	3.41%
Schwepps Ginger Ale	$1.91	$1.92	–$0.01	–0.48%
Pepsi Cola N/R	$2.02	$1.91	$0.11	5.43%
Pepsi Cola Diet N/R	$1.94	$1.82	$0.12	6.23%
Barq's Root Beer	$2.02	$1.81	$0.21	10.25%
Schweppes Tonic N/R	$2.48	$2.30	$0.19	7.52%
Schweppes Diet Tonic N/R	$2.49	$2.32	$0.17	6.76%
R.C. Cola	$2.04	$2.09	–$0.04	–2.14%
A&W Rootbeer Reg	$1.64	$1.75	–$0.11	–6.72%
Sunkist Orange	$2.16	$2.18	–$0.01	–0.57%
Schwepps Ginger Ale	$2.54	$2.34	$0.20	7.73%
Canada Dry Ginger Ale	$2.79	$2.34	$0.45	15.96%
A&W Rootbeer SF	$1.69	$1.73	–$0.05	–2.83%
Diet Coke	$1.94	$1.81	$0.13	6.89%
Column Average	$2.12	$2.02	$0.10	4.10%
Column Median	$2.02	$1.94	$0.12	5.83%
Column Minimum	$1.64	$1.73	–$0.11	–6.72%
Column Maximum	$2.79	$2.34	$0.45	15.96%

Source: Barsky, Robert, Mark Bergen, Shantanu Dutta, Daniel Levy, "What Can the Price Gap between Branded and Private Label Products Tell Us about Markups?" Presented at the NBER Conference on Research in Income and Wealth:Scanner Data and Price Indexes, 15–16 September, 2000 [Revised: 13 September, 2001], Available at: <http://papers.nber.org/papers/W8426>.

5

PRIVATE LABELS AND BRANDED GOODS: CONSUMERS' 'HORRORS' AND 'HEROES'

*Paul W Dobson and Ratula Chakraborty**

A. Introduction

Private label and manufacturer branded goods compete for shelf space and the attentions of consumers. They may have much in common but they can have very different impacts on supplier and retailer competition and ultimately on consumer welfare. This chapter considers the different sides to private labels and branded goods, examining how each type can affect competition in a positive or

* Loughborough University Business School.

harmful way.[1] From the consumer's perspective, the exercise of market power may stifle competition and restrict consumer choice. Different types of brand or private label 'horrors' are considered, where the respective market power of brand producers and retailers can be used in a way that is detrimental to competition and consumer welfare. Equally, though, branded goods and private labels can have a countervailing capacity to stem or neutralize market power and enrich choice with new, innovative products, such that each in their own way have the ability to extend and encourage greater competition and thereby offer important consumer benefits. The chapter considers how and when these goods support effective competition, illustrating the different types of brand and private label 'heroes' that can promote competition and choice to the benefit of consumers. The chapter closes by considering the shape of future competition in light of relentlessly increasing retail concentration and the growing power of large retailers, with possible implications for consumer sovereignty.

B. Brands Versus Private Labels

When one considers the vast number, range, and variety of products typically available in a large supermarket or modern superstore then one might automatically think that the consumers' interests are always being best served. To the extent that consumers have benefited over time from increased choice and more reliable quality then they may evidently be better off than in the past; when stores were typically smaller, there was less product choice, and supply chains worked more slowly. Here, the development of mass retailing—with the move to very large format stores, backed up by continual replenishment utilizing highly efficient logistics systems, with products sourced from ever wider areas, and with

[1] We have deliberately avoided using any technical economic analysis in this chapter and our coverage is also intentionally narrow, allowing us to focus on those issues that we feel merit special attention. For more broad coverage of the competition issues raised here and details of the relevant theoretical and empirical contributions in this field, there are a number of very useful surveys available. For example, see: P W Dobson, 'The Economic Welfare Implications of Own Label Goods' [1998] University of Nottingham Business School Discussion Paper, No 1998:IV; F Berges-Sennou, P Bontems, and V Requillart, 'Economics of Private Labels: A Survey of the Literature' [2004] 2 *Journal of Agriculture, Food and Industrial Organization*, Article 3; K Pauwels and S Srinivasan, 'Pricing of National Brands versus Store Brands: Market Power Components, Findings and Research Opportunities' *Handbook of Research in Pricing* (2008). For a perspective on the US situation, see: R L Steiner, 'The Nature and Benefits of National Brand/Private Label Competition' [2004] 24 *Review of Industrial Organization* 105. Also, there are a number of books that provide a marketing/strategy perspective on private label and brand competition. In particular, we draw on many examples discussed in N Kumar and J-B E M Steenkamp, *Private Label Strategy: How to Meet the Store Brand Challenge* (2007); and K Lincoln and L Thomassen, *Private Label: Turning the Retail Brand Threat into Your Biggest Opportunity* (2008).

huge variety—has unquestionably offered consumers enormous benefits through the productivity improvements it has generated and the greater product choice on offer.

Yet, mass retailing, as with the production of many of the goods sold in these stores, has increasingly become concentrated in the hands of the few. Where once small, independent retailers dominated retailing, for many countries the sector is now largely controlled by a limited number of nationally, and increasingly internationally, operating multiple chain store groups. Consumers may feel that they have enormous choice and variety when they step into a retail store, but the choice over which retail store to use is often now significantly limited.

With retail concentration has come retail power: power not just to influence the choice, variety, and prices on offer to consumers, but power to control the supply chain, dictate the terms and conditions of trade with suppliers, and exploit the retailer as a brand in its own right through the development of private label products. This development of private label has advantages for consumers in that it may challenge the position of established branded goods by offering alternatives for consumers, while also allowing for the opportunity to open up new product areas, with innovative products satisfying previously unserved, latent demand. Yet, it has potential disadvantages for consumers when retailers exploit their vested interest to promote private label (and their own name in the process) at the expense of branded goods by deliberately restricting choice and distorting category price structures to suit their own ends. In this case, competition for shelf space can be an unfair battle where the dice are loaded against manufacturer branded goods.

Only with effective retail competition can consumers be assured that this battle is likely to be played out fairly; where the retailer's self-interest in promoting private label is tempered by the need to meet or better rival retailers' offers. In this regard, the stocking and promotion of branded goods can have an important role to play as they are an obvious instrument by which consumers can immediately compare one retailer against another—as they are the only products guaranteed to be identical from one retailer to another. So, if a retailer wishes to signal its value as a retail proposition, then offering lower prices and more choice on branded goods can be very effective. At the same time, making in-store comparisons between branded goods and its (normally cheaper) private label offering can reinforce this signal, and allow the retailer to appear as the consumer's champion.

But retailers may not have everything their own way. By being limited in number, retailers can often have strong if not controlling positions in their bargaining and dealings with suppliers; skilfully exploiting their gatekeeper role and playing suppliers off one against another to extract the economic surplus that they may generate.[2] However, in some instances, suppliers may have built up sufficiently strong market positions with strong consumer appeal and loyalty that, while not making them entirely immune to retailers' bargaining pressure, will nonetheless ensure their presence on retailers' shelves and allow them to retain much of the surplus they generate. This applies most obviously with those 'must-stock' brands which retailers feel compelled to provide—at whatever the cost—in order to satisfy the needs of their customers or face losing them to rival retailers. In practice, such items may be few and far between—given that even the most well-known brands usually face rivals that can ostensibly act as suitable alternatives for consumers, thereby allowing retailers at least some bargaining scope. Nevertheless, the market power of some leading brands may be sufficient that it allows them largely to call the shots with retailers, providing them with decisive advantages over shelf allocation and positioning and the ability to limit opportunities for rival brands.

With the possibility of major retailers and certain branded goods producers holding significant market power, concern may naturally centre on how that market power is used and whether it can serve to prevent, restrict, or distort competition through how private labels and branded goods operate. From the consumer's perspective, the exercise of market power may stifle competition and restrict genuine choice and value on offer. In this chapter we illustrate the different types of brand or private label 'horrors' that may arise, where the respective market power of brand producers and retailers can be used in a way that is detrimental to competition and consumer welfare.

Equally, though, branded goods and private labels can have a potent countervailing capacity to stem or neutralize market power, such that each type, in its own way, has the ability to extend and encourage greater competition and thereby offer important consumer benefits. The chapter considers how and when these goods support effective competition, illustrating the different types of brand and private label 'heroes' that can promote competition and raise consumer welfare.

In our illustrations of these 'horrors' and 'heroes', we have deliberately chosen names and characterizations that are larger than life. The 'horrors' will be familiar to anyone who has watched B-movie horror films and the like. Here you will meet a cast of characters that may represent consumers' nightmares if they serve to prevent, restrict, or distort competition to the extent of harming quality, choice, and value on offer to consumers.

---

[2] For a discussion on how such retailer bargaining power may work in practice, see: P W Dobson, 'Exploiting Buyer Power: Lessons from the British Grocery Trade' [2005] 72 *Antitrust Law Journal* 529.

Similarly, the 'heroes' we characterize come straight out of Hollywood action and adventure movies. These characters are a force for good, righting wrongs, challenging oppressors, bullies and charlatans, and saving the masses. They provide consumers' sweet dreams when they serve to promote competition and safeguard their interests by enhancing quality, choice, and value on offer.

For illustration and discussion, we provide three examples of each type—horrors and heroes—for both brands and private labels. No doubt readers may think of other examples that reflect our discussion of the merits and concerns about brands and private labels and how well (or otherwise) they serve to spur effective competition to the benefit of consumers.

While our characterizations are intentionally tongue-in-cheek and deliberately exaggerated, their real economic effect is not something to be taken lightly. Daily consumer goods production and retailing represents a multi-billion dollar sector in all major developed countries and one that affects essentially everyone in modern society—given that we all buy and consume these products. Accordingly, even a small restriction or distortion to competition, resulting in consumers paying more than they otherwise would have, can translate into lost consumer surplus in the order of millions of dollars. With so much societal welfare at stake, it is therefore not surprising that the healthiness and effectiveness of competition in this sector takes on considerable interest for policymakers and competition authorities and that the sector is regularly in the glare of the regulatory and media spotlight.

For competition authorities and courts that have to deal with enforcing competition law to protect competition and promote consumer benefits, situations will rarely be as black and white as our characterizations make out. In practice, individual brands and private labels may often have elements that fit both the horror side and the hero side. The challenge will then be to recognize and distinguish between the 'Jekyll and Hyde' sides and ensure that it is the good side of brands and private labels that prevails and that healthy, vigorous competition is pursued to the ultimate benefit of consumers.

In all of this, the battle for shelf space is both ongoing and evolving. Private label goods may have come to challenge and perhaps even lead certain categories, yet branded goods remain key to most product categories. But will this last? Will private label eventually win out to the extent that branded goods eventually disappear from retailers' shelves? In short, are manufacturer branded goods doomed? We consider these questions later in the chapter in relation to the likely shape of future competition in view of the apparently relentless rise in retail concentration and growing power of large retailers and how this may ultimately impact on consumer sovereignty. Here, we draw on the experience in the UK groceries market, which has been at the vanguard of private label development and where brand and private label competition has perhaps been at its most acute but also where the sector has been subject to regular investigations by the UK competition authorities—most recently with the completion in 2008 of a two-year groceries market investigation by the Competition Commission.[3]

C. Brand 'Horrors' and 'Heroes'

Nature of brands

Brands have many virtues in consumers' eyes, which helps explain their continued popularity. Most immediately, consumers benefit from the role brands play in conveying information, providing a quality assurance (which is necessary as part of maintaining brand image), and allowing for quick and efficient comparisons across easily identifiable and trustworthy products. Yet, branding, which allows products to differentiate themselves from one another, offers consumers other economic benefits as well. Brand providers, spurred on by competition and the need to provide adequate returns for shareholders, undertake innovation to improve and further distinguish their product offering, in the process improving product quality and increasing variety and choice, as well as providing enhanced customization to better meet customer needs. At the same time, intense rivalry between brand providers pushes them to improve the value for money in their proposition (through better quality and/or lower prices), whilst driving down costs through improving efficiency and utilizing available economies of scale and scope.

Crucially, effective branding requires identifying, using, and then marketing a key point of distinction or differentiation from other goods serving similar purposes. This applies irrespective of whether the branding is carried out by the producer (with producer branded goods) or the retailer (with private label brands). Private label brands, of course, have their own natural point of differentiation in that they are only available in the retailer (or associated buying group) that bears their name—i.e. the shopper cannot directly compare different retailer private label offerings without having to go to rival retail stores. Yet, for producer branded goods, which sit side-by-side and thereby compete directly on the same supermarket shelf, the point of distinction has to be more immediate—given that the shopper can directly compare the different products on that shelf without even moving.

[3] See: <http://www.competition-commission.org.uk/inquiries/ref2006/grocery/index.htm> accessed 1 April 2008.

With the prospect of direct comparisons being made, some products naturally lend themselves more to branding than others because of the range of separate, identifiable attributes of which they comprise and how they can be packaged and marketed. In this regard, it is therefore not surprising that we see most well-known food brands as being packaged, processed grocery items. Here, the packaging allows for the display of the brand name and where possible logo and characteristic product dressing, including packaging style and format, to reinforce the brand's identity. The processed nature allows for the possibility of developing a distinct recipe, by the specific processing method and the precise combination of different constituents used, to provide a unique product appearance, taste and/or aroma that can be identified solely with that brand.

This inherent 'brandability' applies to other packaged, fast-moving-consumer goods (FMCGs), like household items (e.g. cleaning products), personal care, and hygiene products (e.g. shampoo, toothpaste, sanitary items, etc.), as well as over-the-counter (OTC) medicaments. It applies less easily to simple, unprocessed, minimally packaged items. Nevertheless, it is still observed even on fresh food items, like packaged lettuce leaves and even unpackaged fruit (e.g. Jaffa oranges and Fyffe bananas). It is also widely observed on other standard grocery products, like dairy items (Cravendale milk, Lurpak butter, etc.), meat (e.g. Bernard Matthews turkey), and beverages—even on something as potentially non-differentiable (at least to many palates) as mineral water (e.g. Evian and Volvic).

Accordingly, there appear to be very few product categories where one would not expect to see the presence of producer branded goods. From a consumer's perspective this offers benefits when it provides assurances about quality, reliability, and safety of the product—being backed up by the name and reputation of the producer. However, the consumer may also desire choice and variety, and a cause for concern arises when brands become dominant to the extent that other brands are excluded and brand choice is limited. Here the brand 'horrors' are the situations where powerful brands can restrict or prevent competition to the detriment of consumers. In contrast, the brand 'heroes' are the situations where brands are able to promote and advance competition and choice to the benefit of consumers. We provide three examples of each type.

Brand 'horrors'

The brand horrors described here are all situations where a brand has become so dominant in a product area that competition is weakened and in the extreme eliminated by strategic moves that undermine rivals, enhance barriers to entry, and (for our second and third examples) allow for market power to be leveraged across products to extend domination to the broader category or even multiple-category level. Consumers may then lose out through having to pay higher prices (as retailers have less ability to obtain discounts in bargaining with these brand producers), as well as being faced with less choice (where exit is induced and entry is deterred) and perhaps lower quality (where innovative effort is curtailed) than they otherwise would in circumstances that support more effective competition amongst producers.

'The blob'[4]

This horror facing consumers arises where a brand dominates a product area to such an extent that it smothers all competition, prevents new entry, and restricts innovation. Its means of exercising market power include employing strategic entry barriers to defend its shelf space, outgunning its rivals on advertising for brand recognition, bidding up slotting allowances, and other means of raising rivals' costs, as well as providing financial inducements to retailers for exclusive supply, such as through customer loyalty rebate schemes. It may also use predatory behaviour, such as funding in-store deep discount promotions, to build a reputation for aggressive responses to incursions into its shelf space in order to deter new entry or attempted expansion by its existing rivals, while ensuring that it remains permanently dominant in its product market.

'The giant octopus'[5]

This relates to a multi-product brand producer that has its tentacles everywhere to leverage its market power in one category to another while restricting or killing other (typically specialist) brands that stand in its way to dominating multiple categories. Here, the brand producer seeks to draw on its 'portfolio power' to foreclose market access and raise rivals' costs to restrict or dampen competition. With a portfolio of powerful brands, the producer may have greater opportunities for tying products (as a condition of sale—such as through full-line forcing) or refusing supply (when customers refuse to pay higher prices and accept all or nothing offers), which may serve to drive up prices and restrict competition when it limits opportunities for specialist brand producers.[6]

---

[4] This character features in the eponymous 1955 film *The Blob*, with the fitting promotional tag line '*Indescribable . . . Indestructible! . . . Nothing can stop it!*'—see: <http://en.wikipedia.org/wiki/The_Blob> accessed 1 April 2008.

[5] This creature emerged in the 1954 film *It Came from Beneath the Sea* to attack San Francisco and destroy the Golden Gate Bridge.

[6] Such portfolio power arguments have been used in assessing proposed mergers of complementary consumer goods producers. For example, in *Guinness-Grand Metropolitan*, the European Commission argued that an extended portfolio would increase the scope for tying, making more potent the threat to refuse to deal, and consequently increase support for secondary brands in

'The virus'[7]

Here the brand infects and takes over all shelf space in a category by proliferating spin-off products and variants that serve to kill off and restrict space for smaller, niche brands thus reducing the opportunity for any of these to grow and develop in a way that could challenge its category dominance.[8] Methods include using aggregated rebate schemes where customers are offered discounts for taking the whole product range.[9] In addition, being the leading producer in a category may allow the firm to become a 'category captain' when providing category management services for retailers.[10] This role may afford it greater opportunity for gaining shelf access and better in-store positioning for its new products while restricting the possibilities of other smaller or new contenders to develop.[11]

Brand 'heroes'

While brand strength may be viewed in a bad light when it translates into market power, it should not be forgotten that brands serve an important role in promoting competition and choice for consumers, providing size and scope cost efficiencies, innovative effort, and the capacity to enter and open up new markets. Here, we set out three brand 'heroes', which by their presence help ensure that consumers are well served in the markets in which they operate and which cast brands in a very positive light.

---

a manner that would undermine rivals—Case IV/M938 [1998] OJ L288/24. However, this remains a contentious subject, as offering a wider range of products may simply entail being able to offer customers a more attractive proposition (through single-source supply) than specialist rivals can, while allowing for economies of scale and scope to be realized.

7 This horror has featured in many different contexts, ranging from the spread of an Ebola/Lassa-type virus in *Outbreak* (2005) to more exotic viruses originating from deep space, e.g. *The Andromeda Strain* (1971) and *Virus* (1999).

8 For a discussion of strategic product proliferation and its rationale and potential effectiveness, see: R Schmalensee, 'Entry Deterrence in the Ready-to-Eat Breakfast Cereal Industry' [1978] 9 *Bell Journal of Economics* 305.

9 For example, in the European Commission's case against *Hoffman-La Roche*, the firm was held to have abused its dominant position by offering loyalty rebates to customers who took the whole range of its vitamins—Case 85/76 [1979] ECR 461. More recently, the European Commission has challenged the use of loyalty rebates by Coca-Cola—see: Decision of the Commission of 22 June 2005 in case COMP/39.116 *Coca-Cola* (OJ L 253, 29.09.2005) <http://ec.europa.eu/comm/competition/publications/cpn/cpn2005_3.pdf> accessed 1 April 2008.

10 Category management is essentially a retailer/supplier process of managing in-store product categories as strategic business units, ostensibly intended to produce enhanced business results by focusing on delivering consumer value.

11 For a summary of the potential foreclosure, collusion, and other antitrust aspects relating to category management, see: R L Steiner, 'Category Management—A Pervasive, New Vertical/Horizontal Format' [2001] 15 *Antitrust* 77, and D M Desrochers, G T Gundlach, and A A Foer, 'Analysis of Antitrust Challenges to Category Captain Arrangements' [2003] 22 *Journal of Public Policy and Marketing* 201.

'The protector'

This is where a brand provides value for money through its scale efficiencies as well as offering a quality assurance over product consistency and trustworthiness. These attributes along with its universal availability (being sold in all stores) allow it to serve as the critical benchmark on value and quality for which all other rival products must aspire to match or beat, thus encouraging innovative effort and inventiveness on their part, which in turns keeps the brand producer on its toes and ensures that consumers continue to be well served.[12]

'The pioneer'

Here the brand producer creates new markets through introducing radically new products as well as being first to innovate when consumer tastes change and providing regular innovations to extend markets and cater better for consumers' needs. The pioneer stands or falls by its innovative capacity, taking the risks and earning the rewards from pioneering new market segments and providing additional choice and new experiences for consumers in the process.[13]

'The equalizer'

This brand character enters markets to challenge dominant positions held by established incumbents. This may entail *de alio* entry (i.e. from adjacent product markets) rather than *de novo* (wholly new) entry, where it can draw on its brand recognition and ability to transfer its production or marketing know-how developed in other markets to overcome barriers to entry in new markets. In this way it can neutralize the market power of incumbents and provide consumers with greater choice and better value.[14] It may offer consumers the benefit of standardization to aid price/value comparisons when it consistently provides good value for money across all the market segments it serves.

[12] For example, in the UK, Walkers potato crisps have attained a status and recognition as a trusted, high-quality brand offering consistently good value and regularly coming up with new products and short-run flavour introductions to offer consumers different taste experiences (see: Lincoln and Thomassen (n 1) 180).

[13] A classic example of pioneering brands would be in the development of the premium ice cream market segment led by Haagen-Dazs and Ben & Jerry's. More recently, Red Bull has opened up a new caffeine-based energy drinks category (Kumar and Steenkamp (n 1) 180) and Innocent has led the way in the development of the smoothies market in the UK (Lincoln and Thomassen (n 1) 132). When it comes to constant innovation, Gillette has been in the vanguard of razor developments over many years—providing innovations such as the twin blade floating head, lubrastrip, triple blade, and battery powered wet razors, amongst others (Lincoln and Thomassen (n 1) 175).

[14] For example, Premier Foods, well known for its branded table sauces and pickles, has become an important player in the UK baked beans category with its Branston brand, challenging the long-time leading position of Heinz.

D. Private Label 'Horrors' and 'Heroes'

Nature of private label

The development of private label has been a key element in the retail revolution experienced in most developed countries over the past couple of decades. As large retail chains have emerged to dominate the retail landscape, average store size has increased with the development of the hypermarket and 'big box' store formats, allowing retailers to stock ever wider product ranges. In the process, the opportunity has been taken not just to increase the number of branded goods stocked but also the number of private label goods bearing the retailer's name, facilitated by the scale and reach of the mass retailer's business, and thus offering scale efficiencies in developing private label ranges.[15]

Where once these private label goods were largely generic items or basic 'me-too' copies of leading brands, over time they have become more sophisticated, often rivalling or even exceeding the quality of manufacturer branded goods and also taking on many different forms through sub-branding (with private label appearing in multiple quality tiers and targeting specific consumer segments) as well as being innovative in their own right. As a consequence, retailers' private label products have in many instances become significant brands themselves. This has assisted the retail branding effort by the major store groups, as a means to differentiate themselves from one another (due to the exclusivity of each retailer's private label) while strengthening their customer base and store loyalty. It has also provided a source of bargaining leverage against manufacturers to extract a greater share of the profits generated.

As a result of the success of private label, retailers have moved on from being merely intermediaries in distributing manufacturer-branded items to consumers, to the situation where they take centre stage in the supply chain, controlling the product development and marketing process. In contrast, private label serves to make manufacturers anonymous to consumers, placing them in a more subordinate role and leaving them to serve as mere agents, producing to order for the retailer.[16]

---

15 For instance, Wal-Mart's private label sales totalled $126 billion in 2005, making it 50% bigger than any single consumer packaged goods manufacturer's total brand portfolio. See: Lincoln and Thomassen (n 1) 17–18.

16 The point here is that private labels serve to break the direct link between manufacturer and the consumer (i.e. the bond posted by the brand and reinforced by advertising), and instead allow the retailer to dictate product specification (possibly even determining the nature of production) and take over the role of marketing products, and thereby promote its own retail brand image through the own labels stocked.

Indeed, the situation has become considerably more complex as in effect retailers advancing private-label programmes have become competitors to brand manufacturers as well as their customers, putting them in a 'double agent' position. While brand manufacturers will desire to build a mutually enhancing relationship with retailers, involving cooperation over in-store marketing and sharing complementary information, they will nevertheless be aware that at the same time this relationship is open to potential abuse as the retail customer will have forward information of new products, promotions, and pricing, which may be used to develop new and better private label products.[17] As a result, private-label programmes may benefit from free-riding on investments made by brand manufacturers, where a second mover advantage can arise from foreknowledge of manufacturers' new branded products and marketing plans, allowing speedy mimicking in the development of look-alike products. Additionally, private label products can be further advantaged by the retailer's power to delist branded goods and control over pricing and promotion of branded and private-label products (e.g. allocation of prime display space). These factors increase the retailer's bargaining power over brand manufacturers, while at the same time placing private-label producers in a very competitive situation facing a bidding process to secure contracts to supply the retailer.[18]

Accordingly, the impact of private label on the nature and control of supply chains should not be underestimated. Retailers have the ability to tailor and position their private label products in such a way to enhance their franchise with consumers while also allowing them greater control over both private label and branded goods suppliers.[19] Moreover, this will be undertaken in a manner intended to maximize retailer profits and not necessarily in a manner that best suits consumers or promotes competition.[20] Much may depend on how effective is retail competition in keeping retailers in check and ensuring that there is pressure on them to develop private labels that cater for particular consumer needs,

---

[17] See: R Bell, R Davies, and E Howard, 'The Changing Structure of Food Retailing in Europe: the Implications for Strategy' [1997] 30 *Long Range Planning* 853.

[18] On how the double agent role can be used to exploit retailer buyer power, see: Dobson (n 2). In regard to the effects of increased retailer buyer power on producer and retailer competition with application to the UK groceries market, see P W Dobson and R Chakraborty, 'Buyer Power in the UK Groceries Market' forthcoming in *Antitrust Bulletin*.

[19] On this strategic positioning aspect of private label as a bargaining lever, see: F Scott Morton and F Zettelmeyer, 'The Strategic Positioning of Store Brands in Retailer–Manufacturer Negotiations' [2004] 24 *Review of Industrial Organization* 161.

[20] For example, positioning private label to enhance retail buyer power may mean that consumers are not served with an appropriately competitive choice of products. See: T S Gabrielsen and L Sorgard, 'Private Labels, Price Rivalry, and Public Policy' [2007] 51 *European Economic Review* 403, and R Moner-Colonques, J J Sempere-Monerris, and A Urbano, 'Store vs National Brands: A Product Line Mix Puzzle' [2007] Working Paper AD 2007-10.

otherwise face the risk of losing customer loyalty.[21] Equally effective retailer competition can also help ensure that retailers continue to stock and price fairly a wide range of branded goods and not just emphasize private label to the exclusion of brands.

However, it is not just retail competition that consumers should be concerned about. Producer competition can be distorted by private label developments free-riding on investments undertaken by branded goods producers, thereby affecting future investment incentives and innovative effort. There may also be other vertical impacts through the exercise of buyer power and pressure on suppliers to cut corners (which may affect product quality and safety), accept exclusive supply agreements (which may foreclose access for rival retailers), and pay higher access costs (e.g. higher slotting allowances that raise brands' costs and could feed through to higher retail prices from dampened competition between private label and branded goods).

Nevertheless, it should also be recognized that the development of private label can have both an important role in stimulating competition amongst retailers and also in countering brand producers' market power. Private label offers non-branded goods manufacturers a straightforward and inexpensive means of entering markets as they can supply retailers without having to go through the lengthy and expensive process of developing branded goods of their own. With the scale efficiencies offered by supplying large retailers and without the need for brand marketing support, private label producers can operate with low costs and provide their retail customers with a basis on which they can afford to offer good value for money to consumers and undercut the prices of the leading brands. Moreover, as private label becomes more acceptable to consumers, the challenge will then be on brand producers to lower their prices or face losing significant market share. Perhaps not surprisingly, as Figure 5.1 shows, generally the greater the extent of private label penetration in a category then the lower is the price differential between private label goods and manufacturer brands. Finally, just as brands can be inventive and develop new markets, so can private label be equally innovative with pioneering new product ranges.

Private label clearly offers a mixture of competition effects. As with our discussion on manufacturer brands, we distinguish between these effects by characterizing three examples of private label 'horrors' and 'heroes'. For convenience and

[21] For example, it was noticeable that only with the entry of hard discounters (notably Aldi and Lidl) into the UK market in the mid-1990s did the leading incumbent grocery retailers develop extensive low-priced budget/value private label ranges, i.e. as a response to this competitive threat.

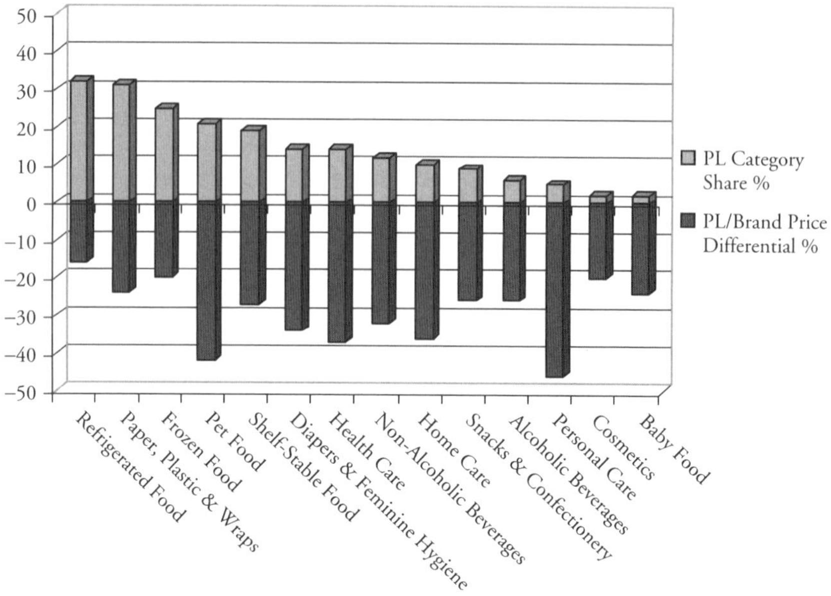

Figure 5.1 Private label category shares and price differentials versus manufacturer brands

Source: Adapted from A C Nielsen, The Power of Private Labels 2005, ACNielsen Global Services, September 2005 (with figures aggregated over 38 countries around the world).

to aid the ensuing discussion, we summarize and contrast these horrors and heroes examples for both private labels and manufacturer brands in Table 5.1.

Private label 'horrors'

Our three private label horrors all work through the harm that they can cause to brands but which in turn then feeds through to consumer detriment. Where private label development entails retailers' free riding on brand investments, brand manufacturers may be less inclined to develop new products (for the fear that they will be unable to fully recover the investment costs) so reducing or retarding new innovations. Also, where retailers promote and push private label at the expense of brands, then the only response for brand manufacturers (given that they have no control over in-store decisions) may be to provide additional marketing support that raises their costs and then means that their prices rise and perhaps private label prices as well.[22] However, even this option may not be

[22] For example, this may arise when retailers take the opportunity to increase private label prices when they shelter under the umbrella provided by the leading brands in respect of category pricing

Table 5.1 Brand and private label 'horrors' and 'heroes'

	Manufacturer brands		Retailer private labels	
	Character	*Features*	*Character*	*Features*
'Horrors' *Consumers' nightmares*	'The blob'	Smothers competition, restricts innovation and deters entry	'The blood sucker'	Bleeds dry innovative effort by free riding on brand investments
	'The giant octopus'	Tentacles everywhere to leverage portfolio power	'The flesh eater'	Slowly devours brands by undermining them in-store
	'The virus'	Proliferates brand variants to spread its category control	'The body snatcher'	Copies then replaces brands with look-alike products
'Heroes' *Consumers' sweet dreams*	'The protector'	Offers quality, value, consistency and trustworthiness	'The underdog'	Takes on the strongest brands to challenge their dominance
	'The pioneer'	Innovates to provide new or improved products for consumers	'The adventurer'	Opens up new product categories with new ranges of products
	'The equalizer'	Enters from adjacent markets to neutralize existing market power	'The revolutionary'	Challenges brands by offering real value and choice for the masses

feasible when it is the retailer's intention to develop and ultimately replace brands with copycat private labels. Then, the brand manufacturer's only hope will be to keep one step ahead of the copycats by continually (and otherwise needlessly) investing in regularly changing its formulation, appearance, and trade dress.

'The blood sucker'[23]

This is where private label feeds off brands' success in creating markets. The private label product deliberately free rides on the marketing, formulation, and packaging of leading brands in the segment. It waits for brand manufacturer investment to create demand in a new area then enters the segment with a 'me-too' private label offering, exploiting its second mover advantage to save on marketing and research and development costs. In the process, this free-riding behaviour undermines brand producers' incentives to innovate and pioneer new

structures and they wish to signal to consumers that their private labels are a similar quality to the leading brands.

23 This horror features in the 1955 film *The Blood Suckers* and a multitude of other vampire films.

segments and invest in improving their products and thus ultimately choking innovation to the detriment of consumers.[24]

'The flesh eater'[25]

The purpose here is to develop and then favour private label through the retailer's control over in-store variables, allowing it to eat into brands' sales. The retailer tries different ways—some subtle, some not so subtle—to persuade consumers to switch to and then keep buying its private label offering. For instance, the retailer may try to undermine brands with poor shelf positioning, artificial price differentials, deliberate stock-outs, and value destroying promotions (such as occasional deep discounts that raise questions in consumers' minds about the true value for money offered by the brands). As such, the retailer exploits its role as a 'double agent', being both the brand producer's customer *and* competitor, using private label as a lever to substitute brand sales with private label sales and in the process extend its buyer power over brand producers (allowing it to obtain more favourable terms, perhaps at the expense of its rival retailers).[26]

'The body snatcher'[27]

This is where private label goes beyond being a 'me-too' offering bearing similarities (such as simple visual cues associated with colours and shapes of packaging) to the leading brands in the category to being a direct copycat or clone of a specific brand. As such, the private label product intentionally mimics and thereby undermines the essential distinguishing features (including its packaging) associated with the brand, often falling short of blatant full reproduction (for legal reasons) but plagiarizing the brand's trade dress.[28] This allows the private label to

---

[24] The 'me-too' private label offering has traditionally been the most common entry route into an established category for a retailer, seeking to emulate the quality and general appearance of the leading brands without having had to go through the long development process and marketing costs required to build up successful brands and develop consumer demand. Previously, brands could be assured of having a significant head start on me-too private labels, as they took time to source and bring to market. However, this time lag has been significantly eroded in recent years with the emergence of sophisticated private label producers and with retailers informed of new brand developments while they are in the pipe line (as a condition of gaining new shelf space when they are launched), with the effect of dramatically improving private labels' speed to market but, in the process, cutting down brands' first-mover advantage and allowing them less time to recoup their initial investment costs.

[25] This horror features in *The Flesh Eaters* (1964) and a host of zombie films, including *Night of the Living Dead* (1968) and *Zombie Flesh Eaters* (1980).

[26] The double agent problem can be particularly problematic for secondary brands that lack the bargaining clout of primary brands, potentially hastening their demise. See: Bell (n 17).

[27] This features in the classic *Invasion of the Body Snatchers* (1956) and *The Stepford Wives* (1975).

[28] In the UK, legal protection for brands is limited unless there is very close copying (through the common law of passing off), an infringement of registered trade marks (Trade Marks Act 1994),

free ride on the image and goodwill that the brand has built up through careful and continual product and marketing investment. Yet, it also means that sales can be diverted to the private label when it misleads consumers into thinking that the product is made by the brand manufacturer or even (by mistake) is the same brand—thereby not just undermining brand investment but also potentially damaging its image and reputation—with the result that the brand loses sales and may ultimately be entirely replaced by the look-alike private label product.[29]

Private label 'heroes'

A common element with private label heroes is that they enhance competition by extending choice and value for consumers. Our examples relate to how they may challenge dominant brand positions, open up new markets with innovative products, and broaden consumer appeal with extended value for money propositions. All of these may be expected to bring significant benefits to consumers and greatly extend and improve their choice set.

'The underdog'

Here, David takes on Goliath. Seemingly against all the odds, the private label good successfully takes on mighty brands that have long dominated a category and in the process extends choice where previously there might have been little. This is often down to the ingenuity and research and production skills of a specialized private label producer that provides its retail customers with products that come close to, or even beat, the quality of the leading manufacturer brands.[30] With the retailer's backing, these private label producers can avoid the marketing expenditure required by branded manufacturers in order to grow as well as avoid

or unfair competition associated with direct consumer confusion (Directive 2005/29/EC of the European Parliament and of the Council of 11 May 2005 concerning Unfair Business-to-consumer Commercial Practices in the Internal Market and Amending Council Directive 84/450/EEC, Directives 97/7/EC, 98/27/EC, and 2002/65/EC of the European Parliament and of the Council and Regulation (EC) No 2006/2004 of the European Parliament and of the Council ('Unfair Commercial Practices Directive') [2005] OJ L149/22). In practice, there have been few successful legal challenges (but some out of court settlements) by brand owners, in large part because of the difficulties in demonstrating direct consumer confusion. However, a notable exception was *United Biscuits v Asda* [1997] RPC 513 (where Asda launched a copycat private label chocolate-coated biscuit called 'Puffin' looking very similar to United Biscuits' brand leader 'Penguin').

29 Private label free riding would normally be expected to reduce brand producers' incentives to invest, but the threat of imitation by private labels may force them to increase (rather than decrease) their investments. However, this may simply result in wasteful over investment from society's perspective; for instance, when it simply amounts to the brand owner being obliged to keep changing its packaging or appearance to stay one step ahead of the clone private label. See: P W Dobson, 'The Competition Effects of Look-alike Products' [1998] University of Nottingham Business School Discussion Paper, No 1998:VI.

30 For some examples, see: Kumar and Steenkamp (n 1) 146–153.

paying slotting allowances to gain and extend shelf space thereby having a better chance than new brands of challenging dominant incumbent brands.

'The adventurer'

This involves boldly going where no one has gone before, developing truly innovative private label products that open up new product categories to serve latent demand. Here, the retailer draws on its ability to provide all the critical in-store elements (including special display units, specific in-store location, adjacent product matching, etc.) to generate opportunities for developing whole new categories served by a wide range of product variants (including different tastes, quality levels, and package sizes) to broaden the appeal to as many consumer types as possible.[31]

'The revolutionary'

The role here is to provide value and choice for the masses. The revolutionary private label product seeks to overturn the old order. For instance, where the category is dominated by high priced branded goods, 'value' or 'budget' private label lines and generics may be sold at a substantial discount to these items, broadening the market to include those consumers on limited budgets. Also, the revolutionary private label product might provide a healthier alternative to the established brands—e.g. low fat, low salt, free from artificial preservatives, organic, and non-genetically-modified—or be more ethically based—e.g. free range, locally produced, fair trade, minimum/recyclable packaging, energy efficient, etc. In all cases, it offers something that broadens the appeal for the product category and caters better for the needs of different consumer segments.

E. Competition between Brands and Private Labels in the UK

From the consumer's perspective, the real champions are those brands and private labels that extend choice, improve quality, and offer enhanced value for money. In respect of brands, consumers can benefit significantly when they offer guaranteed quality and reliability, straightforward price/value comparability, distinct variants to suit different tastes, and regular improvements and innovations. In regard to private labels, consumers will wish to see products that offer genuine value (avoiding brands' 'marketing surcharge'), genuine choice (offering alternatives

31 A prime example has been the pioneering development by Marks & Spencer and other British retailers to introduce and continue to develop extensive ranges of chilled ready meals, which have impacted on the lifestyles of consumers by reducing the time spent on cooking/preparing meals and allowing them greater opportunity to experience new tastes.

to brands), genuine variety (filling gaps), and genuine innovation (catering for latent demand).

The extent to which brands and private labels are fulfilling their ideal roles can be gauged by what has occurred in the market over recent years. Here, we draw on insights from the UK experience.[32]

Despite the emergence of me-too and copycat private labels along with a greatly increased range of private label sub-brands (e.g. budget, premium, healthy, organic, fair-trade, etc.), manufacturer brands continue to be prominent in most product categories in the UK, but to differing degrees in respect of their relative market share positions.[33] For instance, Figure 5.2 shows that brands in 2007 accounted for more than 80 per cent of sales for beers, lager and cider, toiletries, confectionery, and hot beverages, but less than 50 per cent of sales for bakery, dairy, delicatessen, and meat, fish, and poultry.[34]

Furthermore, as Figure 5.2 also shows, over the past decade the shares held by brands and private labels have been fairly stable. Where private label has increased share, the loss to brands has been relatively small, e.g. confectionery, pet food, spirits and liqueurs, frozen, and meat, fish, and poultry. In most other categories, brands have more than held their own, with notable increases in market share in several product categories like table wines. Thus, it would appear that in response to the increasing range and variety of private labels, brand manufacturers themselves have responded well to the challenge, increasing their own ranges and marketing support, and in many cases reducing the price gap between brands and private labels.[35] Moreover, since average store size has increased significantly over recent years in the UK, with the expansion of hypermarkets at the expense of smaller supermarkets, these figures indicate that branded goods have managed to

---

32 Our review of UK developments is necessarily brief. For further analysis on the development of private label and its impact on competition in the UK, see: UK Competition Commission 'Working Paper on the Competitive Effects of Own-Label Goods' (April 2007) <http://www.competition-commission.org.uk> accessed 1 April 2008.

33 The variation in private label share across categories has been studied in a number of empirical papers, e.g. S Hoch and S Banerji, 'When Do Private Labels Succeed?' [1993] 34 *Sloan Management Review* 57, and K Hansen, V Singh, and P Chintagunta, 'Understanding Store-Brand Purchase Behavior Across Categories' [2006] 25 *Marketing Science* 75.

34 Nevertheless, categories can exist which are 100% private label, such as plants and flowers (Nielsen, *State of the Nation 2007*, The Nielsen Company: London, March 2007, p 108).

35 Any narrowing of the price gap between brands and private labels in the UK over recent years may in part be down to brand manufacturers lowering prices in the face of greater competition, but this greater competition has been spurred by the leading retailers launching more premium private labels and specialized sub-brands that compete more closely in quality and price terms with the leading brands. On the relationship between quality and relative prices, see: E Apelbaum, E Gerstner, and P Naik, 'The Effects of Expert Quality Evaluations versus Brand Name on Price Premiums' [2003] 12 *Journal of Product and Brand Management* 154; and Pauwels and Srinivasan (n 1).

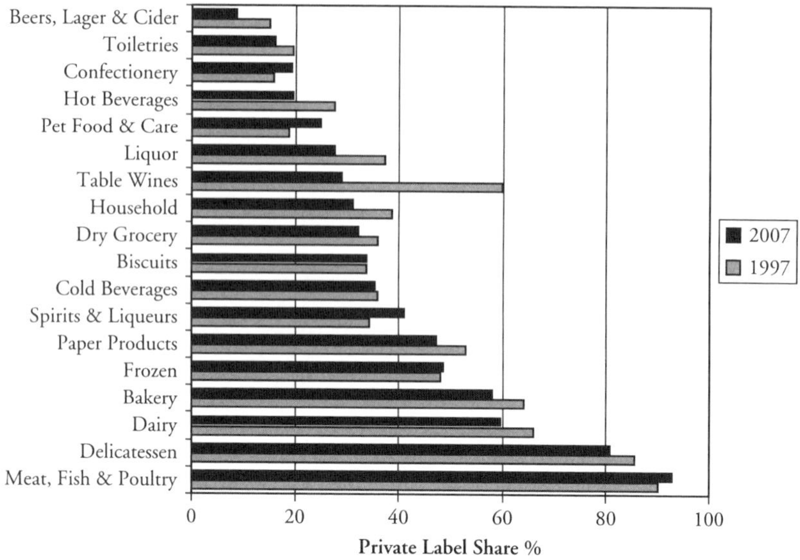

Figure 5.2 Private label category shares in UK grocery retailing, 1997 and 2007.
Source: Nielsen Homescan, based on 52 weeks ending December 1997 and 2007.

capture an increase in this available shelf space roughly proportionate to the increase in that gained by private labels. This may be down to both an increase in the number of 'facings' on a shelf afforded to each item, as well as an increase in the number of brand variants (in respect of different package sizes, different varieties, and different quality levels). So that, just as the number of private label sub-brands have increased over time, so have the number of branded goods variants.[36]

In addition, to private label shares differing across categories, private label shares also differ across retailers. At one extreme, there are supermarket retailers that operate entirely or predominantly with private label—notably Marks & Spencer (exclusively private label, with a 3.8 per cent national market share in the UK) and Aldi (three-quarters private label, with a 1.5 per cent national share). At the other extreme, there are supermarket retailers that operate with low levels of private label—for example Netto (one quarter private label, with a 0.6 per cent national share) and (before it recently exited the market) Kwik Save (around 30 per cent private label). Yet these are exceptions. As Figure 5.3 shows, all of the

[36] To provide just one example, a small convenience store in the UK might only stock one baked beans product—typically Heinz baked beans in its standard 415g tin form. Yet, a visit to a superstore would reveal a multitude of variants of this product on offer. For instance, a Tesco's superstore may stock at least 12 different variants of Heinz baked beans, along with five Branston and eight private label baked beans variants (see: <http://www.tesco.com/todayattesco/pricecheck.shtml> accessed 10 March 2008).

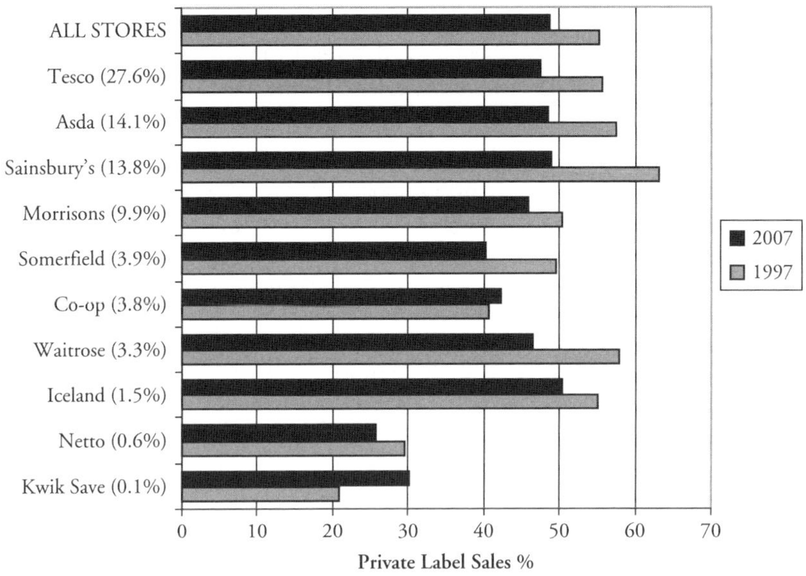

Figure 5.3 Private label shares for various UK grocery retailers, 1997 and 2007.
Sources: Private label from Nielsen Homescan (based on 52 weeks ending December 1997 and 2007); retailer market share figures for 2007 (shown in brackets after retailer's name) from Verdict Research.

other main supermarket groups in the UK now operate with private label shares in the range of 40 to 50 per cent. Interestingly, this range exactly fits with Kumar and Steenkamp's prediction for the upper range for private label for mainstream mass retailers.[37] Furthermore, as evident from Figure 5.3, those retailers that operated with private label shares above this range ten years ago have cut back to fall within this 40 to 50 per cent range.[38] On this basis, it would seem that brands are not about to become extinct in the UK.

Nevertheless, it is clearly not through want of trying that private label shares may have even slightly declined in the UK over the last decade. During this period, the leading retailers have been keen to develop an ever-increasing number of private label sub-brands. An indication of how extensive they have become, moving beyond just a standard private label offering, is shown in Table 5.2. More to the point, the retailers have become very sophisticated in tailoring private label to serve different consumer preferences—both along a quality/price spectrum and

37 See: Kumar and Steenkamp (n 1) 219.

38 The big increase in private label shares in the UK occurred in the 1980s and early 1990s: S Burt and S Davis, 'Follow my leader? Lookalike retail brands in non-manufacturer-dominated products markets in the UK', *International Review of Retail, Distribution and Consumer Research*, vol. 9(2), 1992, 163–185.

on a special needs basis. In particular, they have become very adept at developing premium-positioned private label ranges that more directly target shoppers who might otherwise buy the leading national brands or encourage them to trade up from standard private label—either way the substitution effect is likely to increase retailers' margins. Indeed, Nielsen figures show that in those categories where sub-brands were present (representing some 55 per cent of £81 billion recorded grocery sales), premium private label accounted for 10.9 per cent of sales in 2006, compared to 35.9 per cent for standard private label, 2.1 per cent for budget private label, and 2.8 per cent for healthy private label, leaving 48.3 per cent for branded goods. Yet, it is premium private label that has been growing the quickest (up 8 per cent in 2005 and up a further 10 per cent in 2006, compared to the category average up respectively 3 per cent and 4 per cent).[39] Accordingly, as the number of categories where premium private label is present increases, then this may over time present a greater challenge to the share held by branded goods.

Yet, while private label continues to develop, broadening its consumer appeal through sub-brands and extending its reach by covering new areas and more product categories, its growth potential still appears restricted in the face of three key challenges. First, even if the quality gap is narrowed in taste terms between branded goods and their private label equivalents, an image gap persists. For instance, Nielsen report that 70 per cent of UK shoppers think that their main store's private label products are generally as good as the well-known brands.[40] However, a 2005 survey by Geronimo found that when UK shoppers were asked to name their most desired supermarket brands and the ones they would miss the most if they were not available on the shelves, the top 49 places where taken by manufacturer brands, and only in 50th place did a private label appear (Tesco cheese).[41] Private label goods are clearly liked but not necessarily loved.

Secondly, just as over-extension with too many variants may cause brand fatigue, as consumers grow weary of seeing further extensions of the brand, so private label fatigue may set in when retailers try too hard to push private label products on to customers. The in-store ubiquity of private label and products bearing the retailer's name may count against it if consumers grow resistant to the feeling of being pushed into buying these products and the apparent lack of genuine choice. Sub-branding private label can help, but only to a limited extent as the practice is still about promoting the retailer's name and extending its pervasiveness. Sub-branding also has to be carefully managed to stop one quality tier of private label (say, a standard range) cannibalizing the sales of another tier (e.g. budget

[39] See: Nielsen 2007 (n 34) 112–113.
[40] Nielsen 2007 (n 34) 109.
[41] Kumar and Steenkamp (n 1) 224.

Table 5.2 Private label sub-brands—various UK grocery retailers

	Quality	Price	Kids	Organic	Healthy	Other
Tesco	Finest Bistro Eat me freeze me	Value Mega value	Tesco Kids	Organic	Healthy-living Free from, Reduced Meals for one Food Doctor Carb Control	Italiano Fair Trade Simple Solution Easy steam Grab n go
Asda	Extra Special	Smartprice	great stuff	Organic	Good for you	George
Sainsbury	Taste the Difference	Low price Basics	Blue parrot Café Sainsbury's kids	SO Organic	Be good to yourself Free from Way to S	Italian, Indian Oriental American Easy steam Fair Trade
Somerfield	So Good	Makes Sense			Good Intentions	Al Fresco
M&S	Gastropub		Loved by kids		Count on us	
Waitrose	Bistro		Food explorers		Perfectly balanced	
Co-op	Truly Irresistible Premium	Everyday Value		Organic	Healthy Living	Fair Trade Party
Iceland		Great Value!	Kids Crew		Good Choice	
Morrisons	The Best Luscious Something Special	Farmers Buy Betabuy		Organic	Eat Smart Better for you free from	Quality and Value Vegetarian Italian

Source: Adapted from Jonathan Banks, 'Private Labels: No longer a "lesser brand" in the UK', ACNielsen Consumer Insights, July 2006.

and premium ranges). This may require giving consumers very strong visual cues in terms of the appearance and packaging used for each quality tier. For example, it is not uncommon to find budget private label products deliberately de-marketed (e.g. positioned on the bottom shelf) in intentionally unattractive packaging, in order to attract only those shoppers who are extremely price sensitive and put off all other shoppers in a way that encourages them to trade up to buy the more expensive standard or premium private label equivalent items.[42] However, over time consumers may become increasingly cynical about and resistant to such blatant self-targeting practices, instead preferring the reassurance offered by brands' heritage and trustworthiness (being aware that it is the retailer, not the manufacturer, that controls all the in-store variables from range choice and shelf allocation/positioning to pricing and promotion).

Thirdly, while consumers may desire higher quality private label, their real priority is in obtaining value for money.[43] For a retailer this can be most straightforwardly shown by making price comparisons on like-for-like products across retailers—and it is here that the universal availability of brands has a key role as consumers know for certain that the same quality applies in any price comparisons across retailers. This is not something that can be guaranteed with private label price comparisons. Indeed, the quality of private label can be very variable not just across retailers but also across products within a given retailer.[44] Accordingly, predicting the quality of a private label item by simply observing the retailer's name on the item and its price (both in absolute terms and relative to other items in the product category) may be no easy task. There are no certainties with the quality of private label. All levels and type of private label may disappoint the consumer, given his/her expectations on value for money. Indeed, a poor quality premium sub-brand could do more damage to the reputation of the retailer than a poor quality budget item and serve to enhance consumers' preferences for sticking with trusted manufacturer branded products. So, with consumers perhaps being wary about trying new private label products, the retailer will need to encourage consumers to take the risk and make a first purchase.

[42] For examples and further discussion on this point, see: T Harford, *The Undercover Economist* (2006) 51; and P W Dobson, 'Micro-Marketing and Discriminatory Practices in UK Grocery Retailing' (Report prepared for the Association of Convenience Stores, 2007) 18–21 <http://www.mmc.gov.uk/inquiries/ref2006/grocery/pdf/main_party_submissions_acs_micro_marketing.pdf> accessed 1 April 2008.

[43] For example, IGD find that the most important factor in influencing UK shoppers' choice of main supermarket is 'value for money', with 'wide choice of branded products' ranked third and 'shop's own brand ranges' ranked sixth, and the primary reason that consumers buy private label is because of its lower price—see: Competition Commission (n 32) 3–4.

[44] This point is illustrated in a very interesting and diverse selection of private label quality comparisons undertaken by M Isark, *Supermarket Own Brand Guide* (2006).

This is where the retailer's control of in-store levers over category product range, shelf positioning, product juxtaposition, and pricing architecture (with a clear ladder of prices) come into their own. It is also where brands have the most to lose when the retailer favours its private label products and uses methods like artificial price differences, deliberate stock outs, and delisting minor brands to push consumers into the decision of switching to private label or face switching to another retailer—relying on retailer loyalty being stronger than brand loyalty.[45]

None of these points mean that brand manufacturers can afford to be complacent—they still face the challenge of securing their place on supermarket shelves and not losing out to rival suppliers. However, it does indicate that brands are likely to continue to have an important role for retailers and that consumers will continue to benefit from their wide availability. The exception may be with secondary and tertiary brands that over time become squeezed off supermarket shelves by the pincer movement of primary brands and private labels increasing the extent and depth of their ranges. This should be of concern to consumers not just because it limits their choice over products with distinctly different characteristics, but it restricts their ability to make effective price comparisons (given that its private labels can differ in attributes and quality between retailers and are never, unlike brands, displayed in direct competition with each other in the same store). However, the loss of secondary and tertiary brands may pose a deeper problem for consumers if it serves to dampen competition for shelf space and allow for a cosier and less antagonistic relationship between leading producers and leading retailers, with the possibility of coalescing power working to the disadvantage of consumers when it facilitates higher prices and avoidance of non-price competition.[46]

F. Conclusion

In many respects, consumers have never had it so good. Consumers have choice over which retailer to use, and then abundant product choice when in the store. Indeed, the healthiness and vigour of competition for access to supermarket shelves has helped ensure that consumers are largely well served in respect of the product choice they face. Equally, the battle amongst retailers to attract and retain customers has helped ensure that the prices charged by retailers remain keen. Consumers have also benefited from retail consolidation when it has served to

---

45 For some evidence on the extent of retailer loyalty over brand loyalty, see: L Thomassen, K Lincoln, and A Aconis, *Retailization: Brand Survival in the Age of Retailer Power* (2006) ch 3.

46 For more on this possibility and how coalescing power may operate, see: P W Dobson, 'Competing, Countervailing and Coalescing Forces: The Economics of Intra- and Inter- Business System Competition' [2006] 51 *Antitrust Bulletin* 175, and Steiner (n 1).

increase retailer efficiency and allow for buying power to counter any market power held by suppliers. In all these respects, the development of private label has undoubtedly had a positive impact: it provides additional product choices, it enhances category price competition, and it helps retailers obtain lower prices from suppliers (by enhancing retailers' bargaining power by having credible alternatives).

Yet, there are consumer concerns for the future. In particular, there is the worry that consumer sovereignty may give way to retailer sovereignty if retail consolidation continues apace and remains largely unchecked. Retailer power may counter supplier power (even that held by ostensibly powerful branded goods manufacturers), but what will counter retailer power?

With retailer sovereignty comes the concern that, in an absence of effective retail competition, retailers will be able to undertake actions that serve their own interests and not necessarily those of their customers, who are trapped by their lack of retailer choice. In particular, retailer sovereignty may permit deliberate damage to brand value, restrict product choice (e.g. by delisting non-primary brands and replacing them with leading brand look-alikes), cut corners on private label quality (to save on costs), limit price comparability (by deliberately stocking products that are not like-for-like, e.g. different sizes and quality levels), and allow for the manipulation of prices to distort category price architectures in their favour. In all of this, brands will continue to be stocked, but only when it advances the retailer's interest by being more profitable than replacing with a private label look-alike,[47] superficially enhances choice to placate consumers, helps the retailer to play off suppliers against each other (rather than becoming over-reliant on any one supplier), and perhaps when it aids retailer collusion (e.g. using common category captains as a facilitation device).

Competition authorities and the courts have a crucial role to play in ensuring that such situations do not arise—where competition at both the producer and retailer level is kept fair and keen. Otherwise, over time we may expect to see a greater occurrence of the brand and private label 'horrors' described here, and less of the brand and private label 'heroes' that really benefit consumers and have thus far served them so well. This calls for vigilance and action to tackle anti-competitive practices and prevent situations of single-firm or joint dominance arising and being exploited. More pointedly, it calls for the need to focus on protecting competition in both its horizontal and vertical forms, to ensure that consumers benefit from intense and fair rivalry at each level and between each stage of supply chains.

---

[47] Indeed, it is not necessarily the case that private label is more profitable to a retailer even if gross margins are higher; since brands may offer higher absolute profits through their higher prices and exhibit greater velocity through shelf space turnover. See: K L Ailawadi and B Harlam, 'An Empirical Analysis of the Determinants of Retail Margins: The Role of Store Brand Share' [2004] 68 *Journal of Marketing* 147.

6

PRIVATE LABELS AND ARTICLE 82 EC

*Andres Font Galarza**

The introduction (Section A) will expose Article 82 of the EC Treaty to the explicit but also implicit interests and perceptions of both EU competition enforcers and of the business community. This introduction intends to give a solid understanding to the reader of the interests at stake in the debate on the application of Article 82. The introduction aims to help the reader reach its own conclusions at the end of the chapter, beyond those hinted at by the author, regarding what role, if any, Article 82 should play in dealing with the phenomenon of private labels.

The second part (Section B) will explore Article 82 and private labels from a business to consumer perspective as a pre-condition to the arguments in the third part. Indeed, the consumer is the ultimate subject of protection of the Treaty rule. This part will therefore raise a very intuitive point: whether—in the light of the consumer welfare imperative—the European Commission should ever enforce Article 82 to the private labels offers made by retailers with market power.

* Partner at Mayer Brown International LLP (Brussels). The author wishes to thank Karl Frewein, Arantzazu Golderos, Lisa Lernborg, and Dr Jens P Schmidt for their contribution.

The third part (Section C) will look at the more classical business-to-business perspective to deal with the interpretation and eventual application of Article 82 in the interaction between retailers offering private labels and other competing suppliers who would normally be brand owners.

The fourth and final part (Section D) will put forward a number of tentative conclusions.

A. Legal and Business Perceptions of Article 82

Article 82 of the EC Treaty (hereinafter referred to as Article 82) establishes a quasi-constitutional framework within the European Community for the treatment of unilateral conduct by companies with market power under antitrust law.[1] Article 82 has been interpreted for many years by the European Judiciary in Luxembourg which has created a solid body of case law directly applicable across Europe. Although there are varying opinions as to whether or not EU case law in relation to Article 82 makes modern economic sense, the jurisprudence is largely consistent with little variations or surprises. Oversimplifying matters and in a nutshell, the courts have established the following framework for analysis: if a company happens to be 'dominant' in a given antitrust market, i.e. if it can behave independently in commercial terms, in particular in relation to competitors and customers,[2] then the company has a special responsibility;[3] it must make sure that it competes on the merits[4] through normal commercial practices. If the company

1 EC Treaty (Treaty of Rome, as amended), Article 82 sets out that 'Any abuse by one or more undertakings of a dominant position within the common market or in a substantial part of it shall be prohibited as incompatible with the common market insofar as it may affect trade between Member States.

Such abuse may, in particular, consist in:

(a) directly or indirectly imposing unfair purchase or selling prices or other unfair trading conditions;

(b) limiting production, markets or technical development to the prejudice of consumers;

(c) applying dissimilar conditions to equivalent transactions with other trading parties, thereby placing them at a competitive disadvantage;

(d) making the conclusion of contracts subject to acceptance by the other parties of supplementary obligations which, by their nature or according to commercial usage, have no connection with the subject of such contracts.'

2 The 'independent behaviour' legal test will naturally be analysed with market power indicators such as the existence or absence of competitive restraints and the influence or lack of influence of the company on market prices. The case law legal presumption in terms of market share is obviously another indicator; e.g. Case 27/76 *United Brands v European Commission* [1978] ECR 207; Case 85/76 *Hoffmann-La Roche v European Commission* [1979] ECR 461, [1979] 3 CMLR 211, para 38.

3 Case 322/81 *Michelin v European Commission* [1983] ECR 3461, para 57.

4 The meaning of 'competition on the merits', which is the core-justification of Article 82 and in general of EU antitrust policy, will bring from different authors quite different answers and potentially different outcomes in the Article 82 enforcement debate. Some will favour a test of

does not live up to its responsibilities, and the case law sets out numerous examples of allegedly abnormal behaviours in the market, it could not only be severely fined by competition authorities but, more importantly perhaps, could also be required to change its economic behaviour to re-establish competition on the merits. Although being dominant is not prohibited in itself and will often be the result of entrepreneurial success, which is why the special responsibility of dominant companies described above may be seen as overly interventionist, this special responsibility[5] may make theoretical sense if viewed in the light of protecting the competitive process and ultimately consumers' interests. It sends a clear message to companies with market power that economic dominance is under surveillance for the sake of protecting consumers' welfare in Europe. However, the system puts, more often than not, the competition enforcer in a catch-22 situation as it is not easy to reconcile an economic effects-based analysis of a given behaviour with the legal notion of special responsibility of a dominant company. The enforcer adjudicates justice independently and does not seek to interfere with pro-competitive behaviour.

Some companies perceive that there is a discrepancy in the approach being taken. In simple terms, the dominant company feels that on some occasions it is legally constrained by not being able to behave in certain ways that would make economic sense, e.g. in the light of a profit-maximizing strategy, and which would constitute normal commercial behaviour for such a company when competing in the market. Obviously, this misconception exists with regard to the central grey zone and not at the extremes.

For example, at one extreme, managers of companies with market power are willing to accept that they should not give instructions to their salesmen to visit retailers in order to make sure that the retailers will remove competing products without any objective justification for doing so. In such an example, the companies concerned easily understand that to do so would not amount to competition on the merits. The companies also understand that they cannot fix prices with competitors or evade taxes, despite such practices being profitable and making economic sense but for the threat of being held liable by Government. At the other extreme are companies with very little market power and therefore no special responsibility.

'no-exclusion of equally efficient competitors' or a 'no-economic sense but elimination of competition' standard. Others will emphasize the critical need to keep the structure of the markets open and viable for economic actors that are testing the acceptance of their products against existing or potential demand. There seems to be agreement that more debate is needed on the basic foundations and concepts underlying policy in order to try to reach a common understanding.

[5] Case 322/81 *Michelin v European Commission* [1983] ECR 3461, para 57.

However, between the two extremes, there is a considerably large central grey intersection, which can be reached by meeting competition on prices, tying and bundling strategies, rebates, the 'unrestrained' exercise of intellectual property (IP) rights, or through a range of possible market discriminations, and there is a clear misconception which persists in relation to this area. The fact that these companies are aware of their considerable market power does not imply that they would not feel or actually be threatened by actual or potential competitors. These companies also have difficulties understanding why it is that they should be treated differently by the competition enforcer vis-à-vis behaviour that is permissible for other competitors.[6] In that context the European competition enforcer could have remained in the safe world of *per se* enforcement providing a very predictable framework—perhaps too predictable for it allows for easy adjustment and circumvention—or, in the alternative, turn to the equally safe world of non-intervention at least in the grey area referred to above.

However, it is only fair to recognize that the recent European competition enforcers have nobly been attempting something more difficult but surely more intellectually honest in the public interest: they have been engaging in a continuous process of searching for the right benchmark and intervention standard for each particular case under Article 82 subject to its analysis. The process itself and the willingness of the competition services of the European Commission and of the European Competition Network[7] to produce decisions in this area with the highest legal and economic qualitative standards should be appreciated. There is certainly an effort to understand the economic rationale of a given situation and its impact on the market and consumers. The competition services of the European Commission are not automatically applying rigid rules of law without any regard to what is happening in the market and the effects of their intervention. There does not seem to be a hidden agenda or hidden meta-objectives, neither leading to industrial *mechano* experiments. There are obviously rules but

---

[6] The legal and economic answer to this discriminatory treatment of dominant companies being that competition is already weakened and should not be weakened further to the likely prejudice of the consumer. However, once again one thing is the economic theory and the legal rules and another is the perception of the market players of that economic reality and their corresponding market behaviour. In addition there are behaviours that competitors without market power cannot do or it would not make economic sense to do, e.g. they will not be able to engage in a costly and successful predation strategy followed by recoupment after the competitors' exit. It is not without interest to think in these terms, i.e. what kind of exclusionary or exploitative behaviours can a company with market power do or have the incentive to do in contrast with a company without market power.

[7] The European Commission and the national competition authorities in all EU Member States cooperate with each other through the European Competition Network (ECN). Through the ECN, the competition authorities inform each other of proposed decisions and take on board comments from the other competition authorities. <http://ec.europa.eu/comm/competition/ecn/index_en.html> accessed 2 June 2008.

these are economically informed rules.[8] National Competition authorities[9] and courts are also actively enforcing Article 82 in a coordinated effort. In sum, the EC Treaty has put in the Commission's hands a very powerful legal instrument that, regardless of conflicting opinions on how it should be enforced, is used with caution and responsibility by the competition enforcer given its radical economic potential of regulating certain companies' economic behaviour in a free market economy.[10]

The discussion triggered since 2005 by DG Competition on the application of Article 82 to exclusionary abuses setting out an array of possible theories of harm justifying the enforcer's intervention or abstention in a number of categories of behaviours should be looked at with the above legal and economic dilemmas in mind. However, the Article 82 debate naturally tends to focus on the concerns and implementation difficulties faced by competition enforcers and businesses when they interact. The objective of the rule tends to be forgotten in the battle-field, but it is essential in the legal and economic discussions and should never be forgotten: the subject of protection is the consumer.[11]

B. In the Light of 'Consumers Welfare', Could or Should Article 82 be Enforced against the Private Label Offers by Companies with Market Power?

The above question is necessary because there is a strong perception that private labels are *per se* beneficial to consumers. The consequence being an implicit sort of *estoppel* rule impeding the application of Article 82.

[8] The most clear examples applicable across all antitrust instruments are following: Commission Notice on the definition of relevant market for the purposes of Community competition law [1997] OJ C372/5.

[9] National competition authorities are very active in the enforcement of Article 82 EC since 1 May 2004, pursuant to Article 3 of Regulation No 1/2003 (Council Regulation (EC) 1/2003 of 16 December 2002 on the implementation of the rules on competition laid down in Articles 81 and 82 of the Treaty [2003] OJ L1/1).

[10] See this spirit in the speech: N Kroes, 'Preliminary Thoughts on Policy Review of Article 82' (Speech at the Fordham Corporate Law Institute on 23 September 2005) <http://europa.eu/rapid/pressReleasesAction.do?reference=SPEECH/05/537> accessed 2 June 2008, which triggered the pending discussion on the interpretation of Article 82 EC, the called 'Article 82 review'.

[11] With regard to exclusionary abuses the objective of Article 82 is the protection of competition on the market as a means of enhancing consumer welfare and of ensuring an efficient allocation of resources. Effective competition brings benefits to consumers, such as low prices, high quality products, a wide selection of goods and services, and innovation. Competition and market integration serve these ends since the creation and preservation of an open single market promotes an efficient allocation of resources throughout the Community for the benefit of consumers. In applying Article 82, the Commission will adopt an approach which is based on the likely effects on the market.

Indeed, retailers with market power[12] offering private labels to consumers have a considerable advocacy advantage that has always limited and, to a certain extent manipulated, the competition policy debate in this area. The answer by retailers with buyer power in antitrust cases seems pretty straightforward and is as follows: retailers with alleged market power, by squeezing suppliers' margins, reduce prices downstream in the interest of consumers. Retailers would thereby act as consumer agents. Private labels provide the same product at lower prices than the primary brands. There is eventually fierce horizontal competition downstream when the buyer in turn becomes a seller of the goods or services to consumers. Is the competition enforcer then going to intervene along the lines of rebalancing the market power situation between suppliers and buyers risking putting prices up for consumers? The answer seems to be intuitive—that as long as prices go down, no action will be taken—and many will stop there without any further elaboration. Is this defence maybe too good to be true? The fact that this argument seems to be logical and easy to sell would obviously not be a reason to discard it. So what is the problem under Article 82?

The, at least potential, problem for retailers with market power that offer private labels is that obviously price is not the only parameter to be considered in a competition analysis under Article 82.[13] And even if price were the most prominent competition parameter, short term price beneficial effects on consumers would not be sufficient to discard any, in theory, longer term harmful price effects—if these could be proven.[14] Indeed, there is a policy trade-off between the allegedly insufficient nature of the challenge of short-term effects on consumers and the sometimes speculative nature of the analysis via presumptions on long-term indirect effects on consumers deriving from a given behaviour of a dominant company with possible exclusionary effects on its competitors. The issue

---

12 The goal of consumer welfare is affected by market power. Excessive market power could create a transfer of wealth from consumers to producers. Both concepts, 'market power' and 'consumer welfare', are necessarily linked in an analysis under Article 82 when assessing whether the company is in a situation of dominance and on whether it is abusing its dominant position. The analysis in terms of 'market power' and the analysis in terms of efficiencies coincide for a significant part. Thus, in a market situation with relevant efficiencies, no excessive market power or market dominance can exist, e.g. if a decline of prices or output expansion in favour of consumers can be found. However, this economic aspect which may serve as a defence of those retailers with alleged market power goes beyond the purpose of this chapter.

13 EC Treaty (n 1) Art 82.

14 In general a 'likelihood standard' of proof refers to likely anticompetitive effects, not to actual effects and not to the capability to bring those effects, a quite straightforward standard when dealing with historic past behaviour of the dominant company. In practice, it is not easy to gather the necessary evidence given the difficulty of the enforcer and even the market players to obtain reliable data from the market. The use of rebuttable presumptions when dealing with different categories of abuse such as predation or fidelity enhancing schemes is partially explained by this.

concerning short-term effects on consumers also requires a reflection on how the competition enforcer deals with temporary monopoly power in other areas of EU competition policy. As a conclusion, there is—neither from a legal nor from an economic point of view—no *estoppel* nor any kind of *per se* rule out of the direct consumer's experience[15] or interests that would exclude the impact of private labels from an analysis under Article 82. However, a harmful impact has to be proven.

In an ideal world, the interests of businesses and consumers would coincide and competition authorities would strike the right balance to make business activity thrive in the interest of citizens and consumers whilst protecting them from exploitation. The same applies to the consumer's rights for high-quality and safe products, a wide selection of goods and services, and innovation. The protection of those tangible consumer rights are definitely also part of European competition law and Article 82.[16] Indeed, the focus and diversion of the enforcer's attention has been on the protection of consumer welfare via the protection of competition in the market by preserving and fostering a competitive process with efficient competitors. Here the definitions and concepts used are of the essence. The concept of the consumer in antitrust law and Article 82 of the Treaty has a large scope.[17] In addition, in economic terms, 'pure consumer welfare' is not the same as 'total consumer welfare', 'wealth distribution', or 'fair competition'. Consumer welfare cannot be understood as capturing only effects on prices and/or output but must also be understood to include other competition parameters such as quality, choice, and especially innovation. Consumer welfare is not brought about by having as many horizontal and vertical competitors as possible in following an atomistic approach. The instrument should serve the goal and not the other way round.

15 There is a critical terminological distinction between direct and indirect consumer harm which should be carefully reflected upon and perhaps distinguished from a too easy correlation with the categories of exploitative and exclusionary abuses, i.e. there is scope in the analysis of exclusionary abuses which also prove direct consumer harm.

16 For instance, Case C-7/97 *Oscar Bronner v Mediaprint* [1998] ECR I-7791 para 58, in which Advocate General Jacobs stated that '. . . the primary purpose of Article [82] is to prevent distortion of competition—and in particular to safeguard the interests of consumers—rather than to protect the position of particular competitors'. In analogy with regard to consumer benefits: Guidelines on the Assessment of Horizontal Mergers under the Council Regulation on the Control of Concentrations between Undertakings [2004] OJ C31/5 para 8.

17 See in a parallel legal framework the Communication from the Commission—Notice—Guidelines on the application of Article 81(3) of the Treaty [2004] OJ C101/97 para 84 states that 'The concept of "consumers" encompasses all direct or indirect users of the products covered by the agreement, including producers that use the products as an input, wholesalers, retailers and final consumers.'

Theory is one thing and enforcement practice another. There are no 'Brussels' precedents to the application of Article 82 to retailers with market power—if it was proved under the regular antitrust standards that those retailers actually had market power—that would elaborate on harmful effects of private label offers to consumers, be it in terms of less choice, less quality, or deterrence to innovation. The competition enforcer dealing with manifestations of buyer market power is exposed to the more uncertain, but still relevant, assessment of potentially detrimental non-pricing effects on consumers. This assessment may also be relevant in relation to private label offers analysis under Article 82. As always, the regular and high standards in terms of antitrust evidence should be met.

C. Potential Issues Arising under Article 82 from a Business-to-Business Perspective

In an ideal world, competition authorities would also find the right balance for acceptable levels of natural exclusion of economic players out of the operation of competition. The latter would ensure a fair game between economic operators with different degrees of market power or different positions and economic incentives in the supply chain in the interest of consumers and the competitive process. Against this backdrop, a textbook case is the exercise of buying power by retailers with market power over suppliers. A further refinement would be the analysis of the impact of private labels in that game.

In terms of exclusion of some traditional business players in the vertical chain of supply and even in terms of general output, the phenomenon of buying pools or *centrals d'achat* in combination with the private labels offer is also of interest. Some buyers involved in rather powerful buyer pools are said to put an end to what was traditionally considered to be an efficient accumulation of stocks by suppliers and their eventual distribution to the buyers. Instead, those buyers' pools would at present transmit, on a very short notice, real time orders to the suppliers, based on the instant demand information obtained through their omnipresent network of distribution to their clients. The buyers' platforms would send their own transport to collect the production and then redistribute the goods among the participants in the pool. This vertical and horizontal integration upstream by buyers, with the consequent exclusion of intermediaries in the distribution chain, could be considered as increasing the market power enjoyed by some buyers and the economic dependency of suppliers. Interestingly this aggressive integration upstream could have an impact in terms of the utilization of the suppliers' fixed assets. As a consequence, the suppliers would, in some scenarios, even have an incentive to 'stop the machines' as the planning of production and the management of stocks is no longer in their hands.

The effects on the level of output are interesting from an Article 82 perspective. Obviously, some will see the developments described in the paragraphs above as extremely efficient from an economic point of view, and other chapters of this book will analyse this phenomenon. These referred-to effects and others arising from new models of increased economic power on the buyers' side would be irreproachable if those buyers were the indifferent agents of the ultimate consumers who would, through their day-to-day purchases, determine the right market level of production. However, the buyers' incentives on fostering their private labels' offers cannot be ignored. Consequently many see that the buyers' increasing 'conflict of interests' both upstream and downstream, particularly manifested through their private labels' offer, calls for a careful approach under Article 82 when hearing 'efficiency-enhancing defences', or, in other scenarios, 'efficiency rebuttals' arguing instead the impossibility of challenging abuses of market power by these new buying and selling distribution models.

The new economic incentives created by the private labels' offer by buyers who enjoy single or collective market power opens a number of interesting counterfactuals in the business-to-business economic relationships. A comparison of the traditional approach under Article 82 with potentially abusive behaviours by suppliers with market power on some parallel but still theoretical categories of abusive behaviour appears to be challenging, especially as these circumstances have so far remained untested in the enforcers' decisional practice.

Under the Article 82 basic framework of analysis, a case of collective dominance found on the buyer's side in some product and geographical markets cannot be excluded. Consequently, certain behaviour manifested either collectively[18] or individually[19] from the buyer's side could fall either on the abusive or on the objectively justified side of the framework.

It appears established that there are neither legal nor economic reasons for discrimination, i.e. the enforcer being more lenient or stricter[20]—beyond the specific results of case-by-case analysis—between antitrust situations stemming from excessive market power at buying side or selling side.

---

[18] In practice, it is a 'collective boycott' situation, e.g. with regard to Article 81(1): Case 96/82 *IAZ International Belgium NV v European Commission* [1983] ECR 3369; Case 71/74 *'Frubo' v European Commission* [1975] ECR 563.

[19] T-228/97 *Irish Sugar v European Commission* [1999] ECR II-2969.

[20] However, the theories on economic dependency allow less stringent market power criteria to trigger the dominance thresholds that open the Article 82 analysis.

An extensive practice and literature concerning sellers' predatory tactics[21] has been established in relation to the application of Article 82. Thus, there is no reason—beyond the merits of the specific facts of the case, the compliance with the substantive tests, and the standards of proof—not to develop 'overbidding/overbuying predation' cases in Europe under Article 82.[22]

Article 82 is also an important tool in the enforcement against sellers' price-squeezing tactics and there is extensive practice and literature to this effect.[23] It is therefore suggested that there is no reason—beyond the merits of the specific facts of the case, the compliance with the substantive tests, and the standards of proof—to exclude an analysis in this matter under Article 82 of pricing and non-pricing behaviour of those buyers which are thoroughly vertically integrated. In fact, squeezing incentives for those enjoying market power should be on the rise as suppliers and buyers compete for the vertical control of the chain of supply and those who are excluded from the intermediate steps of the supply chain may also want to enter the downstream levels in defensive moves.

The 'resale below cost' situations, which is a category close to predation, deserve a particular mention. On the one hand, the potential exclusionary effects upstream seem unquestionable. On the other hand, the either beneficiary—in terms of prices[24]—or detrimental effects on the final customer—in terms of choice, quality, and innovation—need further reflection. This all needs to be placed against the backdrop of State pricing legislation that is adopted on *non-standard* antitrust grounds of 'fair competition'.

The use of Article 82 against sellers with market power who would disrupt established patterns of commerce, for example by cutting off supplies,[25] can be

---

21 Case C-62/86 *AKZO Chemie BV v European Commission* [1991] ECR I-03359; Case T-83/91 *Tetra Pak International SA v European Commission* [1994] ECR II-00755; Joined Cases C-395/96 P and C-396/96 P *Compagnie Maritime Belge SA v European Commission* [2000] ECR I-1365; *Deutsche Post AG* [2001] OJ L125/27; *Wanadoo Interactive* [2003] COMP/38.233. In a nutshell the substantive standard being applied in these cases is *selling* below a given measure of cost.

22 In *Weyerhaeuser Co v Ross-Simmons Hardwood Lumber Co*, 549 US (2007), No 05-381 the US Supreme Court has recently established that the test applied to 'predatory-pricing' claims in *Brooke Group* also applies in the case of 'predatory-bidding'. The *Brook Group* test is twofold: first, the plaintiff must prove that the defendant suffered a loss in the short term, and second, that the defendant had a dangerous probability of recouping its loss in the long term.

23 Case 109/75R *National Carbonising Co Ltd v European Commission* [1975] ECR 1193; Case 88/518/EEC *Napier Brown–British Sugar* [1988] OJ L284/41; Case T-5/97 *Industrie des Poudres Sphériques v European Commission* [2001] OJ C134/15.

24 See generally Section B above.

25 Joined Cases 6/73 and 7/73 *Istituto Chemioterapico SpA and Commercial Solvents Corporation v European Commission* [1974] ECR 223; Case 22/78 *Hugin Kassaregister AB v European Commission* [1979] ECR 1869; Case 311/84 *CBEM v CLT and IPB (Télémarketing)* [1985] ECR 3261; Case T-201/04 *Microsoft v EC Commission* (judgement delivered on 17 September 2007).

considered as being an 'antitrust classic'. There is no reason—beyond the merits of the specific facts of the case, the compliance with the substantive tests,[26] and the standards of proof—to exclude analysis under Article 82 resulting from particularly flagrant cases of arbitrary and not objectively justified[27] termination of orders by buyers with market power. In this context, patterns of conduct intended to exclude a second brand for the benefit of the allegedly competing private labels of a buyer enjoying market power upstream and downstream could be seen as an interesting candidate for further antitrust examination.

The above is a non-exclusive list of potential and theoretical candidates for scrutiny under Article 82 in situations involving either a single buyer or a group of buyers behaving in parallel whilst enjoying market power.[28] As part of any antitrust evaluations, private labels will certainly be analysed given their current significant economic and strategic importance—sometimes in the front line, sometimes in the shadow—as a key incentive underlying the rationale of the behaviour examined under Article 82. This is currently happening as a matter of routine in the area of EU Merger Control.[29]

D. Conclusions

1. The EU competition enforcer, as an authority with potentially impressive powers of economic intervention, has chosen, in the realm of application of Article 82, the most difficult but arguably most credible approach that can be taken; the reconciliation of the dictum on special responsibility held by companies with market power and the self-imposed fullest economic justification

[26] In a nutshell *Commercial Solvents* established that refusal to supply a competitor in the downstream market by an undertaking in a dominant position infringes Article 82 if it has the effect of eliminating all competition in the downstream market. However, *Commercial Solvents* may also lead to an obligation to supply a competitor upstream e.g. *IBM* [1984] European Commission's XIVth Annual Report on competition policy, para 94-95; Case C-418/01 *IMS Health GmbH & Co OHG v NDC Health GmbH & Co KG* [2004] ECR I-5039; *Microsoft v EC Commission* (n 25).

[27] See *Tabacalera/Filtrona* [1989] European Commission's XIXth Annual Report on competition policy, para 61. The Commission rejected a complaint with regard to Article 82 made by a Spanish cigarette filter producer, Filtrona Española, against the Spanish tobacco monopoly holder, Tabacalera which decided to stop buying filters from Filtrona. Although, the Commission encountered the issue of buyer's dominance it considered the refusal to be *objectively justified* by economies of sale and cost reductions deriving from an own-filter production.

[28] The buyer who would also enjoy market power downstream should certainly be more careful in terms of its special responsibility under Article 82 including the way its own labels are handled with respect to other brands.

[29] *Akzo Nobel/ICI* [2007] OJ C29/2; *Osram Sunny World* [2007] OJ C290/5; *OEP/MSP-Stiftung/DVG/Dailycer Group* [2007] OJ C286/45; *SCA/P&G (European tissue business)* [2007] OJ C275/1; *Smithfield/Oaktree/Sara Lee Foods Europe* [2006] OJ C280/45; *Procter & Gamble/Gillette* [2005] C239/12.

in terms of effects for enforcement intervention. The same principle applies to the application of Article 82 with regard to buying power and private labels.

2. There is neither legal nor economic *estoppel* from the point of view of the consumer for the application of Article 82 to a situation involving private labels. Furthermore, price is not the only relevant parameter for an antitrust assessment of consumer welfare. However, the required standards of proof of consumer harm have to be met.
3. In business-to-business relations, an Article 82 effects-based evaluation of private labels remains a theoretical case. However, against the backdrop of significant buying power in some retail segments, this market constellation allows for a perfect counterfactual opportunity to reflect on some basic justifications for the treatment of dominance at a European level through application of reverse indicators, i.e. by using classically established selling power indicators in a reverse way. In particular, collective dominance in the area of private labels may lead either to a justification of a particular behaviour or, in the alternative, to a finding of abuse.[30]

30 See generally Section C above.

Part III

VERTICAL RESTRAINTS

7

PRIVATE LABELS, DUAL DISTRIBUTION, AND VERTICAL RESTRAINTS—AN ANALYSIS OF THE COMPETITIVE EFFECTS

*David Gilo**

* Associate Professor, Buchmann Faculty of Law, Tel Aviv University, gilod@post.tau.ac.il. I wish to thank Ariel Ezrachi and Yaron Yehezkel for extremely helpful comments on previous drafts.

A. Introduction

This chapter explores how participation of a retailer in the supplier's market via a private label and participation of a supplier in the retail market via dual distribution impacts on the anticompetitive effects of vertical restraints.

The existence of a private label can impact on the anticompetitive effect of vertical restraints in two principle ways. On one hand, the private label often constitutes presence of the retailer in the supplier's market, thereby creating horizontal competition between the retailer and the supplier in the supplier's market. Restraints limiting the retailer's operation of the private label, therefore, resemble horizontal restraints among competitors and deserve harsher antitrust treatment than purely vertical restraints. On the other hand, as this chapter shows, if a retailer and a supplier adopt vertical restraints that do not limit the retailer's ability to operate his private label, the existence of the private label could actually weaken the anticompetitive effect of all vertical restraints but for exclusive distribution.

Interestingly, in contrast to this latter finding, the EC Commission Block Exemption for Vertical Restraints treats most vertical restraints in the presence of a private label as horizontal in nature, thereby, for the most part, disqualifying them from the exemption. Accordingly, a change in the EC block exemption's application is warranted.

On the other hand, as this chapter shows, the block exemption's treatment of dual distribution cases, in which the supplier party to a vertical restraint also controls a distribution outlet, is too lenient with respect to certain types of vertical restraints. In particular, restraints that eliminate competition between the supplier's retail outlet and competing retailers may harm competition more than similar vertical restraints absent dual distribution. This is particularly shown to be the case when the supplier's profits stem from charging an above-cost price per unit. Similarly, with regard to non-compete clauses and price matching policies, account should be taken of the supplier's retail unit when calculating the percentage of the retail market that is foreclosed from competing suppliers. In fact, exclusive distribution is the only vertical restraint in which the presence of dual distribution warrants a more lenient treatment of the vertical restraint.

B. Why are Vertical Restraints Treated Less Harshly than Horizontal Restraints?

As mentioned in the introduction, one important feature of private labels and dual distribution is that they could turn a supplier and a retailer into competitors in the supplier's or retailer's market, thereby making some of the restraints in their contract 'horizontal' in nature. Accordingly, in order to better understand the way private labels or dual distribution affect the anticompetitive nature of vertical restraints, it should be made clear why vertical restraints deserve a more lenient treatment than horizontal restraints. There are two main reasons for this difference in treatment.

First, when there is a vertical relationship between a supplier and a retailer, the parties can use the legitimate terms of their contract to achieve anticompetitive effects even in the absence of vertical restraints. To illustrate, if a supplier has the power to raise prices and is interested in a high retail price, he can induce retailers buying from him to raise their retail price even without restraints forcing them to do so. All the supplier needs to do is elevate the wholesale price he charges his retailers. This would inflate their marginal costs, thereby compelling them to raise the retail price. Similarly, such a supplier could simply sell his retailers smaller quantities, thereby compelling them to reduce the quantity of the supplier's brand they sell, even absent a vertical restraint imposing maximum quantities upon retailers. This point is especially relevant when the supplier and retailer's contract includes not only a wholesale price per unit but also a fixed fee. In such a case, it is not obvious, for example, that a vertical restraint eliminating competition between retailers, such as dictation of the retail price, or division of retailers into exclusive territories, will raise the retail price. This is because if competition between retailers is eliminated, the supplier is expected to lower his wholesale price per unit, so as to maximize retailers' expected profits. This would enable the supplier to collect a higher fixed fee. Absent the vertical restraint eliminating competition among retailers, retailers do not expect to make substantial profits, and the fixed fee they are willing to pay the supplier goes down. Here, the supplier's profits must stem from an inflated wholesale price. An inflated wholesale price inflates the retailers' marginal costs, and, moreover, creates double marginalization, that typically cause the retail price to be even higher than with the vertical restraint.[1]

The ability to achieve anticompetitive outcomes through legitimate parameters of the agreement such as the wholesale price charged by the supplier and the quantity he sells does not exist with regard to pure competitors. Competitors generally have no such legitimate mechanism that could be used to achieve anti-competitive outcomes. They need explicit restraints, such as cartels, market division, practices facilitating cartels, etc., in order to achieve such outcomes.

1 For more details about this point see Section F below and the literature cited there.

This is one explanation why horizontal restraints deserve more scrutiny: without them, it would be difficult for the parties to harm competition.

The second reason for treating vertical restraints more leniently is that when the supplier derives profits from the wholesale price he charges retailers (i.e., a profit per each unit sold), profit maximization on his part requires him to insist on as much competition as possible among retailers. This is because such competition would increase the number of units sold, thereby elevating the supplier's profits. Similarly, such a supplier would be interested in the retailers providing optimal services (at least from the point of view of the marginal customer—i.e., the first customer to stop purchasing the product if the price were to go up slightly). As for the retailer, since his profits are typically rising when the supplier's power to raise prices is limited, the retailer too would not want to engage in a restraint which enhances the supplier's market power.

The Guidelines on Vertical Restraints[2] acknowledge this second reason for treating vertical restraints leniently and stipulate that:

> Vertical restraints are generally less harmful than horizontal restraints. The main reason for treating a vertical restraint more leniently than a horizontal restraint lies in the fact that the latter may concern an agreement between competitors producing identical or substitutable goods or services. In such horizontal relationships the exercise of market power by one company (higher price of its product) may benefit competitors. This may provide an incentive to competitors to induce each other to behave anticompetitively. In vertical relationships the product of one is the input for the other. This means that the exercise of market power by either the upstream or downstream company would normally hurt the demand for the product of the other. The companies involved in the agreement therefore usually have an incentive to prevent the exercise of market power by the other.

Accordingly, if such a supplier and retailer agree on vertical restraints, this could be explained by the need to alleviate inefficiencies in distribution or supply, such as free riding,[3] hold-out problems, inventory decisions,[4] information problems,[5] moral hazard,[6] or other externalities between the parties causing them to have inadequate incentives efficiently to promote the product absent the vertical

[2] Commission Notice (EC) Guidelines on Vertical Restraints [2000] OJ C291/1, para 100.

[3] See e.g.: L Telser, 'Why Should Manufacturers Want Fair Trade?' [1960] 3 *Journal of Law and Economics* 86.

[4] See e.g.: R Deneckere, H Marvel, and J Peck, 'Demand Uncertainty, Inventories, and Resale Price Maintenance' [1996] 111 *Quarterly Journal of Economics* 885.

[5] See e.g.: P Rey and J Tirole, 'The Logic of Vertical Restraints' [1986] 76 *American Economic Review* 921.

[6] See e.g.: R Romano, 'Double Moral Hazard and Resale Price Maintenance' [1994] 25 *RAND Journal of Economics* 455.

restraint.[7] Alleviation of such inefficiencies in distribution or supply may well be to the benefit of consumers.

C. Harm to Interbrand versus Intrabrand Competition

As is well known in antitrust policy, vertical restraints that harm interbrand competition—competition between competing brands—should be treated more harshly than restraints that merely harm interbrand competition—competition between competing retailers of the same brand. To be sure, as shown in the economics literature, some limitations on interbrand competition may also cause harm to interbrand competition, as will be highlighted in several of the following sections. Nevertheless, it is undisputed that the stronger interbrand competition is to begin with, the smaller the anticompetitive threat of vertical restraints.[8] In what follows we shall examine the various types of vertical restraints and the way the existence of a private label or dual distribution affects their anticompetitive nature.

D. Limits on the Sale of the Private Label

This section considers the competitive effects generated through limitations on the sale of private label itself, when the retailer controls the supply of his private label. When the retailer agrees with a supplier to limit the retailer's ability to sell his private label to consumers, the restraint should typically be viewed harshly, as a horizontal rather than a vertical restraint. In essence, such a restraint resembles the commitment on the part of a potential competitor to limit his ability to compete. Such 'non-competition clauses' or market divisions among competitors or potential competitors are typically dealt with harshly as horizontal restraints.[9]

Note, however, that in order to analyse restraints limiting the retailer's ability to sell his private label it is essential to determine what the private label exactly constitutes. If the retailer purchases his 'private label' from an independent supplier, but just replaces the supplier's brand name with his own label name for

---

[7] See para (6) of the preamble of Commission Regulation (EC) 2790/1999 of 22 December 1999 on the Application of Article 81(3) of the Treaty to Categories of Vertical Agreements and Concerted Practices [1999] OJ L336/21 (hereinafter 'the Block Exemption Regulation') and Commission Guidelines (n 2) para 116.

[8] See: Commission Guidelines (n 2) para 102.

[9] See e.g.: H J Goldschmid, 'Antitrust's Neglected Stepchild: A Proposal for Dealing with Restrictive Covenants under Federal Law' [1973] 73 *Columbia Law Review* 1193; *United States v Topco Associates* 405 US 596 (1972).

the product, then restraints that limit the retailer's ability to sell his private label are almost purely vertical, rather than horizontal, and generally should be treated with the same scrutiny as vertical restraints limiting the retailer's ability to buy from an independent supplier. For example, a retailer's promise to supplier A not to buy from other suppliers (including suppliers who provide the retailer with the product to be branded according to the retailer's 'private label') resembles a so-called vertical non-compete agreement and should be treated as such.[10]

The situation is different, however, when the retailer has substantial control over the operations of the facility supplying the product to be privately labelled. In such a case, a commitment on the part of the retailer to refrain from holding the private label resembles a horizontal restraint to limit the retailer's operation in the supplier's market. This would be the case whenever the retailer's efforts are a key to the very existence of an establishment operating in the supplier's market. From an economic perspective, the retailer's commitment to limit the sales of his private label, in such a case, also may limit the additional capacity and variety of supplies the retailer could have contributed to the supplier's market. In other words, in order to analyse the competitive effects of vertical restraints in the presence of a 'private label' one must distinguish between two different situations: (a) the retailer purchases the product from an independent supplier already operating in the supply market and sells the product under the retailer's own label; and (b) the retailer initiates (or is a key factor in) the production process itself. For example, the retailer invests in expansion of a small supplier's plant so as to accommodate the retailer's requirements for its own label; or the retailer invests in the construction of a new plant to be used to supply the retailer's requirements for its own label, and so forth. Another case that could correspond to possibility (b) is that the retailer adds or helps add capacity to the wholesale level, e.g. by investing in supply channels, warehouses, insurance, packaging, and so forth needed in order to add wholesaling capacity that would accommodate the retailer's need for his own label. The latter type of 'private label' is the one I focus upon here.

In the former type of a 'private label', which I am not focusing upon in this chapter, the retailer is not a key to the addition of new capacity at the supply level. He simply purchases existing capacity from an independent supplier. Presumably, before the creation of the retailer's private label, this independent supplier used its capacity for other channels in the supply market of the product, such as the sale of the product in the branded sector. Once the independent supplier, instead, routes some or all of his capacity to sales ending up as the retailer's private label,

[10] Such a vertical restraint may, according to Article 5(a) of the Block Exemption Regulation (n 7), enjoy the exemption defined by the regulation if it is limited to a five-year period.

his relationship with the retailer is purely vertical and restraints between them, or between this retailer and other suppliers, should be analysed in a similar way to any other vertical restraint. Of course, the fact that the product is sold under the retailer's own label may bear on the analysis of these vertical restraints. For example, to the extent that the retailer's profits from selling his own label are higher than its profits from selling branded goods, the retailer may have an incentive to give more shelf space to his private label and less shelf space to the branded goods.

These, however, are not the type of concerns this chapter focuses on. In essence, when the retailer buys the 'private label' from an independent supplier, and is not a key to the addition of capacity to the supply market due to the private label, it cannot be said that the retailer is really operating in the supply market, and that its relationship with other suppliers is horizontal.

A commitment not to hold a private label

If a retailer commits to the supplier that he will not have a private label, the question is if such a restraint should be treated as a horizontal non-competition clause or a vertical restraint similar to a non-compete clause. Naturally, if the retailer promises not to enter the supplier's market, the restraint resembles a *horizontal* non-competition clause. The restraint prevents the entry of an additional supplier (namely, the retailer) into the supplier's market. Even though this new supplier (the supplier of the private label) may have been focused on selling exclusively to this retailer, interbrand competition is harmed. Suppose, for example, that there are two suppliers, supplier A and supplier B, in the relevant supplying market, and two retailers, retailer A and retailer B, in the relevant retailing market. If retailer A holds his own private label, in addition to supplier A and B's brands, interbrand competition between the different suppliers would intensify, even if the third brand could be found only in retailer A's outlet. Thus, a commitment on the part of the retailer not to hold his own private label potentially harms interbrand competition in a way similar in spirit to a commitment on the part of a potential entrant into the suppliers' market not to enter.

To be sure, when the retailer enters the supplier market with his own label, vertical integration between this retailer and its supply outlet is created. As is well known, vertical integration can at times foreclose competitors.[11] In particular, the retailer will naturally want to dedicate more of its shelf space to its own label, leaving less of its shelf space to other suppliers. When the retailer controls a large

[11] See e.g.: E S Rosengren, J W Meehan Jr, 'Antitrust Policy and Vertical Mergers' [1995] Sep/Oct *New England Economic Review* 27.

portion of retail facilities in the relevant market, this could cause other suppliers to shrink, or at times even exit the market. In the long run, interbrand competition could be harmed, since fewer significant suppliers would be present, despite the new entry of the retailer's private label. On the other hand, vertical integration has its virtues. Because the retailer will purchase the private label at cost, its entry into the supply market eliminates double margins and tends to lower retail prices charged for the private label. Other economic theories show that the presence of the private label (particularly of poor perceived quality) could actually induce branded suppliers to raise their prices.[12]

Entry of the retailer into the suppliers' market, by the introduction of his private label, creates vertical integration. A commitment on the part of the retailer not to introduce a private label prevents such vertical integration. Hence, if we believe the disadvantages of vertical integration outweigh its advantages in a particular case, this factor could work in favour of a commitment on the part of the retailer not to create a private label. Still, such a commitment is horizontal in nature. Absent the commitment, there would have been more brands competing with each other in the supply market. This is why close scrutiny of such a commitment, resembling that of horizontal restraints, is in place.

Financial incentives to sell less of the private label

If the contract between the retailer and a supplier incentivizes the retailer to sell less of the private label (and more of the supplier's brand) this too is quite similar to a horizontal restraint inducing a competitor of the supplier partially to withdraw from the supplier's market. Suppose, for example, that the supplier of a 'must stock brand' offers the retailer bonuses that hinge upon the retailer purchasing a substantial percentage (e.g., above 50 per cent) of his needs in a certain category of products from the supplier. In such a case, the retailer's incentives to distribute his private label are harmed. The effect is similar to a competing supplier receiving a bonus from the supplier for mitigating his sales in competition with the supplier's brand. Such restraints, accordingly, should be treated harshly, as horizontal in nature.

Limitation of shelf space devoted to the private label

A similar result would evolve if the retailer agrees not to devote shelf space above a certain threshold to his private label or devote inferior shelf space to his

[12] See: T S Gabrielson and L Sogard, 'Private Labels, Price Rivalry, and Public Policy' [2007] 51 *European Economic Review* 403, (showing that under certain conditions branded goods are priced at a higher level in the presence of a private label of lower quality).

private label. Such a commitment limits the quantity sold of the private label in a way that also limits its ability to restrain anticompetitive pricing or behaviour by the suppliers of the other brands. It, too, should be treated as harshly as an ordinary horizontal restraint in which a competing supplier agrees to limit his sales in competition with the supplier's brand. On the other hand, the foreclosing effects inherent in the existence of the private brand[13] would also be mitigated by such a commitment. The latter factor could mitigate the potential anticompetitive effect.

Commitment to a minimum price or maximum quantity of the private label

Similarly, if the retailer commits not to charge a price for its private label below a certain floor, or sell quantities of its private label above a certain ceiling, this harms the private label's potential for restraining anticompetitive pricing or quality on the part of competing brands and therefore harms interbrand competition in a way similar to a horizontal price fixing or quantity fixing agreement.

Territorial division with regard to the private label

In the same vein, when a retailer agrees with a supplier to sell his private label only in certain territories and not in others, interbrand competition in the territory in which the private label will not exist due to the restraint may be harmed. In particular, if this territory constitutes a relevant geographic market, consumers in this market find other territories as not interchangeable with this territory. They will enjoy less intense interbrand competition due to the restraint. Such a restraint is similar in nature and effect to a horizontal market division agreement among competing suppliers, which, of course is treated harshly by antitrust law. Again, since such a restraint mitigates the presence of the private label in certain areas, the harsh effects of vertical integration, to the extent they exist,[14] would also be mitigated. This could alleviate at least part of the anticompetitive concerns.

E. Vertical Restraints Not Concerned With the Private Label

The analysis is substantially different when the retailer does not limit its behaviour with regard to its own label but rather engages in vertical restraints not

13 See text above accompanying n 11.
14 See text above accompanying n 11.

connected to the private label, while holding its own label. The way the analysis changes depends on the type of restraint, as the following paragraphs reveals.

Resale price maintenance and exclusive territories

Suppose a retailer is subject to a supplier's dictations as to the resale price or the geographic area (or consumer segment, etc.) in which the supplier's brand is sold by the retailer while, at the same time, the retailer also sells his own private label.[15] How does the fact the retailer holds a private label affect the anticompetitive effect of these vertical restraints?

A formalistic view might treat such restraints more harshly than absent a private label, because the private label supposedly turns the retailer into the supplier's competitor, making agreements between them 'horizontal' in nature rather than vertical. This is a view that classifies a restraint as 'horizontal' or 'vertical' according to the nature of the *parties* rather than the nature of the *restraint*; since the parties compete (in the sense that the retailer also operates in the supplier's market by owning the private label) the formalistic view sees the agreement as horizontal, thereby deserving strict review.

I wish to forward, however, a more substantive view, based on the economic analysis of the situation. When the retailer holds a private label, interbrand competition is by definition more fierce than when the retailer does not hold a private label. Hence, the existence of a private label can only weaken the harm to competition involved in these vertical restraints.

In particular, when the supplier dictates the territory or minimum price in which the retailer may sell the supplier's brand, this could at times cause the price of the supplier's brand (and possibly competing brands) to go up, either because competition among suppliers will be softened due to the elimination of competition among the supplier's retailers,[16] or because the elimination of competition among the supplier's retailers helps the supplier commit to charging higher wholesale prices.[17] But the more fierce interbrand competition is to begin with, the weaker are these price-raising effects and hence the weaker the harm to competition.

---

15 As before, the type of 'private label' I am focusing upon throughout is where the retailer is a key player in the supply market with respect to the private label. As noted above, vertical restraints in the presence of the other type of 'private label'—that purchased from an independent supplier and simply 'stamped' by the retailer as his own—are, from an economic perspective, very similar to regular vertical restraints.

16 See e.g.: P Rey and J Stiglitz, 'The Role of Exclusive Territories in Producers' Competition' [1995] 26 *Rand Journal of Economics* 431.

17 See e.g.: D Gilo, 'Retail Competition Percolating Through to Suppliers, and Using Vertical Integration, Vertical Restraints and Tying to Stop It' [2003] 20 *Yale Journal on Regulation* 25, 57–81.

This is why the existence of the private label is likely to weaken the anticompetitive effect.

Non-compete clauses

Suppose now that a retailer holding a private label promises a supplier that, apart from the supplier's brand and the private label, the retailer will refrain from holding competing brands. Here, again, either a formalistic or substantive view may be applied. According to the formalistic view, the retailer and supplier are competitors on account of the retailer's private label. Hence the agreement between them is between competitors and should be treated harshly, in a way similar to the treatment of horizontal restraints. According to the substantive view, however, which I support, the existence of the private label should generally have an opposite effect on the legal treatment of the restraint.

Absent a private label, the non-compete agreement demands that the retailer hold only the supplier's brand. Hence consumers located in the geographic market or markets in which the retailer operates, particularly those who prefer this retailer over other retailers, will have no choice of brands other than the supplier's brand. Moreover, if the retailer is an important distribution channel for competing suppliers, they might be induced to shrink or exit the market.

With a private label, both these anticompetitive effects are mitigated. Consumers in the retailer's geographic market will have more variety, they can choose between the supplier's brand and the retailer's private label. Also, even if competing suppliers are foreclosed from the supplier's market, at least the private label is not.

The preceding paragraphs have compared the effects of a non-compete agreement without a private label to those with a private label. Another type of agreement that the non-compete agreement with a private label could be compared to is a promise to a supplier to grant him a substantial (although not total) percentage of the retailer's shelf space. Without the private label, when a retailer commits a certain percentage of shelf space to a particular supplier, at least the rest of the retailer's shelf space is open to competing suppliers. If the retailer owns a large percentage of retail outlets in the relevant market, this available shelf space is often important for the viability of competing suppliers. When, on the other hand, the retailer has a private label, a substantial portion of his shelf space would naturally be devoted to the private label. This would leave less shelf space available to other suppliers compared to a retailer that does not own a private label. This factor should be taken into account when assessing such an agreement in the presence of a private label. Still, the point made in the preceding paragraphs is still intact: The non-compete agreement is still less harmful than a full exclusivity non-compete agreement absent a private label. In the latter case, *all* of the retailer's shelf space is dedicated to a single supplier. With a private label, on the other hand, some of the shelf space is dedicated to an independent supplier, and another supplier has access to the retailer's shelf space, namely, the private label, thereby increasing interbrand competition.

Exclusive distribution

Unlike the previous vertical restraints in this section, where the existence of the private label actually mitigated the anticompetitive threat, the anticompetitive effect of an exclusive distribution agreement may be exacerbated with a private label. In an exclusive distribution agreement, the supplier commits to sell his brand solely to the retailer, who also holds a private label. Since this retailer will then be the only retailer pricing and selling the supplier's brand, the retailer is likely to eliminate price competition between the supplier's brand and the private label. In the case of this particular restraint, the horizontal relationship between the supplier and the retailer (in his role as supplier of his private label) is more than a formality. The retailer actually acts as an entity setting retail prices among two rivals in the suppliers' market, and this particular case should be treated with high scrutiny, as other horizontal pricing restraints between suppliers are treated.

Most favoured customer clauses

A most favoured customer clause is a commitment on the part of the supplier not to discriminate against the retailer, i.e., not to grant competing retailers better terms than those of the retailer. This too is a vertical restraint. As the economics literature shows,[18] the anticompetitive threat from such restraints lies in the fear that the supplier will be less inclined to cut prices due to the most favoured customer clause. This may produce both unilateral anticompetitive effects (i.e., prices might rise even absent ongoing collusion) and coordinated anticompetitive effects (i.e., ongoing collusion is liable to be more stable).

The so-called unilateral effects may arise when the most favoured customer clause is retroactive in application, and competition among suppliers is imperfect.[19] By 'retroactive' application it is meant that the supplier promises a retailer (say, 'retailer A') that if at a certain point another retailer receives better terms

[18] See e.g.: J B Baker, 'Vertical Restraints with Horizontal Consequences: Competitive Effects of "Most-Favored-Customer" Clauses' [1996] 64 *Antitrust Law Journal* 517; T E Cooper, 'Most-Favored-Customer Pricing and Tacit Collusion' [1986] 17 *Rand Journal of Economics* 377; A S Edlin, 'Do Guaranteed-Low-Price Policies Guarantee High Prices, and Can Antitrust Rise to The Challenge?' [1997] 111 *Harvard Law Review* 528; Gilo (n 17).

[19] See: Cooper (n 18).

than retailer A, retailer A will not only receive these terms from then on but will also be compensated retroactively for his previous purchases. By 'imperfect competition' among suppliers it is meant that there are only a few suppliers in the relevant market and price, even absent ongoing collusion, does not go all the way down to marginal cost, despite competition, due to market imperfections such as product differentiation,[20] capacity constraints,[21] and so forth.

The coordinated effects of most favoured customer clauses may arise even when they are not retroactive in nature. This is because such clauses could make price-cuts by the supplier more transparent to his rivals, or make price cutting less profitable in other ways, including the prevention of selective price cuts made only to new customers, and so forth.[22]

How does the existence of a private label affect the anticompetitive effects of most favoured customer clauses? Similarly to the vertical restraints discussed in the previous paragraphs, these anticompetitive effects could in fact be mitigated when a private label exists. As explained above, these anticompetitive effects hinge on the imperfect nature of interbrand competition in the supplier's market. The more numerous are substantial competing brands, the weaker the potential price rise within the above-mentioned unilateral effect, and the less likely collusion is to be stable under the coordinated effect. Since the existence of the private label enhances interbrand competition, the above-mentioned competitive threats stemming from most-favoured customer clauses are mitigated.

Price matching

Another type of vertical restraint that deserves consideration is price matching, where the supplier promises the retailer that he will match price-cuts made by competing suppliers. This restraint too may possess both unilateral and coordinated effects.[23] The unilateral effects stem from the fact that the supplier could use price matching in order to grant price concessions and competitive prices only to informed buyers, who 'shop around' for competing offers and utilize the price matching guarantee. This induces the supplier to raise the price it charges uninformed buyers, who do not seek offers from competing suppliers.[24] The coordinated effect of price matching restraints stems from the fact that the supplier's rivals may find deviation from a collusive scheme less profitable, since stealing the supplier's informed buyers would be more difficult. A related threat

20 See e.g.: J Tirole, *The Theory of Industrial Organization* (1988) ch 7.
21 Ibid, ch 5.
22 See: Baker (n 18), Edlin (n 18).
23 Edlin (n 18).
24 Edlin (n 18).

to competition is that the supplier's rivals may be foreclosed from the market by the price matching guarantee, given that many retailers would be induced to stick with the supplier and not transfer their purchases to the competing suppliers.

Again, all of these anticompetitive effects are weaker the fiercer is interbrand competition. Since the existence of a private label intensifies interbrand competition, it can only help alleviate the anticompetitive effect of price matching. Still, when the concern is of suppliers' foreclosure, one should take into account that, in addition to the price matching supplier, to whom the retailer might wish to stick, the retailer is also inclined to devote the rest of his shelf space to his private label. But note that the foreclosing effect is not greater than the one that exists without a private label. Absent a private label, a supplier's price matching guarantee could induce the retailer to devote *all* or *almost all* of his shelf space to this supplier, and foreclosure of other suppliers is as likely.

F. Dual Distribution

Dual distribution takes place when a supplier operates a retail outlet in competition with the retailer. As in the case of a private label, the existence of dual distribution affects the analysis of different vertical restraints in different ways. Let us separate, therefore, the different vertical restraints.

Restraints eliminating or restricting interbrand competition

With regard to vertical restraints that eliminate or limit competition among retailers, the existence of dual distribution could intensify the anticompetitive effect. This is because when the supplier is also a retailer his incentives are changed in a way that favours less competitive pricing and behaviour on the part of retailers than when the supplier does not operate a retail outlet.

This is not to say that the anticompetitive effect of eliminating interbrand competition is the same with dual distribution as with a *purely horizontal* restraint. Still, in certain cases, this anticompetitive effect is stronger than that of *purely vertical* restraints. To see why, recall the two reasons for treating vertical restraints more leniently. The first reason was that when the supplier's contract with his retailers includes a fixed fee and a wholesale price per unit, then absent the vertical restraint, the supplier often can and will cause the retail price to be even higher than with the vertical restraint.

The second reason, which is of particular interest in the current context, was that when the supplier's profits rely on the wholesale price per unit it charges retailers, the supplier should normally not be interested in eliminating competition among his retailers, because this will reduce the number of units sold and harm the supplier's profits. In such a case, as the argument goes, if the supplier did eliminate competition between retailers, it is likely to be due to the supplier's incentive to solve imperfections in distribution, such as retailers' free-rider problem or their lack of sufficient incentives to grant services that consumers want. This latter incentive may at times coincide with consumers' preferences. But it is this second consideration favouring a lenient treatment of vertical restraints that becomes weaker when the supplier also operates his own retail outlet. In such a case, there is another reason the supplier may want to eliminate competition among retailers other than solving imperfections in distribution: his willingness to raise the profits of his retail outlet. The extent to which the second consideration becomes weaker in the presence of dual distribution, however, depends on the circumstances of each case. In particular, the consideration becomes of less weight the more the supplier's profits depend on the wholesale price per unit and the less they depend on the fixed fee. Let us analyse this last point in more detail below.

Ideally, a supplier that eliminates competition among his retailers would maximize his profits by charging retailers a fixed fee that is based on their expected profits, while reducing the wholesale price per unit to the supplier's marginal costs. This would eliminate problems of so-called 'double marginalization' that harm the supplier's and retailers' joint profits. In such an ideal case, the second above-mentioned consideration in favour of treating vertical restraints leniently is irrelevant. Here only the first consideration in favour of the lenient treatment holds. Dual distribution would not change the economic analysis, as will be explained below.

At times, however, due to insufficient information, retailers are not willing to pay a large fixed fee even when competition among retailers is eliminated. For example, a retailer that does not know in advance how high his profits will be may prefer paying the supplier an above-cost wholesale price per unit and a relatively small fixed fee. As mentioned, the more the supplier's profits depend on the above-cost wholesale price per unit and the less they depend on fixed fees, the stronger is the *second* argument mentioned above in favour of a lenient treatment of vertical restraints. Recall that this argument is based on the fact that such a supplier would not be interested in eliminating competition among retailers, and if he does so, it must be to solve distortions in distribution, such as free riding. But, as noted, this second argument is weakened when the supplier is also a retailer, because in his capacity as a retailer the supplier would be interested in eliminating retailer competition.

On the other hand, the less the supplier relies on the wholesale price for his profits vis-à-vis the retailer, the weaker is the second above-mentioned consideration in favour of a lenient treatment for vertical restraints. For example, suppose that with a restraint eliminating interbrand competition the supplier sells to the retailer for a price per unit equal to the supplier's marginal costs of production and derives his profits only from fixed payments (that do not depend on retailer's actual sales) the supplier receives from retailers. In such a case, *even without dual distribution*, the supplier would want minimal competition and maximum profits on the part of retailers. This is because the higher retailers' profits are, the higher are the fixed fees retailers would be willing to pay the supplier.[25]

The foregoing paragraphs imply that the presence of dual distribution does not affect the economic analysis of restraints eliminating competition among retailers when the supplier's profits stem only from fixed fees. On the other hand, when the supplier's profits stem only from the wholesale price per unit, the presence of dual distribution exacerbates the anticompetitive effect of such restraints. Intermediary cases are also possible, where some of the supplier's profits stem from fixed fees and some from the wholesale price per unit. The more they depend on the wholesale price per unit, the more the presence of dual distribution intensifies the anticompetitive effect.

To make things more concrete, let us examine these points with regard to minimum resale price maintenance and exclusive territories separately below.

Minimum resale price maintenance

Suppose that while using minimum resale price maintenance, the supplier relies on an above-cost wholesale price in order to make his profits rather than on a franchise fee. Absent dual distribution, elimination of price competition among retailers by the supplier would have seemed puzzling. Since the supplier makes profits in this example solely from the price per unit he charges retailers, one would expect him not to block competition among retailers so as to maximize the number of units sold. Hence it could be claimed in such a case that elimination of competition among retailers is needed in order to avoid inefficiencies

[25] Here, it is the first above-mentioned consideration justifying lenient treatment of vertical restraints which becomes more pronounced: even without elimination of interbrand competition, the retail price could be equally high, or even higher. This is because with interbrand competition, retailers' expected profits are low, and so are the fixed fees the supplier can collect from them. Accordingly, the supplier is expected to use its market power in order to raise the wholesale price. This will raise retailers' marginal costs and raise the retail price, notwithstanding competition between them. Since retailers too are expected to have a profit margin (assuming competition among them does not drive the retail prices all the way down to their marginal costs), consumers may suffer from a higher price than would be charged absent retail competition, due to double marginalization problems. See: G F Mathewson and R Winter, 'An Economic Theory of Vertical Restraints' [1984] 15 *Rand Journal of Economics* 27.

in distribution. Moreover, due to the supplier's incentive to maximize the number of units, it could be claimed that the dictated minimum resale price is not equal to the cartel-like retail price retailers would prefer, but rather equal to a lower price—the lowest retail price that keeps in tact retailers' incentives to distribute the supplier's product efficiently.

But when the supplier is also a retailer, the profits he makes on account of his retail outlet are those of a retailer. These profits are maximized when the retail price is equal to the cartel price among retailers. This factor could partly offset the supplier's ordinary incentives to keep the retail price as low as possible, so as to maximize the profits of his supplying outlet. The retail price dictated could be higher than the one a supplier not engaged in dual distribution would dictate. Moreover, the restraint may well be motivated by the supplier's eagerness to eliminate retail competition so as to raise the profits of his retail outlet. It is no longer the case, as absent dual distribution, that the restraint could be explained only by the need to improve the efficiency of distribution.

Suppose now that the supplier imposes a minimum resale price and sells to retailers for a price equal to the supplier's marginal cost and that the profits the supplier makes are due to fixed franchise fees the retailers pay him. Here, the claim in favour of a lenient treatment of minimum resale price maintenance is that without it, the supplier will not be able to collect sufficient franchise fees and therefore he will be induced to use his market power to raise the wholesale price per unit above his marginal cost. This will inflate retail costs and prices. Due to retailers' own profit margins, double marginalization could evolve and price could be equal to or even higher than the price with minimum resale price maintenance.

The latter analysis does not change in principle when dual distribution exists. Absent minimum resale price maintenance, the supplier inflates the wholesale price he charges independent retailers and double marginalization evolves. In fact, since the supplier competes with retailers in the retail market, he might even inflate the wholesale price more, in order to grant himself a competitive advantage over independent retailers.[26] With minimum resale price maintenance, the supplier can eliminate double marginalization by lowering the wholesale price per unit he charges independent retailers all the way down to his marginal costs. While the retail margin goes up, due to elimination of price

[26] Compare Y Yehezkel, 'Downstream Competition Between an Upstream Supplier and an Independent Downstream Firm' (working paper, January 2004, on file with author) who shows that a supplier engaged in dual distribution has an incentive to inflate the wholesale price he charges the independent retailer.

competition, the wholesale margin (and retailers' marginal costs) goes down, so that the retail price may well be lower than without minimum resale price maintenance.

Exclusive territories

A similar reasoning suggests that exclusive territories imposed by a supplier engaged in dual distribution could be more anticompetitive than exclusive territories imposed by a supplier who does not operate his own retail outlet, if the supplier's profits include profits per unit and not only fixed fees. Again, absent dual distribution, and when the supplier makes a profit per each unit sold, such a restraint could be explained mainly by the supplier's need to solve imperfections in distribution. When the supplier controls a retail outlet, on the other hand, the profits he makes on account of his retail outlet are enhanced when downstream competition is eliminated. Hence his motivation for imposing exclusive territories may well be the reduction of competition rather than efficiencies in distribution. This mixed motivation bears on the rationale for treating such a vertical restraint differently than a horizontal one.

Suppose, on the other hand, that the supplier imposes exclusive territories upon his retailers and lowers the wholesale price all the way down to his marginal cost, while making his earnings from fixed franchise fees. This time, the main rationale for lenient treatment is that absent exclusive territories the supplier would cause retail prices to be high (or even higher) by raising the wholesale price. Here the existence of dual distribution does not justify harsher antitrust treatment. Without exclusive territories, the supplier would still inflate the wholesale price he charges independent retailers (and possibly even more so, in order to grant his retail unit a competitive advantage), inducing retail prices that could even be higher than those that prevail under exclusive territories.

Restraints limiting the supplier's entry or operation in the retail market

In the same spirit, any restraints limiting the supplier's ability or incentive to enter the retail market are actually horizontal in nature. They are similar to a potential retailer committing not to enter or to limit its operations in the retail market and therefore amount to a horizontal restraint similar to a non-competition obligation, which should be viewed harshly.[27]

---

[27] See n 9.

Non-compete obligations

If the retailer promises the supplier not to buy from competing suppliers (a non-compete obligation) is the anticompetitive effect stronger in the presence of dual distribution? It could be in the following sense. The supplier's retail outlet will be inclined itself to buy only from the supplier and not from competing suppliers. Hence it too is under a *de facto* 'non-compete obligation'. All this means, however, is that the share of the retail market foreclosed from competing suppliers includes the share of the supplier's retail outlet, and not only the share of the retailer subject to the non-compete obligation. Moreover, the harm to product variety in the latter retailer's geographic market should take into account that at least one other retail outlet in the same market, namely, the supplier's retail outlet, is inclined to hold only the supplier's brand.

Exclusive distribution

When the supplier commits towards a retailer that he will sell only to him, but for the supplier's retail outlet, then dual distribution actually mitigates the anticompetitive harm compared to the case of exclusive distribution absent dual distribution. This is because without dual distribution, consumers in the retailer's geographic market will have access to the supplier's brand only in the exclusive retailers' outlet. This is while with dual distribution, consumers can find the supplier's brand both in the retailer's outlet and in the supplier's own outlet.

Most favoured customer clause

Can a most favoured customer clause harm competition more in the presence of dual distribution? Dual distribution does not really have a significant bearing on the anticompetitive effects of most favoured customer clauses. The theories against such clauses hinge on the claim that the supplier will find price cutting less profitable when he has to give the same discount he gives other customers to the customer enjoying the clause. The same theories would exist and be applied similarly when the supplier operates his own retail outlet.

Price matching

The concerns about the anticompetitive effects of price matching are also similar in spirit when the supplier is engaged in dual distribution. These theories hinge on other suppliers hesitating to price cut due to the supplier's price matching policy, on the fear of discrimination between informed and uninformed consumers, and on exclusion of competing suppliers. The latter effect is similar to that of non-compete clauses: the larger the percentage of retail outlets the supplier controls due to his price matching promise, the stronger the anticompetitive effect is. In this context, the supplier's retail outlet should be considered as part of the retail outlets controlled by the supplier, thereby possibly strengthening the exclusionary effect.

G. Implications of the Economic Analysis With Regard to the EC Block Exemption Regulation

Private labels

As shown in Section E above, apart from exclusive distribution, vertical restraints which are not concerned with the private label deserve a more lenient treatment than the same vertical restraints absent the presence of a private label. This implies that EC competition law treats such cases too harshly. In particular, the Block Exemption Regulation[28] exempts, under certain conditions, only vertical restraints between a supplier and a buyer that do not operate in the same level of the supply chain. As Article 2.1 of the Block Exemption Regulation puts it:

> Pursuant to Article 81(3) of the Treaty and subject to the provisions of this Regulation, it is hereby declared that Article 81(1) shall not apply to agreements or concerted practices entered into between two or more undertakings each of which operates, for the purposes of the agreement, at a different level of the production or distribution chain, and relating to the conditions under which the parties may purchase, sell or resell certain goods or services ('vertical agreements').

Moreover, the first part of Article 2(4) provides that:

> The exemption provided for in paragraph 1 shall not apply to vertical agreements entered into between competing undertakings . . .

According to these provisions, when a retailer controlling the supply of a private label operates at the supplier's level of production or distribution, the parties are not eligible for the exemption. This is despite the fact that, as we have shown, apart from the case of exclusive distribution, the existence of the private label mitigates the anticompetitive threat. If the same agreement, with the same market shares of the parties, is exempt in the absence of a private label, I have shown above that this restraint should *a fortiori* be exempt in the presence of a private label.

To be sure, under Article 2(4)(a) of the Block Exemption Regulation, even if the retailer competes with the supplier, their vertical restraint would be eligible for exemption under the Block Exemption Regulation if the retailer has a total annual turnover not exceeding EUR100 million. This qualification, however,

[28] The Block Exemption Regulation (n 7).

does not solve the anomaly described above. On the contrary, the higher the retailer's annual turnover, the more the fact that he operates his private label mitigates the competitive threat of vertical restraints (apart from exclusive distribution). This is because the retailer's private brand acts as an addition to interbrand competition compared to the case without a private label. The larger the retailer's operations, the larger the operations of his private label, hence, the stronger the competing brand the retailer contributes to interbrand competition at the supplier's level.[29]

Dual distribution

The lack of consideration to the pro-competitive effect of the retailer's private label stands out when compared to the specific consideration given in the block exemption to 'dual distribution' cases. According to Article 2(4)(b) of the Block Exemption Regulation, the vertical restraint is *eligible* for exemption if 'the supplier is a manufacturer and a distributor of goods, while the buyer is a distributor not manufacturing goods competing with the contract goods'. First, it is surprising that the other form of supplier—retailer competition—of the retailer also operating in the supply market (i.e. holding a private label), is explicitly ruled out (but for the narrow proviso of Article 2(4)(a) mentioned above) while dual distribution is explicitly ruled in. Moreover, the overall eligibility of the 'dual distribution' case for exemption seems to be too broad and lacks fine-tuning.

In particular, as shown in Section F above, restraints that eliminate interbrand competition such as minimum resale price maintenance and exclusive territories may be substantially *more* anticompetitive when dual distribution exists. This is particularly the case when the supplier's profits stem from an above-cost wholesale price rather than merely from franchise fees. In such cases, the Block Exemption Regulation should not be available to dual distribution cases, and a case-by-case analysis is warranted. In the case-by-case analysis consideration should be given, among other factors, to whether, and to what extent, the supplier makes his profit from above-cost wholesale prices or rather from fixed fees, or a combination of the two.

As to non-compete obligations, in order to take account of dual distribution, it is important to acknowledge the supplier's retail outlet as included in the portion of the retail sector foreclosed from other suppliers. The direct implication is that

29 To be sure, when a retailer is large, concerns such as foreclosure of suppliers that do not gain access to this retailer could arise. Furthermore, the retailer's possession of a private label constitutes vertical integration that itself could foreclose other suppliers. See n 11 and accompanying text. Still, as shown, except for the case of exclusive distribution, the same vertical restraint is typically less anticompetitive with the presence of the private label than without it.

the Block Exemption Regulation's 30 per cent market share threshold should be calculated after taking into account not only the market share of the retailer that gave the non-compete obligation but also as combined with the market share of the supplier's own retail unit. The same is true with price matching policies, especially when one of the concerns is exclusion of competing suppliers. On the other hand, as shown in Section F above, exclusive distribution actually deserves a more lenient treatment when dual distribution is present than when it is not.

H. Conclusion

When a retailer controls the supply of a private label, the economic analysis of vertical restraints in such cases should distinguish between two categories: The first category consists of restraints that limit the retailer's ability to sell the private label. Such restraints should be treated as harshly as horizontal restraints. The second category consists of restraints that are not related to the sale of the private label. As this chapter reveals, antitrust treatment of vertical restraints of the second category should arguably be more lenient than vertical restraints absent a private label. This conclusion stands in contrast to the Block Exemption Regulation provisions. The Regulation does not apply to vertical restraints when the retailer controls the supply of a private label, either in the first or second category of cases, but for the case where the retailer's turnover is limited. As shown, this narrow proviso misses the point, since the larger the private label's turnover, the more lenient the treatment vertical restraints (but for exclusive distribution) deserve. On the other hand, the Block Exemption Regulation applies to dual distribution cases, despite the fact that when some vertical restraints are coupled with dual distribution, they actually possess stronger anti-competitive effects than absent dual distribution. In particular, restraints eliminating competition among retailers are especially harmful with dual distribution, provided that a large percentage of the supplier's profits are from the wholesale price per unit rather than from fixed fees.

8

THE VERTICAL/HORIZONTAL DICHOTOMY IN COMPETITION LAW: SOME REFLECTIONS WITH REGARD TO DUAL DISTRIBUTION AND PRIVATE LABELS

*Ioannis Lianos**

A. Introduction

The vertical/horizontal distinction is an important feature of modern competition law. Undertakings are found to be in a vertical relation when they are present in different levels of the commercialization process, i.e. supply and distribution. They are found to be in a horizontal relation in situations where they produce

* City Solicitors Educational Trust Lecturer in European Union Law, UCL, Faculty of Laws; Jevons Institute of Competition Law and Economics; Emile Noel Fellow, NYU Law School.

substitutable products or services (actual or potential competitors). This chapter will first examine the genealogy of the vertical/horizontal dichotomy in the United States (US) and in European Communities (EC) competition law. It will then analyse the application of the dichotomy in situations of hybrid practices, dual distribution practices, and private labels, where the relation between the supplier and the distributor presents a vertical and a horizontal dimension. The vertical/horizontal dichotomy may find its limits in these situations. After highlighting the reasons and distinct principles that led to the formulation of these specific categories,[1] the study will delve into the utility of the vertical/ horizontal dichotomy and will suggest alternative interpretations of these categories which are both analytically rigorous and consistent with the objectives of EC competition law.[2]

B. Genealogy of the Vertical/Horizontal Dichotomy: Unpacking the Dominant Story

The emergence of the vertical/horizontal dichotomy is fairly recent in competition law. The US Supreme Court employed for the first time the expression 'vertical agreement' in *White Motors Co v US* where vertical territorial restrictions were imposed contractually by a manufacturer on retailers.[3] The court found the concept broad enough to cover forms of cooperation raising issues different from horizontal cooperation arrangements (or cooperation between competitors) as well as from resale price maintenance (that is, vertical price restraints considered equivalent to a horizontal collusion between retailers), both of which were then prohibited *per se* under section 1 of the *Sherman Act*.[4] The court rejected any extension of the *per se* illegality rule to non-price vertical agreements, noting that 'we need to know more than we do about the actual impact of these arrangements on competition to decide whether they have such a pernicious effect on competition and lack of redeeming virtue'.[5]

[1] Jay M Feinman, 'The Jurisprudence of Classification' [1989] 41 *Stanford Law Review* 661, 672–677.

[2] On the importance of classification and categorical analysis in competition law, see: M L Lemley and C R Leslie, 'Categorical Analysis in Antitrust Jurisprudence' [2007] Stanford Law and Economics Working Paper No 348 <http://papers.ssrn.com/sol3/papers.cfm?abstract_id=1026967> accessed 9 April 2008.

[3] *White Motors Co v US* 372 US 253 (1963).

[4] The latter since the seminal decision in *Dr Miles Medical Co v John D Park & Sons* 220 US 373 (1911). The court has recently reversed this decision in *Leegin Creative Leathers Products, Inc v PSKS, Inc* 127 S Ct 2705 (2007).

[5] *White Motors* (n 3) 263.

Subsequent antitrust cases adopted a more hostile approach towards vertical contractual integration. The expression 'vertical restraints', that is vertical agreements found to be infringing competition law, was employed for the first time in *Motor Co v Webster Auto Sales* for non-price and price-related vertical practices.[6] The scope of the *per se* rule was extended to cover customer and territorial restrictions by the US Supreme Court a year later in *Schwinn*.[7] The court's aim was to prohibit restrictions on the freedom of retailers to compete against each other (intrabrand competition), even if the effect of those restrictions was to enhance competition between different suppliers (interbrand competition). In other words, the court applied the same analysis to vertical and horizontal restrictions.

Remarkably, the US Supreme Court overruled *Schwinn* in *Continental TV, Inc v GTE Sylvania*,[8] under the joint influence of the Chicago school of antitrust economics, which recognizes the role of interbrand competition and market power as filters to antitrust enforcement,[9] and new institutional economics, which draw attention to the economic motives of vertical contractual integration.[10] The court held that vertical customer and territorial restrictions should be assessed according to a cost benefit analysis under the rule of reason.[11] Horizontal territorial restrictions should on the contrary be subject to a *per se* prohibition approach.[12] The characterization of a restriction or agreement as being horizontal or vertical has therefore important implications on the outcome of a competition law case.

The introduction of the vertical/horizontal dichotomy is consistent with economic learning. The currently dominant neo-classical economic paradigm recognizes that dealers have significant influence on consumer demand and that distribution services constitute an important input in the commercialization process of a product. It follows that the manufacturer has an interest to coordinate the distribution of its products, in particular as the dealers may have incentives that differ from those of the manufacturer. In this case, a principal-agent (coordination) problem may ensue.[13] Coordination problems may relate to the definition of an optimal level of services to be provided by the dealers, the price

---

6 *Motor Co v Webster Auto Sales* 361 F 2d 874 (1st Cir 1966).

7 *United States v Arnold, Schwinn & Co* 388 US 365 (1967).

8 *Continental TV Inc v GTE Sylvania Incorporated* 433 US 36 (1977) (hereinafter *Sylvania*).

9 See: F Easterbrook, 'The Limits of Antitrust' [1984] 63 *Texas Law Review* 1.

10 See: O Williamson, 'Assessing Vertical Market Restrictions: Antitrust Ramifications of the Transaction Cost Approach' [1979] 127 *University of Pennsylvania Law Review* 953.

11 *Sylvania* (n 8), 49, '... the true test of legality is whether the restraint imposed is such as merely regulates and perhaps thereby promotes competition or whether it is such as may suppress or even destroy competition'.

12 *United States v Sealy Corp* 388 US 350, 352 (1967) (hereinafter *Sealy*).

13 A C M Chen and K N Hylton, 'Procompetitive Theories of Vertical Control' [1999] 50 *Hastings Law Journal* 573, 581.

of the product, and finally the allocation of risks between the upstream and the downstream level of the vertical relation. Vertical integration constitutes a possible solution to this problem.

Monitoring and coordination costs in a vertically integrated entity may, however, be significant.[14] Manufacturers can make instead the choice of independent dealers to distribute their products and may conclude with them contracts that will specify the required services. In certain circumstances, writing contracts may be insufficient to overcome the coordination problems in a vertical relationship, because of the different incentives of the parties and the difficult task of monitoring the performance of these contractual provisions.[15]

The parties will often employ vertical contracts in order to align their incentives, for example by providing dealers with the opportunity to earn additional profits, thus encouraging joint-maximizing behaviour.[16] Vertical contractual integration may also bring allocative efficiency gains, for example by the mitigation of the effects of a successive monopoly, if monopoly power is present at both the upstream and the downstream level of the market,[17] by the protection of retailers' promotional and commercialization efforts from free riding or the appropriation of these investments from other dealers,[18] by the integration by manufacturers of efficient dealers with a reputation in providing quality services in their distribution network,[19] or by the protection of their suppliers' investments from appropriability.[20]

Vertical restrictions may, however, produce anti-competitive effects. Vertical restraints may be used as an instrument to raise rivals' costs[21] and eventually to exclude rivals[22] to enable the firm to exercise market power or more generally to

---

[14] A A Alchian, 'Production, Information Costs, and Economic Organization' [1972] 62 *The American Economic Review* 777; S J Grossman and O D Hart, 'The Cost and Benefits of Ownership: A Theory of Vertical Integration' [1986] 94 *Journal of Political Economy* 691.

[15] B Klein, 'Transaction Cost Determinants of Unfair Contractual Arrangements' [1980] 70 *The American Economic Review* 356.

[16] B Klein and K M Murphy, 'Vertical Restraints as Contract Enforcement Mechanisms' [1988] 31 *Journal of Law and Economics* 265.

[17] J J Spengler, 'Vertical Integration and Antitrust Policy' [1950] 58 *The Journal of Political Economy* 347.

[18] L G Telser, 'Why Should Manufacturers Want Free Trade' [1960] 3 *Journal of Law and Economics* 86.

[19] H P Marvel and S McCafferty, 'Resale Price Maintenance and Quality Certification' [1984] 15 *Rand Journal of Economics* 346.

[20] H P Marvel, 'Exclusive Dealing' [1982] 25 *Journal of Law and Economics* 1.

[21] T Krattenmaker and S C Salop, 'Anticompetitive Exclusion: Raising Rivals' Costs to Achieve Power over Price' [1986] 96 *Yale Law Journal* 209; D T Scheffman and R S Higgins, '20 years of Raising Rivals' Costs: History, Assessment, and Future' [2003] 12 *George Mason Law Review* 371.

[22] P Aghion and P Bolton, 'Contracts as a Barrier to Entry' [1987] 77 *The American Economic Review* 388.

reduce interbrand competition.[23] In the absence of market power (individual or collective) at the upstream or downstream market, vertical restraints will not be harmful to consumers, even if competition between retailers (intrabrand competition) will effectively be reduced.[24] The assumption is that horizontal competition between actual or potential rival suppliers (interbrand competition) will make unprofitable any increase of the price of the good, or reduction of output, quality, and innovation.[25] Resale price maintenance clauses may also facilitate collusion and suppress competition among manufacturers[26] or among dealers.[27] The effect of vertical restraints on consumers is ambiguous and largely depends on the economic context and the specific circumstances of each case. It is not a surprise therefore that vertical restraints came to be seen more favourably in competition law than horizontal restraints. The classification of a restraint as being horizontal or vertical has important implications on competition law enforcement. Professors Lemley and Leslie observe:

> (t)he purpose of distinguishing horizontal and vertical restraints is judicial efficiency. If a restraint is horizontal, then courts are more likely to condemn it under the per se rule. This saves time and resources because such horizontal restraints are likely or almost always likely to reduce competition in a manner that antitrust cares about, while vertical restraints often serve legitimate business purposes. However, given the consequences of a restraint being labelled horizontal, the focus of antitrust litigation often shifts away from whether or not the restraint is unreasonable to whether the restraint is properly categorized as horizontal.[28]

A number of competition authorities have followed US antitrust law in adopting the vertical/horizontal classification as a shortcut to the antitrust assessment of anticompetitive effects. Different presumptions seem to apply, depending on the characterization of a restriction as being vertical or horizontal. The European Commission first referred to the vertical/horizontal dichotomy when it published a *Green Paper on Vertical Restraints* in 1996.[29] The Commission stressed the need

---

23 P Rey and J Stiglitz, 'The Role of Exclusive Territories in Producer's Competition' [1995] 26 *Rand Journal of Economics* 431.

24 M Motta, *Competition Policy—Theory and Practice* (2004) 343.

25 Ibid, 305–306.

26 Ibid, 158.

27 G Shaffer, 'Slotting Allowances and Resale Price Maintenance: A Comparison of Facilitating Practices' [1991] 22 *Rand Journal of Economics* 120.

28 Lemley and Leslie (n 2) 38.

29 Commission of the European Communities, 'Green paper on Vertical Restraints in EC Competition Policy', (22 January 1997) COM (96) 721 final, para 2. See also: Commission Notice (EC) Guidelines on Vertical Restraints [2000] OJ C291/1 (hereinafter *Vertical Restraints Guidelines*), para 6, '[f]or most vertical restraints, competition concerns can only arise if there is insufficient inter-brand competition, i.e. if there is some degree of market power at the level of the supplier or the buyer or at both levels. If there is insufficient inter-brand competition, the protection of inter- and intra-brand competition becomes important'.

to take into account the economic effects of vertical agreements before the finding of an infringement of Article 81. Although the use of a more economic approach was also extended to horizontal agreements,[30] the distinction between horizontal and vertical restraints still plays an important role when it comes to the drafting of block exemption regulations. There are now specific rules applying to vertical agreements,[31] and the characterization of an agreement as being vertical usually triggers the use of a different market share threshold for the application of the exception of Article 81(3) than for horizontal restrictions.[32]

The Commission justified the existence of a more lenient regime for vertical agreements as following:

> (i)t is . . . generally recognized that vertical restraints are on average less harmful than horizontal competition restraints. The main reason for treating a vertical restraint more leniently than a horizontal restraint lies in the fact that the latter may concern an agreement between competitors producing substitute goods/services while the former concerns an agreement between a supplier and a buyer of a particular product/service. In horizontal situations the exercise of market power by one company (higher prices of its products) will benefit its competitors. This may provide an incentive to competitors to induce each other to behave anti-competitively. In vertical situations the product of the one is the input for the other. This means that the exercise of market power by either the upstream or downstream company would normally hurt the demand for the product of the other. The companies involved in the agreement may therefore have an incentive to prevent the exercise of market power by the other (the so called self-policing character of vertical restraints).[33]

One should not, however, overestimate the self-policing character of vertical restraints, in particular in situations where the supplier or the buyer has market power. Vertical restraints could in this context raise strategically rivals' costs, reduce

30 See: Commission Notice (EC) Guidelines on the Applicability of Article 81 of the EC Treaty to Horizontal Cooperation Agreements [2001] OJ C3/2, para 7; Communication from the Commission—Notice—Guidelines on the Application of Article 81(3) of the Treaty [2004] OJ C101/97, para 25.

31 Commission Regulation (EC) 2790/1999 of 22 December 1999 on the Application of Article 81(3) of the Treaty to Categories of Vertical Agreements and Concerted Practices [1999] L336/21 (hereinafter Reg 2790/99).

32 See for instance: Commission Regulation (EC) 772/2004 of 27 April 2004 on the Application of Article 81(3) of the Treaty to Categories of Technology Transfer Agreements [2004] OJ L123/11, art 3 (which provides for a lower market share threshold for agreements between competitors than for agreements between non-competitors in order to benefit from the safe harbour of the block exemption). See also: Commission Notice (EC) Guidelines on the Application of Article 81 of the EC Treaty to Technology Transfer Agreements [2004] C101/2, para 26, '(i)n general, agreements between competitors pose a greater risk to competition than agreements between non-competitors'.

33 Communication from the Commission on the Application of the Community Competition Rules to Vertical Restraints—Follow-up to the Green Paper on Vertical Restraints, COM(98) 544 final [1998] C365/3.

competition, and harm consumers. This generally occurs 'when the upstream and downstream company share the extra profits or when one of the two imposes the vertical restraint and thereby appropriates all the extra profits'.[34]

Although the interests of the parties converge in a horizontal setting, the interests of the parties tend to be divergent in vertical agreements. If both the upstream and the downstream markets are competitive, the gains of suppliers will be losses for the dealers and vice versa. It follows that according to the view defended by the members of the Chicago school of antitrust economics, the interest of the manufacturer will always be to reduce the distribution margin of the retailer at a level that will guarantee the reward of the promotional efforts of retailers up to what is necessary to ensure quality distribution services to the consumers.[35]

Competition between vertical structures will ensure that the manufacturer will choose the optimal level of distribution services. The existence of interbrand competition between manufacturers may mitigate any anticompetitive exercise of market power and therefore preserve consumers' interest. The impact of vertical restraints is, however, ambiguous when competition between the different vertical structures is weak. In this case, the reduction of intrabrand competition from vertical restraints will not be fully compensated by the positive impact of interbrand competition between vertical structures.[36]

Nevertheless, commercial reality is not as straightforward as the preceding paragraphs may indicate. The underlying assumption of these economic models is that vertical restraints are generally imposed by the suppliers/producers to the dealers and that the downstream retail market is perfectly competitive.[37] The reality of the marketplace is obviously extremely different, as large multi-brand retailers may also take the initiative of suggesting or imposing vertical restraints to their suppliers, in particular as the balance of power between the different segments of the vertical chain has in recent years evolved in their favour.[38]

---

34 Ibid, s III(1).

35 R Posner, 'The Rule of Reason and the Economic Approach: Reflections on the Sylvania Decision' [1977] 45 *University of Chicago Law Review* 1; F Easterbrook, 'Vertical Arrangements and the Rule of Reason' [1984] 53 *Antitrust Law Journal* 135, 156–157.

36 P Rey, 'Impact des accords verticaux entre producteurs et distributeurs' [1997] 12(2) *Revue Française d'Economie* 3.

37 W Comanor and P Rey, 'Vertical Restraints and the Market Power of Large Distributors' [2000] 17 *Review of Industrial Organization* 135; OFT 'Vertical Restraints and Competition Policy' (Report prepared by P W Dobson and M Waterson) (December 1996) Research paper 12, 23–25.

38 See: OFT 'Competition in Retailing' (September 1997) Research Paper 13, 46–47: 'over the last decade or so, retailers have tended to become a more important element in the overall value chain, partly at the expense of manufacturers. This change has occurred for various reasons, including: increased retailer size and retail concentration; increased importance of retailer image, which means that own-brand products have become more competitive with branded products; increased

Furthermore, it is not always true that the interests of consumers and producers correspond, as vertical restraints may lead to non-optimal distribution services for certain categories of consumers (in particular infra-marginal consumers), who will pay higher prices for services they feel they do not need.[39] In the absence of sufficient interbrand competition, vertical restraints will harm infra-marginal consumers. Ensuring coordination between the different levels of the vertical chain will not always justify the adoption of vertical restraints.[40]

C. A Heterodox Perspective on the Vertical/Horizontal Dichotomy

Recent economic and management literature presents a more complex story of the economics of vertical relations, which may have important implications on the operation of the horizontal/vertical dichotomy. The new economics of vertical restraints accept that several commercial practices contain both vertical and horizontal characteristics, thus complicating the characterization effort.

The 'new' economics of vertical relations

Robert Steiner has advanced the view that there are two forms of competition that co-exist in vertical structures: First, the horizontal competition between the different vertical structures or between the retailers of the same vertical structure, and second, the vertical competition between the different levels of the vertical structure, such as suppliers versus retailers over the sharing of the profits of the vertical chain.[41] Steiner perceives competition as a struggle between firms aiming to capture a perceptible share of markets from each other (which is the traditional view of horizontal competition) but also an important share of sales or margins.[42]

---

retailer information on consumers' preferences (partly as a result of scanner technology); and increased retailer command of technology.'

39 See: W S Comanor, 'Vertical Price Fixing, Vertical Market Restrictions and the New Antitrust Policy' [1985] 98 *Harvard Law Review* 983; W S Comanor, 'The Two Economics of Vertical Restraints' [1992] 21 *Southwestern University Law Review* 1265.

40 F M Scherer, *Industrial Market Structure and Economic Performance* (3rd edn, 1989), 554 criticized the quality certification argument for resale price maintenance: '. . . what is the wider economic significance of a high-status image that comes from the high prices at which the product is sold, and not from the product intrinsic superiority? If an individual consumer derives utility from exclusiveness, and if the utility declines when a product enters mass distribution, there must be external diseconomies in consumption, violating one of the fundamental assumptions on the basis of which the efficiency of market processes is judged. The argument that product quality certification through resale price maintenance is efficiency-enhancing becomes even more dubious.'

41 R L Steiner, 'Intrabrand Competition-Stepchild of Antitrust' [1991] 36 *The Antitrust Bulletin* 155, 161.

42 Ibid.

It follows that suppliers and retailers engage 'in a form of vertical intrabrand competition by attempting to increase their vertical market share (VMS) at each other's expense', where vertical market share consists in their respective shares of a brand's retail price.[43] Steiner explains:

> The VMS of a brand's retailer is the brand's percentage retail gross margin (%RGM). The latter is the difference between the brand's retail price and its factory, or manufacturer's price—which difference is its dollar retail gross margin ($RGM)—divided by its retail price and expressed as a percent. The VMS of the brand's manufacturer is the ratio of its factory price to its retail price, expressed as a percent, and is also equal to one minus its % RGM. In a dual-stage consumer goods industry firms at one stage can increase their VMS primarily by strategies that intensify horizontal competition among firms at the other stage. This has the result . . . of lowering the margins and the proportion of the final retail price received by firms at the other level . . .[44]

This seems to confirm the self-restricting effect of vertical restraints and the existence of an inverse association between the margins of manufacturers and retailers.

Steiner challenges, however, the dominant view defended by the Chicago school of antitrust economics that relationships between the different levels of the vertical structure are complementary. The Chicago school adopts the assumption that vertical restraints are generally imposed by manufacturers to retailers, and views the relationship between the different levels of the vertical chain as antagonistic. Steiner considers that the retail level is not characterized by perfect competition. It will not be reasonable to assume that the retailers will pass on to consumers the eventual additional margins that will follow from vertical contractual restraints that were adopted to increase interbrand competition. If antitrust enforcement ignores intrabrand competition between retailers, that might lead to higher prices for consumers. The existence of interbrand competition will not be sufficient to preserve consumers' interest. Retailers will not pass on the benefit of increased interbrand competition to the consumers but will instead increase their own margin. Retailers are not passive price takers but they are actively involved in the strategy of increasing their vertical market share. Vertical competition between retailers is as important for consumers as horizontal competition between different vertical structures. Concentration and market power at one stage of the vertical structure may lead to higher margins at this stage and lower margins at the other stage. Empirical research in several markets has confirmed Steiner's intuition.[45]

---

43 Ibid.

44 Ibid, 162.

45 R L Steiner, 'The Inverse Association Between the Margins of Manufacturers and Retailers' [1993] 8 *Review of Industrial Organization* 717; M P Lynch, 'Why Economists are Wrong to Neglect

These findings have important implications on the antitrust assessment of vertical restraints:

> (i)f inter- and intrabrand competition proved to be positively correlated on the industry level, the adoption of vertical restraints will raise margins at both levels and probably unit costs in distribution as well.[46]

As the main objective of competition law is a distributive justice one, the protection of the consumers, it is important to understand how margins can increase in both levels of the vertical chain. According to Steiner:

> the structure of a consumer goods industry and the relative and absolute margins of manufacturers and retailers are largely determined by the magnitudes of two cross-elasticities that define the willingness of consumers to switch stores within brand and to switch brands within store. When the magnitudes are markedly different, margins at the two stages will be negatively related.[47]

It follows that leading advertising brands will have important horizontal market shares as well as higher than average vertical downstream market shares. This may produce the following result:

> . . . their lower relative RGMs (retail gross margins), forces down the factory prices of competing less popular brands in two ways. First, it does not pay retailers to stock slower selling brands unless they provide a higher % and $ RGM than the leading brands. So smaller manufacturers have to have a lower factory price to achieve the same retail price as the leading brands. Second, . . . leading brands develop a 'reputation premium' that requires less popular brands of the same type to sell for a lower retail price than theirs to remain viable competitors, a relationship that further depresses the relative factory prices of secondary brands and raises the margins and horizontal market shares of the leading advertising brands. These dynamics erect significant horizontal mobility and entry barriers for other manufacturers' brands but can prove an incentive for large volume retailers to enter the market as buyers of the leading brands and marketers of their own private label brands.[48]

Vertical market power, defined as the ability to capture vertical market share, may constitute an alternative source of market power that should be taken into account in competition law enforcement. Although it is generally followed by horizontal market power, it is likely that there will be 'a significant time lag before all vertical

---

Retailing and How Steiner's Theory Provides an Explanation of Important Regularities' [2004] 49 *Antitrust Bulletin* 911.

46 Steiner (n 41) 177–178.

47 Steiner (n 45) 718.

48 R L Steiner, 'The Virtual Equivalence of Horizontal and Vertical Competition—An Analysis of the Sources of Market Power in Consumer Goods Industries' (2007 Loyola Antitrust Colloquium) 7 <http://www.luc.edu/law/academics/special/center/antitrust/pdfs/Steiner_Vertical_paper.pdf> accessed 9 April 2008.

competition effects are manifested' in the industry's horizontal concentration levels or market power: 'a manufacturer with a modest horizontal market share but sizeable vertical market shares is one whose horizontal market share and power is in its incipiency and can be expected to grow'.[49]

Steiner suggests an alternative approach for vertical restraints that affect intra-brand competition between retailers. He considers that the 'single-stage paradigm' of vertical restraints, which emphasizes the analysis of the existence of interbrand competition and largely ignores the role of vertical competition, does not correspond to commercial reality. The dual stage model, he suggests, will not only focus on the existence of market power at each level and/or horizontal competition between suppliers or between dealers, but will also examine competitive relationships between manufacturers and retailers.[50] It follows that the 'locus of market power' and consequently the source of the restraint, supplier or retailer market power, should be an important consideration in the enforcement of competition law.[51]

The major implication of Steiner's approach is the proposition that competition law should shift from the static analysis of the existence of horizontal market power to that of negative effects on consumers, following the exercise of horizontal and/or vertical market power. Adopting a broad view of the possible sources of market power, Steiner's analysis may lead to a more agnostic view for the pro- and anti- competitive effects of vertical restraints as it recognizes that the processes of horizontal and vertical competition are similar and they should have an equal importance in competition law assessment. Distinguishing between horizontal and vertical restraints or between interbrand and intrabrand competition does not always operate smoothly as a shortcut for anticompetitive or pro-competitive effects.[52]

---

49 Ibid 9.

50 See: R L Steiner, 'The Evolution and Applications of Dual-Stage Thinking' [2004] 49 *Antitrust Bulletin* 719.

51 See: W S Grimes, 'The Future of Distribution Restraints Law: Will the New Learning Take Hold?' [2006] *Utah Law Review* 885, 889.

52 For a similar criticism of the vertical/horizontal distinction see: W F Baxter and D P Kessler, 'Toward a Consistent Theory of the Welfare Analysis of Agreements' [1995] 47 *Stanford Law Review* 615, the authors conclude that the classification of an agreement as 'horizontal' or 'vertical' provides little guidance as to either its effect on social welfare or its legality under the antitrust laws and they suggest an alternative system that classifies agreements based on the parties' economic relationships as producers of substitutes or of complements. If one follows Steiner's approach, such a categorization will prove particularly difficult as distribution restraints may involve activities that are both complementary and substitutable. See also: I Lianos, 'Commercial Agency Agreements, Vertical restraints and the Limits of Article 81(1): Between Hierarchies and Networks' [2007] 3 *Journal of Competition Law and Economics* 625, 672, emphasizing the organizational form of the particular relation, market, network or hierarchy rather than its vertical or horizontal dimension.

The emergence of hybrid (horizontal/vertical) commercial practices: dual distribution and private labels as an illustration

The vertical/horizontal dichotomy seems also blurred if one examines a number of real life commercial practices that present both, vertical and horizontal, dimensions. This study will focus on dual distribution and private labels.[53]

Dual distribution

'Dual distribution' exists when the manufacturer simultaneously sells to independent dealers and is also present at the distribution level of the commercialization process by supplying customers directly.[54] Dual distribution may take different forms: the manufacturer may operate its own distribution network in competition with other retailers or he may choose to establish an independent exclusive distribution system but will preserve certain territories for his own distribution outlets. To the vertical relation that usually links the manufacturer with independent dealers, dual distribution adds a horizontal layer, as the manufacturer competes with the dealers of his network (intrabrand downstream competition) and with all other dealers in the relevant market (interbrand downstream competition). Unlike the conventional horizontal competition between suppliers, 'the dual distributing manufacturer creates competition with himself by supplying a dealer'.[55] This hybrid relationship has confused competition law authorities and courts, as it is difficult to decide which, horizontal or vertical, dimension should prevail in order to characterize the agreement as being vertical or horizontal. For example, the supplier's suggestion of a resale price and the retailer's acceptance of that suggestion may be qualified as horizontal price fixing, as the supplier and the retailer are also in direct horizontal competition.

There are a number of pro-competitive justifications for dual distribution practices. First, they offer an opportunity for the manufacturer to monitor the performance of his retailers. By being present at the distribution level the manufacturer will be able to collect information on the optimal level and quality of distribution services for the final consumers and will thus take this information into account in order to fine tune his decision to impose vertical restrictions that will provide

[53] Another example of a hybrid, vertical/horizontal practice, is category management, where a retail chain may decide to manage its business on a category basis and appoints the leading manufacturer in the field as Category Captain. The latter formulates a distribution strategy for the presentation and price of all the brands in this specific product category to be implemented by the retailer. See: R L Steiner, 'Category Management—A Pervasive, New Vertical/horizontal Format' [2001] 15 *SPG Antitrust* 77.

[54] This is increasingly the case with e-Commerce.

[55] Phillip E. Areeda, *Antitrust Law* Volume VIII, ¶1606, 91 (Little, Brown & Company, 1989).

adequate competitive incentives at the retail level.[56] Second, the manufacturer will be able to prevent free riding, encourage the provision of presale services, protect his reputation, and avoid opportunistic behaviour by the dealers. Third, dual distribution also increases the opportunities to serve different types of customers, in particular those that the manufacturer's regular dealers do not serve. Fourth, the manufacturer may engage in price discrimination, which in some cases may be beneficial to consumers, in particular if imperfect price discrimination to low value buyers has the effect to increase output. *De facto* discrimination could, however, also be achieved without employing a dual distribution practice. It would be possible to impose intrabrand restraints on independent dealers and maximum resale prices or to charge all dealers the same price and provide a rebate on re-sales to specific categories of consumers. There is no reason to examine dual distribution differently from other vertical restraints, as the same effects may be similarly achieved by more conventional vertical distribution practices.

Dual distribution will not generally increase manufacturer's market power. Herbert Hovenkamp observes that:

> (a) manufacturer who has no market power cannot use dual distribution to create it. Furthermore, even a monopoly manufacturer generally cannot increase its market power by insulating its wholly-owned retail outlets, even if the effect is to injure competing, independent retailers. If the manufacturer has market power, any monopoly profits earned at the retailer level could also be earned at the manufacturer level.[57]

The horizontal dimension of dual distribution may also be a source of anticompetitive effects, in particular horizontal collusion. Nevertheless, collusion at the retail level will not be in the interest of the manufacturer, the latter preferring to limit any possibility of double marginalization and having no interest to participate in a cartel seeking to create market power at the retail level. Most often the reason that manufacturers enter the distribution level is to combat collusion at the retail level.[58] A restriction of intrabrand downstream competition may affect the distribution of profits between the supplier and the retailers but 'will not affect output to consumers since both suppliers and dealers have a considerable

[56] See: Y Yehezkel, 'Downstream Competition Between an Upstream Supplier and an Independent Downstream Firm' Working Paper (March 2003) <http://econ.tau.ac.il/papers/applied/dualdist.pdf> accessed 10 April 2008.

[57] H Hovenkamp, *Federal Antitrust Policy: The Law of Competition and its Practice* (3rd edn, 2005) 490.

[58] Ibid. See also: P M Ippolito, 'Resale Price Maintenance—Economic Evidence from Litigation (Bureau of Economics Staff Report, Federal Trade Commission) (April 1998), 59–60 <http://www.ftc.gov/be/econrpt/232122.pdf> accessed 10 April 2008.

interest in achieving a level of output that maximizes their *joint* profit level'.[59] If one follows this approach, dual distribution agreements should not be treated differently from vertical restraints.

Steiner's analysis may nevertheless shed light into a less anticipated anti-competitive concern raised by dual distribution practices. As it has been previously suggested, competition authorities and courts should adopt a dual stage approach and should examine the effect of vertical restraints on both horizontal and vertical competition. Traditional analysis has focused on horizontal competition at the supplier and the retailer levels and has ignored vertical competition between the supplier and the retailers over the sharing of the profits of the vertical structure. If one takes into account this dimension of competition, the manufacturer may have the incentive to limit vertical competition by imposing price or non-price restraints on the retailers of his network competing with him at the retail level. His incentive will be to limit the retail gross margin and to increase his vertical market share or profits upstream to the detriment of independent retailers. This may harm consumers if the manufacturer's product benefits from an important brand loyalty. These restraints will be particularly harmful if a high percentage of the manufacturer's brands sales are made by manufacturer-owned retail outlets or if the manufacturer imposes a vertical restraint to dealers that sell both his brand and competing brands and therefore reduces interbrand downstream competition.[60]

The supplier may also want to eliminate competition among retailers in order to raise the profits of his retail outlet. The retail price will in this case be higher than in the absence of dual distribution.[61] The anti-competitive effects of dual distribution practices may be stronger than those of purely vertical restraints but they are in any case less harmful for consumers than purely horizontal restraints.

Private labels

Private label is a term referring to all products sold under a retailer's brand, which could be the retailer's own name (store brands) or a brand created by a manufacturer exclusively for the retailer, who defines the characteristics of the

[59] R Zwirb, 'Dual Distribution and Antitrust Law' [1988] 21 *Loyola of Los Angeles Law Review* 1273, 1289.

[60] See for the same approach: National Association of Attorneys General (NAAG) 'Revisions to the National Association of Attorneys General Vertical Restraints Guidelines' (Resolution 1995, *reprinted in* 4 TRADE REG. REP. (CCH) ¶ 13,400), para 2.3. <http://www.naag.org/assets/files/pdf/at-vrest_guidelines.pdf> accessed 10 April 2008.

[61] See: D Gilo, 'Private Labels, Dual Distribution and Vertical Restraints—An Analysis of the Competitive Effects', Chapter 7 above herein.

product (generic brands). Private label products are generally exclusively distributed by the retailer along with national brand products, which are marketed by manufacturers throughout the national market, not only in the specific retailers' outlets. This brings a horizontal dimension in the relationship between suppliers and retailers, as private labels may compete for market share with national brands.

Private label brands' market share has been constantly growing, in particular in the food sector[62] and represents a significant volume of retail sales in Europe.[63] Private labels are generally perceived by consumers of being of lower quality than national brands.[64] In addition, national labels benefit from a 'reputation premium', as a result of more extensive advertising than private labels.[65] This leads to lower prices than equivalent, in terms of quality, national brand products.[66]

Despite this retail price differential, retailer's gross margins for private labels are more important in comparison to national brand products.[67] The commercialization of private labels is thus more profitable for the retailers compared to that of national brands. This constitutes the main reason for the introduction of private labels by retailers and leads often to the exclusion of second-tier national brands from the market.[68] Two reasons explain the higher retail gross margins for retailers. Steiner notes that retailers with strong private labels have more leverage with manufacturers and this helps them to increase their gross margins.[69] Private labels may also enhance consumer loyalty to retail brands and therefore reinforce the horizontal market power of the retailers. This will in turn strengthen the retailers' vertical bargaining power against national brand manufacturers and will enable them to obtain better deals that will increase their profits.[70]

---

62 M B Ward and others, 'Effects of the Private-Label Invasion in Foods Industries' [2002] 84 *American Journal of Agricultural Economics* 961.

63 See: R L Steiner, 'The Nature and Benefits of National Brand/Private Label Competition' [2004] 24 *Review of Industrial Organization* 105, 106; F Bergès-Sennou, P Bontems, and V Réquillart, 'A Survey on the Economic Impact of the Development of Private Labels' Working paper (2003) <http://idei.fr/doc/wp/2003/private_labels.pdf> accessed 10 April 2008. UK Competition Commission, Final Report, Groceries Market Investigation 30.4.2008, available at http://www.competition-commission.org.uk/rep_pub/reports/2008/538grocery.htm, accessed 1 May 2008.

64 T Staahl Gabrielsen and L Sørgard, 'Private Labels, Price Rivalry, and Public Policy' [2007] 51 *European Economic Review* 403, 404.

65 Steiner (n 63) 108.

66 Staahl Gabrielsen and Sørgard (n 64) 404.

67 According to Ward and others (n 62) 962, the gross margins on store brands may be 35% or more.

68 Ward and others (n 62) 963.

69 Steiner (n 63) 113–114.

70 Steiner (n 63) 112–113.

These distributional outcomes are ambiguous from the point of view of the consumers. Steiner observes the generally positive effect of competition between private labels and national brands, what he calls the 'mixed regimen':

> (i)n this structure a group of (national brands) receive vigorous competition from the (private labels) of the major chain retailers—contest that tends to maximize social welfare in consumer goods industries. That is, it brings about a high level of total surplus while also stimulating innovation by manufacturers. It produces these benefits because of a combination of horizontal and vertical relationships that are unique to this structure.[71]

The commercialization of private labels obviously increases consumer choice by offering a lower price substitute to the consumers. The system may also introduce an effective countervailing power for retailers against the market power of national brand owners.[72]

Nevertheless, private labels may also produce important anti-competitive effects, in particular if they finish by dominating the market. Consumer choice and product variety may be affected if private labels exclude all but the leading national brand. This may also increase retail prices for consumers. Robert Steiner explains:

> [private label] retail prices would no longer be constrained by the retail prices of the few remaining [national labels]. Moreover, stores of the same chain do not compete with each other by price on the chain's own label brands—thus eliminating intrabrand competition, the chief force that disciplines retailers' margins. Lastly, rival chains do not stock each other's [private labels], eliminating interbrand competition within store and requiring most interbrand search to take place among stores.[73]

Private labels will increase search costs for consumers and will therefore offer the opportunity for a higher mark-up at the supply or retail level.

Empirical studies have also showed that competition from private labels might not lead to lower prices for national brand products.[74] Consumers with a high degree of loyalty to the manufacturer's brand will not benefit from the introduction of private label products:

> (t)he trade-off for the national brand producer facing a private label is between exploiting the loyal consumers with a high price and competing for the switching consumers with a lower price. When the fraction of loyals is high, the national brand will concentrate on the loyal segment and a private label will be introduced at a

---

[71] Steiner (n 63) 105.
[72] Staahl Gabrielsen and Sørgard (n 64) 404.
[73] Steiner (n 63) 124.
[74] Staahl Gabrielsen and Sørgard (n 64) 404.

> lower price. On the other hand, when the fraction of loyals is relatively low, the national brand finds it optimal to offer an exclusivity contract to the retailer at a low price and no private label is introduced . . . If the national brand producer serves both loyal and switching consumers initially, the price of the national brand will be relatively low. In such a situation private label competition would lead to an increase in the price of the national brand. The reason is that the national brand producer decides not to serve the switching consumers to which the private label is offered and instead sets a high price to serve only loyal consumers . . . Loyal consumers are worse off due to a higher price on the national brand, while switching consumers are better off when offered a low-price private label. It turns out that in some cases consumers on aggregate benefit from private label introduction, in other cases they are worse off.[75]

It follows that the effect of private labels on consumers is ambiguous and largely depends on the characteristics of consumer demand for the specific product. Restricting the commercial freedom of retailers may have, depending on the circumstances, a positive or a negative welfare effect for consumers. As it is also the case for dual distribution agreements, uncovering the vertical or horizontal nature of the restriction constitutes an unnecessary intermediary step in the analysis, as the classification does not bring any particular information on the existence of those anti-competitive effects.

D. The Futile Quest for the Vertical or Horizontal Dimension of the Supplier/Retailer Relationship

It is clear by now that the vertical/horizontal dichotomy does not always offer an adequate criterion in order to define the boundaries of competition law enforcement with regard to hybrid commercial practices. It has been, however, part of the legal landscape for some time now and has exercised a profound influence in competition law jurisprudence on both sides of the Atlantic. Finding analogies between different fact patterns and classifying them in specific categories or conceptual boxes constitutes an essential feature of legal science. Nonetheless, designing adequate conceptual boxes which fit in the reality of the marketplace is not an easy task. The judge is often confronted by accidents of classification, because of the emergence of new commercial practices that require an effort of re-classification. In some cases the conceptual anomaly observed will lead to the emergence of a new classification that will correspond to commercial realities or to the new dominant economic rhetoric. A brief analysis of the US case law and of the European regulatory practice with regard to dual distribution practices may better illustrate the point.

[75] Staahl Gabrielsen and Sørgard (n 64) 406.

Dual distribution in US antitrust law

Since the introduction of the rule of reason for vertical territorial restrictions in *Sylvania* the vertical/horizontal dichotomy came to prominence to the point that a lot of litigation focused on the issue of characterization of the restraint as being horizontal or vertical.[76] Although few cases ruled on the issue of whether the distribution arrangement is by itself legal under competition law, the 'representative dual distribution case' entailed 'a combination of simple dual distribution and additional vertical restraints on competition'.[77]

Prior to *Sylvania*, dual distribution practices were viewed with suspicion as they involved actual or potential competitors at the retail level.[78] The objective was clear: protect the freedom of distributors from the leverage of suppliers' power in the retail sector. The courts focused on the horizontal dimension of the relationship between the suppliers and the retailers and found it identical to a horizontal restraint among distributors.[79] Horizontal territorial restrictions were found to be prohibited *per se* under section 1 of the Sherman Act in *Sealy*, concerning exclusive geographic territorial agreements entered between Seale Corporation and licensees that manufactured bedding products under the Sealy trademark.[80] The court adopted a formalistic approach and considered that, because of licensees' ownership of Sealy's stock, 'it would violate reality to treat (these restrictions) as equivalent to territorial limitations imposed by a manufacturer upon independent dealers'; this left 'little room for debate' and the court characterized the restrictions as being horizontal in nature.[81] The court did not address the obvious efficiency rationales for these restrictions, as the horizontal nature of the restraints precluded any consideration of their economic and business justifications or their impact on the marketplace.[82] In essence, the finding of a horizontal element prevented any analysis of the anti-competitive effects of the restriction and overshadowed the vertical dimension of the relation between the parties.[83]

---

76 *Sylvania* (n 8) 57–59.

77 Zwirb (n 59) 1278–1279.

78 *United States v McKesson and Robbins* 351 US 305, 313 (1956) '... without regard to categories or labels, the crucial inquiry is whether the contracting parties compete with each other...'.

79 *United States v White Motor Co* 194 F Supp 562, 584 (ND Ohio 1961); See also: concurring opinion of Mr Justice Brennan, *White Motor Co v United States* 372 US 253, 274 (1963).

80 *Sealy* (n 12).

81 *Sealy* (n 12) 354 and 352.

82 *Sealy* (n 12) 358.

83 See also: *Interphoto Corp v Minolta Corp* 295 F Supp 711, 718 n 2 (SDNY), aff'd, 417 F 2d 621 (2nd Cir 1969), '[p]roof of the existence of unlawful resale price maintenance, where the manufacturer is also a distributor... makes the antitrust violation even more pernicious... for unlawful cartel activity then co-exists with the attempt to vertically control the discretion of the independent businessman'. The same characterization was also applied in *Hobart Bros Co v Malcolm T Gilliland, Inc*

The same propensity for a formalistic approach in characterizing restraints is found in *Topco*.[84] Independent grocers and supermarkets in different geographic areas had established a buying cooperative, called Topco, in order to buy grocery products cooperatively and to sell them at retail under the private label brand Topco. Topco imposed territorial restraints to its member-supermarket chains, thus restricting the territories within which they could sell Topco-branded goods. It claimed that these territorial restrictions were necessary in order to induce retailers to invest in promotional services and therefore to enhance competition among the Topco members and other supermarkets. The court rejected that analysis because of the alleged horizontal dimension of the relation between the different members of the Topco brand and prohibited *per se* these horizontal territorial restrictions.[85]

The Supreme Court's opinion in *Sylvania* marked the beginning of a different trend. In *Sylvania* the court insisted on the importance of economic analysis in deciding antitrust cases.[86] It affirmed for the first time that vertical territorial (non-price) restraints should be examined according to the rule of reason, although in practice the court's decision meant that non-price restrictions are presumptively legal, with the exception of situations where there is a restriction of interbrand competition. In essence, a vertical agreement will be prohibited only if it is characterized as a horizontal interbrand restraint. This opens the door to a more economic approach and to the consideration of the economic context of the restriction. The court, however, made clear that horizontal territorial restraints are still subject to the *per se* prohibition rule, thus not overruling *Topco*, although it accepted in *Sylvania* the same justifications that it had refused to take into account in *Topco*.[87] It is therefore necessary to distinguish between truly vertical agreements and those that are factually a proxy for a horizontal agreement between distributors.[88] The court did not examine how shifting the focus of the enquiry on the nature of the restraint will affect the characterization of a commercial practice as a dual distribution agreement.

---

471 F 2d 894 (5th Cir), cert denied, 412 US 923 (1973) which involved a territorial restraint imposed by a manufacturer on a distributor who was also producing competing products.

84 *United States v Topco Associates* 405 US 596 (1972).

85 Ibid, 608. See, however the dissenting opinion of Chief Justice Burger (ibid 613) who argued that a rule of reason would have been more appropriate in this case. For a more nuanced analysis of the court's decision see, P Carstensen and H First, 'Rambling Through Economic Theory: Topco's Closer Look' in E M Fox and D A Crane (eds), *Antitrust Stories* (Foundation Press, 2007), 171–203 (suggesting that the territorial restrictions imposed were not necessary for the promotion of Topco's brand).

86 *Sylvania* (n 8), 59 ('departure from the rule-of-reason standard must be based upon demonstrable economic effect rather than . . . upon formalistic line drawing').

87 *Sylvania* (n 8) 50 fn 18.

88 Zwirb (n 59) 1284.

The continuous embracement of the vertical/horizontal dichotomy by the court has ironically led to a reinforcement of formalism, during the same time the court was advocating a more economic analysis in antitrust law. It became necessary for the courts adequately to characterize the horizontal or vertical dimension of the territorial restraint, as this had implications on the antitrust standard they could apply. The recent decision of the Supreme Court in *Leegin* extended the scope of the dichotomy to price restrictions, as vertical resale price maintenance clauses are subject to a rule of reason approach, while horizontal price restrictions are prohibited *per se*.[89] Nevertheless, the recognition of the economic justifications for vertical restrictions has profoundly influenced the way dual distribution practices are perceived and are examined by the courts and has increasingly led to a demise of the previous formalistic approach. Uncovering the vertical or horizontal dimension of a dual distribution agreement requires more than the simple identification of the relation of the parties: it also calls for the identification of the underlying rationale and of the source of the restraint.

Three trends have progressively appeared in the case law. Although some courts, in the immediate aftermaths of the *Sylvania* decision, continued to characterize dual distribution as a horizontal practice and refused to apply the rule of reason approach of *Sylvania*,[90] the majority of the courts classified dual distribution practices as a form of vertical restraint.[91] Some of these decisions focused on a formalistic examination of the type of the relationship that linked the supplier and the retailers, the only difference with the previous approach being the presumption that the vertical dimension was predominant.[92] Other cases have adopted a more economic test that focuses on the source of the particular restraint within the dual distribution agreement.[93] In *H & B Equipment* the Fifth Circuit observed that:

89 *Leegin* (n 4) 2714, '[o]ur recent cases formulate antitrust principles in accordance with the appreciated differences in economic effect between vertical and horizontal agreements, differences the Dr Miles Court failed to consider'. The fact that Leegin's owners possessed some outlets selling their products in competition with other retailers did not occupy the court.

90 See: Zwirb (n 59) 1293–1301.

91 See: *Coca-Cola*, 91 FTC 517, 610-616 (1978), *vacated as* moot, 642 F 2d 1387 (DC Cir 1981); *Data Systems, Inc v Toshiba Am Inc* 663 F 2d 405, 408–409 (2nd Cir 1981); *Graphic Products Distributors v Itek Corp* 717 F 2d 1560 (11th Cir 1983); *Ryko Mfg Co v Eden Serv* 823 F 2d 1215 (8th Cir 1987), *cert denied* 484 US 1026 (1988); *Illinois Corporate Travel v American Airlines, Inc*, 889 F 2d 751, 753 (7th Cir 1989), *cert denied* 495 US 919 (1990); *Smalley & Company v Emerson & Cuming, Inc* 13 F 3d 366, 368 (10th Cir 1993); *Electronics Communications Corp v Toshiba Am. Consumer Prods.*, 129 F 3d 240, 243–44 (2nd Cir 1997); *AT&T Corp v JMC Telecom, LLC*, 470 F 3d 525, 531 (3rd Cir 2006).

92 See: Zwirb (n 59) 1302–1305.

93 See: Zwirb (n 59) 1305–1318.

> (c)onspiracies between a manufacturer and its distributors are treated as horizontal, however, when the source of the conspiracy is a combination of distributors . . . Here the asserted originator of the plan to eliminate *H & B* (distributor) was the manufacturer . . . Consequently, antitrust law treats the conspiracy as a vertical restraint.[94]

As it has been clearly explained by subsequent case law, when a manufacturer acts on its own, in pursuing its own market strategy, it is seeking to compete with other manufacturers and therefore any restraint should be treated as being vertical.[95]

The emphasis put on the source of the restraint makes economic sense. The courts have long recognized that the effects of dual distribution agreements are not very different from those of vertical agreements. The Fifth Circuit clearly explained the rationale of this source test in *Red Diamond*:

> The reason for focusing on the source of restraints on distributors is economic. Distributors have an incentive to agree among themselves to restrict competition, such as by allocating territories, in order to raise the price they receive for their product because to do so normally increases their profits. Such a horizontal conspiracy, which generates simply an increase in prices, is generally detrimental to consumers and is illegal per se. Not only does a horizontal conspiracy among distributors hurt consumers, however; it injures the manufacturer as well because the higher retail price of the product reduces the quantity sold at retail and hence the quantity demanded from the manufacturer. A manufacturer generally prefers that its distributors sell its product for as low a price as possible, given the price at which it sells the product to them, i.e., for as small a mark-up as possible over the wholesale price, because its sales of the products are normally greater the lower the retail price. . . . A manufacturer thus will typically encourage intrabrand competition in order to enhance interbrand competition, i.e., the competitiveness of its product with those of other manufacturers. . . . Because increasing interbrand competition is generally socially desirable and because intrabrand restrictions are generally not socially harmful when there is significant interbrand competition, manufacturer-imposed, i.e., vertical, restraints are governed by the rule of reason.[96]

Identifying the source of the restraint can be a helpful step in the analysis, as restrictions imposed by retailers are more likely to harm consumers than restrictions imposed by manufacturers, if there is sufficient interbrand competition.

---

94 *H & B Equipment Co Inc v International Harvester Co* 577 F 2d 239, 245 (5th Cir 1978).

95 *Krehl v Baskin Robbins Ice Cream Co* 664 F 2d 1348 (9th Cir 1982).

96 *Red Diamond Supply, Inc v Liquid Carbonic Corp* 637 F 2d 1001, 1004 n 4 (5th Cir), *cert denied*, 102 SCt 119 (1981). See also: *Abadir & Co v First Mississippi Corp* 651 F 2d 422, 427 (5th Cir 1981), '(a) particular market-distributing agreement is treated as a vertical agreement if the party imposing the agreement has the potential economic advantages typically available to a supplier in a vertical market-distributing agreement. If these potential economic advantages are absent, then the agreement is horizontal.'

The test may be also criticized for a number of reasons. First, restrictions imposed by retailers do not always produce anti-competitive effects. Contractual restraints introduced because of the existence of countervailing buying power may ultimately benefit consumers. Characterizing the agreement as horizontal and subjecting it to a *per se* prohibition under section 1 of the Sherman Act appears to set an over-inclusive competition law standard. It is in situations where the retailers will benefit from selling power downstream that dealer-initiated restraints may predominately harm consumers.[97] Second, it is not always easy to identify the source of the restraint. A possible option will be to examine the bargaining power of the parties by looking to the existence of horizontal or vertical market power, in other words the location of bargaining power will determine the source of the restriction. Such an approach fits well with recent economic learning on vertical agreements, which insists on the possibility that vertical restraints are imposed by powerful multi-retailers to manufacturers. This approach would, however, also look equivalent to a quick analysis of the anti-competitive effects of the agreement, which is an inquiry that the vertical/horizontal dichotomy attempts to overcome by introducing a proxy for anti- or pro-competitive effects: if the relation is vertical, the (rebuttable) presumption is that pro-competitive effects are predominant; if it is horizontal, the (rebuttable, sometimes irrebuttable—i.e. cartels) presumption is that the commercial practice produces anti-competitive effects.

This illustrates the futility in this case of the characterization of the agreement as being horizontal or vertical. If this classification is only the outcome of an economic approach, the characterization step introduces a degree of formalism which does not accomplish any analytic or instrumental objective. An option would be to adopt new categories (such as dealer-initiated as opposed to manufacturer-initiated distribution restraints) or to simply examine *in concreto* the economic effects of the dual distribution agreement. In any case, the fact finder should, as a first step of the analysis, identify the possible existence of collusion between competitors to adopt hardcore restrictions and apply in this case the *per se* prohibition.[98] There is no reason why the same approach could not apply to private labels.

[97] See: I Lianos, *La Transformation du droit de la concurrence par le recours á l'analyse économique* (2007) 1135–1136.

[98] This test would be particularly significant in situations of hub and spoke conspiracies, where the retailer or the manufacturer operates as a facilitator to a cartel agreement. For an analysis of the vertical/horizontal dichotomy in the context of the definition of collusion, see: I Lianos, 'Collusion in Vertical Relations Under Article 81 EC' forthcoming CML Review (2008), also <http://papers.ssrn.com/sol3/papers.cfm?abstract_id=1089681> accessed 10 April 2008.

Dual distribution in EC competition law

In comparison with the more economic-oriented US approach, the position of EC competition law with regard to the vertical/horizontal dichotomy may appear formalistic. This can be explained by the relatively recent introduction of the dichotomy in EC competition law, following the turn towards a more economic approach in the late 1990s. Introducing specific standards for vertical agreements was an important objective of the modernization process in EC competition law, as opposed to the previous formalistic approach that did not employ that distinction.[99] Although it was clear that the distinction between vertical and horizontal restraints was justified on economic grounds, as it signalled the embracement of an effects-based approach,[100] it was first introduced in EC competition law through the legal instrument of block exemption regulations and not through the more flexible vehicle of case law, as has been the case in the US. The result is that the definition of what constitutes a vertical or a horizontal restraint is formalistic, as regulatory texts make intensive use of categorical distinctions, and do not always take into account the economic context of the specific vertical relation between the parties.

The definition of the scope of Regulation 2790/99 on 'vertical agreements' is of particular interest for our purposes, in particular with regard to the legal regime of dual distribution agreements.[101] According to Article 2(1) of Regulation 2790/99, the concept of vertical agreement is regulation-specific. An agreement will be deemed 'vertical' if, for the purposes of the agreement, the parties act at a different level in the production or distribution chain and the agreement relates to the purchase, sale, or resale of goods and/or services. The block exemption regulation applies to 'vertical restraints', that is restrictions of competition contained in a vertical agreement that fall within the scope of Article 81(1). Restrictions of competition contained in agreements concluded between actual or potential competitors do not fall within the scope of Regulation 2790/99 and may be exempted by the two horizontal cooperation agreements regulations.[102] Article 1(a) of Regulation 2790/99 defines 'competing undertakings' as 'actual or

---

99 See for instance: Commission of the European Communities, 'Commission Evaluation Report on the Transfer of Technology Block Exemption Regulation No. 240/96—Technology Transfer Agreements under Article 81' (December 2001), para 121, <http://ec.europa.eu/comm/competition/antitrust/technology_transfer/> accessed 10 April 2008 ('(a)s regards the potential negative effects on competition, it is necessary to distinguish between agreements where the parties are in a vertical relationship and agreements entered into between competitors').

100 Ibid, para 4.

101 Reg 2790/99 (n 31).

102 Commission Regulation (EC) 2658/2000 of 29 November 2000 on the Application of Article 81(3) of the Treaty to Categories of Specialisation Agreements [2000] L304/3; Commission Regulation (EC) 2659/2000 of 29 November 2000 on the Application of Article 81(3) of the

potential suppliers in the same product market', irrespective of whether or not the suppliers are competitors on the same geographic market.[103]

Pursuant to Article 2(4) of Regulation 2790/99, the block exemption applies also to situations where competitors enter into non-reciprocal agreements when one of the following conditions is fulfilled:

- the buyer has a total annual turnover not exceeding EUR100 million;
- the supplier is a manufacturer and a distributor of goods, while the buyer is a distributor, and not also a manufacturer of competing goods;
- the supplier is a provider of services at several levels of trade, while the buyer does not provide competing services at the level of trade where it purchases the contract services.[104]

The last two conditions cover situations of dual distribution, where the manufacturer of particular goods/services also acts as a distributor of the goods/services in competition with independent distributors of his goods/services.[105] Thus, the regulation applies only in situations where the undertakings are competing distributors, for example independent retailers competing with supplier-owned outlets, but does not cover the situations where the supplier and the retailer are competing manufacturers. This excludes from the scope of the block exemption situations where the retailer sells private labels that compete with the national brand of a supplier, except in circumstances where the distributor provides specifications to a manufacturer to produce particular goods under the distributor's brand name and both parties conclude a subcontracting agreement.[106] In the latter case the agreement falls within the scope of Regulation 2790/99.

Agreements that fall within the block exemption are compatible with Article 81 EC, if they do not contain any hardcore restriction and the market share of the supplier is lower than 30 per cent. If the dual distribution system concerns final goods, 'the market definition and market share calculation need to include the goods sold by the producer and competing producers through their integrated distributors and agents'.[107]

Treaty to Categories of Research and Development Agreements [2000] L304/7; Commission Notice (n 30).

103 *Vertical Restraints Guidelines* (n 29) para 26.

104 *Vertical Restraints Guidelines* (n 29) para 27: '[n]on-reciprocal means, for instance, that while one manufacturer becomes the distributor of the products of another manufacturer, the latter does not become the distributor of the products of the first manufacturer'.

105 *Vertical Restraints Guidelines* (n 29) para 27.

106 *Vertical Restraints Guidelines* (n 29) para 27.

107 *Vertical Restraints Guidelines* (n 29) para 99.

In conclusion, the Commission subjects dual distribution agreements to the more favourable regime of vertical agreements and ignores their horizontal dimension, with the condition that the agreements are not reciprocal. This standard may appear under-inclusive as dual distribution agreements may in certain circumstances harm consumers, in particular if they are initiated by powerful dealers, that is, dealers disposing of horizontal and/or vertical power. Vertical restrictions imposed in the context of private label/national label competition are nonetheless excluded from the scope of the exemption if the supplier's turnover exceeds a threshold set arbitrarily at EUR100 million. There does not appear to be any obvious reason justifying this threshold nor this particularly over-inclusive antitrust standard for private labels. The formalistic approach followed by the Commission does not take into consideration the source of the restraint, manufacturer, or retailer, which could have been a useful indication of the anti-competitive effects of the practice. It also seems to subject dual distribution to more favourable antitrust regime than situations where the retailer develops private labels, without any particular justification.

E. Conclusion

The emergence of the vertical/horizontal dichotomy in modern competition law marks the influence of the Chicago rhetoric of antitrust law and economics that views distribution restraints sympathetically and advocates a less active, if not passive, competition law enforcement against them. The Chicago rhetoric's success has been partly due to the simplification and the clear neo-classical economic-oriented categories it introduced in antitrust law, in contrast to the more chaotic, formalistic, and fact-specific approach of the previously dominant populist school. Judges were in search of clear and easily administrable categories that could make economic sense, and this is what the Chicago school of antitrust law and economics offered them.[108] The success of the Chicago imported vertical/horizontal dichotomy appears to be complete, as the distinction gained momentum not only in US antitrust law, but also in EC competition law. Nevertheless, recent economic learning, frequently referred to as 'post-Chicago', has challenged the simplified world of Chicago antitrust.[109] The new challenge for competition law would be to integrate this new learning without losing the

108 For an analysis see H Hovenkamp, 'The Rationalization of Antitrust' [2003] 116 *Harvard Law Review* 917.

109 H Hovenkamp, 'Post-Chicago. Antitrust: A Review and Critique' [2001] *Columbia Business Law Review* 257; A Cucinotta, R Pardolesi and R van den Bergh, *Post-Chicago Developments in Antitrust Law* (Edward Elgar, 2002).

simplification and increased predictability that was brought in by the Chicago school antitrust revolution.[110] A prerequisite for the introduction of this new learning is critically to assess the different categories or conceptual boxes that are frequently used in competition law jurisprudence. The vertical/horizontal dichotomy seems to be an obvious candidate to this re-consideration of antitrust categories, not least because of the useful contribution of new economics and management learning in the area of distribution restraints.

The competition assessment of hybrid commercial practices in distribution, such as dual distribution and private labels, unveils the conceptual weakness of the vertical/horizontal dichotomy and the risks of a formalistic approach in characterizing the restraints. The main reason for introducing this dichotomy was the shift towards an effects-based economic oriented approach. The labels, vertical and horizontal, do not, however, always correspond to clear presumptions of anti- or pro-competitive effects and are subject to manipulation.[111] The risk is that competition authorities and courts focus on the vertical or horizontal character of the restriction, instead of examining the actual or potential anti-competitive effects and the economic context of the agreement. The categorization process of a conduct as being vertical or horizontal, 'may become the end' instead of being perceived as a means to identify the effects of the conduct on consumers.[112] This is not to say that antitrust categories are not useful. They bring some degree of legal certainty, as 'they provide the basis for bright-line rules'[113] and for the optimal allocation of the burden of proof, and they may lead to an economy of enforcement resources, in particular with the adoption of block exemption regulations and soft law instruments, such as guidelines. Nevertheless, they should be constantly subject to re-evaluation, according to recent economic learning and empirical evidence.[114]

110 H Hovenkamp, *The Antitrust Enterprise—Principle and Execution* (2005) 45–49.
111 See: Lemley and Leslie (n 2) 35.
112 Lemley and Leslie (n 2) 45.
113 Lemley and Leslie (n 2) 71.
114 Lemley and Leslie (n 2) 82.

Part IV

IN-STORE COMPETITION, PRICING, MARKETING, AND ADVERTISING

9

RETAILER AND PRIVATE LABELS: ASYMMETRY OF INFORMATION, IN-STORE COMPETITION AND THE CONTROL OF SHELF SPACE

*Pieter Kuipers**

* Pieter Kuipers is Deputy General Counsel Europe of Unilever. This paper grew out of a few talks I gave, including a presentation at Third Annual Symposium on Retail Competition, St Catherine's College, Oxford, 21 May 2007, organizers: Institute of European and Comparative Law/Centre for Competition Law and Policy. I am grateful to my colleague Sjoerd Schaafsma, Vice-President Customer Development and Michael Hutchings, solicitor in private practice, for their thoughtful comments. Any errors are mine, though. The views presented here are not necessarily those of Unilever. Comments can be sent to: pieter.kuipers@unilever.com.

A. Introduction: The Evolving Role of Retailing, a Network Analogy?

Until a couple of decades ago the grocery retailer's primary business was to be the intermediary between branded firms and consumers in a market where competition in fast moving consumer goods (FMCG) essentially occurred between branded manufacturers. Their other key role was (and still is) the distribution of goods from their central depots to all their shops. However, large-scale retailing has moved beyond this traditional role of making branded manufacturers and consumers meet. Retailers increasingly come into direct competition with their suppliers when stocking own-label products. These products (also referred to as private labels (PLs)) are in fact fast becoming the largest in-store competitor. The PL is often the number-two, or even the number-one product in a category. PL shares of 50 per cent or higher are not unusual and on the increase. In a number of product categories in some countries the PL is often without any competitor inside many stores.[1]

The more own-label products take over from branded goods, the more an analogy comes to mind with network industries, where significant concerns arise over vertical integration. What network regulators aim to avoid is that those who only sell 'independent content', i.e. without owning their own network,

[1] See: UK Competition Commission 'The Supply of Groceries in the UK Market Investigation: Provisional Findings Report' app 8.11: 'Retailer Own-Label Goods' (31 October 2007) <http://www.competition-commission.org.uk/Inquiries/ref2006/grocery/prov_findings/prov_find_app_8_11.pdf> accessed 7 April 2008 ('Own Label Appendix'): 'In 2006 sales of own-label food and drink products were an estimated GBP30.0 billion, representing more than one-third of total food and drink sales'(para 3) and for Tesco, Sainsbury and Waitrose 50% of total food and drink sales were own-label (para 4). An 80% share of PL in ready meals, fresh pasta, chilled pizza, canned vegetables, and fruit juice is reported in para 7. I will comment on this Own Label Appendix a few times: I believe it underestimates risks of distorted competition between PLs and brands.

in the end lack access to consumers. Ten years ago Tran-Thiet pointed out this parallel and voiced concerns about distortion of competition in terms of 'non-discriminatory access to the network' (shelf space) between the network owner's own content (PL) and independent products which compete with it (branded goods). Whilst many of the constraints put on network operators[2] may not be suitable for immediate application in the grocery retail setting, the analogies with network industries can be a source of inspiration for dealing with questions of access to shelf space.[3]

EU Commission President Barroso made interesting remarks in his speech at the press conference on 19 September 2007, presenting the Commission's Energy Package:

> On unbundling, let me first set out the problem we face. If a company sells electricity and gas and at the same time owns the networks, it has every incentive to make sure that its competitors do not get fair access to 'its' grid. . . . It's a bit like a supermarket that has its own brands but does not want to make shelf space available for other brands, let alone build new shelves, or open up new branches. This not only prevents competition from working, it threatens our longer term security of supply and prevents new renewable companies from starting up.[4]

I will share some thoughts on the effects on competition of the, essentially three, intertwining roles of retailers, viz: that of *customer* (i.e. customer of *all* independent branded firms that supply FMCG goods to the retailer); that of *owner* and *provider* of *shelf space* (and as a consequence his *gatekeeper* role: for many products, supermarkets—essentially because of their high volume—are the gateway to the consumer); and, of increasing significance, the *competitor* role with the retailer's own-label products. This chapter will not be about the theme of large retailers being able to negotiate better terms than their smaller rivals and the problems this may cause, in particular in competition between retailers. Nor will it be about the relevance of countervailing buying power, e.g. in the context of suppliers' Article 82 problems when giving bonuses to retailers.[5] I will focus on access to consumers

2 J P Tran-Thiet, 'The Regulation of Networks and Relations between Industry and Trade: a French Perspective' [1998] 19 *European Competition Law Review* 473. As Tran-Thiet emphasizes, network-operators need not be monopolists; the rules often also apply when more networks exist.

3 Ibid.

4 J M Barroso, 'Energising Europe: a Real Market With Secure Supply' (Opening Remarks at Press Conference on the Commission's Energy Package, Speech 07/553 Europa website 2007) <http://europa.eu/rapid/pressReleasesAction.do?reference=SPEECH/07/553> accessed 7 April 2008. Another critical note is a recently adopted European Parliament 'Written Declaration on Investigating and Remedying Abuse of Power by Large Supermarkets Operating in the European Union' (10 October 2007) 0088/2007.

5 On which: P Kuipers, 'Modernisation of EU Competition Law and Article 82' in S Dumoulin, M Raaijmakers, A Tervoort (eds), *Tussen Themis en Mercurius* (Anniversary Book of the Dutch Association of Company Lawyers) (2005),163–187.

for branded products and on in-store competition. I will explain why there are significant risks of distorted competition between branded goods on the one hand and PLs on the other, arising from retailers combining these roles.

B. The Customer Role

Two aspects of the retailer's *customer* role are worth highlighting: the relative economic dependence of suppliers on large-scale retailers; and the retailer's access to confidential information from all of his suppliers, most of which create branded FMCG products.

Relative economic dependence

Paul Dobson speaks and writes often about retailer buyer power. In a contribution to a US symposium on buyer power and antitrust he also wrote about the three interlinked roles of retailers and emphasized the significance of relative economic dependence of suppliers on retailers.[6] Even the largest branded suppliers account for a small proportion of any large-scale retailer's purchases (rarely more than 1–2 per cent). For their part, such retailers frequently account for 10–20 per cent or more of such supplier's sales.[7] Retailers usually have more suppliers to turn to, or they can re-allocate shelf space to a different product category. For their part suppliers usually cannot replace the 10–20 per cent of sales lost from delisting. Other retailers will not be able, even if they wanted, to take over such volumes and it will not be possible for suppliers to capture the bulk of lost sales (i.e. lost consumers who are loyal to the retailer) through alternative outlets or channels.

This relative economic dependence of branded-goods manufacturers on retailers arises at low market shares. The UK Supermarkets Code of Conduct applies where retailers' market share are 8 per cent.[8] Even with retailer market shares of

6 Symposium papers were published in [2005] 72 *Antitrust Law Journal* 505–744; P W Dobson, 'Exploiting Buyer Power: Lessons from the British Grocery Trade' [2005] 72 *Antitrust Law Journal* 529, 535–537.

7 See also the Commission decision in the Procter & Gamble/Gillette merger case: *Procter & Gamble/Gillette* (Case COMP/M.3732) Commission Decision of 15 July 2005, para 125 <http://ec.europa.eu/comm/competition/mergers/cases/decisions/m3732_20050715_20212_en.pdf> accessed 27 May 2007. On the 1–2% see e.g.: UK Competition Commission, 'Supermarkets: A Report on the Supply of Groceries from Multiple Stores in the United Kingdom' [October 2000] at para 2.457 <http://www.competition-commission.org.uk/rep_pub/reports/2000/446super.htm> accessed 25 May 2008 ('UK CC's supermarkets-report'). The average (median) supplier accounted for only 0.01% of Tesco's purchases.

8 The Code came into force in 2002, following the UK CC's supermarkets-report recommending a code to put relations between supermarkets and suppliers on a clearer, more predictable basis (<http://www.oft.gov.uk>).

10 per cent the loss of turnover can have a significant impact on the profits of delisted suppliers.[9] The Rewe/Meinl-merger decision acknowledged that switching 5–10 per cent of turnover can be difficult. This decision and that in Carrefour/Promodes acknowledge that at a level of 22 per cent of turnover a supplier will even face a serious risk of bankruptcy.[10] Conversely, for the retailer the potential impact of delisting on his profit is usually very limited because he can so easily fill the shelf space with another product or his PL-version of a delisted product. Hence *relative* economic dependence.

Relative economic dependence therefore exists at levels well below the traditional levels of dominance and it even applies to large suppliers.[11],[12] This is pertinent to merger control in the retail sector. Concerns of substantial lessening of competition may well arise at levels below the traditional dominance levels. The issue exists despite fierce downstream competition between retailers. In fact fierce competition increases the retailers' search for differentiation, which in turn stimulates PLs at the expense of branded goods. Branded goods' access to consumers is an issue despite retailers' competing hard amongst each other and despite market shares being well below the usual levels of dominance. In the context of retailer mergers, substantial lessening of competition may well occur already at market shares below traditional dominance.

Access to confidential information, asymmetry of information: a head start for private labels

The second point about the retailer as customer is its access to confidential information. It knows of new product developments (NPDs), promotion plans, prices etc., of the branded firms. It needs to know this, because promotions and NPD-introductions require planning. Decisions on listing suppliers' NPDs have

---

[9] See W S Grimes, 'Buyer Power and Retail Gatekeeper Power: Protecting Competition and the Atomistic Seller' [2005] 72 *Antitrust Law Journal* 563, 563–564 and 580–581.

[10] Commented on by Dobson (n 6) in fn 22, p 536. See: *Rewe/Meinl* (Case IV/M.1221) Commission Decision 1999/674/EC [1999] OJ L274/1, para 97 for the 5–10% and para 101: 'on average 22% of turnover is a figure which a customer can replace only at the cost of very heavy financial losses'.

[11] Grimes (n 9) 563–564: 'The second theme I explore is the unique power large retailers wield over suppliers. Abusive exercises of retailers' gatekeeper power can occur even if a retailer has a market share of 10 percent or less and even if the sellers are large and oligopolistic. These issues [are] inadequately acknowledged in the case law.'

[12] To put things further into perspective: retailers are not small businesses compared to their multinational branded suppliers. Table 1.1 in N Kumar and J B E M Steenkamp, *Private Label Strategy: How to Meet the Store Brand Challenge* (1st edn, 2007) shows that the annual USD-turnover of each of Wal-Mart, Carrefour, Metro-group, and Tesco is larger than that of Nestlé, Altria, P&G, Johnson&Johnson, or Unilever. PL-only turnover of Tesco equals the whole of PepsiCo's global turnover.

to be made (sometimes a year) in advance. This 'asymmetry of information' between retailers and their suppliers has been acknowledged in the P&G/Gillette merger.[13]

Because the retailer has advance knowledge of NPDs, introductions of new variant, plans for promotions etc. of *all* his suppliers, including the pricing of their products, he knows more than any of his 'in-store competitors'. He gets that information legitimately as customer, but can and does use it as competitor, from time to time, to plan development of equivalent own-label products or variants (with knowledge of the cost of suppliers' products) and to determine his own promotional plans and pricing and so on.

The UK Competition Commission (CC) has, in a way, acknowledged the risks associated with this, where, in the context of innovation issues, it refers to a Mintel report 'which points out that in many sectors own-label products still play the role of innovation follower. In particular, own-label products will generally introduce an own-label variety for any new branded product that proves successful.'[14] The CC carries on to say: 'We are aware that some suppliers are becoming more careful about releasing commercially-sensitive information about new products to retailers. It seems that these suppliers have identified an advantage in limiting the sensitive information that is provided to retailers and it is consistent with what we expect would be normal commercial practice surrounding the R&D of new products.'[15]

I agree, branded firms will do as much as they can to protect commercially sensitive information, but often this is just not possible. Knowledge of NPD-launches is commercially sensitive but you simply have to tell your customer about it in order to plan things.

Leaving aside examples of cases where the launch of the PL-version took place even before the branded-NPD launch, there is a much broader implication that warrants emphasis. The point is this. Because of his advance knowledge, the retailer will virtually always be able to be second in the market. He has a strategic competitive advantage over all other (branded) competitors and is able to develop and introduce own-label versions much sooner than branded competitors, clearly a risk of distorted competition, due to insider knowledge.

---

[13] *P&G/Gillette* (n 7) para 124. See also: A Gorrie, 'Competition Between Branded and Private Label Goods. Do Competition Concerns Arise When a Customer is also a Competitor?' [2006] 27 *European Competition Law Review* 225.

[14] Own Label Appendix (n 1) para 41.

[15] Own Label Appendix (n 1) para 42. I will return to the issue of R&D protection when discussing whether branded firms should engage in own-label production.

Put differently: insider knowledge, acquired as customer, provides the PL/retailer as competitor with a second-mover advantage, potentially even with a first-mover advantage.

C. Owner of Shelf Space and Gatekeeper Role

Access to consumers; alternative channels as an 'escape'?

Because of their gatekeeper role, retailers are an important platform for access to consumers. Grimes puts it as follows:

> The realities of a retailer's gatekeeper power can be summarized briefly. For most sellers, creation of their own retail outlets is not a satisfactory option. Sellers of less-expensive consumer products ranging from groceries to appliances to apparel will end up relying in whole or in part on the retailers that sell the bulk of these goods in a multi-brand setting. These retailers are the gatekeepers: unless a retailer carries the seller's brand, the brand will be relatively inaccessible to customers who usually shop at that retailer's outlets. The power that a gatekeeper retailer exercises may be local, national, or international in its reach.[16]

When I talk about the topics of this paper, I am often asked: but if there is consumer demand for branded products (NPD or otherwise), surely they will find their way into the market via other routes? More often than not the answer is no. The bulk of many branded grocery products are sold in what is often referred to as the 'one-stop-shop setting' of large-scale retailers. Without access to large-scale distribution, sufficient critical and sustainable mass may not be achievable. If a product is not stocked by major retailers, it simply may not be able to survive or even reach profitability.

The 'relative-economic-dependence' phenomenon confirms that sales lost from delisting by a large-scale retailer cannot usually be captured otherwise. As Grimes says, unless a retailer carries the sellers' products, these will be relatively inaccessible to consumers who usually shop at that retailer's stores. Not only can lost sales not be replaced in the *same* channel, it will be impossible to redirect the bulk of sales to *other* channels. It should, therefore, not be taken for granted that, after delisting of products for which there is consumer demand, such products will find the customers via other routes.

Likewise NPDs need listing by major retailers to get a chance. The decision by one or two major retailers not to stock them can have a material impact on their survival, which can often not be resolved by introducing them in other channels.

16 Grimes (n 9) 583, 585; Dobson (n 6) 531; and *P&G/Gillette* (n 7) para 125. See also EU-Parliament Declaration (n 4) B.

Having seen advertising, consumers expect to find new products in shops of major retailers and if they don't, chances of success diminish. The higher the retailer's share of large and high volume stores, the more important this effect is. Large (high volume) stores are key to NPD-introduction, particularly at the early stages. That is where people buy new products and where you achieve sufficient levels of weighted distribution to, for example, justify national advertising and promotion campaigns. Moreover, different channels may require different products or product-formats. Not every product (format) can be launched in every channel.

This side of branded firms' dependence is not always recognized in retailer mergers. When looking upstream, competition authorities sometimes assume that 'the market for the procurement of daily consumer goods comprises the sale of such goods directly from the producers to customers such as wholesalers, retailers and other firms (cafés, hotels, restaurants)'. This was taken from a questionnaire in a recent retailer merger. However, this approach produces (buying) shares of retailers on the procurement market that are substantially below the market share in their own down-stream (e.g. one-stop-shopping) market. This hugely underestimates their gatekeeper function in their own sales channel, both in terms of existing products and NPDs.

Quite rightly the Rewe/Meinl-merger decision emphasized the 'close interdependence between distribution market and procurement market' such 'that different sales channels are not readily interchangeable and that there are strong arguments that the procurement market may have to be subdivided according to sales channels'.[17] Indeed, where the downstream channels for finished goods are different markets, the same holds true for the procurement market immediately upstream from the retail level. If one also realizes that limited assortment discounters (LADs) hardly stock branded products and their shelf space is not at all available for introduction of *innovations* the dependency on other retailers increases even further. If anything, the buying shares in the procurement market of retailers that do stock branded goods should be recorded as *higher, not lower* than their own downstream market share.[18]

EU vertical merger guidelines: input foreclosure

Considering the retailer as provider of shelf space to branded firms, while being their major competitor as well, the vertical merger guidelines adopted by the

[17] *Rewe/Meinl* (n 10) para 72.

[18] One does not, however, see this consequence of the Rewe/Meinl-decision reflected consistently in subsequent retailer-merger decisions. Since the points are unlikely to be put forward by merging retailers themselves, it would be good if authorities ensured consistency with previous decisions, if only by asking the right questions in supplier-questionnaires.

Commission on 28 November 2007 are of interest (the guidelines).[19] Were branded goods to have insufficient access to consumers with PLs taking their place, there are issues of 'input foreclosure'.

Shelf space is a key input for branded firms, because without shelf space, branded products 'could not be . . . effectively sold on market'.[20] The guidelines also confirm that foreclosure may take more subtle forms, e.g. 'degradation of quality of input'.[21] The quality of shelf placement does spring to mind when business colleagues are dismayed because of products having been put on 'death row', or on the 'slipped-disc shelf'. Retailers' control of shelf space is further discussed in Section D below.

Incentives to foreclose and to mimic brands

About *incentives* to foreclose, the new vertical merger guidelines make an interesting point: the diversion of downstream demand away from foreclosed upstream competitors increases if products are 'close substitutes'.[22] Focusing on PLs, this implies and indeed contributes to an economic incentive for retailer own-label products to mimic brands and to persuade shoppers that branded and own-label products are equivalent: *perceived* quality is an important driver of PL-success.[23]

Such practices do occur quite often. The key thing to note is that these retailer practices are not just about the question whether consumers are confused as to *origin* of product. This tends to be the primary focus of intellectual property (IP) litigation. However, the real point (not dealt with by IP law) is that these practices are part of a wider economic drive of retailers to divert volume away from branded products and towards their own label products.[24] Additionally, the customer relationship increases branded firms' barrier to litigate, be it over copycatting, misleading consumers, or use of confidential information.

Of course this does not occur with each and every own-label product but it happens regularly enough. The argument put forward by retailers that they have

---

19 Commission Notice: Guidelines on the Assessment of Non-horizontal Mergers Under the Council Regulation on the Control of Concentrations Between Undertakings <http://ec.europa.eu/comm/competition/mergers/legislation/nonhorizontalguidelines.pdf> accessed 27 May 2008.

20 Ibid, para 34. Footnote 24 of the guidelines confirms that 'the term "inputs" is used here as a generic term and may also cover services [and] *access to infrastructure*' (emphasis added).

21 Ibid, para 33.

22 Ibid, para 42.

23 Kumar and Steenkamp (n 12) 92–97, 102–103.

24 Cf Own Label Appendix (n 1) para 9: '(e) Own-label sales are stimulated when consumers cannot tell an own-label product from a branded product due to similarity in packaging, and when consumers believe that own-label products are produced by the manufacturer of the branded product.'

no incentive whatsoever to copycat, because they should rather differentiate their products from the branded ones, is not as compelling as the UK CC likes to believe in its Own Label Appendix. Both at the initial stages of PL (getting consumer used to them and endorsing the picture that PL is equivalent to brands), or when they do a PL-version of a successful branded product, retailers have every incentive not to differentiate too much (except on price), but rather create as close a substitute as possible, as the vertical merger guidelines indicate.

Kumar and Steenkamp confirm that copycatting is an effective retailer strategy to decrease the perceived quality gap with (and the price premium of) manufacturer brands; and: '[t]he copycat strategy accounts for more than 50 percent of the store brand introductions in the CPG industry.'[25]

Even if PL has become a more mature brand in its own right,[26] whenever it seeks to build on the success of a branded innovation, there will always be an economic incentive to mimic elements of the branded success and to tag on to and free-ride on the investments of successful brands. In that sense PL is no different from how branded competitors (mis)behave at times. However, as said, branded firms will not hesitate to take a branded competitor to court—with a competitor who is also a major customer and gatekeeper to the channel, engaging in legal proceedings is not as straightforward.

The CC rejects the arguments put forward by the British Brands Group, wrongly in my view. Even if it were correct that copycatting 'on its own' is unlikely to provide a sustained basis for the success of an own-label product, that does not mean it should be dismissed altogether. One has to take into account all aspects of competition by PL and even if one aspect, taken in isolation, is not the decisive factor, it nonetheless remains relevant to the whole picture. I totally disagree that 'any negative effect on competition is unlikely'.[27]

---

25 Kumar and Steenkamp (n 12) 102–103, referring to: F S Morton and F Zettelmeyer, 'The Strategic Positioning of Store Brands in Retailer-Manufacturer Bargaining' [2000] National Bureau of Economic Research, Working Paper 7712.

26 Which they have: Kumar and Steenkamp (n 12) 9.

27 Own Label Appendix (n 1) para 19. The CC's liberal approach to copycatting is in marked contrast with its view on mislabelling: a label had indicated that the product was from British/UK origin, whilst in fact it was from overseas origin and had only been packaged in the UK. The CC rebuked: 'This practice distorts competition as it provides those retailers that are carrying out this practice with an advantage over those retailers that behave honestly', see: UK Competition Commission, 'The Supply of Groceries in the UK Market Investigation: Provisional Findings Report' app 8.10: 'Supply Chain Practices of Grocery Retailers' (31 October 2007) item ID40 in annex 3 <http://www.competition-commission.org.uk/Inquiries/ref2006/grocery/prov_findings/prov_find_app_8_10.pdf> accessed 27 May 2008. I agree this reprimand concerns distorted competition between retailers, but likewise distorted competition between PL and brands occurs with deliberate copycatting, misleading of consumers, or use of suppliers' confidential information.

Kumar and Steenkamp write that one of three important obstacles to successful new branded products is: 'The intellectual property protection process, because the new product was rapidly imitated by retailers'.[28]

D. Retailers' Control of Shelf Space and In-Store Positioning of Brands and Private Labels

To recap: the combined customer/competitor roles bring about risks of reduced, distorted competition between brands and PLs. Factors discussed above were: (i) asymmetry of information, providing PLs with a competitive advantage, based on insider knowledge, over their branded competitors in terms of being able to be (at least) second in the market; and (ii) the PL having more room to free-ride on the success and goodwill of brands. Additional factors are: retailers set in-store consumer prices of branded as well as own-label products; and retailers determine listings and in-store positioning of branded and own-label products. In-store pricing will be discussed in Section G. I will now turn to the latter ('input foreclosure').

Growth of private labels at the expense of brands; increased choice?

Retailers determine if and how their shoppers, the consumers, will have access to products in store. In determining whether or not to list certain products and, if listed, their on-shelf positioning, they will, understandably, have a natural inclination to prioritize own-label products over branded goods.[29] To paraphrase EU Commission President Barroso, one might say that supermarkets have every incentive to, where possible, deny competitors access to the infrastructure of shelf space in the same way as its own-label products get access. And if stocked, the retailer can still give own-label products better in-store treatment, resulting in higher PL shares.[30]

To come back once more to the copycatting issue, it is important to keep in mind that the kind of distortion discussed here will not depend on whether or not the PL is a mature brand. The PL being a mature brand, and not just another copycat, does not at all remove the incentive for the supermarket to give PL on-shelf priority.

---

28 Kumar and Steenkamp (n 12) 169–170.

29 Kumar and Steenkamp (n 12) 18.

30 Kumar and Steenkamp (n 12) 94–95 (cf p 18) point out that (while one group of shoppers consistently prefers PLs, another prefers branded products) one of the key battlegrounds is for 'random buyers'. 'Random buyers can be attracted to the [PL] by using in-store stimuli that guide the shopper to the [PL], such as favourable shelf facings, shelf tag-ons, and end-of-aisle displays.' Giving PLs favourable shelf space pulls in a hefty share of random buyers, giving high PL market shares in certain categories.

As long as own-label products take a modest share of sales in the store, the risk of this distortion may still be limited as the retailer cannot do without branded products to fill the shelves properly and attract shoppers. However, the larger the share of PL within a retailer, the less the supermarket depends on branded turnover and the more the 'network risk' identified by President Barroso becomes real.

In its Own Label Appendix the UK CC describes trends of own-label sales in an attempt to determine whether PLs are performing at the expense of branded goods and whether this has reduced innovation from branded products.[31] The CC believes this is not the case. In so doing, it emphasizes that PL penetration varies significantly from category and that at category level PL shares have increased, but sometimes also have decreased again.

Be that as it may, it is undeniably true that overall the share of PL has grown. Increases of PL penetration clearly outnumber any decreases. The CC reports that PL represents more than one-third of total food and drink sales and that for Tesco, Sainsbury, and Waitrose 50 per cent of total food and drink sales were own label.[32] All that did not happen at once—these shares grew over time. Indeed, the CC reminds us that 'The sale of own-label products as a share of total grocery sales has increased substantially since their widespread introduction in the 1960s'.[33] There is a correlation between increased consolidation in the retail and the propensity of PL.[34] I do not think it is really denied that PL has grown at the expense of branded goods, in fact:

> Morrisons viewed the grocery market as increasingly concentrated by primary and own-label brands, at the expense of secondary and tertiary brands and for the benefit of consumer choice. Morrisons considered that own label has provided better competition for the brands, than tertiary brands because they are generally better marketed, better packaged and challenge the ability of the brands to dictate prices. Secondary brands tend not to have the marketing support of the brand leaders and find it difficult to compete against own-label products. Own-label products acquire the well-known reputation of the retailer, which promotes sales over less well-known secondary and tertiary brand reputations.[35]

It is not clear on the basis of this statement why PL increased choice. The choice issue seems neutral at best, the one replacing the other(s). As noted by Dobson,[36] increasingly retailers stock one or two A brands of a particular product in

31 Own Label Appendix (n 1) paras 33 *et seq* and para 45.
32 Own Label Appendix (n 1) paras 3–4.
33 Own Label Appendix (n 1) para 34.
34 Cf Kumar and Steenkamp (n 12) 17.
35 Own Label Appendix (n 1) para 25.
36 P Dobson, 'Competition and Mergers in Consumer Goods Industries: The Case of Pet Food' [2001] 22 *European Competition Law Review* 443–457.

addition to their own PLs, resulting in a decline of secondary (B and C) brands and smaller A brands. The CC itself identified the following practice and marked it as 'possibly problematic': 'Delisted any suppliers of branded products in favour of your nearest own-label equivalent.'[37]

Of course this does not happen all at once, nor will retailers necessarily replace an entire branded range. They are more likely to put their own version of the most-sold branded variety alongside it initially. Over time they may replace it, while keeping some other branded variants. Even if the brands as such remain listed, you may find that in the retailer's smaller shops, where there is less shelf space available, or where he has a local monopoly of time-driven shopping trips, he can afford to favour his PL. All this typically involves a very subtle, refined, and gradual process. As the CC said, it took PLs from the 1960s to get to where they are today.

Kumar and Steenkamp report an increase of PL in Germany from 12 per cent to 34 per cent over the last three decades at the expense of (non-premium) brands.[38]

Certainly, PL taking over from brands is not always a problem. If there is less consumer demand it is entirely legitimate that retailers should delist. However, delisting products for which consumer demand does exist is more likely to be a problem.[39] It is not easy to establish this though. An unfavourable in-store treatment can 'stimulate' reduction of branded product sales. Also suppliers will be very reluctant to give authorities examples, simply because they do not want to upset a major customer, but it is a concern worthy of recognition by authorities.

Before moving on, let me quote some concluding remarks from an article on the economics of PLs, based on a survey of ten years of literature:

> PLs are frequently considered as additional goods that allow the retailer to increase his profit to the detriment of the upstream producer, either by decreasing the wholesale price or by capturing a larger share of the surplus of the industry.

---

37 See: Appendix 8.10 (n 27) item ID31 in Annex 3.

38 Kumar and Steenkamp (n 12) 4–6, 186–188.

39 In December 2004 the Dutch competition authority NMa issued a guidance paper (in Dutch) on buyer power ('Visiedocument Inkoopmacht' <http://www.nmanet.nl> accessed 7 April 2008) ('NMa-paper'). I briefly discussed it in Kuipers (n 5) 175–177. The NMa-paper acknowledges that if a powerful retailer buys less of a particular product or products, e.g. in order to force better conditions from his supplier/s, but *without* market circumstances giving rise to the retailer's lowering his purchases (notably: consumer demand for the product has not gone down in the retailer's downstream market), consumers might be worse off because they will face less choice in the shop. In addition the price of products which were delisted may even go up in the market, because a lower volume of buying will also mean a lower volume of sales in the downstream market (NMa-paper paras 72, 92, 94).

> Consumers benefit from the increase in the number of goods available and from the positive impact of the reduction in double marginalisation. However, in practice, a PL generally replaces another product, [e.g.] a regional brand. In this case the positive impact of having a larger number of goods available for the consumers disappears. Moreover, the strategic choice of product quality by a retailer or a producer is not identical. For a given quality of the [branded product], the retailer designs a less differentiated good than an upstream producer would. Therefore the consumer will benefit from an increase in competition between PLs and [brands] but could be penalised by the lower degree of differentiation between products. Thus, in a more realistic framework, it is not certain that the introduction and development of PLs lead to an increase in consumer surplus and to an increase in welfare.[40]

Innovation and private labels: 'asymmetric' access to market/consumers

Earlier we saw the UK CC's reference to a Mintel report pointing out 'that in many sectors . . . own-label products will generally introduce an own-label variety for any new branded product that proves successful'. On the whole, ideas for own-label products are derived from elsewhere. Significant research and development is not really part of the retailer's (price/cost-focused) business model. This continues to come from branded industry (with much more differentiation/added-value focus). As Bergès-Sennou et al. express it: the strategy of retailers to develop 'me-too' products 'is nothing more than free-riding on research and development of new products. Such free-riding will discourage the efforts devoted to the development of new products in the long term.'[41] The potential for free-riding will increase the threshold of innovation and over time may affect innovation rate. Of course branded firms shall have to innovate continually in order to survive, but if branded innovations either do not get a chance to reach the consumer or do not get enough time to earn the investments back, overall levels of innovation are bound to be affected.

That said, next to a majority of innovation-followers, there have been PL-introductions which, even though not driven by fundamental research and development, did create new product segments. The chilled ready-meals category is a case in point. However, this does not remove the concerns of distorted competition. The point to make is this.

Where it is the PL that has driven a new in-store product category, it is no wonder that PL will typically make out 100 per cent or the vast majority of that

40 F Bergès-Sennou, P Bontems, and V Réquillart, 'Economics of Private Labels: a Survey of Literature' [2004] 2 *Journal of Agricultural and Food Industrial Organisation*, Article 3, s 5.

41 Bergès-Sennou, Bontems, and Réquillart (n 40) further on in the concluding remarks section of their article. Compare above quotes from Kumar and Steenkamp (n 12) 102–104, 169–170.

product category. The chilled-meals segment in many large-scale retailer stores tends to be dominated by own-label products. However, if branded manufacturers wanted to move into that category, they will find that getting access to the chilled-meals shelves is far from easy. The company I work for has indeed experienced such difficulties.

More generally where PLs have captured a category, it will be an uphill battle for branded NPDs, even if the quality is better, to find their own place on the shelves in that market. Put differently: it is much easier for PLs to find their way into a product market populated by branded goods, than it is for branded goods to find their way into a market dominated by PLs. This is another 'asymmetry', so to speak, of competition between PLs and brands.

What about 'must-stocks'?

An argument often heard (or implied) is that branded goods are must-stocks and that retailers cannot do without them. Let me say this. When my business colleague reviewed a draft of this paper, he told me that the proper definition of a must-stock is (likely to be) an equation: 'brand loyalty ≥ store loyalty'. Because it is an equation, each of the level of store loyalty and brand loyalty are relevant. Both will be different for different products, even for different shopping trips.

Which product or brand is a 'must-stock', is highly dependent on the retailer's business model and how he attracts shoppers. Take the LADs, e.g. Aldi and Lidl. Essentially they have no supplier-branded must-stock products. Their PLs are their must-stocks. With PLs increasing their market shares, these are becoming the real must-stocks for retailers.

Second, even products which are considered 'must-stocks' are not immune to retailers' strategic behaviour. These too are delisted, as was specifically confirmed in the P&G/Gillette merger decision:

> retailers have indicated that even in the case of increasing margins for branded products they would not consider stopping buying private label

and:

> the market investigation has shown that retailers *delisting* policy applied also to P&G's or Gillette must-stock brands, although retailers reported that delisting these brands might entail a risk of losing customers and significant costs.[42]

42 *P&G/Gillette* (n 7) para 126, 127. Retailers replacing/delisting must-stocks, will find it even easier to replace products which are not must-stocks, particularly with PLs.

Last but not least one should also be mindful that a branded 'must-stock' is by no means the same as the product or brand being dominant.

Advertising of brands: a barrier to private labels, or brands catching up?

Advertising by branded manufacturers is often referred to as a significant barrier to own-label sales.[43] However, there is another side to branded advertising in the context of competition with PL. Advertising of specific products is an essential mechanism for branded firms to attract consumers. Branded products require the support of advertising to be attractive for a retailer to stock them. By contrast own-label products do not require advertising to be accepted for listing, as it is the retailer who decides himself and uses stores as his advertising and promotional media. Indeed, as Morrisons' view cited by the CC stated, 'own-label products acquire the well-known reputation of the retailer'. Naturally the retailer will have to develop a product which consumers will buy, but he reduces his risk by building on experience gained with the success of—and therefore also on investments made by—brands. Once the retailer has taken the decision to develop its PL, there is no doubt he will stock it and only delist if it turns out to be unsuccessful. The branded firm will have to wait and see if and how long retailers will stock its products.

E. The Private Label/Retailer Business Model, Choice and In-Store Competition

The (vertically-integrated) private label/retailer business model

Building on the point made in the last paragraph, we should be mindful that a retailer, even when its PLs have become mature brands, is not 'just another branded competitor'. PL/retailers' business model differs from that of branded firms, essentially because brand ownership and retailing are vertically integrated. Because of this, retailers, when advertising and promoting their store banners, at the same time advertise their PLs, and *vice versa*. Retailers need not engage in significant *product-* or even *category*-specific advertising. Costs are spread over all product categories. Own-label products acquire the reputation of the retailer and benefit from the same brand, the retailer/banner name.

Because they must advertise and promote their store banner anyway, retailers *de facto* only have distribution costs for whatever PLs they stock. By contrast

43 E.g. CC reference to report at Own Label Appendix (n 1) para 9(d).

branded goods have distribution costs *and* advertising costs. And insofar as distribution costs are concerned, branded firms shall have to pay retailers somehow or other for being inside the store, be it through listing fees or other financial terms and discounts, costs which do not apply to own-label goods.[44] With a view to the network parallel, one might ask: 'listing fees, margin squeeze'?

As Kumar and Steenkamp put it: 'the retailer will capture most of the total system profits, resulting in high retailer gross margins on private labels'.[45] They do emphasize though that higher gross margins do not necessarily make PLs more profitable for retailers. Dollar profit per square foot is the measure of profitability that retailers should focus on. The difference on net margins is usually much less; the absolute dollar profit per unit sold may be higher for brands than for PLs; and last but not least shelf turnover (velocity) of branded good may be higher, overall resulting in higher profits generated by brands.[46]

Branded firms need scale to be able to advertise and to achieve lower prices. Therefore brands mostly also require availability in more than one retailer. As Grimes, cited above, said: for branded manufacturers, creating their own retail outlets is not an option. Indeed, '[i]t is hard to imagine a major retail chain being acquired by a branded manufacturer in consumer packaged goods'.[47]

Put differently, the vertical integration model of PL/retailer is not an option for branded firms. Foreclosure from retail outlets, arising from increased PL/retailer integration is a real threat. Is that a problem? This depends on how important one considers issues like in-store consumer choice and in-store interbrand competition.

Shopper trips

Whilst this may sound counter-intuitive, consumers have sometimes complained not about too little choice, but about an excessive abundance of choice. This issue has a time-driven dimension, though, and it also depends on the role of the store in consumer's shopping strategies. Consumers make different types of shopping trips, each having different time constraints. For example, consumers on weekly 'bulk-shopping' trips know what they need and they want to get their usual choice of things without too much distraction. They just want to get efficiently

44 Cf Tran-Thiet (n 2) 473, who refers to 'distortion of competition in relation to shelf space', arising from costs which brands have to make but PLs do not.

45 Kumar and Steenkamp (n 12) 111. Bergès-Sennou, Bontems, and Réquillart (n 40) (at para 3.2) also refer to literature showing 'that the introduction of a PL always diminishes the joint profit of the channel, compared to selling the second national brand'.

46 Kumar and Steenkamp (n 12) 112 *et seq*.

47 Kumar and Steenkamp (n 12) 168.

what is on their shopping list. When on a top-up shopping trip to buy this evening's meal, the shopper is in another mode/mood, does not have time to shop around at all, and he will buy something that is available. By contrast, when on an 'indulgence' or fun-shopping trip, consumers will shop around, enjoy a wide choice, and take their time.

The issue of too much choice, e.g. if shopping under time pressure or similar constraint, has been a trigger for category management. Category management techniques[48] allow retailers to take informed decisions on rationalization of product portfolios, improving the revenue from shelf space without consumers suffering from (a perception of) reduced choice. Which portfolio to keep in store is, of course, a matter of careful balancing. As Professor Marcel Corstjens (INSEAD) remarked at the Oxford symposium, there is a cost to choice. Indeed there is and if it becomes too high, rationalization is essential. However, this is all about striking the right balance—after all, there is also a cost to *lack* of choice.

Two types of choice: range of one brand versus range of different brands

When it comes to the question of in-store choice, there are two types of choice: first the choice provided by the varieties within the range of *one* particular brand (be it branded or PL); second is a choice between *two or more* competing brands. If choice offered by the range from one brand is sufficient, there may be no need for more choice and the second brand is superfluous. Query, however, whether choice, quality, and price of products remain at the level preferred by consumers, once no in-store competitor is left. With less in-store competition, I believe the laws of economics indicate that, eventually, choice might well go down and prices up.

Moreover, most consumers prefer to have a choice in the store at which they usually shop, e.g. in the one-stop-shop or bulk-shopping trip. Consumers will not take the trouble of buying one product in one store, another in another store, a third in a third store, and so on, even when they might have preferred the other products. They may pay regular visits to a couple of different large stores, but there is a limit, and they will not switch stores only for a couple of products, nor will they travel a long way to get the groceries they want.

Having choice within the store, therefore, provides a benefit to the consumer. The costs (including time spent) for the consumer to switch *between* stores is higher than choosing between different products *in* store. This is precisely why

[48] Important deliberations about category management can be found in *P&G/Gillette* (n 7) paras 134–151. The CC dedicated app 7.1 of their Provisional Findings Report (n 1) to category management. See also: J Davey, 'Category Management' [2004] 25 *European Competition Law Review* 479–484.

authorities express concerns about single-branding obligations, in particular at the retail level:

> In case the buyers are retailers selling to final consumers the foreclosure may also lead to a loss of in-store inter-brand competition[49]

and:

> For final products, foreclosure is in general more likely to occur at the retail level, given the significant entry barriers for most manufacturers to start retail outlets just for their own products. In addition, it is at retail level that non-compete agreements may lead to reduced in-store interbrand competition.[50,51]

Imagine a vertically-integrated (private label-only) world: once more the network parallel

If PLs did replace brands altogether and all stores would only stock PL, there would be no *in-store* competition left. Only competition *between* stores would remain. This may sound far-fetched and indeed it is an extreme scenario, but not ruled out if one takes into account (i) that this is, as said, the case already in a number of product categories in some countries; and (ii) that the advance of LADs in Europe (which by and large stock only their own-label products) is significant.

The trend of retailers increasingly championing their PLs is illustrated by a test carried out in 2006 in the Netherlands, when Albert Heijn (part of Ahold) opened one or two shops in which it exclusively stocked own-label products. The test was not yet an absolute success, but tests like this, which one day may work, or may work for a particular kind of store, do underline retailers' increasing emphasis on PL and resources put behind advancing PL sales and market position.

Clearly a PL-only scenario leaves brand ownership and retailing fully vertically integrated: in-store competition would vanish. To return once more to the network analogy, the PL-only scenario is comparable to what network regulators

---

49 DG Competition Discussion Paper on the Application of Article 82 of the Treaty to Exclusionary Abuses (Public Consultation, December 2005), para 139 <http://ec.europa.eu/comm/competition/antitrust/art82/discpaper2005.pdf> accessed 27 May 2008.

50 Commission Notice (EC) Guidelines on Vertical Restraints [2000] OJ C291/1 at para 148.

51 After all, this is why Unilever was required to abandon exclusivity of free-on-loan ice-cream cabinets in 'solus outlets' in Ireland. Agreed, that was about contractual exclusivity, which is not the issue with PLs. However, economics-wise, the issue still is: do competitors have access to (infrastructure necessary to reach) the consumer. Cabinet exclusivity was held to foreclose access to the Irish impulse-ice-cream market, comprising small outlets with no space for competitors' cabinets. Wouldn't it be odd if no concerns arose over insufficient access for all branded competitors to the much larger shops of the collective large-scale retailers, all essential for consumers' regular shopping trips?

do want to avoid, namely that those who only sell 'content' independently, without owning their own network, in the end lack access to consumers.

Certainly, there are more retailers who compete amongst themselves, each with their own-label ranges. However, even if a sufficient number of retailers would remain with a sufficiently wide range of products to provide consumers with enough choice at local level, one could say, with a wink to Article 81 that the network effect of retailers' all deciding to only stock PL, that there is no more room left for branded products: no access to consumers for brands, despite the existence of several networks.

Branded firms' mergers

There are many more things that can be said; for now there is one more thought I would like to leave with you. With growing PL shares and (to borrow from Morrisons' view as reported by the CC) the grocery market becoming increasingly concentrated by primary and own-label brands, and with fewer brands in store, it is only logical that concentration in the branded goods industry continues. So long as competition authorities are not concerned by PLs taking increasingly strong positions in product categories, they should be consistent and not be too worried either about high market shares arising from mergers between branded firms.

The Irish competition authority went some way to acknowledge this recently. It approved the takeover of the soft drinks business of C&C Group plc by Britvic plc, despite this leading to a combined share of nearly 70 per cent of the squashes market. Besides the fact that the two merging brands were not each others' closest substitutes, significant value was attached to the proliferation of retailer own brands and discounter brands, which essentially occupied the remaining 30 per cent. This was taken as evidence of ease of entry in the squashes market.[52]

F. Is the Answer: Branded Manufacturers to Engage in Private Label Production?

Manufacturing own labels

It is a common misperception[53] that own-label products are often produced by manufacturers of branded equivalents. As said in connection with the vertical

[52] Irish Competition Authority, 'Determination of Merger Notification M/07/027—Britvic/C&C: Proposed Acquisition of the Soft Drinks Business of C&C Group plc by Britvic plc' (13 August 2007), paras 43–45 <http://www.tca.ie/MergersAcquisitions/MergerNotifications/MergerNotifications.aspx?selected_item=348> accessed 27 May 2008.

[53] Even in economic literature! See Bergès-Sennou, Bontems, and Réquillart (n 40) para 5.2.

merger guidelines, retailers have every incentive to endorse that impression. However, for branded firms this is a delicate issue and these days PL is mostly produced by dedicated PL manufacturers (often former second or third-tier branded firms).

Production of own-label products for retailers requires a business model which is different from that of manufacturing one's own branded products. Own-label manufacturers have to have focus on lowest possible cost and low overheads; conversely branded manufacturers need to invest more in research and development and promotion and advertising. As said, ideas for PL developments by and large find their inspiration elsewhere: trends spotted and products seen in other (geographic) markets. Fundamental research and development investment is not really part of their cost-focused business model.

Second, producing PL as well as branded equivalents creates pressure from retailers to produce PLs which, quality-wise, are as close to the brands as possible. This raises issues of protection of know-how, in addition to higher risks of PL diverting volume away from the manufacturer's own branded goods (remember the vertical merger guidelines) when PLs actually do come from the same source.

Third, competing retailers may see the manufacturer as an ally of the other retailer, which may trigger strategic decisions not to list brands of PL manufacturers.[54] More generally, manufacturing PL makes the branded firm even more dependent on the retailer than he already is for the sale of his branded products; it contributes to the vertical integration process.

Manufacturing PLs mostly makes sense if a separate unit is created within the branded firm's group. This, however, results in reduced or limited synergies between PL and branded production. Because of the potential downsides and complexities involved, branded firms tend to produce PLs very selectively, in particular to (temporarily) fill excess capacity.[55]

It is of note that branded firms are *not* primarily competing with PL-*manufacturers*—competition is against the PL-*owner*. The essence of branded firms' existence is their creation of brands, not their manufacturing capability (which they can and do outsource, like retailers do). Brands compete with brands and the issues addressed in this paper arise from competition of (independent) brands versus

54 Cf Kumar and Steenkamp (n 12) 19: 'Mainstream retailers can react strongly to brand manufacturers supplying to other retailers, most notably hard discounters.' This is about supply of branded goods, but similar concerns arise over PL-supply.

55 On the pros and (particularly) cons ('the vicious circle of dual strategy') of PL-production by branded firms see: Kumar and Steenkamp (n 12) 132–146.

(PL-)brands. Issues which may arise at the manufacturing level are derivative of the *brands* competing, not the other way around.

New emerging business model: collaborative differentiation

That said, there is an alternative, new business model emerging in the groceries industry. One of the reasons why PLs have grown to be so important is that they help retailers to differentiate themselves from one another.[56] Retailers who all sell the same branded products, can, for those products, essentially only compete on price. Some stock a wider range of products than their competitors. This and higher service levels add to their differentiation. To the extent that the assortment is similar, however, retailers can only compete on price, which is why they use PLs as a differentiating tool.

Collaborative differentiation is another way of achieving pro-competitive differentiation between retailers. The essence of co-differentiation is captured as follows in an article describing the case of Seven-Eleven Japan (SEJ):

> Unlike most other retailers, who have focused on the development of private brand products, SEJ collaborates with national brand manufacturers to develop new products that are sold under the manufacturers' brand names—though only at SEJ stores. . . . SEJ's approach to innovate goes beyond the product itself to include the product's supply chain and sales processes. This combination of approaches means that SEJ can differentiate its customer offering in a way which its competitors find very hard to copy.[57]

The article describes a number of other, highly successful examples. The technique also emerged in Europe. It is based in part on consumer and shopper segmentation.[58] Modern shopper research has generated insights into why shoppers buy which products at which stores on which occasions. Different shopping occasions generate different shopper behaviour, even of the same person. Likewise, retailers attract shoppers for different reasons or even for different products, and therefore they each have a specific shopper segment profile. Research in these areas delivers new insights, and co-differentiation makes it possible for branded firms to develop specific products which precisely fit the characteristics of the shoppers and shopping occasions at each retailer he works with.

Like retailers can and do engage in co-differentiation at the same time with different branded firms for different products, branded firms also work with

---

56 See also: Kumar and Steenkamp (n 12) 118–120.

57 H Matsuo and S Ogawa, 'Innovating Innovation: The Case of Seven-Eleven Japan' [2007] 7 *ECR Journal: International Commerce Review* 104.

58 S Schaafsma and J Hofstetter, 'Raising the Game to a New Level' [2005] 5 *ECR Journal: International Commerce Review* 66–69.

different retailers at the same time, each in respect of products (or variants of products) which are important to their respective profiles. The exclusivity of products can last for a number of years, but it can also be shorter.[59]

G. Retailers Set Consumer Prices of All Products

Risks of private label/retailer strategic pricing behaviour

I will now move on to my last topic of PL/brands competition: in-store pricing. In their article on this topic Olbrich and Buhr summarize their findings as follows:

> This paper shows that the competitive chances of private labels in comparison with the industry's branded goods are considerably different and very much favour private labels. In its core this phenomenon is rooted in the prohibition of resale price maintenance which weakens the industry's set of pricing policy instruments and which in return has practically helped the pricing policy options for private labels to come to full flower.[60]

Olbrich and Buhr explain why PLs are subject to less competition than branded goods. Inside stores branded goods face competition from each other as well as from PLs. PLs for their part, of course, also face competition from branded goods, at least from those which the retailer chooses to stock (after all, retailers do pick their own in-store competitors). However, PLs do not face in-store competition from *other* PLs. Because competition *between* PLs only takes place at the level of competition between different retailers and their banners, PLs do not among each other face intra-store interbrand competition.

Second, again because PLs are only present in retailers' own stores, PLs do not face *intrabrand* competition either. This is again contrary to branded products, where intrabrand competition results from the very fact that brands are present in shops of different retailers who compete with one another.

Moving on to the pricing issue, retailers determine in-store consumer prices of own-label and branded products. This creates a risk of strategic pricing behaviour

59 Kumar and Steenkamp (n 12) 157–160 describe a number of successful examples (though they do not use the expression 'co-differentiation') and recommend: 'Rather than developing exclusive brands, we believe it is preferable for manufacturers to offer dedicated SKUs consistent with the individual retailer's strategy.' This may also provide an answer to introducing branded products at LADs, resulting in incremental brand sales volume, rather than diverting volume away from other retailers (163–164).

60 R Olbrich and C C Buhr, 'Who Benefits from the Prohibition of Resale Price Maintenance in European Competition Law?—The Case of Food Retailing' [2005] 26 *European Competition Law Review* 705.

and retailers' pricing decisions can be a source of distortion. Olbrich and Buhr describe this risk of manipulation.

Retailers can set artificially high prices for branded goods: 'umbrella pricing' makes PL more price-attractive to consumers.[61] This could, in principle, be dealt with since maximum resale prices have been allowed in the (2000) vertical restraints block exemption and guidelines.

However, retailers also offer branded goods at extremely low prices, even below purchase price, particularly for 'traffic building' purposes: to attract shoppers. 'Traffic-building by loss-leading' can, however, have a devastating effect on the brand. Let me explain why.

Why brands are affected by (extremely) low pricing

First and foremost, branded firms develop differentiated assortments of products, each with their own 'positioning', including price-point positioning. In terms of price positioning: budget, standard, and premium-positionings are common. Branded firms develop assortments along these and other criteria. Via advertising and other means they communicate their products positionings directly to the consumer. Branded firms have a legitimate interest that carefully developed positionings are not destroyed and that a premium positioning does not, because of the retailer's in-store pricing, change into a *de-facto* budget image.

In the fashion industry one can imagine that the goodwill of Gucci and Louis Vuitton brands could be severely damaged if these goods could regularly be bought at heavily discounted prices. Likewise significant brand value can be destroyed in the branded groceries industry. Olbrich and Buhr: 'a uniform market appearance of a product is an important factor for its success on the market and the price is a significant component of this market appearance'.[62]

Second, low in-store pricing of branded products affects not only their positioning, but eventually also their sales/turnover. This is not obvious, because one would expect low in-store prices to generate higher in-store turnover. This may indeed be true for sales to (and by) the loss-leading retailer (provided he keeps sufficient stock). However, other retailers may not be willing or indeed be able to meet this extremely low price. In that case, they will delist the product. This way branded manufacturers of loss-leading products are exposed to significant loss of turnover.

---

[61] Cf Kumar and Steenkamp (n 12) 104: 'sometimes retailers disfavour manufacturer brands that they imitate by charging higher prices, while lowering the price of manufacturer brands that they do not imitate.'

[62] Olbrich and Buhr (n 60) 712. See also quote from Zachariah Chafee in: F Alese, 'Unmasking the Masquerade of Vertical Price Fixing' [2007] 28 *European Competition Law Review* 514, 515.

Traffic-building by loss-leading is in fact another way to free-ride on goodwill and investments of brands. Retailers make use of the name and fame of brands to attract shoppers. The losses on those products are earned back on other products (including PLs). By offering brands at below-value prices, goodwill value is affected both in terms of brand positioning and because of delisting by other retailers.

The US Leegin case: resale price maintenance now subject to rule-of-reason

The recent break-through decision of the US Supreme Court in the *Leegin* case replaced the rule of *per se* illegality of minimum resale price agreements under US antitrust law by the rule-of-reason, requiring assessment of economic effects of this practice.[63] Put very briefly the Supreme Court found that:

- price-related vertical restraints are no different from non-price-related vertical restraints;
- resale price maintenance (RPM) stimulates *inter*brand competition by reducing *intra*brand competition, and it can encourage retailers to invest in services or promotional efforts (other retailers, when discounting, could free-ride on the investments of the higher priced retailer);
- there are other legitimate means to reach the same result;[64] and
- the latter might lead to inefficient vertical integration that might otherwise not take place (and which in turn even eliminates *all* intrabrand competition).

RPM has *potential* downsides too, which of course have to be monitored carefully. On balance, however, the Supreme Court held that there are ample pro-competitive rationales to allow the rule-of-reason.

An often-heard objection to RPM is that it will produce an upwards pricing effect in the market, suggesting that the price will go above the competitive level. However, as the Supreme Court specifically reasoned, where markets are competitive there is no reason to assume that branded firms would set the minimum resale price above the competitive level. That would make competitors step up their effort to steal volume from the highly-priced product. Indeed the Supreme Court held that even where RPM leads to less *intra*brand competition, it increases *inter*brand competition.

---

63 *Leegin Creative Leather Products Inc vs PSKS Inc* 551 US__(2007). Alese (n 62) was under publication in March 2007 when the law changed in the US. The article argues in favour of the position ultimately taken in the *Leegin* decision. M Kneepkens, 'Resale Price Maintenance: Economics Call for a More Balanced Approach' [2007] 28 *European Competition Law Review* 656 also argues in favour of adopting the new economic US approach in Europe.

64 Consider: retailer as agent, 'shop-in-shop', practically selective distribution, and franchising go a long way. Unilateral RPM-policy was already allowed in US law.

To borrow another thought from Olbrich and Buhr, if fixed resale prices were allowed, pricing competition between branded firms 'would also be promoted, because the industry could then advertise a defined price which is contractually agreed with the retailers'.[65]

Another usual objection against RPM is that it would keep out discounters. For the grocery industry it is clear that this is no issue. LADs (e.g. Lidl and Aldi) have established themselves firmly across Europe, entirely on the basis of their own-label assortment. This does confirm that PL takes an important position in Europe and is a significant and effective competitive constraint on the market as a whole and on brands in particular. The risk that RPM by branded firms would either stop discounters coming in, or would lead to a super-competitive price level in Europe and its Member States, is negligible. This unfounded fear does not justify a continued *per se/hard-core* prohibition of RPM. As the Supreme Court found, RPM is no different from other vertical restraints and should be judged on that basis.

How about Europe?

It would be good if RPM were treated the same way as other vertical restraints: block exempt up to 30 per cent market share. When judging pro- and anti-competitive market shares above 30 per cent, the PL situation might be relevant for two reasons:

- it would at least remove one source of potential distortion of competition between brands and own-label;
- PLs will keep brands from pricing above the competitive level anyway; the larger the share of PLs, the more a competitive constraint PLs will be.

In 1997 the US Supreme Court had already replaced the rule of *per se* illegality of *maximum* RPM by the rule-of-reason. Europe followed in 2000 with its more economic vertical restraints regulation and guidelines. These are due for renewal by 2010 and we could draw inspiration from the US again. Minimum RPM would allow an increase of in-store competition between branded and own-label goods, and it would allow branded firms to advertise pricing of their respective products.

Increase of head-on in-store interbrand competition—who would not be in favour?

[65] Olbrich and Buhr (n 60) 711. At p 712 they explain that it 'is by no means undisputed in academic discussion' that the prohibition of RPM 'leads to an increase of welfare'. It might often be the opposite.

H. Conclusion

The role of retailing is to make a choice of products available to consumers. Retailers are gatekeepers to consumers: without sufficient access to retail outlets, products will not reach the consumer. In addition to branded products, retailers increasingly stock own-label products (PL). PLs are fast becoming the largest in-store competitor of branded products.

The combined customer-competitor role brings about risks of reduced and distorted competition between independent brands on the one hand and PLs on the other. There is also an increasing risk of reduced in-store interbrand competition.

This chapter reviewed a range of variables which affect the nature of retail competition. These include, among other things, the asymmetry of information (insider knowledge, acquired as customer, provides retailers with a strategic advantage in the competition between their PLs and independent brands), the retailers' control of access to consumers, pricing, and their control over in-store positioning of branded and own-label products.

Other areas of 'asymmetry' include retailers' lower risks when introducing PL products, room to free-ride on the success and goodwill of independent brands, and PL's 'immunity' from delisting.

As to pricing, there is a reasonable case for saying that, in the interest of interbrand competition, resale price maintenance should be treated the same way as other vertical restraints and that, like in the US, the rule of *per se* illegality of minimum resale price agreements should be replaced by a rule-of-reason type of approach.

Overall the trend is that retailers increasingly champion their PLs, with the risk of compromising their function as efficient gatekeepers to final consumers. Looking at retailer mergers (both national and cross-border), substantial lessening of competition may well occur when retailers' market shares are well below traditional dominance. With increased concentration of the retail, these concerns are worthy of recognition by competition authorities in the interest of interbrand competition.

10

MISLEADING PACKAGING, COPYCATS, AND LOOK-ALIKES: AN UNFAIR COMMERCIAL PRACTICE?

*Ulf Bernitz**

A. Introduction

Private brands, i.e. retailers own-label products, play a particularly great role in the UK grocery trade[1] and constitute a widespread practice in Western Europe. Private brands are sometimes strong brands in their own right having distinct and well-known features and not likely to cause confusion with other brands in

* Director, The Wallenberg Foundation Oxford/Stockholm Association in European Law, Institute of European and Comparative Law, University of Oxford. Professor of European Law at Stockholm University

1 According to the UK Competition Commission, 'The Supply of Groceries in the UK Market Investigation' (Final Report) app 9.10: 'Own-Label Goods' (30 April 2008) <http://www.competition-commission.org.uk/rep_pub/reports/2008/fulltext/538_9_10.pdf> accessed 2 June 2008, sales of own-label food and drink in the UK in 2006 were an estimated £30.0 billion, representing more than one-third of total food and drink sales.

the market, such as leading brands of the manufacturers. However, the realities are often different. It is the practice of many retailers, partially including major retail chains, to market private labels carrying trade symbols and packaging which bear strong resemblance to those used for well-known branded products, often leading brands. The private labels might be of inferior quality, although this does not have to be the case,[2] and are normally sold at a lower price. The practice is by no means special for the UK but well known also in other EU countries and to a certain extent also in the US.

In general terms, these types of private brands (private labels) constitute imitations. They are also designated as look-alike products, shorter look-alikes, or copycats. The latter term has a somewhat pejorative connotation but has become widely used. In the following I will use the terms *copycat* and *look-alike*. Copycat normally indicates a deliberate imitation, while look-alike points at the factual similarity between the trade marks and/or packaging used. However, largely the terms cover the same realities.

For the brand owner, imitations of this sort can cause serious problems.[3] The marketing of the imitations might have negative effects on the goodwill of the brand and might reduce sales volumes. Copycats and look-alikes also cause problems for the consumers. They will normally not be properly informed about who the producer is and will often either be misled to believe the look-alike is the original brand or made to believe it has the same origin as that brand or some commercial connection to the producer of the latter.

From a legal point of view, trade mark law constitutes the basis. However, trade mark protection is often not broad enough to catch the use of copycats and look-alikes. They often avoid being so confusingly similar that they would constitute trade mark infringement. In this regard, it is of fundamental importance to which extent there exist principles of unfair competition law suitable to the problems. On this point, the law is far from uniform. The possibility of taking successful legal action against the practice seems to be particularly restricted in the UK; English law on passing off tends to require proof of actual misleading. In other countries, e.g. Germany and the Nordic countries, unfair competition or marketing law offers wider possibilities for successful legal action in these kind of cases.

---

[2] To a certain extent, major brand manufacturers also manufacture the products sold under retailers own-labels.

[3] A Gorrie, 'Competition between Branded and Private Label Goods. Do Competition Concerns Arise When a Customer is also a Competitor?' [2006] *European Competition Law Review* 217. See also: P Kuipers, 'Retailer and Private Labels: Asymmetry of Information, In-store Competition, and the Control of Shelf Space', Chapter 9 herein.

However, the recent EC Directive 2005/29 on Unfair Commercial Practices has changed the basic legal perspective substantially.[4] Misleading packaging is one of the issues the Directive is addressing specifically. In the following, I will discuss the Unfair Commercial Practices Directive and its importance for the possibility of curbing private labels in the form of copycats and look-alikes. The objective of the Directive is no less than full harmonization of the law of the EU Member States in the area of unfair commercial practices.

However, before discussing the scope of the Directive (Section D) and its applicability to copycats and look-alikes (Section E), it seems appropriate to present in short what are the major functions of trade marks and brands from a legal perspective (Section B) and the different types of legislation on unfair competition related to imitations (Section C).

B. The Major Functions of Trade Marks and Brands

In a legal context, one normally distinguishes between the terms trade mark and brand. *Trade mark* is the legal term, used in legislation and legal practice. An undertaking can acquire an exclusive legal right, a kind of property right, to a trade mark, either by registration or by extensive use. *Brand* is primarily a marketing term with a less distinct definition. Many legally protected trade marks have only little economic value, sometimes a trade mark is not even actually in use. The term brand seems to be used primarily to connote trade marks of a more significant economic value used as a marketing device. However, there are no sharp distinctions, to a large extent the terms trade mark and brand are used synonymously. However, when dealing with the legal protection of marks, the term trade mark should be preferred as having a distinct legal meaning.

The primary function of trade marks is to enable undertakings to individualize goods and/or services supplied by that business.[5] Thus, the interests underlying

---

4 Directive 2005/29/EC of the European Parliament and of the Council of 11 May 2005 Concerning Unfair Business-to-consumer Commercial Practices in the Internal Market and Amending Council Directive 84/450/EEC, Directives 97/7/EC, 98/27/EC and 2002/65/EC of the European Parliament and of the Council, and Regulation (EC) No 2006/2004 of the European Parliament and of the Council [2005] OJ L149/22 (Unfair Commercial Practices Directive). V Marsland, 'Unfair Commercial Practices: Stamping out Misleading Packaging' in S Weatherill and U Bernitz (eds), *The Regulation of Unfair Commercial Practices under EC Directive 2005/29: New Rules and New Techniques* (2007) 191.

5 On the function of the trade mark system, see: J Phillips, *Trade Mark Law: A Practical Anatomy* (2003) ch 2 and A Gowers, 'The Gowers Review of Intellectual Property' (December 2006) <http://www.hm-treasury.gov.uk/media/6/E/pbr06_gowers_report_755.pdf> accessed 1 July 2008.

the protection of trade marks are primarily the interests of the proprietor of the mark in protecting that which individualizes and distinguishes his goods or services. However, it is also in the interest of society at large, consumers, and other undertakings that goods and services supplied by a particular undertaking are individualized. Modern techniques of advertising and marketing would be almost inconceivable if it would not be possible to distinguish goods and services from different sources in this fashion. Selling of anonymous goods is rare nowadays; fruit and vegetables being somewhat of an exception.

As follows from what has been said, trade marks fulfil an important communication function by enabling consumers to identify goods or services sought. Without being able to rely on trade marks, the consumers' search for the goods and services he or she is looking for would be much more difficult, if at all possible in modern self-service stores. In this way, trade mark protection is also fulfilling important competition-enhancing functions. Closely related is the guarantee function of the trade mark.[6] In order to secure the competitive and informational functions, it is strongly in the interest of the trade mark owner to maintain the product's homogeneous quality and general standard. For the owners of well-known brands, this is particularly so. In addition, the trade mark often functions as a vehicle for the undertaking's legal liability for its products, e.g. tort liability for damage caused by goods to which the mark has been attached.[7]

However, trade marks do not only individualize products coming from different undertakings but also differentiate the products in the eyes of the consumer. It is generally acknowledged that consumers, through the influence of advertising, often prefer goods or services marketed under well-known trade marks to similar products which are objectively of approximately the same standard and quality (e.g. prestige trade marks for clothing). Advertising and other marketing

---

6 The importance of the guarantee function is stressed by the European Court of Justice in the Arsenal case, in which the court stated:

> the essential function of a trade mark is to guarantee the identity of origin of the marked goods or services to the consumer or end user by enabling him, without any possibility of confusion, to distinguish the goods or services from others which have another origin. For the trade mark to be able to fulfill its essential role in the system of undistorted competition which the Treaty seeks to establish and maintain, it must offer a guarantee that all the goods and services bearing it have been manufactured or supplied under the control of a single undertaking which is responsible for their quality', Case C-206/01 *Arsenal Football Club plc v Matthew Reed* [2002] ECR I-10273 para 48.

7 Council Directive 85/374/EEC of 25 July 1985 on the Approximation of the Laws, Regulations and Administrative Provisions of the Member States concerning Liability for Defective Products [1985] OJ L210/29, art 3.

activities are often aimed at establishing or enhancing trade mark preferences amongst consumers. This mechanism of trade mark differentiation functions as a key element to the establishment of successful brands. Such well-known brands might enjoy a somewhat secured market position, often allowing the maintenance of a higher price level than objectively similar but less known competing products.

The *goodwill* attached to well-known brands often has a very significant economic value and might even constitute an undertaking's most important asset. The legal basis of the value of the goodwill is primarily the trade mark owner's exclusive right in the trade mark. The goodwill may be exploited by the owner or his affiliated companies themselves or through trade mark licences and can also be assigned to others. Particularly well-known examples are the trade marks Coca-Cola and Coke which, together with their protected get-up, probably constitute the Coca-Cola Company's most valuable assets which, as such, are licensed to the manufacturers of soft drinks the world over, in conjunction with the sale of the drink extract. The good-will of well-known trade marks can also be exploited in a wider sense, through the licensing of the trade-mark to companies in other branches of industry for use in relation to other goods or services where the trade mark's image is regarded as appealing. This is known as brand stretching or logo licensing. Examples are trade marks for clothing also used for perfumes or vice versa.

If we look against this background at private labels having the character of copycats and look-alikes, the problems are evident. The private labels might imply a misuse of the information, communication, and guarantee functions of the trade mark by misleading consumers to believe the products are those of the owner of the original brand or have some other kind of commercial relation to that brand. In addition, the marketing of a look-alike involves an element of appropriation of the goodwill attached to the original, in other words a 'free ride' on the cost expended by the manufacturer of the original in development and marketing of the imitated symbol(s). The practice might cause a decrease in the value of the goodwill of the brand by reducing its image or prestige. If copycats are of poor quality and/or sold in premises of a less attractive character, the practice might be a real threat to the goodwill of the original.

C. Unfair Competition Law and Passing Off

The exclusive right to a trade mark is generally only affording protection in relation to undertakings in the same or a similar branch and to marketing of goods and services of the same or a similar type using a confusingly similar, distinctive symbol.[8] As a general rule, it is free for everyone to copy or reproduce marks and packaging which do not enjoy trade mark protection. However, imitations which do not infringe trade mark rights or other intellectual property rights might constitute an unfair commercial practice, also characterized as acts of unfair competition.

Unfair competition is covered by the Paris Convention for the Protection of Industrial Property, the major international treaty on industrial property rights, originally of 1883 and revised many times. This Paris Convention has a nearly worldwide coverage, including the EU Member States and the US. According to Article 10bis of the Convention, there is an overall obligation to 'assure effective protection' to nationals of participating companies against unfair competition. Unfair competition includes 'any act of competition contrary to honest practices in industrial and commercial matters'. There follows in Article 10bis a list of prohibited acts, which include:

1. All acts of such a nature as to create confusion by any means whatever with the establishment, the goods, or the industrial or commercial activities of a competitor.

The obligations under the Paris Convention have been reaffirmed, much more recently, by the TRIPs Agreement[9] of 1994. This international agreement is also of a nearly universal character, including the EU countries and the US. It is stated explicitly in Article 2.1 of TRIPs that Members shall comply with Article 10bis of the Paris Convention.[10]

These international treaty obligations indicate clearly that the intellectual property protection of trade marks is intended to be supplemented by protection against acts of unfair competition, amongst those acts such acts that create confusion with the goods of a competitor.

---

[8] The First Council Directive 89/104/EEC of 21 December 1988 to Approximate the Law of the Member States Relating to Trade Marks states in art 5 (1):

'The registered trade mark shall confer on the proprietor exclusive rights therein. The proprietor shall be entitled to prevent all third parties not having his consent from using in the course of trade:

(a) any sign which is identical with the trade mark in relation to goods or services which are identical with those for which the trade mark is registered;
(b) any sign where, because of its identity with, or similarity to, the trade mark and the identity or similarity of the goods or services covered by the trade mark and the sign, there exists a likelihood of confusion on the part of the public, which includes the likelihood of association between the sign and the trade mark.'

[9] Agreement on the Trade Related Aspects of Intellectual Property Rights.

[10] C Correa, *Trade Related Aspects of Intellectual Property Rights: A Commentary on the TRIPS Agreement* (2007), 44.

In most of continental Europe, Germany being the primary example, slavish copying can be prohibited by the courts as a type of act constituting unfair competition. It is usually necessary to establish that there is a danger of the original being confused with the copy. The primary sanction is normally an injunction against continued use of the copying. Damages may also be claimed. In the Nordic countries, similar results can be reached on the basis of the legislation on marketing practices.[11]

In the common law countries, the concept of unfair competition has never become firmly established. In England there has not developed any coherent legal principle of unfair competition and existing consumer legislation on unfair practices is scattered and lacking systematization.[12] Of particular relevance is the tort of *passing off*. Basically, an action for passing off allows trader A to prevent a competitor B from passing off its products as those of A's.[13] It is the official attitude normally taken that the law on passing off would satisfy the UK's international treaty obligations under the Paris Convention and TRIPs to offer protection supplementing trade mark law against acts creating confusion with the goods of competitors. However, the scope of protection offered in the UK under passing off law is often quite limited, as the courts in most cases take a rather restrictive general attitude and demand proof of actual misrepresentation (normally of the origin of the products) in the individual case. A successful passing off action requires that a party is able to establish goodwill or reputation attached to the goods or service so that it is recognized by the public as distinctive specifically of the products of the party. It also requires that the party is able to demonstrate that there has been a misrepresentation by the other party leading or likely to lead the public to believe the products offered by the other person are those of the party. Finally, the party must show it has suffered damage. This means appropriation of competitor's goodwill connected to the brand or the packaging without causing confusion is normally not contravening the law on passing off. The relatively limited protection available in the UK through the law of passing off, compared to what normally is the state of the law in many other EU countries, in

---

[11] See: A Bakardjieva Engelbrekt, 'An End to Fragmentation? The Unfair Commercial Practices Directive from the Perspective of the New Member States from Central and Eastern Europe' in S Weatherill and U Bernitz (eds), *The Regulation of Unfair Commercial Practices under EC Directive 2005/29: New Rules and New Techniques* (2007) 47, and C Wadlow, 'The Case for Reclaiming European Unfair Competition Law from Europe's Consumer Lawyers' in S Weatherill and U Bernitz (eds), *The Regulation of Unfair Commercial Practices under EC Directive 2005/29: New Rules and New Techniques* (2007) 175.

[12] S Weatherill, *EU Consumer Law and Policy* (2005), 191.

[13] See for an overview of the law of passing off in the UK, e.g. L Bently and B Sherman, *Intellectual Property Law* (2nd edn, 2004) 707 ff; W Cornish and D Llewelyn, *Intellectual Property: Patents, Copyrights, Trademarks and Allied Rights* (6th edn, 2007) 627.

combination with the particularly high concentration of private label in the UK, presents particular problems for brand owners in relation to the use of copycats and look-alikes.

In the UK, a comprehensive government report on the functioning of the intellectual property law and the need for reform was published in 2006, The Gowers Review of Intellectual Property.[14] The Gowers Review includes a section entitled 'Copycat packaging'.[15] Information contained in the Review makes it clear look-alikes, which are generally cheaper than the original branded products, have a very significant economic effect, and this to the detriment of the brand owner whose packaging is imitated. Gowers believes that the law of passing off does not go far enough to protect many brands and designs from misappropriation. It points out the difficulties for brand owners to demonstrate consumer confusion in court, and substantial evidence may be required to bring a successful passing-off action. Also, if copycats appear on the market before the defendant has built up goodwill in a certain appearance, the brand owner cannot rely on the law of passing off. This is especially relevant to smaller producers who are at risk of their designs being copied before they are able to establish a reputation in the marketplace.

The Gowers Report noted in particular the new European Directive on Unfair Commercial Practices, at that time in the process of being transposed into UK law, would tackle practices that mislead or confuse consumers. Gowers recommended the Government to monitor the success of these measures, and, if changes would be found to be ineffective, Government should consult on appropriate changes.[16]

We will now turn to the Unfair Practices Directive and its possible effects in relation to the problem discussed.

D. The EU Unfair Commercial Practices Directive—An Overview

The Unfair Commercial Practices Directive, required to have been implemented by the EU Member States by 12 December 2007, constitutes a major new piece of European legislation.[17] Few directives in the consumer law field have such a

[14] The Gowers Review of Intellectual Property (n 5).

[15] The Gowers Review of Intellectual Property (n 5) ss 5.82–5.88.

[16] C Morcom, 'Gowers: A Glimmer of Hope for UK Compliance with Article 10bis of the Paris Convention' [2007] 29 *European Intellectual Property Review* 125.

[17] Unfair Commercial Practices Directive (n 4). See: J Stuyck, E Terryn, and T van-Dyck, 'Confidence Through Fairness? The New Directive on Unfair Business-to-consumer Practices in the Internal Market' [2006] 43 *Common Market Law Review* 107.

broad scope of application and represent such a high level of legislative ambition, aiming at full harmonization. However, the scope of the Directive is limited to business-to-consumer (B2C) transactions; the consumer being defined as a natural person acting for non-business purposes.[18] Business-to-business-transactions (B2B) have been left out of the Directive[19] and in this area the far less ambitious elder 1984 Directive on Misleading Advertising is continuing to apply, however including a comprehensive addition in 1997 on Comparative Advertising.[20]

This solution has been the object of much criticism. It is in particular contrary to the German concept of a unitary unfair competition law which has been largely accepted in a substantial number of continental EU countries.[21] Historically, the German unfair competition concept has focused on protection against unfair practices in B2B transactions, but it has gradually been widened and the new German Unfair Competition Act of 2004 aims at offering B2B and B2C protection on the same level, balancing conflicting business and consumer interests, when necessary. Also in the Nordic countries the marketing practices legislation comprises both B2B and B2C protection, albeit with a more pronounced emphasis on protection of consumers than has been the case in Germany.

The fairly quick and smooth acceptance of the European Parliament and the Council of the Commission's proposal for such a comprehensive directive is a remarkable achievement. A primary explanation why the Commission was able to succeed so well is probably the decision taken not to follow the model of any particular EU country but to found its proposal for the Directive[22] on a new systematic formation, based on functional considerations fitting the EC law.

18 Unfair Commercial Practices Directive (n 4) art 2 (a).

19 Recital 6 of the Directive states that the Directive neither covers nor affects the national laws on unfair commercial practices which harm only competitors' economic interests or which relate to a transaction between traders.

20 Council Directive 84/450/EEC of 10 September 1984 relating to the Approximation of the Laws, Regulations and Administrative Provisions of the Member States Concerning Misleading Advertising [1984] OJ L250/17 as amended by Directive 97/55/EC of European Parliament and of the Council of 6 October 1997 Amending Directive 84/450/EEC Concerning Misleading Advertising so as to Include Comparative Advertising [1997] OJ L290/18.

21 See in particular on national unfair commercial practices law in the EU Member States R Schulze and H Schulte-Nölke, 'Analysis of National Fairness Laws Aimed at Protecting Consumers in Relation to Commercial Practices' (study for the EU Commission, June 2003) <http://ec.europa.eu/consumers/cons_int/safe_shop/fair_bus_pract/green_pap_comm/studies/unfair_practices_en.pdf> accessed 1 July 2008. The study includes a number of national reports, among them S Weatherill's Report on the UK and my own Report on Sweden. See also, e.g., H Micklitz and J Kessler, *Marketing Practices Regulation and Consumer Protection in the EC Member States and the US* (2002).

22 Commission Proposal for a Council Directive Concerning Unfair Business-to-consumer Commercial Practices in the Internal Market and Amending Directives 84/450/EEC, 97/7/EC and 98/27/EC (the Unfair Commercial Practices Directive) COM (2003) 356 final (18 June 2003) (Proposal).

From this perspective, it was probably wise to limit the Directive's scope to B2C transactions harming consumers' *economic* interests (Article 1), a limitation well in line with its primary harmonization object. Thus, the Directive excludes practices affecting matters of taste and decency where the requirements are said to vary widely between the Member States.[23] By concentrating on the consumer protection aspect, the Directive establishes a strong connection to other consumer law directives, e.g. the E-Commerce Directive[24] and make it part of the quickly developing European consumer law. In addition, by using a new systematic, the Commission was able to adapt its model to the particular needs of removing barriers to cross-border advertising and marketing, thus furthering European integration.

The Directive gives a broad definition of what is a commercial practice, including all types of advertising, marketing, or commercial communication.[25] It requires full harmonization on the basis of Article 95 EC (the functioning of the internal market), aiming at creating a single regulatory framework regulating all aspects of unfair commercial practices across the EU.[26] This is claimed to create a high common level field of consumer protection[27] and eliminate the barriers stemming from the present fragmentation of the rules on unfair commercial practices.[28] Thus, the Directive compels Member States to bring their legislation fully in line with the provisions of the Directive.

In order to reach a result, the Commission had to compromise and drop its original proposal to introduce the country of origin principle into the marketing practices field. The main thrust of the original Green Paper on Commercial Communication in the Internal Market of 1996[29] was the liberalization of commercial communication and promotion of free movement of advertising and marketing services throughout the Community, using the principles of country of origin and mutual recognition as main instruments. This principle was introduced and accepted in the E-Commerce Directive of 2000: 'Member States may not, for reasons falling within the coordinated field, restrict the freedom to provide information services from another Member State'.[30] However, although

23 Unfair Commercial Practices Directive (n 4) Recital 7.

24 Directive 2000/31/EC of the European Parliament and of the Council of 8 June 2000 on Certain Legal Aspects of Information Society Services, in Particular Electronic Commerce, in the Internal Market [2000] OJ L178/1 (Directive on Electronic Commerce).

25 Unfair Commercial Practices Directive (n 4) art 2 (d).

26 Unfair Commercial Practices Directive (n 4) Recital 12.

27 Unfair Commercial Practices Directive (n 4) Recital 11.

28 Unfair Commercial Practices Directive (n 4) Recital 12.

29 Green Paper from the Commission on Commercial Communication in the Internal Market COM (96) 192 final (8 May 1996).

30 E-Commerce Directive (n 24) art 3 (2).

kept in the Green Paper of 2001 on EU Consumer Protection[31] and in the proposed text of the Unfair Practices Directive as first presented, the country of origin-principle stumbled on massive critique from certain Member States wanting to have the possibility of enforcing stricter national standards. As the Directive prescribes total harmonization, there should be no room for such differences except in such cases in which differences could be established between Member States in consumers' perception or understanding of a certain type of marketing practice.[32]

The primary aim of the Directive is liberalization and enhancing open markets. An important factor, explaining the Commission's interest in having the Directive enacted, is the object of achieving deregulation of national unfair competition law in such Member States where the applied standards have been regarded as too strict and restrictive, thus eliminating barriers to the development of the internal market. The primary target in this regard has undoubtedly been the traditionally restrictive German Unfair Competition Act as applied in the case law. The fundamental idea behind the directive is to create a common level playing field throughout the Union for advertising and marketing.

The architecture of the substantive provisions of the Directive is based on a division into four parts:

(I) a general clause prohibiting unfair commercial practices contrary to the requirements of professional diligence, provided the practice is able to distort consumers' economic behaviour (Article 5);

(II) a prohibition on misleading commercial practices, divided into two statutory provisions, one on misleading actions (Article 6) and another on misleading omissions (insufficient information, Article 7);

(III) a prohibition on aggressive commercial practices, likewise divided into two statutory provisions, one directed against the use of aggressive commercial practices (Article 8) and the other against the use of harassment, coercion, and undue influence (Article 9);

(IV) a black list comprising 31 types of commercial practices considered to be prohibited as unfair in all circumstances (Annex I). Thus, the black-listed practices are prohibited *per se* and do not require an assessment in the individual case of their effects.

The prohibited practices described under II to IV are particularly important examples of unfair commercial practices. It seems somewhat unclear to what

31 Green Paper from the Commission on European Union Consumer Protection COM (2001) 531 final (2 October 2001).

32 The architecture of the Directive is analysed in Stuyck, Terryn, and van-Dyck (n 17) 115.

extent the general clause in Article 5 is intended to be independently applicable to practices which fall outside the scope of the specific prohibitions, in particular in relation to cases where the commercial practice would be of a different type. This is probably an issue which has to wait for clarification by the European Court of Justice (ECJ). Primarily, the general clause can be expected to cover practices which are well in line with such practices that fall under any of the two prohibitions on misleading and aggressive practices or the black listed practices but do not fully fit the specific criteria of these provisions. However, it will be perfectly possible for the ECJ to find the general clause applicable to other types of commercial practices regarded as contrary to the requirements of professional diligence, in particular if the court finds the unfairness of the practice to be a widely held view in the EU Member States.

E. Copycats and Look-Alikes under the Directive

When taking a closer look at the provisions of the Directive, the exclusion of B2B relations is not as total as one might be inclined to think. Many marketing practices are unfair both from the viewpoint of the competitors or other business firms and from a consumer protection perspective, albeit often with a somewhat different emphasis in the assessment of the character of the unfairness. Such practices are normally covered by the Directive; the sometimes heard view that the Directive fully disregards B2B transactions is not correct. It is noted in the recitals that unfair advertising, which directly harms consumers' economic interests, indirectly also harms the economic interests of legitimate competitors.[33] This indirect protection of the interests of competitors has different facets. Often, the same advertising or other type of marketing practice is directed to consumers and to other customers, and in such cases national law based on the directive will in effect offer protection covering a broader circle of addresses. Misleading advertising, having consumers as well as commercial purchasers as addresses, is the obvious example. Another aspect is the indirect beneficial effects for those competitors who stick to honest practices. As stated in the recitals, the Directive protects indirectly 'legitimate businesses from their competitors who do not play by the rules in this Directive'.[34]

The object of the Directive to offer, within its general limits of application, protection also of the interests of competitors and the business community in general is demonstrated clearly by the provision that competitors, as well as

33 Unfair Commercial Practices Directive (n 4) Recital 6 first sentence.
34 Unfair Commercial Practices Directive (n 4) Recital 8.

organizations, shall be regarded under national law as having a legitimate interest in combating unfair practices. This shall include the right to take legal action against such practices and to initiate other appropriate legal proceedings.[35] Orders for the cessation of unfair commercial practices shall be available.[36] The wording and structure of the Directive does not support the proposition it would be sufficient to offer competitors the possibility of submitting claims to administrative authorities in charge of consumer protection. I will come back to this issue in relation to the UK implementation of the Directive.

There are certain practices, explicitly included in the Directive, which have a particularly strong link to the interests of competitors and which might be regarded as inclusions of protection of unfair B2B practices in the Directive. Thus, the use of brands, trade-names, packaging, etc. which are misleading the average consumer about the commercial origin of the products and causing him or her to purchase the products on the basis of that misconception (passing off in a general sense) is covered by the Directive.[37] The black list includes as a prohibited practice the promotion of a product similar to a product made by a particular manufacturer in such a manner as deliberately to mislead the consumer into believing that the product is made by the same manufacturer when it is not.[38] Obviously, the Directive includes the packaging (get-up) of products. Of particular practical importance would be misleading advertising or misleading exposure of products or their packaging in sales outlets causing consumers to purchase look-alikes.

The standard of assessment is touched upon in one of the recitals which declares it is not the intention of the Directive to reduce consumer choice by prohibiting the promotion of products which look similar to other products unless this similarity confuses consumers as to the commercial origin of the product and is therefore misleading.[39] This recital can be read as a pronouncement in favour of a rather restrictive view on the scope of protection offered, indicating the priority of consumer perception and thus possibly reducing the application of the Directive to instances of clear deception of consumers looking for a particular

35 Unfair Commercial Practices Directive (n 4) art 11 ('Enforcement'). Recital 21 first sentence has to be understood in the light of the text of the Directive itself.

36 Unfair Commercial Practices Directive (n 4) art 11 (2) (a).

37 See, in particular, Unfair Commercial Practices Directive (n 4) art 6 (2) (a) which comprises 'any marketing of a product, including comparative advertising, which creates confusion with any products, trade marks, trade names or other distinguishing marks of a competitor'. See also art 6 (1) (b), referring to misleading information about commercial origin of a product.

38 Unfair Commercial Practices Directive (n 4) Recital 13. This black list rule seems to be similar to the requirements for passing off under English law.

39 Unfair Commercial Practices Directive (n 4) Recital 14.

brand or the like. This would be more in line with the rather restrictive view on passing-off prevailing in English law than with the elaborate German case law. In this much observed and economically important area, it will be the task of the ECJ to clarify and develop the legal standards to be applied. Most likely, the ECJ will use its present trade mark law jurisprudence on confusion and deception as an important point of departure.

Misleading use of attributes and misrepresentations about geographical origin, connections to other undertakings, ownership of intellectual property rights, etc., constitute typical examples of unfair B2B practices.[40] However, they are also misleading consumers and fall under the Directive as long as they are contrary to the standards laid down in the Directive of what is misleading to the consumer and having an economic effect.

When assessing whether a commercial practice is misleading or not, *the average consumer* will function as the benchmark. On this point, the case law already established by the ECJ will constitute the basis. This case law is characterized by a free competition approach and a reaction against the German case law on unfair competition, which the ECJ seems to regard as too far-reaching and protective.

An illustrative European case about labelling is the *Estée Lauder* case.[41] A company was labelling a firming cream, marketed in different countries, as 'lifting'. The Estée Lauder Cosmetics Company argued before a German court that the use of the term 'lifting' was misleading because it gave the impression that the use of the firming cream would obtain results identical or comparable to surgical lifting. The ECJ, asked for a preliminary ruling, was obviously not impressed by the argument and stated, citing in particular another well-known case in the same field, *Gut Springenheide*:[42]

> . . . when it has fallen to the Court, in the context of the interpretation of Directive 84/450 [on misleading advertising] to weigh the risk of misleading consumers against the requirements of the free movement of goods, it has held that, in order to determine whether a particular description, trade mark or promotional description is misleading, it is necessary to take into account the presumed expectations of an average consumer who is reasonably well informed and reasonably observant and circumspect.[43]

The ECJ continued:

> Although, at first sight, the average consumer—reasonably well informed and reasonably observant and circumspect—ought not to expect a cream whose name

40 Unfair Commercial Practices Directive (n 4) art 6 (1).
41 Case C-220/98 *Estée Lauder Cosmetics v Lancaster Group* [2000] ECR I-117.
42 Case C-210/96 *Gut Springenheide and Tusky* [1998] ECR I-4657.
43 *Estée Lauder Cosmetics* (n 41) para 27.

> incorporates the term 'lifting' to produce enduring effects, it nevertheless remains for the national court to determine, in the light of all the relevant factors, whether that is the position in the case.[44]

Another example, among rather many, is the *Hartlauer* case[45] on comparative price advertising. This case is about the interpretation of the provisions on comparative advertising which were made part of the Misleading Advertising Directive in 1997 and which will continue to be in force also in relation to B2C advertising. The *Hartlauer* Company, a well-known price-cutter marketing spectacles in Austria, had made a direct price comparison with spectacles sold by the Pippig Company at a much higher price. Without going into the details, the ECJ, asked by the Austrian court for a preliminary ruling, basically accepted the type of comparative advertising at issue and underlined Member States were precluded from applying stricter standards as far as the form and content of the comparison was concerned. Referring to the *Estée Lauder* case, the ECJ noted the national court should take into account the presumed expectations of an average consumer who is reasonably well informed and reasonably observant and circumspect.

Characteristic for the cases mentioned, and many others, is the pro-competition approach taken by the ECJ and its policy not to apply too strict a standard when assessing whether or not consumers are likely to be misled.

These basic features of the case law have been carried forward into the new Directive which is referring to the average consumer as benchmark. The general clause on unfair commercial practices and the prohibitions in the Directive on misleading and aggressive practices all refer to the average consumer as the person likely to be mislead, having his freedom of choice restricted etc.[46] The recitals are referring to the notional, typical consumer and the benchmark is described as:

> The average consumer, who is reasonably well-informed and reasonably observant and circumspect, taken into account social, cultural and linguistic factors, as interpreted by the Court of Justice.[47]

As is explicitly stated in the recitals, the average consumer test is not a statistical test. National courts and authorities will have to exercise their own faculty of judgment to determine the typical reaction of the average consumer.[48] The ECJ has taken a reserved attitude towards statistical market surveys as evidence in the

44 *Estée Lauder Cosmetics* (n 41) para 30.
45 Case C-44/01 *Pippig Augenoptik v Hartlauer Handelsgesellschaft et al* [2003] ECR I-3095.
46 See: Unfair Commercial Practices Directive (n 4) arts 5 (2) (b), 6 (1) and 8.
47 Unfair Commercial Practices Directive (n 4) Recital 18.
48 Unfair Commercial Practices Directive (n 4) Recital 18.

Gut Springenheide and *Estée Lauder* judgments and the Directive confirms this sceptical position.

Normally, the traders carry the burden of proof as to the accuracy of factual claims they have made.[49] However, it is for national law and courts to determine where to place this burden and it is to be expected that differences between national procedural law in the Member States will have an impact on this issue.

Further, in order to curb over-excessive use of fairness standards in Europe, e.g. in Germany, the Directive requires material distortion of consumer economic behaviour as a prerequisite for considering a commercial practice to be unfair.[50] This requirement of commercial effect functions as a threshold and constitutes a *de minimis* rule. It requires a commercial practice to cause or be likely to cause the average consumer to take a transactional decision he would not have taken otherwise.[51] The requirement excludes misleading representations of an irrelevant or petty character. The material distortion requirement is applicable also to omission of relevant information. According to the text of the Directive, omission of information is prohibited only if the omission causes or is likely to cause the average consumer to take a transactional decision he would not have taken otherwise.[52]

Taking a tolerant position, the text of the Directive talks explicitly about:

> The common and legitimate advertising practice of making exaggerated statements or statements which are not meant to be taken literally.[53]

What does this mean for the protection of brand owners against copycats and look-alikes? As mentioned, the primary ambition of the Directive is to establish a European standard which would make it possible for companies to follow only one set of EU rules when branding, packaging, and marketing goods and services in the EU Member States. It will take time to get this standard fully established in practice. However, the text of the Directive and the already existing ECJ case law has drawn up the major principles. The main thrust of this case law is pro-competition and consumer orientation. Commercial practices are assessed based on their effects on consumers rather than competitors. The benchmark is the average consumer, 'reasonably observant and circumspect' to quote the often used phrase of the ECJ. The use of copycats and look-alikes does not constitute unfair commercial practice as such; an element of misleading seems to be required.

---

49 Unfair Commercial Practices Directive (n 4) Recital 21.
50 Unfair Commercial Practices Directive (n 4) art 5 (2) (b).
51 Unfair Commercial Practices Directive (n 4) art 6 (1).
52 Unfair Commercial Practices Directive (n 4) art 7 (1).
53 Unfair Commercial Practices Directive (n 4) art 5 (3) *in fine*.

F. A Critical Assessment

In 2008, the Competition Commission in the UK published a major report, The Groceries Market Investigation.[54] The Commission found that, in many important respects, competition in the UK groceries industry is effective and delivers good outcomes for consumers. However, the Commission had concerns in two principal areas. Several grocery retailers were found to have strong positions in a number of local markets. The transfer of excessive risk and unexpected costs by grocery retailers to their suppliers through various chain practices would have an adverse effect, if unchecked.[55]

The Commission also studied the importance of own-label goods and copycat packaging. Here, the Commission came to different conclusions from the Gowers Report, discussed in Section C, above. The Commission noted copycat packaging might induce consumers mistakenly to purchase own-label products or assume that the own-label good has the same reputation as a branded product. The Commission also noted that where own-label packaging is similar to that of branded products it will simulate own-label success. However, the Commission draw the conclusion that packaging on its own is unlikely to provide a sustained basis for the success of an own-label product when competing with a branded product. Over time customers are able to distinguish copycat packaging for any particular product. The Commission found any sustained negative effect on branded goods unlikely to be the result of copycat packaging.[56]

This approach does not seem acceptable. It is based on the idea that consumers will probably learn the hard way, by their own mistakes, to distinguish copycats from the original branded products. Supposing this is correct, the Commission finds the copycats harmless. However, this approach is definitely not in line with the Unfair Commercial Practices Directive, discussed in Sections D and E, above. The Directive is based on the idea consumers should be correctly informed in order to be able to take well-considered decisions as purchasers. Misleading practices related to the marketing of copycats and look-alikes are explicitly covered by the Directive. As was clarified above, although the Directive is aiming primarily at consumer protection, it also offers brand owners (as well as all other undertakings) protection against misleading practices. The opinion of the Competition Commission that a certain amount of deception of consumers can be tolerated because it might not be

54 The Groceries Market Investigation Final Report (n 1).

55 The Groceries Market Investigation Final Report (n 1), summary of the Report, paras 2–3.

56 Appendix 9.10 of the Report (n 1) para 19.

harmful in a broader economic perspective is based on different perceptions than those which have now become accepted all over the EU.

The Unfair Commercial Practices Directive should by now have been implemented in all EU Member States. In the UK it was transposed into the Consumer Protection from Unfair Trading Regulations 2008, which came into force on 26 May 2008.[57] The new UK Regulation closely follows the text of the Directive; contrary to what is the case in many or most other EU countries it has not been integrated into a more comprehensive statute on consumer protection or marketing practices, and certainly not in a German type of unfair competition statute. A particular feature of the UK Regulation is the treatment of the enforcement issue. The Regulation only includes rules on public enforcement by government agencies or officers.[58] In practice, the enforcement will primarily be the task of the Office of Fair Trading (OFT) and the Trading Standards Authorities. It is not likely they will pay particular attention to the marketing of copycats and look-alikes. In short, the UK has chosen a minimalistic approach to the implementation of the Directive.[59]

As mentioned above, competitors as well as private organizations shall have the right under the Directive to take legal actions against unfair commercial practices in court or bring such actions before an administrative authority competent to take actions. Contrary to most other EU countries, Ireland included, the UK has chosen only to permit the latter type of private activity. It seems doubtful that this will be found to be a sustainable solution in a somewhat longer perspective.

There is a strong case for a fairly uniform application of unfair commercial practices law throughout the EU. Advertising and other marketing activities, e.g. advertising campaigns, are increasingly run cross-borders. As was proposed in the Green Papers mentioned in section D above, it is the ambition for commercial communication to meet the standards of its EU country of origin and the EU Directives should be considered acceptable all over the EU without having to satisfy additional or different national restrictions. This idea will in all probability be the loadstar of the case law due to develop during the coming years on the basis of the new Directive, based as it is on the principle of full harmonization. Thus, we will see the emergence of a more uniform European approach to marketing practices, including copycats and look-alikes. In all likelihood, the new European case law, based on the provisions of the Directive, will be less permissive towards copycats and look-alikes than the present UK approach, but, on the other hand, it might very well be less restrictive than the present German unfair competition law.

57 Available on <http://www.oft.gov.uk>.
58 The Consumer Protection from Unfair Trading Regulations 2008, Part 4, s 19.
59 On the legal remedies in the UK, Marsland (n 4) 194.

11

PRIVATE LABELS, PRODUCT VARIETY, AND PRICE COMPETITION—LESSONS FROM THE GERMAN GROCERY SECTOR

*Rainer Olbrich, Gundula Grewe, and Ruth Orenstrat**

* University of Hagen, Germany. The authors are grateful to Information Resources GmbH (IRI) which provided scanning data for this study.

A. Introduction

For several years now, a proliferation of private labels has been evident in European consumer goods retailing. A 'hotbed' for the proliferation of private labels has been created by the restriction on vertical price fixing under Article 81 EC. The prohibition of resale price maintenance has restricted the pricing policy tools available to manufacturers and has, in its wake, considerably broadened the range of pricing policy options for private labels. In particular in the food retailing sector for some considerable time now, private labels have been foreclosing competition and circumventing the price maintenance regulations simultaneously. Here, 'price sceneries', i.e. artificially-generated pricing comparisons for certain goods, are playing an ever increasing role.[1]

A topical example from food retailing shows the form in which 'price sceneries' are currently embedded in business practices. In advertising leaflets provided by the retailer REWE, its own labels and national brands are directly compared against one another in terms of price and quality.[2] Here, the intended effect of the comparison aims not only at a direct increase in sales of the private labels, but also at the retailer's profile in comparison with that of other retailers that still sell a considerable number of national brands.

In the context of this 'hotbed' effect, the judgement pronounced by the US Supreme Court on 28 June 2007 regarding vertical pricing agreements is of particular significance. In it, the US Supreme Court overturned the former *per se* prohibition of vertical minimum pricing agreements and instead introduced case-by-case assessment ('rule-of-reason').[3]

In consideration of legal issues, the following chapter explores the proliferation of private labels and the impact it has on competition. We start by outlining the study which covers data from three outlet formats in Germany (Section B). Following this, we review the impact generated by legislation and German Federal Court ruling and its impact on the market power of retailers (Section C). The proliferation of private labels in the German grocery sector is then considered (Section D). After that, we discuss the relevant literature and derive hypotheses (Section E).

[1] Cf R Olbrich, 'Mehr Wettbewerbschancen für die industrielle Marke durch Aufhebung des Preisbindungsverbotes! Zur Frage der Abschottung von Wettbewerb durch "private labels"' in D Ahlert, H Evanschitzky, J Hesse, and A Salfeld (eds), *Exzellenz in Markenmanagement und Vertrieb* (2004) 169, 170.

[2] Regarding a critical perspective see G Hanke, 'Kölner Mimikry' [2007] *Lebensmittelzeitung*, No 23, 8 June 2007, 31.

[3] Cf *Leegin Creative Leather Products, Inc v PSKS, Inc* 551 US 28 (2007).

Using empirical data referring to the German grocery sector, we demonstrate selected effects of this proliferation in the product group studied and reflect on the welfare effects of the proliferation of private labels (Section F). Finally, we point out the risks of further crowding-out of branded goods (Section G).

B. On the Proliferation of Private Labels: The Study

Our study included the analysis of a group of products from the ready-meals category. It was conducted over a total period of 312 consecutive calendar weeks between 2000 and 2005, and was based on almost seven million data records. One data record covers sales and turnover of a national brand or private label per calendar week and retail outlet. The scanning data on which the study is based originated in the outlet formats 'discount store', 'supermarket', and 'hypermarket' (with 24 outlets each). All analysed stores are located in Germany.

The selected product group from the ready-meal category was particularly appropriate in view of the objective of the study, that is, to investigate the consequences of the proliferation of private labels: it is exemplary for a product group which at one time was mainly supplied by the branded goods industry, but is nowadays increasingly dominated by private labels. This is a prime example of the strategy of the retail trade of substituting national brands by private labels.

This study is the first to make a long-term analysis covering a long period (six years) and several outlet formats. As indicated below, previous studies have predominantly been static or short-term and in generally cover just one outlet format. One disadvantage of short-term studies is the fact that they only reveal temporary upward or downward 'leaps'. The long-term course of developments is left untracked. As a result, the danger of misinterpretation in short-term studies is significantly higher compared to long-term studies. Such a risk is avoided in a long-term study as this is.

C. Legislation and German Federal Court Ruling as a 'Motor' for the Growing Market Power of Retailers

Current legislation in Germany, combined with the Federal Court ruling, has given the highly concentrated retail sector even more comprehensive room for manoeuvre, in particular referring to its marketing mix.

The litigation of the Markenverband e.V. (the German brands association) versus the drugstore chain Müller, is illustrative in this respect as it has significant repercussions both for the retail sector and the (branded goods) industry. The litigation between the Markenverband e.V. and drugstore retailer Müller Ltd & Co KG was triggered by an advertising leaflet published in 2002 by Müller, which runs one of the four largest drugstore chains in Germany.[4] The advert in the leaflet showed a systematic comparison with their branded 'counterparts' and the low price of the private labels clearly highlighted.

In this case the drugstore chain Müller had cleverly used its large room for manoeuvre in the fields of product, pricing, and advertising policy: The range, consisting of national brands and private labels, was priced according to its own calculations and aggressively advertised in a sales brochure. The special point referring to this case is that the prices which were being compared were actually those prices set by the advertiser himself.[5] Such conduct was classed as anti-competitive by the branded goods industry and gave rise to a five-year-long litigation which was finally ruled in Müller's favour in the spring of 2007 by the German Federal Court of Justice (FCJ).[6] Prior to that, the Higher Regional Court in Stuttgart had ruled in favour of the brands association and judged the comparative advertising of the prices of private labels and national brands to be anti-competitive. However, from the point of view of the Federal Court judges such comparison did not infringe upon the German Act against unfair Competition (UWG).[7] The pronouncement of judgement stated that the fact that advertisers compare prices which they themselves have set for their private labels and for national brands is not an unfair practice.[8] The judges were of the opinion that no reasons had been advanced that could be proven to represent a case of unfairness.[9] Furthermore, lists of price comparisons are not judged illegitimate even if branded goods are included. The side-by-side comparison of private labels and national brands is regarded as necessary in order to enable a distinction between compared products and to ensure effective competition.[10] No unfair exploitation of reputation was associated with this action.[11] Any possible damage of brand equity must be accepted by the competitors.[12]

[4] See also: Table 11.1.

[5] What is known as the 'Double agent in terms of freedom in pricing' results from the prohibition of resale price maintenance (art 81 EC). Cf in this context also the statements in Section A.

[6] Cf FJC (German Federal Court of Justice), judgment of the 1st Civil Senate dated 21 March 2007, I ZR 184/03; C Murmann, 'Drogerie Müller siegt vor BGH' [2007] *Lebensmittelzeitung*, No 13, 30 March 2007, 30.

[7] Cf FJC, judgment of the 1st Civil Senate dated 21 March 2007, I ZR 184/03.

[8] Ibid, 1.

[9] Cf ibid, 9 ff.

[10] Ibid 12.

[11] Cf ibid.

[12] Cf ibid, 13.

The court judgement indicates that the applicable legislation in Germany is not a sufficiently effective instrument with which to combat this kind of conduct by retailers. On the contrary, individual regulations (such as the prohibition of resale price maintenance) and 'retailer-friendly' FCJ judgements promote retailers in their efforts to constantly expand their market power and to exploit it in the interests of their own business objectives.

Federal Court ruling paving the way for anti-competitive business practices by the retail trade

The basic implication of the Federal Court judgement for retailers and manufacturers is demonstrated by the business practices of the REWE Group. In 2007—shortly after the FCJ judgement—the powerful retailing group[13] introduced its new private label range. This initiative was accompanied by comprehensive leaflets, advertising, and television commercials intended to make the general public aware of the new product range. As in the Müller case, a widespread advertising campaign was rolled out with quality and price comparisons between the national brands and the private label 'counterparts'. Compared to the example of the drugstore chain, however, one peculiarity of the REWE case further intensifies the debate about such practices. Whilst taking a casual look at the REWE brochure, certain products draw immediate attention. Such eyecatchers are REWE's private labels that closely imitate the trade dress of competing branded goods.

The comparison of both types of brands is obviously aimed at initiating an image transfer from the original brand to REWE's private label, to be translated into increasing sales figures for the comparatively cheaper REWE products. As a result, consumers suffer the risk of making purchasing decisions in favour of the look-alike ('copycat') brands (at the expense of the original products) due to false assumptions. These false assumptions can concern both the manufacturer and the quality characteristics of the private labels.

The examples of Müller and REWE clearly show the extent of the current imbalance of market power between the highly-concentrated retail sector and the branded-goods manufacturers. Intensifying concentration in the retail sector is resulting in a further consolidation of the unbalanced relationship of dependency between producers and retailers at the expense of many manufacturers. As a consequence, retailers have an ever-increasing threat potential that considerably diminishes the room for manoeuvre of many branded-goods manufacturers. In some cases, the fear of shelf-space loss or complete delisting of their lines runs so deep that manufacturers affected simply (have to) accept unfair practices by retailers.

---

13 Regarding various indicators of market power cf Table 11.1.

Table 11.1 Select key figures from the drugstore chain Müller and the REWE Group

	Müller Ltd. & Co. KG	REWE Group
Outlet format (retail)	Drugstores	DIY stores, cash & carry, discount stores, specialist stores, garden centres, drinks stores, supermarkets, tourist shops, hypermarkets
National markets, 2006	AT, CH, DE, ES, HR, HU, SI	AT, BG, CH, CZ, DE, FR, HR, HU, IT, RO, RU, SK, UA
Total turnover (net) in billions of EUR, 2006	2,0	43,5
Number of outlets, 2006	470	11.948
Degree of concentration on the basis of turnover quota (by rank), given in per cent, 2006	Schlecker (40.6) + dm 20.4) + Rossmann (16.7) + **Müller (13.3)** = 91% (Drugstore market in Germany)	Edeka Group (17.55) + Metro Group (15.18) + **REWE Group (14.9)** + Schwarz Group (11.31) + Aldi (10.16) = 69.1 % (Grocery sector in Germany)

Source: Metro Group, Metro-Handelslexikon 2007/2008—Daten, Fakten und Adressen zum Handel in Deutschland, Europa und weltweit (2007), 21; EHI Retail Institute, Handel aktuell. Struktur, Kennzahlen und Profile des deutschen und internationalen Handels (2006), 125, 132, 237; Trade Dimensions, TOP-Firmen 2007 (2006), V.3.

Finally, predominant retailers such as Müller or REWE are prepared to accept the displeasure of many branded-goods manufacturers, provided that their activities promise benefits in terms of profiling and/or profits.

The substantial market position of Müller and REWE in their respective sectors is demonstrated in Table 11.1.

The levels of concentration in the drugstore and food market (see Table 11.1) indicate the growing market power of the retail sector at the expense of manufacturers. The REWE Group example shows how in Germany the existing legal framework in conjunction with the Federal Court ruling and increasing retail concentration favours the introduction of private labels in general and own-brand look-alikes in particular.

D. On the Proliferation of Private Labels in the German Grocery Sector

For several years now, a proliferation of private labels has been evident in German food retailing. The inclusion of private label products in a range has, in many cases, led to a delisting of national brands due to limited shelf space. This has resulted in the proportion of listed national brands being reduced ever further in favour of private labels. The proportion of listed private labels in German food outlets already often amounts to more than 30 per cent. A high proportion of listed private labels is particularly evident in 'discount stores'.[14]

This development is also reflected in the point of sale (POS) scanning data investigated here. Figure 11.1 shows the proportions of listed national brands and private labels in a product group from the ready-meals category, recorded during the course of 312 successive calendar weeks between 2000 and 2005. The ready-meals studied were mainly meat-based meals. The basic scanning data comes from 24 outlets of the format 'discount store', 24 outlets of the format 'supermarket' (sales area < $800m^2$), and 24 outlets of the format 'hypermarket' (sales area > $800m^2$). The proportions of listed national brands and private labels at all stores studied in one calendar week are illustrated by means of a bar chart.

Figure 11.1 shows that the proportions of listed private labels in 'discount stores' rose from 0 per cent in 2000 to more than 20 per cent in 2005. In the outlet formats 'supermarket' and 'hypermarket', the proportions of listed private labels also rose from below 10 per cent in 2000 to more than 20 per cent in 2005.

E. Discussion of the Consequences of Private Labels in the Scientific Literature and Derivation of Hypotheses

In literature, on the one hand pro-competitive, pro-consumer effects are attributed to the proliferation of private labels. On the other hand, however, anti-competitive effects detrimental to consumer and to public welfare are identified, at least in the long term.[15] This contradiction in the results can be attributed to

---

[14] Cf R Olbrich and CC Buhr, 'Handelsmarken, Wettbewerb und Wohlfahrt' in H Prießnitz (ed), *Markenführung im Billigzeitalter, Wertevernichtung—Spirale ohne Ende* (2006) 21; R Olbrich, G Grewe, and D Battenfeld, 'Sortimentsgestaltung durch Herstellermarken oder Handelsmarken—zu den betriebswirtschaftlichen Grenzen der Verbreitung von Handelsmarken' in R Olbrich (ed), *Marketing-Controlling mit POS-Daten—Analyseverfahren für mehr Erfolg in der Konsumgüterwirtschaft* (2006) 326 f, and R Olbrich and CC Buhr, 'Handelskonzentration, Handelsmarken und Wettbewerb in der Konsumgüterdistribution—Warum das Verbot der vertikalen Preisbindung abgeschafft gehört' in M Schuckel and W Toporowski (eds), *Theoretische Fundierung und praktische Relevanz der Handelsforschung* (2007) 492 f.

[15] Cf regarding a comprehensive analysis of a multitude of sources R Olbrich and others, 'Die Folgen der zunehmenden Verbreitung von Handelsmarken für den Wettbewerb und den Verbraucher' in R Olbrich (ed), *Berichte aus dem Lehrstuhl für Betriebswirtschaftslehre, insb. Marketing* (Forschungsbericht No 11, 2005) s 4.1.1.

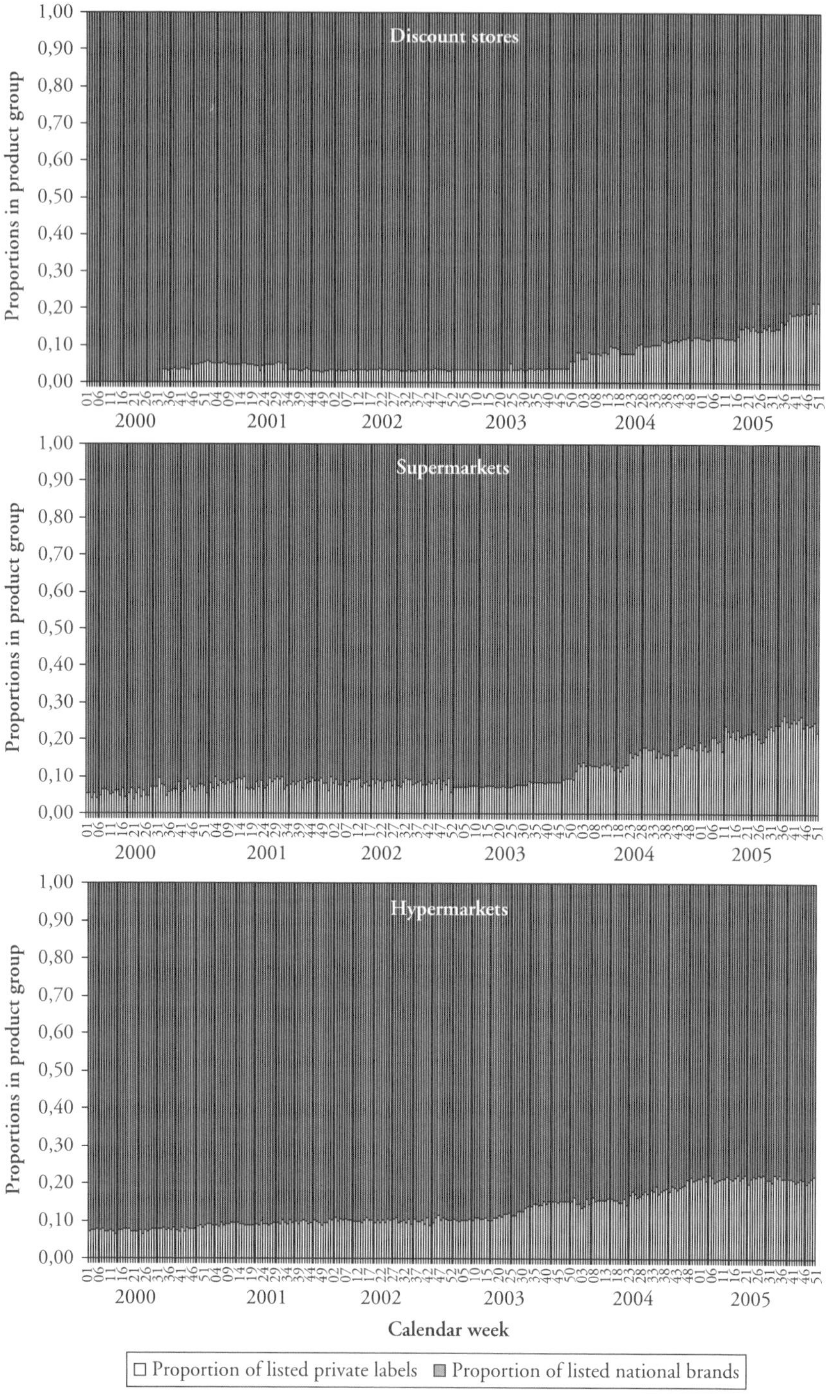

Figure 11.1: Proportions of listed private labels and national brands per calendar week and outlet format

the varying lengths of the studies. While in short-term studies only temporary upward or downward 'leaps' can be determined, long-term studies enable the observation of development paths.

The effects of the proliferation of private labels in view of the welfare indicators 'variety of products', 'prices', and 'market volume' discussed in literature are illustrated in the following sections.

Variety of products

In some instances the same authors expect there to be both a reduction and an increase in the *range of different products available*. Dobson (1998) and (1999), Vogel (1998), and Dobson, Clarke, Davies, and Waterson (2001) assume that a proliferation of private labels can bring about both a reduction in the range of different products available[16] and a greater variety of products.[17]

By contrast, the following authors or institutions take a clearer stance: Mills (1995) also assumes a reduction in the range of different products as a consequence of the increased distribution of private labels, as do the European Commission (1997), the Competition Commission (UK) (2003), the Nordic Competition Authorities (2005), and the Federal Competition Authority of the Republic of Austria (2007).[18] Almost all of these cite as their reason the fact that an increase in private labels automatically entails the delisting of national brands, in particular those of second- and third-tier national brands. Raju, Sethuraman, and Dhar (1995) and Ward, Shimshack, Perloff, and Harris (2002) have been

---

16 Cf PW Dobson, 'The Economic Welfare Implications of Own Label Products' [1998] School of Management and Finance Discussion Paper IV, 25; L Vogel, 'Wettbewerbsrecht und Einkaufsmacht: Es ist Zeit für eine neue Betrachtungsweise' [1998] *Wirtschaft und Wettbewerb* 48, 1163; Dobson Consulting, 'Buyer Power and its Impact on Competition in the Food Retail Distribution Sector of the European Union' (prepared for the European Commission—DG IV, Study Contract No. IV/98/ETD/078, 1999) 160 <http://ec.europa.eu/comm/competition/publications/studies/bpifrs/> accessed 4 April 2008; and PW Dobson and others, 'Buyer Power and its Impact on Competition in the Food Retail Distribution Sector of the European Union' [2001] 1 *Journal of Industry, Competition and Trade* 247, 276.

17 Cf Dobson (n 16) 2, 26, 28 f, 33; Vogel (n 16) 48, 1163; Dobson Consulting (n 16) 190; and Dobson and others (n 16) 277.

18 Cf B Mills, 'Own Label Products and the "Lookalike" Phenomenon: A Lack of Trade Dress and Unfair Competition Protection?' [1995] 17 *European Intellectual Property Review* 116; European Commission 'Green Paper on Vertical Restraints in EC Competition Policy' (22 January 1997) 66; UK Competition Commission 'Safeway Merger Inquiries: Remedies Statement' (24 June 2003) <http://www.competition-commission.org.uk/press_rel/archive/2003/jun/pdf/21-03.pdf> accessed 30 May 2008; Nordic Competition Authorities, 'Nordic Food Markets—a Taste for Competition' [2005] 1, 89; Federal Competition Authority of the Republic of Austria, 'Allgemeine Untersuchung des österreichischen Lebensmitteleinzelhandels unter besonderer Berücksichtigung des Aspekts der Nachfragemacht' [2007], 20.

able to provide empirical evidence for this position with studies from American supermarkets, Baker, Baltzer, and Møller (2006) on the basis of questionnaire survey results from Danish producers and retailers from the food sector and Bergström, Daunfeldt, and Rudholm (2006) with reference to data from the Swedish food retailing.[19]

By contrast with this, however, there are comparatively few (and generally older) works to be found in which there is any reference to a rise in the variety of products on sale as an effect of the proliferation of private labels. Call (1967) uses a study carried out by the National Commission on Food Marketing (1966) to indicate that retailers extend their product range by using private labels.[20] Täger (1998) highlights new ranges of goods and low-priced private labels as one positive aspect of the concentration process in the retail sector.[21]

This apparent contradiction in the development of the range of products as a reaction to the increased proliferation of private labels is in particular attributable to a failure to take into account the dimension of time. Different trends can be observed short-term and over a longer period. Directly after the introduction of new private labels, overall more products exist. Therefore during this period a more extensive range of products is available.[22] The assumption of a wider choice not only relates to product characteristics, but also to prices, as private labels, at least in the short term, affect prices.[23]

In terms of the variety of products on offer, this may be another reason why an increase in choice, i.e. an increase in the number of different products on offer, can only be assumed for some consumers for a short period of time. In the long term, a reduction in the absolute number of different products available can be expected due to the crowding-out of industrial brands by private labels. From the point of view of all consumers, the diversity in the outlets they actually frequent would also decline.

---

[19] Cf J S Raju, R Sethuraman, and S K Dhar, 'The Introduction and Performance of Store Brands' [1995] 41 *Management Science* 957, 974; M B Ward and others, 'Effects Of The Private-Label Invasion In Food Industries' [2002] 84 *American Journal of Agricultural Economics* 961, 972; D Baker, K Baltzer, and A Møller, 'Branding Behavior in the Danish Food Industry' [2006] 22 *Agribusiness* 31, 45; and F Bergström, S O Daunfeldt, and N Rudholm, 'The Times, they are a Changing: What's new in the Swedish retail trade market?' [2006] 52 *European Retail Digest* 37.

[20] Cf D L Call, 'Private Label and Consumer Choice in the Food Industry' [1967] 1 *The Journal of Consumer Affairs* 149, 151 f; and National Commission on Food Marketing, 'Private Label Products in Food Retailing' [1966] Technical Study No 10, June 2006.

[21] U C Täger, 'Hohe Wettbewerbsintensität in der Warendistribution der Europäischen Union' [1998] *IFO-Schnelldienst* 51, 7.

[22] Cf e.g. Dobson (n 16) 25.

[23] Cf e.g. Dobson Consulting (n 16) and Dobson and others (n 16) 277.

Against this background, the following basic hypotheses can be set out in terms of the development of item diversity in consumer goods retailing:

> *Hypothesis 1:*
> *Over time, the number of private labels listed continuously increases.*
>
> *Hypothesis 2:*
> *Over time, the number of listed national brands continuously declines.*
>
> *Hypothesis 3:*
> *Over time, the total number of listed products continuously declines.*

In the context of our statistical study (Section F), a hypothesis is considered to have been proved, if the regression coefficient sign points in the expected direction and the value of the significance level is below 5 per cent.

Prices

Assessments also vary concerning the effects of the increase in private label products on the *level of prices* in the retail sector. Several authors consider (long-term) rising and (short-term) falling prices to be likely and had observed such effects 'to some extent'. In the majority of cases, the price level of *all* products has not been studied, only the prices of national brands. In a few studies, however, the effects on prices of private labels and the level of prices as a whole have also been examined.

Lower prices as a consequence of the proliferation of private labels are mainly expected in older studies and generally in studies that do not include any empirical research.[24] To justify the assumption of, in particular, short-term[25] *falling prices*, on the one hand reference is made to the fact that national brands have been undercut by competing private labels.[26] The price pressure generated in this way by private labels[27] might lead as a whole to a cheaper range of products.[28] On the other hand, it is also debated whether falling prices could be a consequence of the passing on of more favourable purchasing terms and conditions to consumers.[29] It is true that even a few recent sources do report

---

24 Cf S J Hoch and S Banerij, 'When Do Private Labels Succeed?' [1993] 34 *Sloan Management Review* 57–67; P W Dobson and M Waterson, 'Countervailing Power And Consumer Prices' [1997] 107 *The Economic Journal*, 418–430; Dobson (n 16); Vogel (n 16) 48, 12; Dobson Consulting (n 16); R Wieser, K Aiginger, and M Wüger, 'Marktmacht im Einzelhandel', *Österreichisches Institut für Wirtschaftsforschung* [1999].

25 Cf Dobson Consulting (n 16) 4 f.

26 Cf e.g. Dobson (n 16) 20 f.

27 Cf Wieser, Aiginger, and Wüger (n 24) 65.

28 Cf Vogel (n 16) 1163.

29 Cf Dobson and Waterson (n 24) 428.

price reductions: According to Bergström, Daunfeldt, and Rudholm (2006), a 10 per cent increase in the market share of private labels leads to a 3.4 per cent reduction in price level in the Swedish food retailing.[30] The Nordic Competition Authorities (2005) also assume, without any empirical study having been carried out, that a rising percentage of private labels goes hand in hand with a reduction in price levels.[31]

Falling prices in the wake of an increase in private labels have seldom been proven empirically. Cotterill and Putsis (2000), in a study of American supermarkets, discovered lower prices in national brands and private labels where the market shares of private labels were higher.[32] Chintagunta, Bonfrer, and Song (2002) also studied, among other things, the effects of the introduction of private labels on the prices of national brands and found price reductions of approximately 7 per cent.[33] These authors are the only ones who used a sample period (275 weeks) that is comparable to this study (312 weeks). However, they only determine supermarkets of a particular chain and only have a very limited data basis. Furthermore, they only analyse the prices of national brands and total sales. The product variety, the prices of private labels, the entire price level, the sales and turnovers of private labels and national brands, as well as total turnovers are not in the focus of their investigation. Therefore, their analysis contains considerably less welfare-related indicators compared to this study.

Both price increases and reductions are considered by Dobson (1998) and Wieser, Aiginger, and Wüger (1999) to be possible effects of the proliferation of private labels.[34] A general rise in price level is attributed by Wieser, Aiginger, and Wüger (1999), among other things, to retail oligopolization caused by private labels.[35] They explain price reductions on the basis of pricing pressure exerted by the private labels on national brands.[36]

Putsis (1997) and Putsis and Cotterill (1999) report contradictory empirical results in the pricing response of national brands and private labels to the

[30] Cf Bergström, Daunfeldt, and Rudholm (n 19) 38. The authors also refer in this context to the following source: Handelns Utredningsinstitut, 'The Effects on Prices, Margins and the Range of Products of Private Labels in Swedish Retailing' [2005] Report for Project No 83/2003, Swedish Competition Authority.

[31] Cf Nordic Competition Authorities (n 18) 89.

[32] Cf R W Cotterill and W P Putsis, 'Market Share and Price Setting Behavior for Private Labels and National Brands' [2000] 17 *Review of Industrial Organization* 17, 33.

[33] Cf P K Chintagunta, A Bonfrer, and I Song, 'Investigating the Effects of Store-Brand Introduction on Retailer Demand and Pricing Behavior' [2002] 48 *Management Science* 1242, 1255.

[34] Cf Dobson (n 16) 20 f and 33; Wieser, Aiginger, and Wüger (n 24) 65, 67.

[35] Cf Wieser, Aiginger, and Wüger (n 24) 67.

[36] Cf Wieser, Aiginger and Wüger (n 24) 65.

proliferation of private labels. They determine, in the context of their studies in the American food retail sector, increasing prices of private labels and reduced prices of national brands.[37]

Bonfrer and Chintagunta (2004) discovered varying results in the prices of national brands on the basis of data from the American food retailing sector. Across the product groups, they observed price increases as a consequence of the introduction of private labels. However, when they looked at specific product groups, approximately 50 per cent of the 104 product groups recorded price increases, and price reductions for the other 50 per cent.[38]

In particular, more recent non-empirical and empirical studies unanimously expected and observed increasing prices of national brands to be a negative consequence of the proliferation of private labels.[39] The degree of price increase according to some authors is dependent on various factors. Bontemps, Orozco, Réquillart, and Trevisiol (2005) assume that the intensity of the price reaction of national brands depends on the type of private labels the national brands are competing with.[40] Bontemps, Orozco, and Réquillart (2006) moreover determine that the prices of leading national brands have been more greatly affected in the wake of the introduction of private labels than the prices of second-tier brands.[41]

To sum up, it can be stated that the consumer, at least in the long term, faces the risk of higher prices across the board. This trend is further encouraged by the risk of a dwindling intensity of competition between retailers.

---

37 Cf W P Putsis, 'An Empirical Study of the Effect of Brand Proliferation on Private Label—National Brand Pricing Behavior' [1997] 12 *Review of Industrial Organization* 355, 367; and W P Putsis and R W Cotterill, 'Share, Price and Category Expenditure—Geographic Market Effects and Private Labels' [1999] 20 *Managerial and Decision Economics* 175, 183.

38 Cf A Bonfrer and P K Chintagunta, 'Store Brands: Who Buys Them and What Happens to Retail Prices When They Are Introduced?' [2004] 24 *Review of Industrial Organization* 195, 212.

39 Cf regarding empirical results from the American foods retailing sector R W Cotterill, W P Putsis, and R Dhar, 'Assessing the Competitive Interaction Between Private Labels and National Brands' [2000] 73 *Journal of Business* 109, 133; Ward and others (n 19); and A Bonanno and R A Lopez, 'Private Label Expansion and Supermarket Milk Prices' [2005] 3 *Journal of Agricultural and Food Industrial Organization*, Article 2, 14. Empirical results from the French food retailing sector are given in C Bontemps, V Orozco, and V Réquillart, 'Confirming the Price Effects of Private Labels Development' [2005] IDEI Working Paper, No 367, Institut d'Économie Industrielle (IDEI) 14; C Bontemps and others, 'Price Effects of Private Label Development' [2005] 3 *Journal of Agricultural and Food Industrial Organization*, Article 3, 14; and C Bontemps, V Orozco, and V Réquillart, 'Private Labels, National Brands and Food Prices' [2006] IDEI Working Paper, No 402, Institut d'Économie Industrielle (IDEI) 22. Cf regarding theoretical results T S Gabrielsen and L Sørgard, 'Private Labels, Price Rivalry, and Public Policy' [2007] 51 *European Economic Review* 403, 414.

40 Cf Bontemps, Orozco, and Réquillart 2005 ibid; Bontemps and others ibid.

41 Cf Bontemps, Orozco, and Réquillart 2006 (n 39) 22.

Against this background, with regard to price level trends in consumer goods retailing during the period studied, the following hypotheses can be set out:

> *Hypothesis 1:*
> *Over time, the average prices of private labels continuously increase.*
>
> *Hypothesis 2:*
> *Over time, the average prices of national brands continuously increase.*
>
> *Hypothesis 3:*
> *Over time, the average prices of all goods continuously increase.*

In this context it should be noted that the third hypothesis cannot be falsified if the first two hypotheses can be well-proved.

In the context of our statistical studies (Section F) a hypothesis is considered to have been proved if the regression coefficient sign points in the expected direction and the value of the significance level is below 5 per cent.

Market volume

In the scientific literature, the growing significance of private labels, in particular in European but also in American consumer goods retailing, is unanimously exposed with reference to increasing market shares of private labels. Comparatively rare in this connection are studies on the effects of the increase in private labels on market volume. Market volume may be determined both in terms of quantity of sales and in terms of value of turnover.

In terms of the key figures studied in the literature, it can therefore be stated that predominantly only sales and turnover *shares* have been evaluated. Effects of private labels on absolute sales and turnover by contrast are seldom the focus of study. For an evaluation of the effects of private labels on market volume—and therefore on the supply of goods to consumers—a study of the absolute sales and turnover figures is, however, essential.

None of the sources explains how turnover of private labels and national brands have developed in the wake of the proliferation of private labels. However, it can be assumed from them that the increasing sales of private labels and declining sales of national brands has ultimately resulted in corresponding trends in turnover.

Total sales and turnover have also rarely been the focus of study. In the few sources that do deal with this, however, either increasing market-related figures are determined empirically (Chintagunta, Bonfrer, and Song (2002)[42]) or else forecasted without such trends being empirically demonstrated (McGoldrick (2002) and

42 Chintagunta, Bonfrer, and Song (n 33).

Gilbert (2003)[43]). Solely Raju, Sethuraman, and Dhar (1995)[44] empirically determined neither a significant positive nor a negative effect of the introduction of private labels on total sales in the product group.

Against this background, with reference to the development of market volume in consumer goods retailing in the sample period, the following hypotheses can be set out:

> *Hypothesis 1:*
> *Over time, sales and turnover of private labels continuously increase.*
>
> *Hypothesis 2:*
> *Over time, sales and turnover of national brands continuously decline.*
>
> *Hypothesis 3:*
> *Over time, total sales and turnover continuously increase.*

In the context of our statistical studies (Section F), a hypothesis is considered to have been proved if the regression coefficient sign points in the expected direction and the value of the significance level is below 5 per cent.

F. Empirical Results Regarding the Welfare Effects of the Proliferation of Private Labels

Decreasing variety of products

Figure 11.2 first shows the number of all products (overall) in the years 2000 to 2005. The graph shows that the number of listed national brands declined considerably in the sample period in all three outlet formats, whereas the number of listed private labels has increased. The sharp decline in listed national brands has not been balanced out by the addition of new private labels. The absolute number of different products in the product group therefore has been reduced overall, caused by the crowding-out of national brands by private labels. There has been a dramatic reduction of the variety of different products in the product group, to the detriment of the national brands.

Thus, the figure illustrates the fact that the number of products—when considered cumulatively between all outlet formats—declined sharply over the sample period. Consumer choice is therefore becoming ever more restricted.

Table 11.2 gives an overview of the results of the bivariate linear regressions considered across all outlet formats.

---

43 P McGoldrick, *Retail Marketing* (2nd edn, 2002); D Gilbert, *Retail Marketing Management* (2nd edn, 2003).

44 Raju, Sethuraman, and Dhar (n 19).

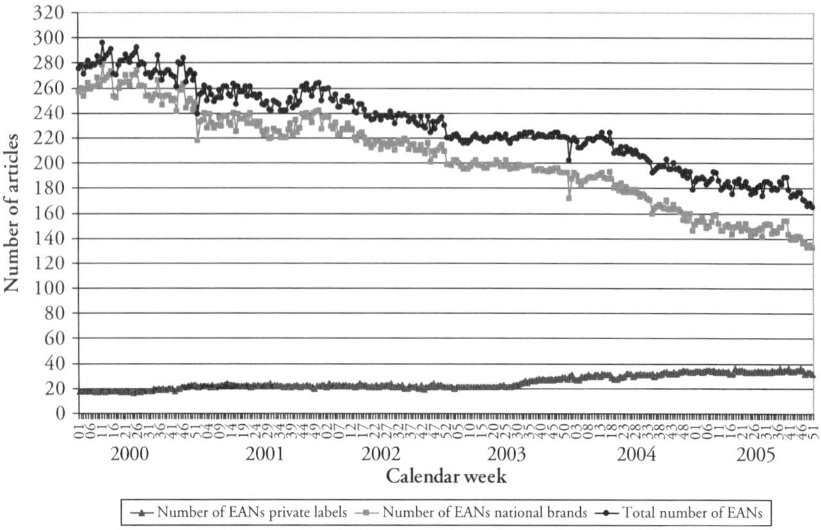

Figure 11.2: Cumulative number of different products per calendar week across all outlet formats

Table 11.2 demonstrates that all standardized regression coefficients have the expected sign. The t-values, moreover, show that the results are highly significant. Beyond this, all of the coefficients of determination are quite high. The hypotheses can be described therefore as proved statements.

Table 11.2 Results of the regression analyses with the number of listed products as regressands studied across all outlet formats

Dependent variable	Expected sign	Standardized regression coefficient	t-value	Significance	R^2	proved?
Number of products private labels	+(H 1)	+0.910	38.728	0.000	0.829	yes
Number of products national brands	−(H 2)	−0.981	−88.806	0.000	0.962	yes
Total number of products	−(H 3)	−0.976	−78.300	0.000	0.952	yes

Rising prices

In order to eliminate the fact that the price increases were attributable to increased packaging sizes, a study was carried out taking the prices per kg

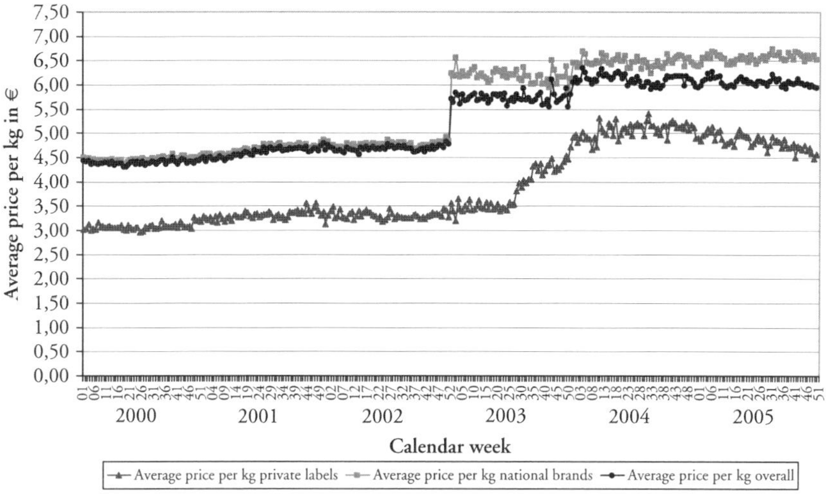

Figure 11.3: Average prices per kg and per calendar week studied across all outlet formats

into consideration. Figure 11.3 shows the development of the average prices per kg during the period of the study across all outlet formats.

The graph shows that both the average price per kg of private labels, as well as that of national brands, increased significantly during the period studied, with the increase in national brand prices being sharper than that of private labels.

The rate of price increase of the private labels in the product group studied is significantly above the 6.4 per cent rate of inflation for meat and meat products (2000–2005).[45] The average private label price per kg rose between 2000 and 2005 by 51.32 per cent, therefore exceeding the rate of inflation by 44.92 percentage points.

In this context it is remarkable that the average prices per kg of the private labels were kept well below those of the national brands by the retailers. The retailers in this way apparently attempt to demonstrate to the consumer the inexpensiveness of their own brands (at least compared to the national brands). The fact that both, the prices per kg of private labels as well as those of the national brands, have practically continuously increased over recent years and that the prices per kg of the private labels in 2005 were approximately at the level of the prices per kg of the national brands in 2000, is generally overlooked by consumers.

45 Cf German Federal Statistical Office, Statistical Yearbook [2006] 506.

Presumably the consumers do not make any detailed records of the prices of the foods they have purchased over a period of six years. Consumers generally only see the current prices on the shelf and therefore only notice that the prices per kg of the private labels are currently below those of the national brands. Whether they notice the significant price increases in both types of brand over the sample period at all is debatable for the aforementioned reasons.

The perception of low cost private labels retained by many consumers only persists because national brands are frequently used by the retailers as reference products when setting prices. This means that the prices per kg of private labels are constantly kept below those of the national brands, although at an increasingly high level. In this context it is a point of controversy that the retailers have been given this opportunity only by the prohibition of vertical price fixing and the associated freedom of price fixing on two levels.[46]

Table 11.3 gives the results of the bivariate linear regression across the outlet formats with the average prices per kg as regressands.

Table 11.3 shows that there is a highly significant positive relation between average prices per kg and time. Besides that, the high values of the coefficients of determination of around 0.8 and above and that the majority of the overall scattering can be explained by the variables being studied.

In the long term, therefore, a considerable rise in prices of national brands and private labels can already be discerned which, in terms of competition

Table 11.3 Results of the regression analyses with the average prices per kg as regressands in a study across all outlet formats

Dependent variable	Expected sign	Standardized regression coefficient	t-value	Significance	R^2	proved?
Average price per kg private labels	+(H 1)	+0.889	34.267	0.000	0.791	yes
Average price per kg national brands	+(H 2)	+0.925	42.926	0.000	0.856	yes
Average price per kg all products	+(H 3)	+0.927	43.398	0.000	0.859	yes

[46] Cf e.g. R Olbrich, 'Der "Double-Agent-Approach" in der Konsumgüterdistribution—die Verschiebung des "strategischen Machtgefälles" zwischen Markenartikelindustrie und Handel durch die zunehmende Verbreitung von Handelsmarken' in V Trommsdorff (ed), *Handelsforschung 2001/2002* (2001) 161–181; Olbrich (n 1) 165–178; and Olbrich and Buhr (n 14) 485–505.

policy, must be considered as negative due to the associated disadvantages for the consumer.

Decreasing market volume

The top section of Figure 11.4 shows that the cumulative total turnover across all outlet formats is in decline in the period of the study. This is particularly apparent as the prices in the same period of time increased significantly (see Figure 11.3). As a consequence, the falling turnover is caused by declining sales, as is illustrated in the lower section of Figure 11.4.

These results point to the fact that intensive price increases—at least to some extent—have resulted in non-consumption.

Table 11.4 indicates that corresponding and highly significant results can also be discerned in the context of bivariate linear regressions.

Table 11.4 shows that only hypotheses 1 and 2 can be described as proved statements. The correlation between time and total turnover or total sales is negative, by contrast with the hypothesis set out above. Hypothesis 3 is therefore rejected in each case. These results clearly show that the increasing proliferation of private labels, in general, is causing a reduction in market volume.

The increasing proportions of listed private labels are not accompanied by positive trends in total turnover in the product group. However, this does not necessarily mean that profits are also in decline.

It is to be expected that retailers are achieving higher profit margins with private labels than with national brands, due to lower procurement costs.[47] To this extent it is possible that the retailers will achieve lower turnover figures with higher proportions of private labels being listed, but, due to higher profit margins of private labels, will achieve a higher contribution margin. Accordingly, it may be attractive for retailers, at least to some extent, to forego higher turnover figures in favour of higher contribution margins.

However, whether the decline in total turnover of the product group is overcompensated by higher marginal contributions from private labels is highly questionable. It is therefore an obvious assumption that the retailers, by selling private labels, are—at least in short term—not pursuing the aim of increasing profits at all, but are following other objectives. At this point we particularly refer to

[47] Regarding a cost-oriented evaluation of national brands and private labels see: L Müller-Hagedorn, 'Handelsmarke oder Herstellermarke?—Überlegungen zur ökonomischen Effizienz' in M Bruhn (ed), *Handelsmarken* (3rd revised and amplified edition, 2001) 99–112.

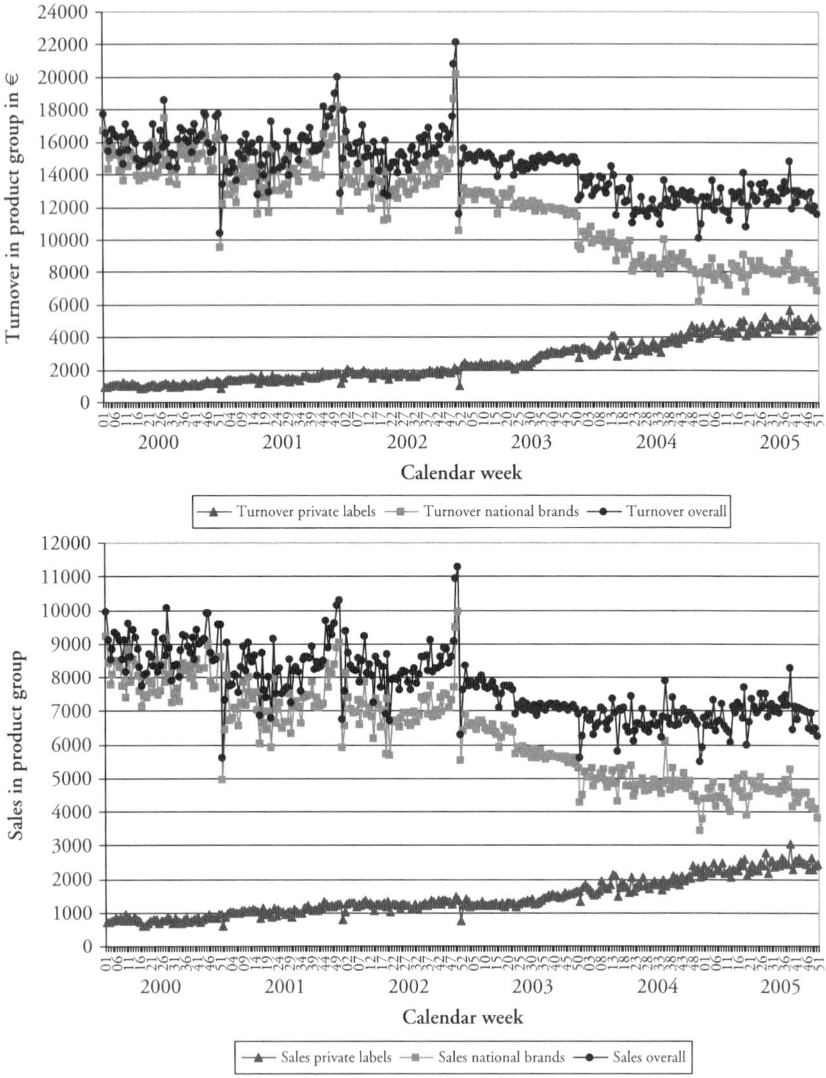

Figure 11.4: Cumulative turnover and sales per calendar week across all outlet formats

the crowding-out of smaller brand manufacturers. The existence of smaller manufacturers which do not have strong brands is in particular threatened by the delisting of second-tier and third-tier brands in favour of private labels. It is therefore to be expected that the number of branded-goods manufacturers will diminish due to fierce competition from private labels. By doing so, retailers

Table 11.4 Results of the regression analyses with turnovers and sales

Dependent variables	Expected sign	Standardized regression coefficient	t-value	Significance	R^2	proved?
Turnover of private labels	+(H 1)	+0.956	57.463	0.000	0.914	yes
Turnover of national brands	−(H 2)	−0.874	−31.731	0.000	0.765	yes
Total turnover	+(H 3)	−0.693	−16.935	0.000	0.481	no
Sales of private labels	+(H 1)	+0.943	49.662	0.000	0.888	yes
Sales of national brands	−(H 2)	−0.891	−34.588	0.000	0.794	yes
Total sales	+(H 3)	−0.730	−18.800	0.000	0.533	no

are presumably expecting to achieve a strengthening of their negotiating power with branded-goods manufacturers and a reduction in the costs of negotiating and reaching agreements.[48] Moreover, large manufacturers can, because of the economies of scale, in some circumstances produce at lower costs, which promises the opportunity successfully to negotiate additional potential profits for the retail trade. Short-term turnover and profit losses are apparently considered acceptable in the interests of this long-term objective.

Should the crowding-out of manufacturers succeed, the process of concentration at manufacturing level would be driven forward and the horizontal pressure of competition at that level would abate. From the perspective of individual manufacturer, however, it might seem a short-term advantage to a certain (small) number of surviving companies to belong to this group, due to the associated gain in power. In the medium to long term, however, even the position of those remaining manufacturers would be very much at risk due to the flexibility of retailers' ranges. From the consumer's point of view, this would further increase the risk that prices will increase ever more while the variety of products on sale diminishes. Such trends must therefore be evaluated as being negative from the point of view of competition policy.

48 Cf R Olbrich and others (n 15) 85; Olbrich and Buhr (n 14) 39; and Federal Competition Authority of the Republic of Austria (n 18) 11.

G. Conclusion

The empirical results make clear that the feared negative effects on consumer welfare of a proliferation of private labels in terms of variety of products, price level, and market volume in the product group studied—at a time when the increased distribution of private labels has presumably by no means reached its peak—can already be discerned.

The descriptive results show that in all studied outlet formats, clear reductions in the diversity of products can be observed—brought about by the delisting of national brands only partially being replaced by newly listed private labels. Moreover, in all outlet formats studied, there is evidence of significant price increases.

Moreover, the results of regression analysis show that the hypotheses demonstrated above, with regards to product diversity and the price level per kg, should be classed as proved statements. With regard to market volume, the results are particularly controversial: both total turnover and total sales figures are in sharp decline, by contrast with previous hypotheses. These developments indicate that consumers are restricting their consumption, or may in some cases even have completely ceased to consume, in the wake of the proliferation of private labels.

Corresponding results concerning the range of different products on sale are, according to Information Resources GmbH (IRI), discernible throughout the food retail sector. According to IRI, the number of products in food retailing declined by almost 10 per cent between 2002 and 2007.

At the same time, the empirical results indicate that retailers are further extending the proportion of private labels listed even though there are no positive turnover trends associated with such a course of action. It can only be supposed that the retailers are selling their private labels—at least to some extent—with the aim of ousting smaller branded-goods manufacturers from the market. As a consequence of the reduced number of manufacturers, an increased concentration process at manufacturer level is to be expected.

Competition in the distribution of consumer goods distorted by the *per se* ban on vertical price fixing therefore already seems—at least to some extent—to have resulted in vertically-integrated retailing groups carving off an exclusive market for themselves as they seek to create customer loyalty by selling private labels.

The disappearance of many national brands is causing a reduction of the consumers' freedom of choice. It is a burning issue that consumers are being given the impression, at least indirectly, by means of the continuous expansion of sales areas (in all outlet formats) in recent years, that a wider choice of products is being offered to them.[49]

It is to be assumed that the outlined negative effects on consumer welfare as a result of the diffusion of copycat brands is intensifying. The example of the REWE Group indicates that the legislators, to some degree, are acting as a 'compliant tool' in the rise to power of the retail sector, and in the marketing of own-label look-alikes. The 'scooping' of such room for manoeuvre can only primarily serve to achieve microeconomic objectives. Therefore it has to be assumed that consumer interests are only of secondary importance when it comes to the planning of the assortment.

The repeal of the *per se* prohibition on vertical minimum price agreements in June 2007 by the US Supreme Court seems, in the context of the empirical results found here, to be a first step in the 'right direction' and towards at least balancing out the disadvantages for the manufacturer. If a similar statutory framework was created within the EU, the rules of the game in the consumer goods sector would once again offer incentives to perform, as it is to be expected that some manufacturers of national brands and some retail outlet formats would benefit from the system. A concentration-inhibiting effect in the retail sector could then be expected in the medium term as some extreme pricing tactics (such as aggressive price-cutting policy with branded goods) could be restrained.

---

49 Cf regarding this data EHI Retail Institute, 'Handel aktuell. Struktur, Kennzahlen und Profile des deutschen und internationalen Handels' [2006] 231.

12

ADVERTISING, PROMOTIONAL CAMPAIGNS, AND PRIVATE LABELS

Ariel Ezrachi and Jonathan Reynolds***

A. Introduction

In recent decades retailers have become significant economic and social actors within the value chain in most developed economies. In conjunction with this development, advertising and promotion of retailers as brands, and of retailers'

* Slaughter and May Lecturer in Competition Law, The University of Oxford; Fellow, Pembroke College, Oxford; Director, The University of Oxford Centre for Competition Law and Policy.
** University Lecturer in Management Studies, Saïd Business School, The University of Oxford; Fellow, Green Templeton College, Oxford; Academic Director, Oxford Institute of Retail Management.

private label brands, has taken on greater importance and sophistication. These campaigns now run alongside the promotional efforts of supplier firms. For example, the combined advertising expenditure by the top 50 UK retailers in the last three months of 2006 was £530 million, a 41 per cent rise since the same period in 2003.[1]

In this chapter we explore the interaction between retailers and suppliers in advertising and promotion. In the first two parts of this chapter we review the goals and economic rationale of advertising and promotions and their use in the retail sector. Following this we explore how advertising and certain forms of promotion may affect competition, including a review of the limited number of cases in which the European courts and Commission considered these effects.[2] We then move to consider the unique characteristics of retailers' private labels and reflect on the interrelationship between advertising, brand competition, and private labels.

B. The Roles of Advertising and Promotion

Advertising is generally defined as 'any paid form of non-personal presentation and promotion of ideas, goods, or services by an identified sponsor'.[3] This definition differentiates advertising from other forms of promotion such as direct marketing, or telephone sales which target individuals or small groups of individuals.

Advertising in a competitive market seeks first and foremost to maintain any brand's broad salience—that is to say the consumer awareness of that brand compared to others—in order that the consumer may consider buying, or re-buying it. This process works by prompting memory associations with the brand and a 'share of brand' in the mind, leading to familiarity and a degree of brand assurance.[4] Conventionally, advertising has also been thought to play a powerful persuasive role for consumers: providing an incentive or reason for them to change their attitudes toward a brand, or their actual purchasing behaviour. Indeed, this view forms the basis and rationale for the historic growth and

[1] Quoted in C Grande, 'TV advertising lines up festive boost' *Financial Times* (London, 9 November 2007).

[2] Note that the debates surrounding 'advertising and unfair competition', 'misleading advertising', and 'joint brand advertising' are outside the realm of this chapter; as are the direct marketing activities practised by many retail firms.

[3] P Kotler and K L Keller, *Marketing Management 12e* (12th edn, 2006).

[4] J Romaniuk and B Sharp, 'The Concept of Brand Salience and Implications for Measurement' (In Proceedings of the European Marketing Academy 31st Annual Conference, Braga, Portugal: University of Mino, 2002).

dominance of the advertising industry, and most definitions found in literature allude to this persuasive role: 'persuasion is the only mode [of advertising] worthy of consideration'.[5]

However, this so-called 'strong' view of advertising has been called into question. Arguably, brand advertising works mainly by creatively publicizing the brand, without persuading people that the brand differs from other brands, or is superior to them.[6] 'Fairly few advertisements actually feature potentially persuasive inducements for their brand. Nor do they usually appear to change people's opinions.'[7] In addition, doubts may be raised as to the real benefit of advertising in light of the potential 'wear-out' of persistent attempts to persuade.[8] For example, evidence suggests that short-term advertising elasticities are small and decrease during the product life cycle.

The contribution of advertising may also be questioned in light of the role of prior experience in purchase of the brand, particularly within a mature economy. In practice, and particularly for frequently bought products, repeat buying is the main determinant of sales volume. In such cases advertising must seek to be reinforcing rather than persuasive. Furthermore, evidence also suggests that in mature, frequently purchased packaged goods markets, the effectiveness of advertising diminishes fast; a small frequency may be sufficient for advertising an established brand.[9]

Doubts about the true contribution of advertising means that, in many sectors, advertising is no longer *the* dominant form of marketing communication for retail firms. Although still a significant component in the promotional tool-box, advertising is commonly used alongside other promotional channels. These may include, among other mechanisms, direct marketing and in-store sales promotion. The latter is used considerably and may involve product displays, in-store promotional material, shelf-edge displays, store design, and the overall ambience of the store itself.[10]

---

[5] J Meyers-Levy and P Malaviya, 'Consumers' Processing of Persuasive Advertisements: An Integrative Framework of Persuasion Theories' [1999] 63 *Journal of Marketing* 45.

[6] A Ehrenberg and others, 'Brand Advertising as Creative Publicity' [2002] 42 *Journal of Advertising Research* 7; J Jones 'Advertising: Strong Force or Weak Force? Two Views an Ocean Apart' [1990] 9 *International Journal of Advertising* 233.

[7] Ehrenberg ibid.

[8] C Pechmann and D W Stewart, 'Advertising Repetition: A Critical Review of Wearin and Wearout' in J H Leigh and C R Martin (eds), *Current Issues and Research in Advertising* (1988) 285–330.

[9] D Vakratsas and T Ambler, 'How Advertising Works: What Do We Really Know?' 63 [1999] *Journal of Marketing* 26.

[10] Contrast the ambience of an Aldi limited line discount store with that of an up-market department store, but where in both cases the store is deliberately designed to communicate the points

C. Advertising and Promotion by Retailers

The role of advertising and promotion are in general terms no different in retailing, but conceal two distinctive characteristics of the retail promotional environment.

First, retailers provide readily identifiable locations where final consumers enter into transactions by which they acquire goods and services manufactured by suppliers, but identified and sourced by the retailer. Consumers therefore see advertising for products designed by manufacturers but which are only available through retail stores (or their online equivalents). In addition to providing the 'lens' through which to view manufacturers' brands, retailers also advertise both themselves as well as their own private label brands. This provides for a complex mix of marketing communications for consumers.

Secondly, retailers by their very nature have access to a broader range of resources for their marketing communications, in comparison with manufacturers. Recall that, unlike conventional product advertising and promotion, promotional activity undertaken by the retailer can take place in the store itself and can make use of its characteristics and environment. Within their stores, retailers work to facilitate and encourage such transactions by providing support services of various kinds, including product displays, stocks, cash, and credit facilities.

Just like suppliers' marketing communications, retailers' advertising and promotion activities must be undertaken in the context of and be consistent with the firm's strategic marketing objectives. McGoldrick identifies five possible goals for retail advertising:[11]

1. to win new customers (in most cases from competitors in an area, particularly in the context of a new store opening);

of difference about the retailer as a brand. In this respect, Aldi UK's marketing communications suggest: 'We cut out anything that increases costs and pushes up prices. That includes elaborate displays, fussy presentation and in store gimmicks. It keeps overheads to a minimum so you pay for food, not unnecessary frills.' <http://www.aldi.co.uk/uk/html/company/all_about_aldi.htm> accessed 13 April 2008. Whilst the department store Harvey Nichols' award-winning new Istanbul store proclaims: 'fit for a pasha, this store has the glamour of crystal in its windows and a showy yet sophisticated gilded interior that will make shoppers feel they have been transported back to the days of the Ottomans'. <http://www.harveynichols.com/output/Page175.asp> accessed 13 April 2008. Interestingly, research suggests that it is the visit to the store which appears to have the most influence on a retailer's price image amongst consumers. UK Competition Commission, 'Groceries Market Inquiry: Prices Practices' (working paper, 23 January 2007) <http://www.competition-commission.org.uk/inquiries/ref2006/grocery/pdf/emerging_thinking_pricing_practices.pdf> accessed 14 April 2008.

[11] P J McGoldrick, *Retail Marketing* (2nd edn, 2002).

2. to increase expenditure by existing customers (by targeting specific customer segments or raising awareness of new features, product ranges, or special offers in store);
3. to increase store traffic (during otherwise quiet trading periods, through promoting discounting or special events);
4. to increase product sales (to promote new lines or unrealized characteristics of branded or private label products or clear unsold inventory); or
5. to develop a store's image (building the longer term reputation of a store for a particular market positioning around—say—price, quality, or service expertise).

Advertising undertaken by retailers themselves has evolved in its sophistication to match the growing professionalism found more broadly within the sector, especially amongst the largest firms. Nevertheless, simple is sometimes best. For example, reference price campaigns are still employed by retailers and have been shown to not always be ineffective (reference price campaigns involve value cues provided by the retailer, such as: 'Regular price £9.95, Now £4.95'). Interestingly, reference pricing appears to result in favourable price perceptions and store shopping intentions only when consumers are shopping for the product in question (and it is therefore immediately relevant to their needs) and have to be combined with limited-time availability information ('offer ends on Saturday') in order to generate more favourable price perceptions and change store destination intentions.[12]

However, the traditional dominance of simplistic comparative 'product-price' announcements had served to reinforce commentators' views that the sector was a relatively unprofessional proponent of marketing principles: 'Each store sings the same song ... "here tomatoes are cheaper". The result is a poor attribution of advertising claims and some lack of credibility.'[13]

This is in part because the evidence suggests that the opportunity to shop across retail stores reduces the effect of comparative price claims on consumers' estimates of lowest price for a particular item, but has less impact on their estimates of the store's regular price.[14] And so, whilst there are still examples of isolated product-price claims, as retailers have come to control more of the supply chain, becoming large and more corporate enterprises, and have come to face more

[12] D J Howard and R A Kerin, 'Broadening the Scope of Reference Price Advertising Research: A Field Study of Consumer Shopping Involvement' [2006] 70(3) *Journal of Marketing* 185.

[13] J-N Kapferer, 'Beyond Positioning: Retailer's Identity' in *Retail Strategies for Profit and Growth* (1986) 167–175.

[14] E A Blair, J Harris, and K B Monroe, 'Effects of Shopping Information on Consumers' Responses to Comparative Price Claims' [2002] 78 *Journal of Retailing* 175.

competition in maturing markets, retail firms have come to develop increasingly coherent and sophisticated communications campaigns. These include longer term campaigns to build price image, including the communication of so-called Every Day Low Price—EDLP—marketing strategies.

Finally, it is interesting to note that whilst generic advertising spending by retailers has increased over the long term, it is still smaller than the advertising budgets of other sectors such as consumer products and automotive. It has also shared in the secular decline which has affected conventional advertising spending more generally in response to the fragmentation of promotional channels, including the growth of the Internet. Nevertheless, in 2005, retail advertising in the US comprised USD19.1 billion, or 12.8 per cent of total advertising spend in that year, whilst the retail sector itself generated some 9.2 per cent of the country's GDP.[15] However, there appears to be no consistent relationship between firm size and advertising budget in the sector. For example, Wal-Mart (the world's largest retailer) was out-spent by Sears, Target, Home Depot, Macy's, and JC Penney in 2006. Macy's alone spent 30 per cent more on advertising than Wal-Mart, despite only generating 11 per cent of the US sales of Wal-Mart.

D. Possible Effects on Competition

In this part we will take a broad view of the range of possible effects that promotion campaigns and advertising may have on competition generally, and in the retail sector specifically.

Promotion and advertising campaigns generally strive to foster brand recognition and create consumer loyalty toward branded goods. Campaigns may affect demand characteristics, pricing, market foreclosure, and barriers to entry and expansion, thereby affecting competition on the market, as we shall illustrate below.

Information flow

It has long been recognized that information is a key component in a competitive market and that it is a valuable attribute of consumer welfare.[16] The flow of

[15] L Hristov, R Cuthbertson, 'Food Retailing: Impact on society and the economy' [2004] 4 *Executive Outlook* 3, 38–51.

[16] G J Stigler, 'The Economics of Information' [1961] 69 *The Journal of Political Economy* 213; OECD, 'Price Transparency' (OECD Roundtable on Competition, DAFFE/CLP(2001)22, 2001) <http://www.oecd.org/dataoecd/52/63/2535975.pdf> accessed 14 March 2008; R Nitsche, N von Hinten-Reed, 'Competitive Impacts of Information Exchange' [2004] CRA Paper <http://ec.europa.eu/comm/competition/antitrust/others/maritime/elaa_proposal/note_on_information_exchange_en.pdf> accessed 29 May 2008.

information through price and non-price promotion assists consumers in making better choices regarding the purchase of goods by identifying sellers, providing terms of sales, and providing information on products, their quality, characteristics, and price.

The flow of information through advertising and promotions facilitates competition by widening the range of known substitutes that the consumer takes into account. The increase in the size of the consideration set *increases* the consumer's *sensitivity to price changes* for any one brand.[17] However, as will be discussed below, loyal customers may be willing to pay more for what they perceive as a superior, distinguishable product, thus allowing the manufacturer to increase the price of the branded product.

In addition, the flow of information increases market transparency and makes it easier for consumers to compare the prices of advertised goods between outlets, thus making it harder for retailers to increase the price of advertised goods.[18] In this respect, advertising serves as a significant contributor to competitive markets.

Note, however, that by their very nature advertising and promotions are neither neutral nor objective. They may often encompass biased, asymmetric information which may not provide consumers with accurate quality data about the goods or service, particularly in comparison with the offerings of competitors. Whilst promotional claims can be regulated by national standards authorities, and certain practices can be prohibited in certain jurisdictions, advertising and other promotions inevitably only serve as an imperfect vehicle for disseminating product information.

An effective illustration of this can be seen in the way in which retail advertising is used, within existing regulations, to make price claims against a competitor. Two leading grocery retailers in the UK—Tesco and Asda—have vied for price leadership in the public's mind over the past eight years. Amid renewed concentration in the sector and to support price promotional activity involving strategic price 'rollback' campaigns, advertising has been developed to signal the dominance of one firm over another in terms of the scale of price competitiveness (rather than in relation to the prices of specific goods sold in the store). The objective of both retailers is to create an *image* of good prices built upon independent

[17] Ibid.

[18] A Mitra and J Lynch, 'Towards Reconciliation of Market Power and Information Theories of Advertising Effects on Price Elasticity' [1995] 21 *Journal of Consumer Research* 644; A Kaul and D Wittink, 'Empirical Generalization about the Impact of Advertising on Price Sensitivity and Price' [1995] 14 *Marketing Science* 151.

third party evidence of price comparison information; not to focus upon individually identifiable branded or private label products. Tesco's campaign in 2007 involved the use of a 'swingometer'—a device used in the UK during the broadcasting of election results—to demonstrate the overwhelming price leadership of Tesco over its main rivals. In 2008, Asda launched its own price image campaign, 'Why Pay More', to draw out the distinctions with Tesco's manufacturer-branded products in particular.

Exchange of information between undertakings

In addition to their impact on consumers, advertising and promotion play an important role in the relationship between undertakings. They affect price signalling, investment decisions, incentives to innovate, and decisions concerning entry, exit, or expansion. It is important to note, however, that information exchanged through advertising, which by its nature is general and available to both undertakings and consumers, is not likely to result in excessive market transparency. As such it differs from information exchange arrangements and is not likely to remove uncertainties inherent in the process of competition.[19]

Brand awareness and loyalty

Advertising and promotions are aimed at building brand awareness and primarily brand loyalty. In essence, brand loyalty leads consumers to attribute value to the brand and favour it over other products which are distinguishable, albeit at times being of similar quality or nature. As such, these promotion channels can work to affect the nature of consumer demand, making it *less elastic and less sensitive to price variations*.[20]

The lower elasticity in demand, which characterizes loyal customers, implies that they would not consider other products as equal substitutes to the advertised brand and would be reluctant to switch to other products even when faced with an increase in price. Subsequently, a promotional campaign which succeeds in fostering brand loyalty shields the brand owner from the forces of competition to some extent, enabling it to charge a price premium over other competing products.[21]

---

[19] These anti-competitive effects will materialize depending on the nature and intensity of information exchange and the market characteristics; UK OFT, 'Guidelines on Agreements and Concerted Practices' (OFT 401, 2004) 3.17–3.23 <http://www.oft.gov.uk/shared_oft/business_leaflets/ca98_guidelines/oft401.pdf> accessed 14 March 2008; Case T-34/92 *Fiatagri UK Ltd and New Holland Ford Ltd v Commission* [1994] ECR II-905; Case C-89/85 *Ahlström Osakeyhtiö and others v Commission* [1993] ECR 1307, [1993] 4 CMLR 407.

[20] Note, however, that a brand loyal consumer is not necessarily less price sensitive.

[21] In *BBI/Boosey & Hawkes* [1987] OJ L286/36, these were among the factors used to assess the market power of Boosey & Hawkes (para 18).

For example, UK variety store Marks & Spencer's 'M&S Food' campaign launched in 2005 was deliberately developed to differentiate the complete food offer within Marks & Spencer from that of other retailers and to generate customer loyalty. The advertising declared that 'this is not just food—this is M&S food'. Although designed to promote the entire range, individual private label products were selected as part of a featured menu. One featured chocolate pudding increased its sales as a result by some 3,500 per cent. As the Marks & Spencer Marketing Director commented: 'that chocolate pudding was just sitting on the top shelf like a sad old magazine, but it was a pudding with a personality. It made you want to lick the telly!'[22] The top three words consumers associate with the Marks & Spencer food brand are: 'expensive', 'reliable', and 'exclusive'. The evidence suggests that Marks & Spencer is seen by customers a retailer of 'expensive, aspirational treats in an attractive and caring environment'.[23]

Brand loyalty affects not only the price of the advertised product but can also affect its availability. In some circumstances, heavily advertised products are more likely to register in consumers' minds as 'must-have' products which the retailer is expected to stock. The pressure on the retailer to stock the brand may in turn affect its bargaining position with the 'must-have' brand producer. This may be particularly the case in markets where the retailer's buying power is less concentrated, such as in the retailing of electrical goods, where large, global manufacturers continue to dominate the value chain. It may also be a characteristic of markets, such as toys or entertainment products, in which fads and fashions in purchasing can be readily generated.[24] For example, the popularity of the Nintendo Wii games console led to 17.5 million consoles being sold worldwide by March 2008. The manufacturer considered withdrawing its advertising in the UK before Christmas 2007 because of a potential inability to meet the demands of retailers and customers: 'as we are keen to act responsibly we are potentially looking at moving some advertising on some products into early 2008'.[25] Limited substitution, which results from brand loyalty, improves the producer's bargaining position vis-à-vis the retailer. In this case, customers and retailers were less interested in the more readily available games consoles from competitors: the Wii was the 'must-have' product.

---

22 Marks & Spencer Marketing Director Steve Sharp quoted in: J Martinson, 'Steve Sharp: Shy Marketing Whizz Creating Sparks at Marks' *Guardian* (London, 23 June 2006) <http://www.guardian.co.uk/media/2006/jun/23/marketingandpr.marksspencer> accessed 14 April 2008.

23 Mintel, *Own Label Grocery Retailing in Europe* (Mintel Oxygen, March 2007).

24 B Lilly and T R Nelson, 'Fads: Segmenting the Fad-buyer Market' [2003] 20 *Journal of Consumer Marketing* 252.

25 BBC News, 'Nintendo Mulls Pulling Wii TV ads' (7 December 2007) <http://news.bbc.co.uk/1/hi/business/7132935.stm> accessed 14 April 2008.

Also illustrative in this respect are comments made by the European Court of Justice (ECJ) in *United Brands v Commission*.[26] There, the ECJ considered the impact of United Brands' (UBC) large scale advertising campaign of its 'Chiquita' brand of bananas. The court noted that the large-scale repeated advertising and promotion campaigns have induced brand loyalty in spite of price differentiation and transformed UBC's bananas into a 'must-have' brand:

> UBC has made this product distinctive by large-scale repeated advertising and promotion campaigns which have induced the consumer to show a preference for it in spite of the difference between the price of labelled and unlabelled bananas . . .[27]
>
> it has thus attained a privileged position by making Chiquita the premier banana brand name on the relevant market with the result that the distributor cannot afford not to offer it to the consumer.[28]

The impact of advertising on brand loyalty, and the impact of the latter on competition may vary and depend generally on the intensity and nature of the advertising campaign and on the product and market characteristics. For example, some evidence suggests that overly repetitive advertising for some products can result in 'wear-out', with the consumer tiring of the frequent use of a particular campaign and perhaps even developing negative attitudes towards a brand as a consequence.[29]

Generally, the more loyalty is fostered, the less elastic is the demand and the more likely it is that the brand producer will be sheltered from the forces of competition.[30] Further, at times brand loyalty may lead to the creation of barriers to entry, as discussed in the following section.

Barriers to expansion and entry

Advertising, which often accompanies product differentiation, may have an entry deterrent effect. Subsequently, it has, at times, been viewed as a barrier to entry.[31] This may be the case where large-scale advertising by a powerful

[26] Case 27/76 *United Brands Continental BV v Commission* [1978] ECR 207.

[27] Ibid, para 91.

[28] Ibid, para 93.

[29] C Pechmann and D W Stewart, 'Advertising Repetition: A Critical Review of Wearin and Wearout' in J H Leigh and C R Martin (eds), *Current Issues and Research in Advertising* (1988) 285–330.

[30] Note however that in some circumstances brand loyalty may make market segmentation profitable and encourage entry. See: J Gabszewicz, L Pepall, and J F Thisse, 'Sequential Entry with Brand Loyalty Caused by Consumer Learning-by-using' [1992] 40 *Journal of Industrial Economics* 397; on price elasticity also see generally: L C Telser, 'Advertising and Competition' [1964] 72 *Journal of Political Economy* 537.

[31] R J Van den Bergh and P D Camesasca, *European Competition Law and Economics: A Comparative Perspective* (2nd edition, 2006), 145; J Farrell, 'Moral Hazard as an Entry Barrier'

incumbent makes competitors' expansion or entry difficult or impossible. In such instance the incumbent's ongoing advertising campaign increases customers' loyalty and shrinks the residual demand that a potential entrant would face, thus making entry more costly and risky.[32] For example, the two market leaders in the US home improvement retailing market are Home Depot and Lowe's. These firms spent USD1.1 billion and USD838 million on advertising respectively in 2006.[33] It is not unreasonable to assume that the 'share of mind' that such large scale campaigns command amongst consumers would make it hard for a new entrant to make its presence felt and build brand awareness, other things being equal.

In its Discussion Paper on the Application of Article 82 of the Treaty to Exclusionary Abuses the European Commission notes, when considering barriers to entry, that:

> it may be difficult to enter an industry where experience or reputation is necessary to compete effectively, both of which may be difficult to obtain as an entrant. Factors such as consumer loyalty to a particular brand, the closeness of relationships between suppliers and customers, the importance of promotion or advertising, or other reputation advantages will be taken into account. Advertising and other investments in reputation are often sunk costs which cannot be recovered in the case of exit and which therefore make entry more risky.[34]

European case law also makes reference, albeit scarcely, to the possibility of advertising forming a barrier to entry. For example, in *United Brands v Commission*[35] the ECJ noted, while considering the barriers to entry to the banana market, that these include, among other things, 'very large-scale advertising campaigns'.[36] In *Kimberly-Clark/Scott Paper*[37] the Commission assessed consumers' loyalty to branded tissue products and noted the importance of advertising expenditure for branded products. The Commission then noted that 'the establishment of a new brand would require heavy investment in advertising and promotion in order to

[1986] 17 *Rand Journal of Economics* 440; J S Bain, *Barriers to New Competition* (1956); R Schmalensee, 'Entry Deterrence in Ready-to eat Breakfast Cereal Industry' [1978] 9 *Bell Journal of Economics* 305; OFT, 'Barriers to Entry and Exit in UK Competition Policy' (Office of Fair Trading Research Paper 2, March 1994) s 2.3.2.

32 OFT Research Paper 2 ibid s 2.3.2

33 Advertising Age, *Datacenter: Marketer Profiles Yearbook* (31 December 2007).

34 European Commission DG Competition, 'DG Competition Discussion Paper on the Application of Article 82 of the Treaty to Exclusionary Abuses' (Public consultation, December 2005) para 40 <http://ec.europa.eu/comm/competition/antitrust/art82/discpaper2005.pdf> accessed 11 April 2008.

35 *United Brands v Commission* (n 26).

36 Ibid, para 122.

37 Case IV/M623 *Kimberly-Clark/Scott Paper* [1996] OJ 183/1; also note Case IV/M190 *Nestle/Perrier* [1992] OJ L356/1.

persuade brand loyal customers to switch away from their usual brand. Such expenditure is a sunk cost and adds to the risk of entry.'[38] In *Nestlé/Perrier*[39] the Commission assessed the competitive environment in the bottled source water market. It noted that heavy advertising by the three leading French suppliers may act as a barrier to entry as the establishment of a new brand would require heavy investment and risk.[40]

It is important to stress that the possibility of finding advertising as a barrier to entry is limited to cases where the incumbent advertiser benefits from distinct economies of scale, the advertising campaign established long term consumer brand loyalty which enables it to earn high profits, and the advertising expenditure is sunk and hence cannot be recovered or transferred.[41] Moreover, in the case of retailing, where barriers to entry are in practice quite low (as, also however, are barriers to exit),[42] advertising's contributory role as a barrier is likely to be proportionally less than for product manufacturers.

Advertising, retail profit margins, and price

A large volume of literature has been dedicated to exploring the way in which advertising may affect retail price and profit.[43] In what follows we briefly outline the main possible effects of advertising and promotion.

Following a promotion campaign and the creation of brand loyalty, the producer may be able to charge a price premium over its rivals. This is often referred to as a reputation premium, which consumers are willing to pay for a product they perceive as superior or desirable.[44] Accordingly, following a successful promotion campaign, prices charged for the advertised product may *increase*, in *absolute* terms.

---

[38] *Kimberly-Clark/Scott Paper* ibid, para 211; See similar Comment on advertising expenditure being a sunk cost which adds to the risk of entry in Case IV/M430 *Procter & Gamble/VP Schickedanz* [1994] OJ L354/32 (para 99).

[39] *Nestlé/Perrier* (n 37).

[40] *Nestlé/Perrier* (n 37) paras 33, 97.

[41] Note that advertising expenditures are endogenous sunk costs; see: OFT research paper 2 (n 31) s 2.3.2; Also see generally: Discussion Paper on the Application of Article 82 of the Treaty to Exclusionary Abuses (n 34) para 40; Van den Bergh and Camesasca (n 31).

[42] According to BERR statistics, retail insolvencies run at around 10% of all business failures in the UK.

[43] See e.g.: M Levy and others, 'Emerging Trends in Retail Pricing Practice: Implications for Research' [2004] 80 *Journal of Retailing* 165; R N Bolton and V Shankar, 'An Empirically Derived Taxonomy of Retailer Pricing and Promotion Strategies' [2003] 79 *Journal of Retailing* 213; Steiner (n 48).

[44] A V Abela and P W Farris, 'Advertising and Competition' (Darden School of Business Administration, University of Virginia) (15 December 1999) <http://faculty.darden.virginia.edu/farrisp/personal/pdf/AdvCompFinal.pdf> accessed 2 April 2008; A V Abela and P W Farris, 'Advertising and Competition' in R Hovland, J Wolburg and E Haley (eds), *Readings in Advertising, Society, and Consumer Culture* (2007).

On the other hand, in certain circumstances, advertising may lead to a *decrease* in price. As indicated above, brand recognition and loyalty results in price transparency, enabling consumers more easily to compare different outlets' prices of the branded goods. This transparency limits outlets' ability to increase the price charged for the branded goods above competitive levels and exerts pressure on retailers to lower their prices. Failing to observe a competitive price for branded goods may result in customers switching outlets within brand rather than switching the brand within the outlet.[45] A typical example of this can be found in the product-price advertising commonly conducted for audio-visual and electrical goods. For such generally higher involvement goods, consumers may have already selected their desired brand and be seeking the cheapest available incidence of the model. A retailer may seek to encourage store switching and reassure the consumer with a combination of price-matching and non-price features, such as extended warranties.

The price of the advertised brand also affects the pricing of its substitutes.[46] Non-advertised brands use the advertised brand price as a reference point and may sell at a discounted price to maintain sales volume. One would therefore expect to see a gap between the price of the leading brand and other substitutes. Note, however, that this *relative* gap between the brand leader and the price of non-leading brands does not imply lower or higher prices in *absolute* terms. It only implies that customers may be willing to pay a premium, above market price, for the advertised brand which they will not pay for non-leading brands.

The increase in demand for advertised products is also likely to affect the retailers' pricing strategy and their willingness to lower their retail gross margins.[47] A successful advertising campaign results in *less elastic demand* for the product and subsequently increases the producer's market power at the expense of the retailer. Accordingly, as emphasized by Steiner, a strong negative correlation exists between the weight of the brand advertising and the retailer's margins.[48] Manufacturers, through successful advertising, can force retailers to become more competitive

---

45 R L Steiner, 'The Virtual Equivalence of Horizontal and Vertical Competition—An Analysis of the Sources of Market Power in Consumer Goods Industries' [2007] Working paper presented at the Annual Loyola Antitrust Colloquium.

46 *Kimberly-Clark/Scott Paper* (n 37); in this merger decision the Commission approved the transaction following in-depth investigation. In its decision, the Commission noted the role played by the advertised leading tissue brand and its impact on the price of private label tissue.

47 M S Albion and P W Farris, 'Manufacturer advertising and Retailer Gross Margins' in P N Bloom (ed), *Advances in Marketing and Public Policy: A Research Annual* (1987).

48 Steiner (n 45); R L Steiner, 'Manufacturer's Brand Advertising and how it Influences Manufacturers' and Retailers' Margins' [2001] 7 *Journal of Marketing Communications* 35.

and command lower retail gross margins for the advertised brand.[49] In other words, vertical bargaining between the retailer and the producer of an advertised brand is likely to result in lower gross margins for the retailer without significant effects on consumers.[50]

E. Advertising, Promotion, and Private Labels

The tale of advertising, promotion, and competition takes an interesting turn when looking at private labels. The supermarkets' control over shelving, in-store promotion, and pricing of branded and own-label goods and their superior access to consumer data has the potential of changing the power balance between the producer and distributor and between the private label and branded good. The interaction between the upstream producer and downstream distributor is explored below.

Profit margins, market transparency, and price

As indicated in Section D above, the flow of information through advertising and promotion affects vertical bargaining between the retailer and the producer of the advertised brand and is likely to result in lower gross margins for the retailer.[51]

Not surprisingly, the retailer's position differs when selling its own private label. The retailer, being in control of the costs associated with the development of a private label product, including those of advertising and promotion, is in principle able to retain high profit margins on account of the private label's producer, whose prices are lower. Assuming that both the private label and branded product in a certain category are equally fast selling, the difference in profitability creates a strong preference for the retailer to promote the private label on account of the advertised branded goods.

The price of the leading advertised brand directly affects the price of substitutions, among them the private label. As noted by the Commission in the

[49] Steiner, ibid; R L Steiner, 'Does Advertising Lower Consumer Prices?' [1973] 37 *Journal of Marketing* 19; R L Steiner, 'The Evolution and Applications of Dual-stage Thinking' [2004] *Antitrust Bulletin* 877; M P Lynch, 'Why Economists are Wrong to Neglect Retailing and How Steiner's Theory Provides an Explanation of Important Regularities' [2004] 49 *Antitrust Bulletin* 911.

[50] On the other hand, non-advertised brands are likely to result in larger retailer margins on account of the producer's margins; R L Steiner, 'The Third Relevant Market' [2000] 45 *Antitrust Bulletin* 719; Steiner (n 48).

[51] Steiner's Dual Stage Model (n 49); Steiner, 'The Third Relevant Market' (n 50) 719; Steiner (n 48).

Procter & Gamble/Gillette decision,[52] the retailers have the advantage to be in a position to fix the prices for their own private labels in reaction to the producers of branded products. 'In contrast, these producers are not able to readjust their prices to the retailers' private label prices. Therefore, the retailer has the capacity to counteract efficiently against the leading brands of the parties with its own private labels, whilst the parties have an asymmetry of information vis-à-vis prices for private labels.'[53]

The correlation between the price of the branded product and the private label means that an increase in the branded product's price will affect the value perception of the private label and will subsequently allow the retailer to increase the price of its own private label.[54] Subsequently, the retailer may have an incentive to push up the price of the advertised brand.[55] When the manufacturer and retailer both have market power, the launch of a quality-equivalent own brand by the retailer can lead to higher average prices in a category.[56]

In practice, there may be constraints on these kinds of behaviour. The first comes from the different kinds of marketing objectives sought by the retailer in the context of its private labels. For example, a retailer may have different pricing strategies for its private label goods depending on the role that they are designed to play. 'Value' private labels play a different role from private labels deliberately designed to compete with the leading manufacturer's brand. Indeed, a single retailer, especially in European grocery retailing, may maintain several tiers of private labels simultaneously, each targeted at different groups of consumers.[57] Secondly, market transparency and the consumer's ability to compare the price of the branded goods to other outlets are also likely to curtail this incentive. The retailer is aware of the fact that consumers are more likely to choose a store to shop in on the basis of criteria other than their own private label products. Research into the UK grocery retailing market has shown that it is the accessibility and

52 *Procter & Gamble/Gillette* (Case COMP/M.3732) Commission Decision of 15 July 2005 <http://ec.europa.eu/comm/competition/mergers/cases/decisions/m3732_20050715_20212_en.pdf> accessed 27 May 2007.

53 Ibid, para 124.

54 *Kimberly-Clark/Scott Paper* (n 37); N Levy, 'Kimberly-Clark/Scott and the Power of Brands' [1996] 17 *European Competition Law Review* 403; K Namwoon and P M Parker, 'Collusive Conduct in Private Label Markets' [1999] 16 *International Journal of Research in Marketing* 143.

55 Ibid.

56 D A Soberman and P M Parker, 'The Economics of Quality-equivalent Store Brands' [2006] 23 *International Journal of Research in Marketing* 125.

57 H Laaksonen and J Reynolds, 'Own Brands in Food Retailing Across Europe' [1994] 2 *Journal of Brand Management* 37. Many studies, based on the private label growth experienced by grocers and supermarkets in the US, make the assumption that private labels only occupy a very low price positioning; see e.g.: D A Soberman and P M Parker, 'Private Labels: Psychological Versioning of Typical Consumer Products' [2004] 2 *Quantitative Marketing and Economics* 347.

convenience of the store and its layout, followed by overall perceived price levels of branded goods, followed by the public image of the retailer which are likely to determine store choice, rather than the store's private label products alone.[58] Competitive pressure would therefore push the retail price down.[59] Thirdly, the brand owner is likely to react to the increasing threat from private labels by providing sale price reductions or engaging in non-price promotional activities.[60]

Brand advertising can therefore retain a degree of competitive pressure on a retailer, even if it offers its own private label. Advertising and promotion campaigns of the leading brand and the market transparency they foster limit the outlets' ability to increase the price charged for the branded good and serve to push down the prices of both branded goods and private labels, to the benefit of consumers.

Interestingly, the lack of price transparency of private labels between retailers stands in sharp contrast to that of branded labels. The consumer is likely to find it difficult, if not impossible, to compare directly the price of private labels offered by different retailers due to the product differentiation of these private labels. Subsequently, the market transparency, from which consumers benefit when choosing between branded goods, is diluted in the case of private labels.

Yet again, the retailer's ability to benefit from the lack of transparency may be curtailed by the price of the branded goods serving as a focal point. Interestingly, the largest retailers who have extensive ranges of private label products are well-placed to present the consumer with real choice between differently priced private label goods, without reference to branded products. For example, in a recent promotional campaign by Tesco for eggs, the voiceover describes the 12 different types of private label eggs typically offered by the firm, each designed for a different use, from a basic egg for a cake to a Finest Free Range egg 'for a treat'. These internally-referenced marketing communications play a powerful role in reinforcing the retail brand's credentials as a 'one stop shop', match the growing sophistication of consumers in wanting to make informed choices about products, and exclude discussion of branded equivalents.

Barriers to entry and foreclosure effects

In the majority of categories the retailer's control over the distribution channel, pricing, and in-store promotion enables it to bypass many of the barriers faced by

58 Groceries Market Inquiry: Pricing Practices working paper (n 10).

59 Lynch (n 49).

60 M B Ward and others, 'Effects of the Private-Label Invasion in Food Industries' [2002] 84 *American Journal of Agricultural Economics* 961.

other producers. The retailer's control over the outlet dramatically reduces the risk of unsuccessful entry, retaliation, and post-entry competition. In this respect private labels act as a counter force to heavily advertised goods.

This effect is, however, confined to the relationship between the private label and the leading must-have brand. When one considers the availability of substitutes in the outlet, it is apparent that second-tier, slower selling, national brands are dropped in many categories to give way for the private label. The foreclosure effect may eventually result in reduced choice for consumers.[61]

Subsequently, heavy advertising has limited effects on the availability and success of private labels, but may have a detrimental effect on the availability of other slower selling brands. To be more precise, it is the introduction of the private label alongside the advertised brand which is likely to increase the foreclosure effect. Only the fast selling, advertised brands will find their ways to the shelves alongside the private label, pushing out slower selling brands. As a result, advertising, in a 'private-label-environment' plays a pivotal role and is more likely to form a barrier to entry.

It is important to note one caveat. In some product markets it is possible that the incumbent brand producer exerts such market power which would make it unprofitable for the retailer to introduce a private label. Such may be the case when a brand dominates a product or service category to the extent that the private label would find it difficult to develop sufficient sales volume which would justify its launch, or where consumers would doubt a retailer's capability or expertise to launch products of an acceptable standard.[62] Retailers have not sought to sell private label cars, for example. Such markets are increasingly hard to find, however. Indeed, many consumers place sufficient trust in retailers as brands to encourage their diversification into selling an even wider range of products and services. A 1998 McKinsey survey sought to understand the extent to which consumers felt that US brands could be further leveraged. One conclusion was that 60 per cent of respondents felt that Wal-Mart had the skills to expand successfully into activities ranging from restaurants to travel to insurance and even television broadcasting.[63]

---

[61] Ibid.

[62] R L Steiner, 'The Nature and Benefits of National Brand/Private Label Competition' [2004] 24 *Review of Industrial Organization* 105, 119, citing N Borden, *The Economics Effects of Advertising* (1942) 589.

[63] J S Eagle, E E Joseph and E Lempres, 'From Products to Ecosystems: Retail 2010' [2000] 4 *McKinsey Quarterly* 108.

Market share, brand loyalty, and outlet reputation

It is generally accepted that there is an inverse relationship between the advertising intensity of branded goods and the private label's market share.[64] The private label, at least at its infancy, targets those consumers who are not brand loyal, offering them a similar, yet cheaper alternative to the branded product. Absent advertising to support the private label or the creation of certain reputation, the private label mostly satisfies the generic demand for goods of a particular class. Therefore, the intensity of advertising by the leading brand dictates the private label's market share.

In the last two decades the quality of private labels has improved due to technological advantages and production by name-brand firms. The quality improvement has enabled private labels to replicate national brands and develop their reputation.[65] This, together with the support of advertising and the outlet reputation, has led to increased market power for the private labels, placing them in direct competition with branded goods.

A distinct advantage which supports the increased market power of private labels is the use of the outlet's reputation to promote the label across categories. The retailer's advertising campaign is cost effective, as, for example, in the case of grocery retailing, it often promotes both the supermarket as an outlet and its private label range as a quality and/or low price alternative. Such campaigns facilitate the creation of a 'reliability umbrella' for the private label, increasing the volume of sales by enticing customers to trust the label either for its high quality or its guaranteed low price across the range.

The supermarket's position enables it to create a brand image for the private label range which is then deployed in different product markets.[66] Its unique position enables the supermarket to achieve economies of scale and invest in the reputation of its private label range rather than in the advertising of a particular product. This stands in contrast to the majority of branded goods advertising in which investment is sunk and often non-transferable to other categories. For example, Procter and Gamble sought to transfer its expertise within areas as diverse as

---

64 Steiner (n 62), citing studies by V J Cook and T F Schutte (1967), S J Hoch and S Banerji (1993), S K Dhar and S J Hoch (1997), and F Scott Morton and F Zettelmeyer (2001).

65 Ward and others (n 60).

66 See e.g. comments made by Morrisons: 'Own-label products acquire the well-known reputation of the retailer, which promotes sales over less well-known secondary and tertiary brand reputations.' UK Competition Commission, 'The Supply of Groceries in the UK Market Investigation: Provisional Findings Report' app 8.11: 'Retailer Own-Label Goods' (31 October 2007) para 25 <http://www.competition-commission.org.uk/Inquiries/ref2006/grocery/prov_findings/prov_find_app_8_11.pdf> accessed 7 April 2008.

personal care, household cleaning, and disposable nappies into soft drinks through the acquisition of Sundor Brands, manufacturer of the Sunny Delight fruit-flavour drink in 1989. The product range was launched in the UK in 1998, but, despite a £10 million promotional campaign, was unsuccessful for a variety of reasons and the brand was eventually sold on.[67]

In-store promotional activity

The retailer's control over the outlet, both in terms of shelf space allocation, visual merchandising, and promotion, provides additional opportunities for determining the nature and extent of marketing communications in relation to private labels in ways which are not immediately available to suppliers. It is important to note that a high proportion of consumer decision-making, particularly for low involvement goods, is made in store. For example, US studies have shown that only around one third of grocery store purchases are planned in advance.[68] Retailers make increasingly effective and innovative use of their store environments to enhance the promotion of both products and services. Displays can be used to affect the ways in which consumers perceive products, by manipulating the area devoted to the product, the incidence and nature of adjacent products, and the size and layout of the overall display.[69] A product's absolute and relative shelf position may have an appreciable effect upon consumer choices and product sales levels.[70] Factors include the horizontal and vertical placement of products, in relation to both product size and the eye level of the customer. Consequently, considerations of in-store promotion take on a particular importance for both producers and retailers. This has become sufficiently important for many producers to have shifted promotional spending from generic advertising to in-store promotional programmes, which include shelf space management.[71]

Access to data

The ability of many retail firms to utilize data from their own databases to target specific consumers creates a distinct advantage for the retailer over

---

67 J Clayton, 'The Rise and Fall of Sunny Delight' *BBC News* (London, 3 December 2003) <http://news.bbc.co.uk/1/hi/business/3257820.stm> accessed 14 April 2008.

68 J Dagnoli, 'Impulse Governs Shoppers' [1987] *Advertising Age* 93.

69 X Drezé, S J Hoch, and M E Purk, 'Shelf Management and Space Elasticity' [1994] 70 *Journal of Retailing* 301.

70 C Chung and others, 'Economic Evaluation of Shelf Space Management in Grocery Stores' [2007] 23 *Agribusiness* 583.

71 See the discussion in Chapter 9 herein which focuses on in-store competition and the control of shelf space.

brand owners.[72] Electronic point-of-sale (EPOS) data is now available to the majority of retailers in developed markets. By contrast, the producer relies on secondary data, perhaps supplemented by some retailer-supplied EPOS data, in its attempt to track the sales and changes in the nature of the market for its branded goods. For example, Wal-Mart's Retail Link e-collaboration platform accommodates over 100,000 registered users, 40,000 supplier companies, and a 600 terabyte database containing 104 weeks worth of point-of-sale information. Suppliers can download sales and inventory data which can be analysed in a variety of ways and, in particular, can be used to assist in forecasting demand.

The availability of such data has allowed some retail firms to develop promotional mechanisms designed to enhance customer loyalty by means of reward or incentive programmes, including the provision of discount vouchers to be set against future purchases. When combined with personal information from customers, such data can be used to understand buying behaviour, to make much more specific sales forecasts, and to deliver significantly more relevant and personalized marketing communications.[73] The UK's Tesco operates a Clubcard scheme which mails 13 million Clubcard holders on a quarterly basis with up to £1 billion in vouchers and coupons for both private label and branded goods.[74] Some £4 out of every £5 spent by Tesco shoppers in the UK is spent under the auspices of a Clubcard, meaning that the company is able to gain insights into the buyer behaviour of up to 80 per cent of its shoppers. Some commentators[75] have suggested that the economic effect of such schemes is to increase overall price levels in stores, but this has yet to be independently confirmed.

F. Conclusions

Advertising and other forms of promotional activities generate a mixture of welfare effects. On one hand they facilitate information exchange and transparency, thus creating competitive pressure and lowering prices. By empowering the manufacturer and improving its bargaining position they can work to curtail some of the downstream market power exhibited by private label owners.

---

72 On the asymmetry of information note the Commission's comment in *Procter & Gamble/Gillette* (n 52).

73 M Stone and others, 'The Effect of Retail Customer Loyalty Schemes—Detailed Measurement or Transforming Marketing?' [2004] 12 *Journal of Targeting, Measurement and Analysis for Marketing* 305.

74 See a description of the origins, development, and application of the Clubcard programme in T Hunt, C Humby, and T Phillips, *Scoring Points: How Tesco Continues to Win Customer Loyalty* (2006).

75 See e.g.: Consumers Against Supermarket Privacy Invasion and Numbering (CASPIAN), <http://www.nocards.org> accessed 14 April 2008.

On the other hand, at times, advertising may lead to price increases, although one should acknowledge that this will only be the case when consumers value the reputation premium of the brand concerned. When successful, such campaigns may give rise to foreclosure effects or even create barriers to entry. This may especially be the case in a 'private label environment' where private labels dominate the shelf space.

Looking forward, it is important to recognize that the promotional environment within which retailing operates is undergoing significant evolution, in common with the impact being experienced by other business-to-consumer firms. Advertising is no longer a dominant form of marketing communication for retail firms. Most commentators note a secular shift away from conventional advertising vehicles (such as television and press) into new promotional channels, including those provided by mobile phones and the Internet. Direct marketing—including that associated with the promulgation of loyalty card schemes—in-store sales promotion, as well as more novel promotional mechanisms, including sponsorship, have also become important elements in the retailers' tool-kit. More broadly, the need for greater accountability of promotional expenditure has encouraged many consumer-facing firms, including retailers, to reallocate budgets away from non-personalized toward more personalized marketing communications. Similarly, for many retailers and suppliers, this means that the move toward more sophisticated sales promotion mechanisms is likely to continue.

The shift toward in-store promotion provides greater control to the retailer and may tilt the balance in favour of own-labels on account of branded products. The future impact of these shifts on the pricing of own labels and consumer welfare will deserve further scrutiny.

Part V

RETAIL CONSOLIDATION AND THE USE OF REMEDIES

13

RETAIL CONSOLIDATION: THE IMPLICATIONS OF MERGERS AND BUYING ALLIANCES

*John Ratliff**

A. Introduction

The object of this paper is to outline the typical considerations which competition regulators have in relation to mergers (and acquisitions) and buying alliances in the retail sector. The author's principal reference is EC Competition law, although reference is also made to UK competition law. Private label is part of those typical considerations, but not usually the central one. The perspective offered is that of a legal practitioner, who is necessarily led to look at both sides. The aim here is, as far as possible, to set out the main principles based on

* Partner, Wilmer Cutler Pickering Hale and Dorr LLP (WilmerHale), Brussels. The views expressed in this paper are personal and do not necessarily reflect those of WilmerHale. This paper is a revised version of the presentation made on 21 May 2007 to the Oxford Retail Competition Symposium. With thanks to Anastasios Xeniadis for his assistance in researching this paper.

experience, rather than offering a detailed survey of the case law or the very extensive literature on such issues.[1]

The plan of this chapter is to deal first with mergers (Section B), then buying alliances (Section C), then comment on consolidation of these two aspects (Section D). The most recurrent themes in the author's view are then highlighted (Section E), with finally some conclusions (Section F).

B. Retail Mergers: Typical Competition Considerations

There have been a number of EC merger control cases dealing with retail concentration. The main EC cases are: *Kesko/Tuko*,[2] *Rewe/Meinl*,[3] *Carrefour/Promodes*,[4] and *Blokker/Toys R' US*,[5] with *Rewe/Meinl* still the leading precedent. Buyer power is also dealt with in the European Commission's Horizontal Merger Guidelines.[6]

Leading cases in brief

Kesko/Tuko was a case involving the merger of two Finnish retail chains, which accounted for some 55 per cent of sales of daily consumer goods and which was almost three times larger than its nearest competitor. The Commission found that the new entity would have unique purchasing power, reinforced by various specific factors, and that, after the merger, Kesko would be able to obtain lower

1 See generally, L H Röller, 'Buyer Power in the EU' (Presentation at the American Antitrust Institute Conference on 'Buyer Power and Antitrust', Washington DC, 22 June 2004) <http://ec.europa.eu/dgs/competition/economist/buyer_power.pdf> accessed 30 May 2008; J Ratliff, 'Buyer Power' (Presentation at the IBC Competition Law Conference, London, 9 May 2000) <http://www.wilmerhale.com/files/Publication/0f4ec90e-8095-46f2-965e-62ab2d97ae7c/Presentation/PublicationAttachment/b21830fe-303c-401f-9742-6387855fd646/Ratliff_Slides_LondonConf_BuyerPower_May2000.pdf> accessed 31 May 2008; the ABA Symposium on Buyer Power and Antitrust [2005] 72 *Antitrust Law Journal*; C D Ehlermann and L Laudati, *Proceedings of the European Competition Forum* (1997); OECD, 'Buying Power of Multi-Product Retailers' (Policy Roundtables, 1998) <http://www.oecd.org/dataoecd/1/18/2379299.pdf> accessed 31 May 2008; Dobson Consulting, 'Buyer Power and Its Impact on Competition in the Food Retailing Distribution Sector of the European Union' (Report for the European Commission, May 1999) <http://ec.europa.eu/comm/competition/publications/studies/bpifrs/> accessed 31 May 2008; J Faull and A Nikpay (eds), *The EC Law of Competition* (2nd edn, 2007) paras 7.301 *et seq*.

2 *Kesko/Tuko* (Case IV/ M.784) [1997] OJ L110/53.

3 *Rewe/Meinl* (Case IV/M.1221) [1999] OJ L274/1.

4 *Carrefour/Promodes* (Case COMP/M.1684), 25 January 2000 <http://ec.europa.eu/comm/competition/mergers/cases/decisions/m1684_6_fr.pdf> accessed 31 May 2008.

5 *Blokker/Toys R' US* (Case IV/M.890), 26 June 1997 <http://ec.europa.eu/comm/competition/mergers/cases/decisions/m890_19970626_664_en.pdf> accessed 31 May 2008.

6 Guidelines on the Assessment of Horizontal Mergers under the Council Regulation on the Control of Concentration between Undertakings [2004] OJ C31/5, paras 61–67 ('The EC Horizontal Merger Guidelines').

prices from producers to an extent that none of its competitors would be able to match. This would make it difficult for competitors to compete actively on price and also would make new entry on the market more difficult. The Commission prohibited the transaction in 1996.

Rewe/Meinl was a case involving a merger of a German/Austrian retailer and an Austrian retailer, which accounted for some 30 per cent of retail food sales in Austria. The Commission noted that food retailing was highly concentrated there. The Commission found that the transaction would increase the already strong position of Rewe further, with particular strength in certain regions and areas. The merger was also found to create or strengthen dominant positions on some nine Austrian purchasing markets. The transaction was cleared in 1999, but only after Rewe offered undertakings which meant that it acquired only 162 out of 341 Meinl shops, accounting for some 34 per cent of Meinl's food retailing turnover and 2.5 per cent as opposed to 7 per cent market share.

Carrefour/Promodes was a food retail concentration related to France, Spain, Portugal, Italy, and Greece, which the Commission cleared as part of a 'Phase 1' preliminary investigation in 1999, after undertakings were given. There are three main features of the case of interest: First, Carrefour gave up a minority stake in a rival group controlling the competing Cora chain. Second, the Commission referred certain parts of the transaction to the national competition authorities in France and Spain, because of local effects. This is interesting, given that generally the Commission considers markets to be local (based on driving distance for consumers) but overlapping and hence broader, especially given centralized (national) sales strategies of suppliers. Third, in considering the purchasing strength of the new entity the Commission also noted the significant shares of the rival purchasing groups Lucie and Opera, combining two different groups of other significant retailers.[7] The Commission considered that it could not exclude that Carrefour would have dominant positions on certain purchasing markets, which prompted the undertakings offered.

Blokker/Toys 'R' Us was a case involving two Dutch toy retailers, one part of a broader Dutch retail group, the other being the Dutch operations of a US-based toy retail group. Even before the transaction, Blokker was found to be dominant on the market for specialized retail toy outlets. By itself, Blokker was found to have some 55–65 per cent of Dutch toy sales, with the nearest competitor only on 10–20 per cent. Blokker was also found to have significant scale advantages through branded and unbranded goods and to have the advantage of offering several different outlet formulae, to which Toys 'R' Us 'megastores' would be a further

[7] See: *Carrefour/Promodes* (n 4) paras 48 and 76 *et seq.*

complement. Some suppliers also said they would not introduce new products in the Netherlands, unless they were in Blokker outlets. The Commission found that the transaction strengthened Blokker's dominance, making it even more difficult for others to compete, and prohibited it in 1997.

Core principles

The European Commission (the Commission) generally carries out a two-fold structural assessment, looking at the procurement markets (i.e. from which suppliers do the merging entities purchase goods) and the downstream supply markets to consumers, in which the merging entities operate.[8] These aspects are looked at separately and then together insofar as they are interdependent.

A prominent consideration for the Commission on the procurement side has been whether suppliers are so *dependent* on the merged entity that they will have to give in to the merged entity's demands; notably, if it would be difficult for a supplier to find alternative sales channels to the merged entity and the supplier might even go bankrupt if it were to lose the merged entity's business.

For example, in *Rewe/Meinl*, the Commission noted:[9]

> It must be borne in mind here firstly that, when they lose a major customer, producers do not have much in the way of alternatives. In the food-retailing trade, especially if the firm concerned is already on the list of the leading competitor Spar, only small competitors are left, and they are hardly in a position to take up a large share of turnover. Switching to other sales channels is difficult, costly and, in the short term at least, generally impossible. Switching to exports, mentioned by the parties as an alternative, is likewise not feasible in the short term. To build up export markets, an on-the-spot presence and an intensive, costly canvassing of the market are normally necessary. The Commission has information in its possession which indicates that it can take about five years to attain a satisfactory level of exports, to Germany for example. The upshot is that already on the supplier side there is a strong dependence on Rewe/Billa/Meinl, a dependence which will grow as a result of the merger.
>
> Rewe/Billa and Meinl, on the other hand, are not dependent on individual suppliers. The leading supplier to the Rewe group (the Nestlé group) covers, according to the notification, only about [. . .]% of the volume of purchases. In the case of Meinl, the leading supplier covers approximately [. . .]% of the volume of purchases. The result is a much heavier dependence of the supplier side on Rewe/Billa/Meinl than the other way round. This is the norm, moreover, with large food retailers . . . Range flexibility in the trade is far greater than the flexibility of producers in production and distribution. Hence it is much easier for the trade not to buy something than it is for the producer not to produce it . . .

---

8 See e.g.: *Kesko/Tuko* (n 2) para 38.
9 See e.g.: *Rewe/Meinl* (n 3) paras 102–103 (footnotes omitted).

In this context, there is discussion of the so-called '*threat point*' of the supplier (being the amount of business which could drive a supplier to bankruptcy if lost) which, it has been suggested, should be some 22 per cent of sales.[10] However, lower figures for market power are also suggested, starting from the 5–10 per cent level.

By classic supply side merger control approaches, these are not levels suggesting concerns about dominance. Nevertheless, clearly such structural implications are taken seriously, insofar as dependencies are created or strengthened.

Considerable care is required on market definition here. On the one hand procurement markets may be wider than they appear at first sight, diluting market shares and reasons for concern. On the other hand, regulators may define procurement markets more narrowly into certain product categories.[11] Clearly the categorization may be very important to assess any market power.

In considering such retail mergers, the Commission talks of a so-called '*spiral effect*'. This is the idea that the merged entity will have greater purchasing power, which will lead to greater downstream sales power, which will in turn lead to greater purchasing power.[12]

In *Rewe/Meinl*, the Commission put it like this, in what is still a classic statement of its approach:[13]

> The exercise of buyer power which leads to the securing of a more favourable purchase deal is not to be considered per se detrimental to the economy as a whole. Especially where the supplier side is itself highly concentrated and powerful buyers are faced with effective competition in their own selling market and hence are compelled to pass on any savings to their own customers, buyer power can prevent monopoly or oligopoly profits from being earned on the supply side . . . However, if the powerful buyer himself occupies in his selling market a strong position which is no longer kept sufficiently in check by the competition, any savings can no longer be expected to be passed on to customers.
>
> In the retail trade there is a close interdependence between the distribution market and the procurement market. Retailers' shares of the distribution market determine their procurement volume: the bigger the retailer's share of the distribution market, the larger the procurement volume. And the larger the procurement volume, the more favourable as a rule are the buying conditions which the trader obtains from his suppliers. Favourable buying conditions can in turn be used in various ways to improve one's position in the distribution market (sometimes through internal or external growth, but also through low-price strategies targeted at competitors).

---

10 See e.g.: *Rewe/Meinl* (n 3) paras 97 and 101, *Carrefour/Promodes* (n 4) para 52 *et seq*.

11 See e.g.: *Rewe/Meinl* (n 3) para 77.

12 See e.g.: *Rewe/Meinl* (n 3) paras 55 and 71–73.

13 *Rewe/Meinl* (n 3) paras 71–74.

> The improved position in the distribution market is itself reflected in a further improvement in buying conditions, and so on.
>
> The spiral described above leads to ever-higher concentration both in distribution markets and in procurement markets. In the short term, final consumers may benefit from the process, as there may be a period of intense (predatory) competition in the distribution market during which the powerful buyer/trader is forced to pass on his savings to consumers. But this will last only until such time as a structure (as in this case, an individual dominant position) is arrived at in the distribution market which leads to a clear reduction in competitive intensity. At this stage, any consideration for the final consumer goes by the board, as he is left with few alternatives.
>
> Buyer power also gives a trader considerable influence over the choice of products which come to market and hence are obtainable by consumers. Products which are not bought by a dominant buyer have practically no chance of reaching the final consumer as the supplier lacks alternative outlets. Lastly the dominant buyer determines the success or otherwise of production innovations.

The spiral effect described is therefore generally considered to be positive, *provided* that a retailer is not, or does not become, individually dominant, or collectively dominant (with others) on both the upstream purchasing and the downstream supply markets. If that were to happen, there is concern that the gains of the increased purchasing power will not be passed through to customers and that the dominant firm will be able to squeeze existing competitors in the downstream market, or even oust them completely from the market. Moreover, to quote the jargon of these cases, there is concern that the retailer may be or become the 'gatekeeper' of access to the market.[14]

Otherwise one may add that there is a tendency to narrow market definitions at least insofar as retail competition may be measured very locally (i.e. as the outlets in driving distance of certain consumer groups, or in a certain region), or particular types of supermarket or store.[15]

Further, in assessing retail competition, the Commission may look at the degree of concentration in the upstream supply markets[16] (in other words, how concentrated are the suppliers to the merging entities).

Overall the key issue is whether there will still be effective competition downstream after the merger. The Commission can be expected to look at a variety of factors, including whether the competitors in the downstream market have different profiles, whether the market is still growing, and whether market entry or market expansion for competitors is still possible. Moreover, the Commission

---

14 See e.g.: *Toys R' Us* (n 5) paras 59 and 67; J Faull and A Nikpay (n 1) para 7.346.
15 See e.g.: *Kesko/Tuko*, (n 2) paras 18–20.
16 See: *Rewe/Meinl* (n 3) paras 72–73.

can be expected to pay attention to routes to the market concerned and neighbouring markets, for example whether the merging entities are also operating in other retail markets (e.g. smaller supermarkets and/or cash & carry).[17]

As regards private label, there are usually two considerations: whether the private label brand is on the same market as branded products (which may be the case if the quality is comparable); and whether the fact that the retailer offers private label products makes it stronger. As regards the latter, in the cases, the Commission has found that it does: the private label profile of the retailer may be viewed as increasing its buyer power, especially as regards the brands of the weaker suppliers—partly because of increased economies of scale and partly because direct price comparisons on unbranded goods are more difficult, so higher margins may be charged.[18] Private label offerings may also be seen as a further negotiating tool vis-à-vis suppliers to achieve additional concessions on price or increased marketing support.[19] The presence of a retailer in buying alliances may be seen as a concern, as the Commission questions whether such cooperation may inhibit potential market entry where the retailers are sharing private label brands.[20] However, such purchasing cooperation may also be considered positively, as helping to counterbalance larger competitors, or supply-side concentration, or simply giving greater efficiencies.[21]

Remedies in EC merger control cases in the retail sector can be both 'soft' and 'hard'. In the 'soft' category are, for example, situations where the Commission has 'taken note' of statements that a merged entity would not consolidate its suppliers for five years, or in one case would continue to buy the vast majority of Irish products in Ireland.[22] In the 'hard' category are, for example, requirements to sell stores, to divest holdings in competing chain stores, and prohibition of the merger.

C. Retail Buying Alliances: Typical Considerations

Thus far, the regulatory framework has been the EC merger control rules (or equivalent). As we turn to the issue of buying alliances, we now have to consider the general rules on EC Competition law, as they apply to so-called 'horizontal'

17 See e.g.: *Kesko/Tuko* (n 2) para 38 and *Carrefour/Promodes* (n 4) para 56 et seq.
18 See e.g.: *Toys R' US* (n 5) para 63 et seq, *Rewe/Meinl* (n 3) paras 51 *et seq* and 112–113.
19 See e.g.: *Kesko/Tuko* (n 2) para 133.
20 See: *Kesko/Tuko* (n 2) para 160.
21 See: the discussion of buying alliances in *Carrefour/Promodes* (n 4) at para 76 *et seq.*
22 See e.g.: *Tesco/ABF* Case IV/M.914, 5 May 1997 para 28 *et seq*, <http://ec.europa.eu/comm/competition/mergers/cases/decisions/m914_en.pdf> accessed 31 May 2008.

agreements, meaning those between companies at the same level of trade, which may be competitors (or not) depending on the facts. These rules are now conveniently summarized in the European Commission's Horizontal Cooperation Guidelines.[23]

The assessment of the competitive impact of buying alliances in the retail sector generally comes into play at two levels: purchasing cooperation amongst large integrated chain stores, i.e. (sometimes international) purchasing groups amongst the *large* retailers; and purchasing cooperation amongst *smaller* rivals, which are trying to stay within a competitive range of the prices which the larger chains can obtain (although their costs may still be higher).

Such purchasing cooperation may be pro-competitive, offering real distribution efficiencies, new product offerings, greater investments through joint procurement, and the sponsoring of new supplies into the market.

However, such cooperation may also be anti-competitive. For example, such cooperation could also involve purchasing cartels offering no real efficiencies.[24] There are also usually concerns about risks of market sharing and collusion (e.g. where there is one participant per EU Member State). There may also be concerns that shared common costs may lead to reduced competition and that products may be standardized, reducing innovation. There are not many such cases at EC level and usually they have involved small groups (see e.g. *Eudim*[25] and the *EEIG Orphe*[26]).

Under the EC rules, there is what lawyers tend to call a 'safe harbour' for purchasing groups as regards structural issues. Such a horizontal cooperation is considered lawful if the combined market share of the parties to the cooperation accounts for less than 15 per cent market share on the upstream purchasing market and their combined market share is also less than 15 per cent market share on the downstream supply market.[27]

If the companies have more than that market share, a more detailed assessment has to be done, to see if there is a competition issue within Article 81(1) of the EC Treaty, or which can be cleared under Article 81(3) of the EC Treaty. In other words, one looks in detail at issues such as whether the companies compete in

---

23 See: Commission Notice (EC) Guidelines on the Applicability of Article 81 of the EC Treaty to Horizontal Cooperation Agreements [2001] OJ C3/2 paras 115–138 (EC Horizontal Cooperation Guidelines).

24 See e.g.: the recent *Spanish Raw Tobacco Purchasing Cartel* [2007] OJ L102/14.

25 *Eudim* [1996] OJ C111/8; J Ratliff 'Major Events in EC Competition Law, 1996' [1997] 2 International Company and Commercial Law Review 43.

26 European Commission, *1990 Annual Report on Competition Policy*, para 102.

27 EC Horizontal Cooperation Guidelines (n 23) para 130.

the first place, what is the supply side concentration, whether the cooperation offers efficiencies, and whether it may eliminate competition in a substantial part of the market.

This 'safe harbour' is clearly conservative (as one would expect from such a concept). It may well be, as the EC Horizontal Cooperation Guidelines also note, that there is *no* concern about such market shares. The key point is, however, that then companies are expected to do a more detailed self-assessment as to whether they are infringing the competition rules and, if so, to adapt their behaviour accordingly.

One should also recall that under the EC rules a double review may be required: 'horizontal' cooperation issues under the EC Horizontal Cooperation Guidelines and 'vertical' supply issues (e.g. selling, distribution, and supply to consumers or, as appropriate, the next layer of the supply chain) under the EC Vertical Restraints Guidelines and Block Exemption.[28]

Interestingly a recent RBB Economics report for the UK Office of Fair Trading[29] suggests that the downstream 'safe harbour' ceiling should be 25 per cent of the downstream market (in line with the EC merger control presumption that there is no concern below 25 per cent market share and because purchasing groups are less integrated than single companies). It is also suggested that, on the upstream side, more than 15 per cent market share could also be appropriate. However, RBB Economics notes that *cumulative* harmful effects need to be considered (e.g. if several buyers and buyer groups all operate similar purchasing policies).

There are some aspects of buying alliances which appear to involve difficult decisions in terms of regulatory treatment. For example, if members of a purchasing group are required to buy through the group, that makes it more efficient and gives more buyer power (which may be considered pro-competitive, if it leads to the passing on of benefits gained to consumers). If, however, the purchasing commitment to the group is more open, the group's buyer power is weakened, but the members' freedom to purchase as they please is greater (so the cooperation is less restrictive in that sense).

There are various cases on this in EC law. Notably, the 'Danish Cooperatives' case, *Gøttrup-Klim*[30] in which a significant purchasing cooperation was considered outside the competition rules, to be contrasted with other cases, where

---

28 EC Horizontal Cooperation Guidelines (n 23) para 117.

29 See: Office of Fair Trading, 'The Competitive Effects of Buyer Groups' (Economic discussion paper) (January 2007) paras 1.84 and 1.85 <http://www.oft.gov.uk/shared_oft/economic_research/oft863.pdf> accessed 31 May 2008.

30 Case C-250/92 *Gøttrup-Klim v Dansk Landsbrug* [1994] ECR-I-5641.

commitments to the group may be treated as within the competition rules (e.g. in the context of insurance pools).

Otherwise, the structural assessment of buyer alliances is similar to that of retail mergers, explained above, although in general in the EC cases, buying alliances are viewed as weaker than the chain stores because they are only cooperations of independent firms, not integrated companies. This is partly because they are perceived to have less ability to introduce private label brands than integrated chain stores.[31]

Recently there has been discussion as to whether the buyer power of such groups raises smaller rivals' costs (called colourfully the 'waterbed theory').[32] The idea is that a supplier will seek to recoup concessions given to large customers by raising prices to smaller ones. The term 'costs' here is to be interpreted in the broad sense, meaning not just prices, but also in terms of attention or service insofar as it is argued that larger 'key accounts' receive better prices and supplier attention.

It is not clear to what extent this happens or is harmful. Notably it is not clear that suppliers will charge more of their smaller customers in this way, because there may be other factors in play. For example, the higher costs of supplying the smaller purchasers may explain the higher prices, if any. Otherwise, a supplier's desire to keep the best coverage of the market may lead him to encourage smaller retailers to hold his product longer if required, by charging less and within a competitive price range of the larger retailers. As RBB Economics note, the buying group's gains may also be beneficial to consumers.

D. Consolidation Issues: Cumulative Effects

The next issue is to think about what all this consolidation means overall. In a sense, this will be done already through the market structure assessment already built into both the EC merger control and general competition rule assessments outlined above. However, a few further specific comments may be useful.

First, it appears that there is a trend for the bigger to become bigger and, as noted above, to move into related and neighbouring markets. This may not be a concern. It may be pro-competitive, offering clear efficiencies. However, some argue that this may also raise issues of market access. In other words, entering the market, or related markets to obtain a foothold to move into others, may be more difficult, if such markets or related markets are already contested by large retail 'conglomerates'.

---

31 See e.g.: *Rewe/Meinl* (n 3) paras 49 *et seq*.

32 See: the RBB Economics OFT Report (n 29) para 1.61 *et seq* and 6.24 *et seq*; and see the EC Horizontal Cooperation Guidelines (n 23) paras 126 and 135.

Second, there may also be a supply side 'spiral effect', insofar as more retail concentration promotes more supplier concentration and the cycle repeats itself, as suppliers seek to have the strongest brand portfolios, in part to have the best negotiating positions with ever larger retailers.

Third, interestingly, it appears that regulators are still finding scope for more intense retail competition despite concentration. Notably, in its 2007 'Groceries Market Investigation', the UK Competition Commission found that the real price of food had fallen by 7 per cent since 2000, while the number of stores had fallen.[33] In short, concentration may have more to do with market modernization in competition terms than anything else.

Fourth, the cumulative effect of consolidation of chain stores and purchasing groups may be an issue for some third parties. For example, where a new retail franchise network seeks to enter an already densely concentrated market, some argue that the consolidated market position can be a 'wall' for new retail entrants (although a counter argument may be that if there is a different, successful competitive format, there will still be openings).

A similar point is also made by suppliers, concerned that if all the leading retailers want only the top one or two brands on their shelves, together with one or two private label own brands (one high quality, another a deliberately cheap product) then there is no scope for additional suppliers to obtain access to the largest consumer retail platforms. In other words, what do you do if you are the number three or four supplier? (Although a counter argument may be again to say that suppliers should innovate in product or supply terms, or in supply channels and/or even vertically integrate downstream to the extent possible.)

As already noted, there may also be dependency issues where a supplier is heavily committed to several large retailers in a given market and would face serious problems if delisted by any one of them, in terms of finding alternative outlets;[34] although it may be said, as a counter argument, for example, that these are just normal commercial risks, which suppliers have to address by diversifying their customer base.

Fifth, retail concentration can be a compliance headache for allegedly dominant suppliers. The classic scenario is where a supplier has significant market share on its product market (say more than 50 per cent), but represents only 1 per cent or less of a large retailer's turnover. The retailer may want certain brands and it may

33 UK Competition Commission, 'Groceries Market Investigation: Emerging Thinking' (23 January 2007) para 10 <http://www.competition-commission.org.uk/inquiries/ref2006/grocery/pdf/emerging_thinking.pdf> accessed 31 May 2008.

34 See e.g.: *Carrefour/Promodes* (n 4) para 97.

be argued therefore that they are 'must have' or 'must stock' products, giving the supplier 'dominance'.[35]

However, in practice, if measured in terms of an ability to raise prices, the supplier may be far from dominant, as the large retailer demands high rebates, with threats of punishment, or actual punishment, through delisting of these products or other items which the supplier offers, if the rebates are not given.[36] Insofar as the supplier only accounts for, at most, 1 per cent of sales a retailer may also use arguments beyond the product group (e.g. 'I can make more profit per square metre from another product group, if necessary you know . . .'). Or the retailer may be able to use private label as a counter, simply saying that he will do without the 'key brand', if prices are not reduced.

Dominant companies are generally advised *not* to do precisely what the large retailer may seek: non-cost justified rebates on total turnover, or at least across more than one product family. However, suppliers find this odd when they see themselves as far from dominant, in bidding markets, seeking the limited shelf opportunities outlined above. Predictably, in that context, suppliers tend to see themselves as not dominant as regards these large retailers, but rather as competing and negotiating in the ordinary (non-dominant) way for their potential customers' demand.

All this is still not clear on the European Commission's rules. Some structural situations are addressed through merger control, where buyer power may be accepted. However, in the general competition rules applicable to 'dominant' companies, we do not see cases distinguishing between large and small retailers on a basis of countervailing buyer power, even though that would appear overdue. The impression given is that the Commission is caught in a dilemma as to whether to allow such arguments because, if accepted, it is thought that there would be competitor foreclosure issues (although in the DG Competition Discussion Paper on Article 82 of the EC Treaty there was discussion of distinguishing customers into strong and weak buyers).[37]

Finally, the Commission's recent *Coca-Cola* settlement has also not made matters simpler, insofar as the Commission appears to have objected to rebates on product families, if they link leading products/brands with others within

---

[35] See: European Commission DG Competition, 'DG Competition Discussion Paper on the Application of Article 82 of the Treaty to Exclusionary Abuse' (Public consultation, December 2005) para 143 <http://ec.europa.eu/comm/competition/antitrust/art82/discpaper2005.pdf> accessed 31 May 2008; and *Clearstream* Case COMP/38.096, 2 June 2004 paras 241 and 287 <http://ec.europa.eu/comm/competition/antitrust/cases/decisions/38096/en.pdf> accessed 31 May 2008.

[36] See: the EC Horizontal Merger Guidelines (n 6) para 65.

[37] See DG Competition Discussion Paper (n 35) para 42.

the family.[38] Previously, it was thought that rebates based on sales in a 'product family' should be safe, or at least that this was a good compliance guideline. Now, even though this was only a settlement case, rather than a full procedure and decision, it appears that a closer examination may be required.

E. Some Recurrent Themes

It may be useful to highlight what are, in the author's view, the most recurrent themes to watch in the competition assessment of retail concentration, whether through mergers or buying alliances/groups.

First, it is argued that a retailer cannot be expected to stock all products, because they cannot. There is a physical constraint in issue. Therefore, even though suppliers may badly need large retailers and, in some cases, be dependent on them, it may be difficult to argue that it is abusive not to buy. This may be behind the reluctance of competition authorities to intervene in many cases, together with the general view that, provided there is sufficient downstream competition, there should be no structural concern, because benefits gained from suppliers will have to be passed through to consumers. More specific abusive conduct is therefore likely to be required to justify intervention.

Second, the 'bidding competition' which suppliers face for hypermarket 'slots' may not have been sufficiently recognized in the application of the competition rules. Notably, to some extent, it is reflected in EC merger control review, but appears not to be a feature of Article 82 EC 'dominance' cases. There are only a few places on the relevant shelf and, as explained above, competition for them is intense.

Third, whilst clearly there is much scope for debate on the competitive effects of mergers and buying alliances, regulatory intervention should be in order to protect scope for market dynamics (at retail and supplier level), but not to stop the efficiencies which come with larger scale organization.

Fourth, it may be useful to recall the view of some of the older studies (e.g. by Dobson, Waterston, and Chu for the Office of Fair Trading (OFT))[39] that to see if there is a retail concentration problem, there should be a focus on increases in large retailer margins. If not, market modernization may be just that and not a concern

[38] See *Coca-Cola* [2005] OJ L253/21 (the commitments and a non-confidential version of the Commission's commitments decision is available on the Commission's website <http://ec.europa.eu/comm/competition/antitrust/cases/decisions/39116/commitments_fr.pdf> accessed 31 May 2008.

[39] P Dobson, M Waterston, and A Chu, 'The Welfare Consequences of the Exercise of Buyer Power' (Research Paper 16 prepared for the Office of Fair Trading, September 1998) <http://www.oft.gov.uk/shared_oft/reports/comp_policy/oft239.pdf> accessed 31 May 2008.

(although some still argue that this leads to an unacceptable reduction in consumer choice if only the leading brands are repeatedly selected, as discussed above).

Fifth, market definition is very important in these retail cases and can be complex. Markets may be national or local (or with elements of both). Markets may be focused (e.g. by channel, such as kiosks or cash & carry). They may be broad or narrow, from competition for shelf space in general, to competition for a particular product 'shelf' (such as in a cool shelf), or just certain product 'slots'. Assessments may also need to be more in terms of 'closest competitors' under the general competition rules, as is now happening under the more modern merger control rules which focus on 'significant impediment to effective competition'.

Sixth, the place of 'private label' competition in all this is a specific topic whose scope is broader than the structural assessment overview which the author has been asked to contribute. Notably there are, in some national competition systems, specific rules on economic dependency. For present purposes, the key point is that private label supply is considered to give purchasers more power, because it gives the retailer more ability to say it does not need the supplier's branded products and also because of the economic scale advantages noted above. Clearly that also raises other competition issues, as the retailer has become the *competitor* as well as the distributor of the supplier.

Finally, although this paper has focused on the competition assessment of retail mergers and buying alliances, it should be stressed that some of the issues raised and solutions found to retail concentration are simply not related to competition law, for example, legislation on pricing, exemptions for small and medium enterprises, transitional periods for supply renegotiation/replacement, and 'buy local' soft undertakings.

F. Conclusion

Retail concentration is a controversial topic which is likely to be with us for many years. Within that development, structural competition factors, buyer power, and private label are likely to continue to loom large as points of debate.

Provided market access remains open (if necessary through competition regulatory intervention) usually retail concentration may be seen as healthy, albeit that the resulting power vis-à-vis suppliers should not be underestimated, and continued scope for both retailer and supply dynamics remain critical.

14

RETAIL COMPETITION: THE USE OF EX-ANTE AND EX-POST REMEDIES

*Alastair Gorrie**

* Partner at Orrick, Herrington & Sutcliffe, London. With thanks to Harsharon Kundan and Stuart Jansze for their assistance in preparing this paper.

This chapter looks at remedies in merger cases involving the supermarkets and groceries sectors and goes on to consider other ex-ante remedies (market investigations) and ex-post remedies (Articles 81 and 82).

The plan of this chapter is to consider first remedies in merger cases (Section A), then other ex-ante remedies arising out of market investigations (Section B), then remedies in Article 81/Chapter 1 cases (Section C), other ex-post remedies (Section D) and drawing a few conclusions in Section E.

A. Ex-Ante Remedies—Merger Control

Consolidation in the supermarket sector

A marked feature of the supermarket grocery sector across Europe has been a continuing trend towards consolidation through mergers and acquisitions, between both horizontal and vertical entities. An inherent attraction exists to such consolidation, whereby supermarkets merge horizontally or with upstream/downstream suppliers or distributors to benefit from synergies achieved through economies of scale, the manufacturing or sourcing of private label products, the widening of logistical networks, and expansion of geographic coverage of the supermarket's brand.

Within this trend towards consolidation there are, potentially, a number of negative implications, specifically, that consolidation augments the anti-competitive effects arising from the role of large supermarket retailers as 'gatekeepers'. This role occurs where a concentration of buyer power permits the supermarket(s) to establish an enhanced bargaining position as 'customer', increasing negotiating pressure upon upstream suppliers, as consolidation narrows the potential routes to market for such suppliers. As a 'competitor' to suppliers, the consolidated supermarket can further build upon its financial ability and size to engage in aggressive pricing tactics, setting the pricing of its increased private label capability below that of branded producers. In relation to the consolidated supermarket's role as a 'supplier' of shelf space, the power to provide suppliers with retail area and shelf space, at point of sale to the end customer, becomes concentrated. The potential for the supermarket to engage in commercially unfair practices, such as the levying of increased fees upon suppliers vying for prime shelf space and higher marketing support charges becomes acute.

The possibility of such practices arising in the context of supermarket retail consolidation has raised competition concerns at both European and domestic State level. These concerns have been addressed through the regulatory mechanism of merger control. Such issues were examined by the European Commission (the Commission) in three prominent supermarket merger investigations over the last decade. The issues have since been looked at more frequently at State level, where domestic merger control procedures have been utilized.

Remedies in merger control

The types of remedial conditions and obligations that the European Commission or Member State regulators may impose in exercise of their merger control powers upon the consolidating entities can be broadly categorized into three types:

(1) structural remedies involving divestiture of businesses or assets;
(2) other (non-divestiture) structural remedies; and
(3) behavioural remedies.

Divestiture usually involves the compulsory sale of businesses as a going concern or assets belonging to the merging entities to a suitable purchaser which has the credentials to be an effective long term competitor. Other types of structural remedies imposed have in the past included the removal of links with competitors through the sale of shareholdings. Behavioural remedies may consist of the undertaking providing competitors with access to its infrastructure, mandatory termination of exclusive supply or distribution arrangements, commitments not to raise prices or bundle products, or the creation and institution of information firewalls, to bolster a competitive environment.

The Commission sets out its approach towards the remedial commitments required from the undertakings in its notice on remedies.[1] The preferred remedy, across all industries and sectors and not just in the grocery retail sector, is divestiture[2] as it is perceived to be the most effective way to restore effective competition by creating the conditions for the long-term emergence of a new competitive entity or to strengthen an existing competitor,[3] at either a horizontal or vertical level. The divested entity must be sufficiently preserved prior to transfer so that post-transfer it can compete effectively and independently of the merging parties. Other types of structural remedies may be deemed suitable where their effects are thought to be equivalent to divestiture.

---

1 Commission Notice on remedies acceptable under Council Regulation (EEC) No 4064/89 and under Commission Regulation (EC) No 447/98 [2001] OJ C68/3; See Draft revised Commission Notice on remedies acceptable under the Merger Regulation (dated 24 April 2007) <http://ec.europa.eu/comm/competition/mergers/legislation/draft_remedies_notice.pdf>accessed 2 June 2008.

2 Notice on remedies (n 1) para 13; Draft revised Commission Notice (n 1) para 22.

3 Notice on remedies (n 1) para 13.

The Commission's approach towards behavioural remedies has historically been reluctant,[4] depicted to be acceptable in only exceptional circumstances to deal with particular types of effects.[5] The rationale for such approach is based upon the administrative difficulties related to effective implementation and monitoring of long term behavioural remedies vis-à-vis divestiture. In contrast, critics have argued that a more flexible 'effects' based approach can or should be taken instead, moving away from the structural/behavioural dichotomy that the Commission has long advanced.[6] This criticism has been amplified more recently by the European Court of First Instance in *Tetra Laval*[7] which reiterated that categorizing proposed commitments as behavioural or structural was 'immaterial' and that 'commitments which are prima facie behavioural . . . may also be capable of preventing the emergence or strengthening of a dominant position'.[8] Furthermore, the Commission's own review of its remedies policy[9] concluded that the remedy of divestiture has resulted in significant shortcomings with 'serious design and implementation issues affecting the effectiveness of remedies', which unresolved mean that '. . . the competition concerns likely remain partially or fully unaddressed'.[10] Behavioural remedies do not necessarily require intensive regulatory monitoring, as has been the Commission's apprehension, with measures allowing third parties to enforce commitments themselves through arbitration mechanisms being increasingly used.

Nevertheless, the historical and current position of the Commission is that divestiture is the remedy of choice and any other structural or behavioural remedies will usually only be considered as a package of required commitments, in conjunction with divestiture. Such approach was demonstrated in three of the Commission's most prominent supermarket merger control investigations. Interestingly, in comparison, the domestic regulatory bodies have in a number

---

4 In the DG Competition, European Commission 'Merger Remedies Study' (public version, October 2005) <http://ec.europa.eu/comm/competition/mergers/legislation/remedies_study.pdf> accessed 2 June 2008, of the 227 remedies imposed in all merger control investigations between the years 1996–2000, 56% were remedies of a structural nature, see chart 2, p 13.

5 Draft revised Commission Notice (n 1) para 17.

6 P Papandropoulos and A Tajana, 'The Merger Remedies Study—In Divestiture We Trust?' [2006] *European Competition Law Review* 443, 449 para 3.2. See also: International Bar Association—Antitrust Committee, 'Submission of the IBA Working Group on the European Commission's Draft Notice on Remedies Acceptable under Council Regulation (EEC) No 139/2004 and under Commission Regulation (EC) No 802/2004 <http://www.ibanet.org/images/downloads/lpd/Submission-20070629_final%20_3_.pdf> accessed 2 June 2008, p 7, para 33.

7 Case C-12/03P *Commission of the European Communities v Tetra Laval BV* [2005] ECR I-987, paras 85–89.

8 Ibid, para 86.

9 Merger Remedies Study (n 4).

10 Merger Remedies Study (n 4) 139, Part V, para B1.

of supermarket merger investigations adopted a broader, more expansive approach to the types of divestiture commitments that they have been willing to accept.

Supermarket consolidation—appraisal and remedies

This section considers experience at both EU and national level.

The European Commission experience

Kesko In the *Kesko/Tuko* case,[11] the acquisition of Tuko, active in the Finnish wholesale and retail markets, by Kesko, active in the retail, cash and carry, and procurement markets, was subject to outright prohibition by the Commission. Upon investigation, the Commission found significant competition concerns discernible from all three aspects of the combined undertaking as 'gatekeeper'.[12]

Assessment by the Commission of the potential combined undertaking's buyer power in its downstream 'customer' role and seller power in its upstream 'supplier' role yielded the most concern. The Finnish retail market for daily consumer goods was one of the most concentrated in the EU, in which Kesko's market share would rise to 55 per cent post-acquisition, three times larger than the size of the nearest competitor in the retail market, and to 80 per cent in the cash and carry market. The Commission commented[13] that the combined effects of the size and capacity of the retail outlets, the high level of membership of its customer loyalty scheme, the scope of its distribution network, and its position as the central procurement institution for itself and its 'block' of contractually bound downstream retailers, would give the combined undertaking 'unique purchasing power'[14] that would reinforce its dominant position in both the retail and cash and carry markets. Further, there was considerable economic dependency upon Kesko and Tuko demonstrated by the suppliers, who were reliant upon them for between 50 per cent to 75 per cent of all Finnish sales. Whilst such suppliers had limited alternative distribution routes to market, Kesko and Tuko were in a significantly more powerful position in being able to substitute suppliers[15] and exercise an enhanced bargaining position in negotiations, in respect of product pricing, availability of discounts, and marketing support fees.

The Commission rejected Kesko's proposed commitments outright, which included divestiture of assets to restructure the cash and carry market to create a new competitor: 'Newco', with a projected 11 per cent market share.

---

[11] *Kesko/Tuko* (Case IV/M784) Commission Decision 97/277/EC [1996] OJ L110/53.
[12] Ibid, para 133.
[13] Ibid, para 106.
[14] Ibid, para 133.
[15] Ibid, para 150.

The Commission found that the proposed commitments were insufficient, as the stores offered as part of the divestiture were regionally skewed to south west Finland and were *de facto* non-profitable, thereby putting any suitable purchaser at an immediate competitive disadvantage. Furthermore, there were no commitments offered to counteract the anti-competitive issues identified in the retail market.

Rewe In the *Rewe/Meinl*[16] case, the Commission approved, subject to remedial conditions, the acquisition of Meinl, a groceries retailer operating in Austria, by Rewe, a groceries retailer in Germany and Austria. Rewe was held to occupy a dominant position in the concentrated groceries retail market in Austria, where its post-acquisition market share (excluding discount stores) would be between 38 per cent and 48 per cent of the market, giving it a market share advantage of at least 25 per cent over its competitors.[17]

The Commission evaluated the implications for the combined undertaking's exercise of buyer power as a result of its dominant position, identifying the emergence of a potential 'spiral effect' in both the retail and procurement markets.[18] This occurs when the enhanced size of the merged entity would lead to larger volume-related discounts being negotiated from upstream suppliers, enabling this cost saving to be passed to the consumer in the form of lower prices, undercutting competitors at a horizontal level, thereby increasing the merged entity's market share over time. This would subsequently lead to larger volume discounts again being extracted and a cyclical creeping type of consolidation to become entrenched in the market. The Commission warned against this 'spiral effect' of buyer power in general; however, in the facts of the Rewe/Meinl case, there was a countervailing concentrated supply side in many product groups.

Rewe's role as a 'competitor' to the same suppliers against whom favourable buying conditions could be extracted by virtue of consolidation of buyer power was also assessed by the Commission, given its substantial own-label capability. Concerns regarding the possible practice of arbitrary delisting of secondary supplier brands and replacement with own-label products, together with the use of the private label portfolio strategically to reduce the combined undertaking's dependence on producers, were considered.[19] Such commercial practices were likely to take place in the context of a perceived economic dependency by the suppliers upon Rewe, there being evidence that the combined undertaking would account for a very large proportion of the suppliers' sales, but that the suppliers'

---

16 *Rewe/Meinl* (Case IV/M1221) Commission Decision 1999/674/EC [1999] OJ L274/1.
17 Ibid, 7, para 24.
18 Ibid, 18, paras 71–73.
19 Ibid, 29–30, paras 111–114.

sales would account for a much smaller percentage of the combined undertaking's purchases.

The acquisition was approved subject to Rewe abiding by various commitments. These included 117 Meinl outlets outside of the defined geographical area of Eastern Austria and 45 Meinl outlets in the whole of Austria being limited to operational use only as drug stores and not food retail outlets, for an unlimited period. Where the conversion of such stores into drug stores was commercially unviable, Rewe had to offer to close, divest, or sub-lease such stores to competitors.

Carrefour/Promodes The merger control investigation in *Carrefour/Promodes*[20] assessed the impact of the US$17 billion acquisition by Carrefour of Promodes in relation to dominance in the local French and Spanish groceries retail markets. On a global scale, the acquisition would result in a combined undertaking comprising the world's second largest groceries retailer.

The Commission again considered the 'spiral effect' paradigm in respect of buyer power, as earlier discussed in *Rewe/Meinl*, and went on to identify a quantitative threat point of 22 per cent—being the point at which buyer power is detrimental to upstream suppliers as the relative bargaining position becomes skewed heavily in favour of the retailer. This detriment was conceptualized as the maximum revenue share that a supplier could afford to forgo without being put at risk of insolvency.

The Commission imposed a number of structural remedies to authorize part of the merger, whilst referring the remainder of the merger control investigation back to the respective French and Spanish competition authorities for localized authorization. The Commission required the divestiture of Carrefour's 42 per cent stake in French competitor Cora, which had a 5 per cent market share in the French retail market. This was in addition to Carrefour's earlier concessions to the Commission to divest four retail outlets in France and four in Spain.

Member States' experience

The United Kingdom One of the key merger decisions in the supermarket retail sector in the UK in recent years has been the conclusion of the Competition Commission's merger inquiry[21] into the acquisition of Safeway Plc, pursuant to a

20 *Carrefour/Promodes* (Case IV/M1684) [2000] OJ C164/5.

21 UK Competition Commission 'Safeway plc and Asda Group Limited (owned by Wal-Mart Stores Inc); Wm Morrison Supermarkets PLC; J Sainsbury plc; and Tesco plc: A Report on the Mergers in Contemplation' (September 2003) <http://www.competition-commission.org.uk/rep_pub/reports/2003/481safeway.htm#full> accessed 2 June 2008.

referral under the UK's merger regime of the Fair Trading Act 1973. The Competition Commission assessed whether the structural implications of the proposed merger in the domestic grocery retail sector would operate against the public interest—as Safeway Plc was, at the time, the UK's fourth largest supermarket.

In the course of its analysis the Competition Commission evaluated the effect of the proposed mergers on competition at a national and a local level, together with any perceived associated effect on buyer power and suppliers, thereby considering many of the issues that arise in the 'gatekeeper' dichotomy. One of the Competition Commission's findings in relation to buyer power, in its role as 'customer', was that the acquisition was 'expected to aggravate further the imbalance in the respective bargaining positions of the acquiring party and its suppliers'.[22] The Competition Commission found that greater financial difficulty was likely to be experienced by suppliers, hindering investment in new products, techniques, and adversely affecting product diversity. Whilst at the same time, the respective bargaining positions of the acquiring supermarket would be likely to be exacerbated. Suppliers were expected to secure less disadvantageous terms with four national grocery retailers than with three, with no expectation that the procurement cost savings derived from such increased buyer power would be passed on fully to the consumers in the form of lower prices.[23]

The Competition Commission concluded that the proposed acquisitions of Safeway Plc by its biggest three competitors (Asda, Sainsbury's, and Tesco) should be prohibited, as each of these proposed acquisitions would have involved a reduction of the total nationwide supermarket chains from four to only three and would, therefore, operate against the public interest. Such prohibition extended to any 'Safeway asset', namely, any retail store or other property, including logistical sites and distribution depots, utilized by Safeway Plc in the course of its grocery retailing business. In contrast, this prohibition did not extend to the fourth interested acquirer, Morrisons, which was permitted to proceed with the acquisition, subject to a number of store divestitures (48 'one stop' stores each with a floor area in excess of 1,400 square metres and five smaller stores), as such sale would establish it as a fourth strong national competitor. It was felt that approval of the acquisition by either Asda, Sainsbury's, or Tesco, qualified by forced divestiture of certain outlets, was inadequate as a remedy, as such disposals were required on a large scale and there was no certainty that the competitive structure would be adequately addressed equivalent to restoring a fourth competitor at national level.

22 Ibid, 8, para 1.20.
23 Ibid, 8, para 1.20.

Germany On 8 April 2008, Germany's Federal Cartel Office announced its intention to block a joint venture between supermarket chains owned by Edeka and Tengelmann in its current form. The office said it had considered not only the national market, where the merger would have made Edeka pre-eminent, but more than 100 local markets, in which the merger would result in a single dominant player. The office observed 'that price competition would not be sufficient to limit the incentives for Edeka to behave anti-competitively'.

The transaction, announced in November, would see Edeka's discount supermarket subsidiary Netto merge with Tengelmann's Plus discount chain, in a joint venture with a turnover of EUR11 billion per year. Edeka, which has a 25 per cent market share in German supermarkets, would own 70 per cent of the joint venture.

Portugal The acquisition of Carrefour (Portugal) Sociedade De Exploracao de Centros Comerciais SA by Sonae Distribuico was not opposed by the Portuguese Competition Authority, subject to a number of structural and behavioural conditions being imposed upon the concentration to guarantee effective competition.[24] The investigation concluded that the merger was liable to create or strengthen a dominant position that could result in significant barriers to effective competition, particularly in the retail food markets in specifically identified Portuguese localities.

The commitments required from the concentration by the regulator were categorized by location and included divestiture of specified built and proposed stores, restrictions upon applying for new food retailing licences, caps upon any increase in total retail food sales area, and compulsory conversion between types of retail outlet, i.e. from hypermarket to supermarket.

Spain In November 2007 the Spanish Competition Commission approved the EUR200 million acquisition of Plus Supermarkets by DIA (a subsidiary of French retailer Carrefour) at the end of Phase I after accepting undertakings.

DIA controlled over 2,800 retail outlets across Spain and proposed to acquire 251 further outlets from Plus 251, as well as 56 projected outlets. The merger clearance required the divestiture of seven stores.

Switzerland The acquisition of discount retailer Denner by Switzerland's largest supermarket group, Migros, in September 2007, was qualified with the imposition of conditions by the Swiss Federal Competition Commission. Migros was perceived as dominant in a rapidly consolidating Swiss retail supermarket

24 Autoridade Da Concorrencia, 'Competition Authority authorizes Sonae Distribuico/Carrefour merger operation, with conditions attached' Press Release No 22/2007 (27 December 2007).

sector; Migros and its nearest rival, Coop, together possessed nearly one third of total market share in Switzerland.

The types of remedies imposed by the Swiss regulator were expansive—being a package of structural, behavioural, and temporal conditions, exemplifying the most vigorous and comprehensive range of merger remedies used to counteract potential anti-competitive effects of supermarket consolidation by a regulator to date.

Structurally, Denner was bound to remain legally, organizationally, and operationally independent for a period of seven years unless otherwise stipulated. Such independence is reinforced through a prohibition on Denner stores being converted into Migros stores; the majority of Denner's board of Directors, including the president, having to be independent of Migros; Migros Union being prohibited from acquiring further retail food outlets in Switzerland; and Migros being prohibited from opening any further M-Budget shops.

In terms of behavioural remedies, potential misuse of buyer power vis-à-vis suppliers was addressed through the imposition of extensive conditions upon the combined undertaking relating to how it can negotiate with suppliers, to ensure that plurality of supply is maintained and any foreclosure effect is minimized. Denner was not permitted to terminate contracts with its suppliers without good cause; Migros was permanently prohibited from entering into any exclusive agreements with product suppliers; and procurement of products by Migros and Denner from suppliers must be carried out separately and not jointly.

Interestingly, in comparison to the 22 per cent 'threat point' in the *Carrefour/Promodes* decision, at which threshold supplier 'economic dependency' is seemingly established, the Swiss regulator has opted for a higher quantitative threshold of 30 per cent. Denner is not permitted to replace suppliers that have achieved an average of more than 30 per cent of their turnover from Denner in the period 2004–2006 (provided such supply is of quality commensurate of the market) and at a competitive price. Where Denner wishes to delist a product from its range, but the supplier is willing and able to continue to supply at market quality and competitive price, Denner/Migros must mandatorily undertake to find an individual solution for the supplier concerned if such supplier would otherwise go out of business as a direct result of the merger. Hence, although the Swiss regulator has established the 'threat point' at a higher threshold, once such threat point is achieved a highly paternal responsibility towards the supplier is invoked.

B. Ex-Ante Remedies—Market Investigations

Market investigations are increasingly used for the enforcement of competition law in the armoury of competition law enforcement bodies. Market investigations are not used to address the anti-competitive behaviour of individual firms in relation to specific competition legislation, but to address other aspects of potential market failure, to the ultimate benefit of consumers. Typically, market investigations address key aspects pertaining to a market, including its structure (for example, market concentration, market share, or buyer power), the conduct of its suppliers, and the conduct of the buyers and customers within that market. As such, the market investigation is a potentially useful and flexible tool permitting investigation into a broad range of market-wide issues and associated behaviour.

Further, the relevant regulatory body responsible for conducting a market investigation generally has a wide discretion as to the type and manner of remedies to be imposed in response to the actual or perceived market threats. Such remedies may be structural (designed to make instant and direct changes to a market's structure, for example, divestment of a business or assets), behavioural (imposing or restraining specific company conduct, for example, ensuring notice is given of all price changes), or monitoring (requiring adherence to specified regulatory matters, for example, providing the regulatory body with regular pricing information). Yet despite the potential of the market investigation as a tool to address competition issues within markets prior to the BAA airport case, at least, doubts remain over the effectiveness and potency of the enforcement remedies which have to date been imposed.

The 2000 supermarkets investigation

In its 2000 supermarkets market investigation the Competition Commission (CC) concluded that:

> five multiples (the major buyers—Asda, Safeway, Sainsbury, Somerfield, and Tesco), each having at least an 8 per cent share of grocery purchases for resale from their stores, have sufficient buyer power that 30 of the practices identified, when carried out by any of these companies, adversely affect the competitiveness of some of their suppliers and distort competition in the supplier market—and in some cases, in the retail market—for the supply of groceries.[25]

And further:

> that the exercise of 27 of these practices by the five major buyers meeting the 8 per cent criterion operates against the public interest.[26]

The remedy decided upon by the CC to best combat these anti-competitive market features was the imposition of a supermarkets code of practice (SCOP).

---

25 UK Competition Commission, 'Supermarkets: A Report on the Supply of Groceries from Multiple Stores in the United Kingdom' [October 2000] <http://www.competitioncommission.org.uk/rep_pub/reports/2000/446super.htm> accessed 25 May 2008, 6.

26 Ibid, 7.

The CC stated that the SCOP should be non-voluntary and that any multiple meeting the '8 per cent criterion' should automatically be required to give undertakings to comply with the SCOP. Further, the SCOP should be designed to prevent the supermarket multiples from exploiting their excessive buying power.

The SCOP was eventually introduced in March 2002, forming part of the statutory undertakings given to the Secretary of State for Trade and Industry under section 88(2) of the Fair Trading Act 1973. It applied to Sainsbury's, Asda, Safeway, Tesco, and latterly Morrisons (since their takeover of Safeway in 2003). The SCOP itself aimed to rebalance the position of suppliers with supermarkets in terms of negotiation and general dealings by requiring transparency and uniformity with regards to terms of business, payment times, prices, promotions, compensation, payments for consumer complaints, third party dealings, supermarket staff training, and dispute resolution.

Effectiveness of the remedy?

Since introduction, the SCOP has been dogged with criticism for being too weak and of not working effectively. A key concern of suppliers was that the SCOP was different to that originally recommended by the CC in that it permitted supermarkets to request certain payments or contributions from suppliers for promotions or similar, provided such requests were 'reasonable'.

The Office of Fair Trading (OFT) has undertaken, or commissioned, various studies to assess the impact and effectiveness of the SCOP, the first being published in February 2004[27] and the second being in March 2005.[28] Both studies remained inconclusive as to the actual effectiveness of the SCOP, but stated that the belief among suppliers that the SCOP was not working remained unabated. By and large, it was found that supermarkets had generally complied with the SCOP, but the concept of 'reasonableness' seemingly remained a thorn in the side of suppliers by favouring, they felt, the supermarkets in negotiations. Further, suppliers were apparently fearful of complaining due to the potential threat of product delisting by the supermarkets. The effectiveness of the SCOP was considered further under the auspices of the 2006 Investigation, considered below.

[27] Office of Fair Trading, 'The Supermarkets Code of Practice: Report on the Review of the Operation of the Code of Practice in the Undertakings Given by Tesco, Asda, Sainsbury and Safeway to the Secretary of State for Trade and Industry on 18 December 2001' (February 2004) <http://www.oft.gov.uk/shared_oft/reports/consumer_protection/oft697.pdf> accessed 2 June 2008.

[28] Office of Fair Trading, 'Supermarkets: The Code of Practice and Other Competition Issues' (March 2005) <http://www.oft.gov.uk/shared_oft/reports/comp_policy/oft783.pdf> accessed 2 June 2008.

The 2006 groceries investigation

On 9 May 2006, the supply of groceries[29] by retailers in the UK was referred to the CC for investigation by the OFT, under section 131 of the Enterprise Act 2002 (EA). The CC published its report on 30 April 2008.

The CC concluded that there were features of the markets for the supply of groceries by retailers in the UK, either alone or in combination with each other, that prevented, restricted or distorted competition in connection with the supply or acquisition of groceries by retailers.[30] A finding of an 'adverse effect on competition' (AEC) under section 134(2) of the EA was made.[31]

These anti-competitive features included: the significant number of local markets with high levels of concentration; the UK planning regime and the manner in which it is applied by local planning authorities; the control of land in highly-concentrated local markets by the large supermarket operators; and the exercise of buyer power by the leading supermarket operators in relation to their suppliers, particularly the growing practice of transferring excessive risk and unexpected cost to the suppliers.

In accordance with Section 134(6) of the EA, the CC, in choosing appropriate remedial action, shall 'have regard to the need to achieve as comprehensive a solution as is reasonable and practicable to the [AEC] and any detrimental effects on customers' resulting from it. In its notice of possible remedies,[32] the CC stated that in considering the effectiveness of different possible remedies, it would have regard to the individual cost of such remedies, their benefits, and the overarching principle of proportionality.

The CC has developed a package of remedial measures to address concerns as to competition in concentrated local markets and the relationships between supermarket operators and their suppliers.

29 'Groceries' include food (other than that sold for consumption in the store), pet foods, drinks (alcoholic and non-alcoholic), cleaning products, toiletries, and household goods, but excludes petrol, clothing, DIY products, financial services, pharmaceuticals, newspapers, magazines, greetings cards, CDs, DVDs, videos, audio tapes, toys, plants, flowers, perfumes, cosmetics, electrical appliances, kitchen hardware, gardening equipment, books, tobacco, and tobacco products. See: The Groceries Market Investigation, June 2006, Statement of Issues, 1.

30 UK Competition Commission 'The Supply of Groceries in the UK Market Investigation' (30April2008) <http://www.competition-commission.org.uk/rep_pub/reports/2008/fulltext/538.pdf> accessed 2 June 2008.

31 UK Competition Commission, 'Groceries Market Investigation: Notice of Possible Remedies under Rule 11 of the Competition Commission Rules of Procedure' (31 October 2007) <http://www.competition-commission.org.uk/inquiries/ref2006/grocery/prov_findings/notice_of_remedies.pdf> accessed 2 June 2008, 1.

32 Ibid.

To address the issue of supermarket operators consolidating or increasing their position of dominance in local grocery markets, the CC has concluded that a 'competition assessment' should be implemented within the planning system where local planning authorities (LPAs) are assessing planning applications for new large grocery stores. The CC has further recommended that the OFT act as 'statutory consultee' to the LPAs during this assessment, to ensure that LPAs take account of competition issues under its guidance. The assessment will apply to all grocery store developments, new stores, extensions, mezzanines, or store relocations, above 1,000 square metres.[33] Further, for new developments, the assessment would take account of a combination of fascia and an assessment based on market share (most probably grocery floor space), with the results of any competition assessment remaining valid for five years. No further amendments were recommended to the planning system.

In relation to land controlled by the large supermarket operators, the CC has imposed behavioural remedies in relation to restrictive covenants, restrictive agreements, and exclusivity clauses. In areas of high concentration, supermarket operators will be required to release existing restrictive covenants as soon as possible, with a total ban on future restrictive covenants which restrict grocery retail use. Supermarket operators will also be required to lift exclusivity arrangements which have been in place for more than five years and will be prevented from entering into, or enforcing any exclusivity arrangements in the future for longer than five years. In addition, the CC has also recommended to the Department for Business, Enterprise and Regulatory Reform that the current Land Agreements Exclusion Order should be amended so that agreements which restrict grocery retailing should no longer benefit from exclusion from the Competition Act.[34]

Interestingly, the CC has fallen short of the originally proposed structural remedy of land divestiture to counter the supermarket operators growing control of 'landbanks'. On review, apparently only 19 land bank sites in total were identified as actually acting as barriers to entry in highly concentrated markets.[35] Yet again the CC has proven wary of imposing any form of structural remedy under their market investigation powers.

Perhaps one of the most far reaching remedies proposed by the CC is in relation to supply chain practices and the creation of a new Groceries Supply Code of Practice (GSCOP) to replace the existing SCOP. The substantive provisions of

33 The Supply of Groceries in the UK Market Investigation (n 30) 182.
34 The Supply of Groceries in the UK Market Investigation (n 30) 209.
35 The Supply of Groceries in the UK Market Investigation (n 30) 227.

the GSCOP will mostly mirror those of SCOP but with important amendments.

The GSCOP will be extended to all UK grocery retailers that are part of corporate groups with a turnover in excess of £1 billion.[36] Supermarket operators will be made to institute improvements in internal practices with regards to their relationships with suppliers, including appointing an in-house GSCOP compliance officer, improving their supplier contract records management arrangements and automatically providing suppliers with information on contractual terms. In addition, they will be prohibited from making any outright changes to previously agreed terms of supply.[37]

Further, the CC has recommended that a post of groceries supply code ombudsman be created to arbitrate disputes between retailers and suppliers, publish guidance on specific provision of the GSCOP, investigate alleged breaches, and report to both the public and the OFT on retailers' compliance with the GSCOP.

Aftermath of 2006 investigation

Coinciding with the publication of the CC's final report came initiation of an OFT investigation into price coordination by the supermarkets in the supply of grocery and health and beauty products and facilitation of that coordination by suppliers.[38]

As part of the 2006 Investigation, the CC requested emails between Asda and Tesco and their suppliers between 18 June 2007 and 22 July 2007. The aim was to investigate the price war between these two retailers which started on 15 June 2007. As a result of this information, the CC identified the following potential competition and supply chain concerns:

- exchange of information of competitor pricing and promotion;
- contribution to costs of promotions; and
- wastage and product quality complaints.

This information was made available to the OFT. There are also newspaper reports that Asda applied for immunity for any resultant finding of the infringement in exchange for additional information and evidence on these arrangements.

---

36 This will include the 'Big Four' (Tesco, Sainsbury's, Asda, and Morrisons), plus Waitrose, Somerfield, Marks and Spencer, Co-op, Aldi, Iceland, and Lidl.

37 The Supply of Groceries in the UK Market Investigation (n 30) 232.

38 See, e.g., reports appearing in the Sunday telegraph on 27 April and 4 May 2008.

C. Ex-Post Remedies—Article 81/Chapter I

Supermarkets, anti-competitive agreements, and concerted practices

The supermarket and grocery sector more generally is under considerable scrutiny with recent or current investigation under Article 81 of the EC treaty (and equivalent powers under national laws) in several EU Member States. The function of Article 81(1) is to prohibit all agreements between undertakings, decisions by associations, and concerted practices which may affect trade between EU Member States and which have as their object or effect the prevention, restriction, or distortion of competition within the common market. Such agreements and practices have been investigated in the supermarket sector in the form of collusion to coordinate prices, the exchange of sensitive commercial information, and the formation of buying groups. In the event that contravention of Article 81(1) (or an equivalent national power) is found any such offending agreement is void[39] and the competition authority may levy a fine of up to 10 per cent of turnover for the infringement.

Buying groups

Buying groups are formed to take advantage of enhanced economies of scale in procurement, with the collective being able to negotiate better terms and conditions with suppliers through enhanced buyer power, as compared to the individual entity. Such buyer groups may be subject to the Article 81 regime where negative effects upon competition are deemed to be discernible. The Commission notice[40] provides guidance on the types of characteristics that an infringing buying group would be likely to possess:

- the participants of the group are large commercial entities, with relatively large market shares (collectively);
- the participants are restricted from sourcing supplies through means other than the joint purchasing arrangements;
- ancillary restrictive practices exist between the participants to the group, in addition to the joint purchasing arrangements.[41]

Where such type of characteristics is in evidence, the buying group is likely to be in contravention of Article 81(1), particularly if the parties to the joint

---

[39] Art 81(2) EC.
[40] Commission Notice (EC) Guidelines on the Applicability of Article 81 of the EC Treaty to Horizontal Cooperation Agreements [2001] OJ C3/2.
[41] Ibid, sec 4.

purchasing agreement have a combined market share significantly in excess of 15 per cent in both the relevant purchasing and relevant selling markets.[42]

In such event, the buying group may be eligible to meet the requirements of the Article 81(3) exemption, namely, that the participants to the group will pass the benefits of joint procurement to the downstream customer. Where, instead, the joint purchase agreement obliges the participants to source only through the agreement, places caps on procurement price and volume on the participants or ancillary restrictions are in place, then the availability of the exemption will not be likely.

The formation of buying groups by large supermarket retailers has not been a frequent occurrence particularly in the UK, due in probability to the risk of contravening Article 81(1) by attaining a combined market share in excess of 15 per cent in both the relevant purchasing and relevant selling markets. However, there has been the controversial joint venture between French supermarkets Auchan and Casino, where a buyer group in all but name was created but was not subjected to Article 81 scrutiny by the Commission. The purpose of the joint venture was cited as a project to 'contribute to the internationalization of small businesses by facilitating their access to export markets, with *Auchan/Casino* providing advice, to look for new suppliers, to combat unjustified price differences that result from the national compartmentalization of markets and to prevent large suppliers practising unjustifiable discrimination to the detriment of the parties'.[43] These characteristics of a buying group were counterbalanced, however, in that both Auchan and Casino retained their respective purchasing independence and remained competitors in their home French market.

Exchange of information

The coordination of competitive behaviour arising from the exchange of information between competitors compromises the principle that entities in the market should operate independently of one another and not interdependently. The sharing of information between competitors may in certain circumstances, therefore, constitute an infringement of Article 81(1).

The Commission's 1968 notice[44] provides guidance that certain types of information exchanges are unlikely to transgress the Article 81(1) prohibition, except where the data exchange restricts competition in an oligopolistic market for homogenous products and where the communication between the undertakings is a 'device for facilitating either the coordination of their commercial behaviour

42 Ibid, sec 4, paras 130–131.
43 Notification of a Joint Venture (Case COMP/D3/A38576) [2003] OJ C54/2.
44 Commission Notice on Cooperation Agreements [1968] OJ C75/3, para 11.

or the adoption of a common industry response to market indicators'.[45] Hence, determining the sensitivity of the content and intent of the information exchange, together with the market structure in which the communicating parties operate is imperative. Information which is historical and anonymized is unlikely to offend Article 81(1), however, detailed commercial data relating to future sales and delivery, pricing, terms of trade, product composition, and territorial market strategy will be more likely to result in infringement.

The unique juxtaposition of the three roles of the supermarket 'gatekeeper' means that although the initial information exchange downstream from supplier to supermarket as 'customer' is for the purposes of developing effective marketing strategies to attract consumers at point of sale, the same information is appropriated for an unintended function, namely, by the supermarkets in their 'competitor' role, providing them with valuable commercial information to help set pricing and promotional strategies for their private label products. This innate tension was acknowledged in two merger control investigations in both *Kesko/Tuko*[46] and later in *Proctor & Gamble/Gillette*.[47] The Commission expressly noted the inherent competitive advantage that is endowed upon a supermarket in its role as 'gatekeeper', in respect of access to commercially sensitive information:

> ... private label development is a key element in the power wielded by retailers vis a vis branded daily consumer-goods producers. It enables retailers, who are inevitably privy to commercially sensitive details regarding the branded good producers' product launches and promotional strategies, to act as competitors as well as key customers of the producers. This privileged position increases the leverage enjoyed by retailers over branded-good producers.[48]

The subversion of sensitive information received from upstream suppliers by the supermarkets to then coordinate and align the marketing and promotional strategies of their private label goods to augment their competitive position against those very suppliers at a horizontal level, is of concern to the competition authorities. A particular trepidation expressed in *Proctor & Gamble/Gillette* is the supermarkets' ability to fix the prices of their private label goods pegged against the branded labels, potentially in a predatory manner:

> ... Since retailers know the prices of the goods offered by the parties, they have the advantage to be in a position to fix prices for their own private labels in reaction to the producers of branded products. In contrast, these producers are not able to

45 *CEPI-Cartonboard* (Case IV34.936/E1) [1996] OJ C310/3, para 18.

46 *Kesko/Tuko* (n 11).

47 *Procter & Gamble/Gillette* (Case COMP/M.3732) Commission Decision of 15 July 2005, para 125 <http://ec.europa.eu/comm/competition/mergers/cases/decisions/m3732_20050715_20212_en.pdf> accessed 27 May 2007.

48 *Kesko/Tuko* (n 11) para 152.

> readjust their prices. . . the parties have an asymmetry of information vis a vis prices for private labels.[49]

The application of Article 81(or equivalent) competition powers to combat the internal exploitation of commercially sensitive information by a supermarket 'gatekeeper' in this way is untested as yet.

This is in contrast to exchange of information between competitors (horizontally and vertically) where the purpose of such communication has been to engage in anti-competitive behaviour, such as price fixing. A supermarket sector related example is the recent price coordination finding by the OFT in the British dairy market and other investigations discussed below. In this case, the collusion between the supermarkets and dairy processors involved the sharing of commercially sensitive information, including details of the levels of price increase to be set to the retail consumer, over a period of two years. Similarly, in *Argos/Littlewoods*, the fixing of retail prices for toys was facilitated through the supplier, Hasbro, who received information from Argos and Littlewoods as to each retailer's respective future pricing strategy, and who then communicated such information between the two. Although there was indirect contact between Argos and Littlewoods, the channelling of information through the mutual upstream supplier had the effect of influencing future conduct in the horizontal market, specifically in the setting of prices. In both instances, such behaviour was held to be in direct contravention of the UK's Chapter 1 of the Competition Act 1998.

Price-coordination

The UK's OFT has developed a body of cases investigating whether retail prices have been manipulated by the indirect exchange of pricing information using a vertically related retailer or a manufacturer as a conduit.

A recent example of price fixing by supermarkets, both vertically as 'customers' and horizontally as 'competitors', has been in the UK. The OFT, the UK's competition enforcement authority, provisionally made a finding pursuant to Chapter 1 of the Competition Act 1998, that the five largest domestic supermarket retailers in their 'customer' capacity, colluded with five upstream dairy processors to increase the retail prices of liquid milk, value butter, and cheese. The cost of the collusion to consumers was estimated at £270 million.[50]

The OFT concluded early resolution agreements with six of the named parties who admitted infringement of Chapter 1 and agreed to pay individual penalties,

---

49 *Procter & Gamble/Gillette* (n 47) 21, para 124.

50 OFT, *OFT Issues Provisional Decision Against Supermarkets and Dairies over Price Fixing* Press Release 134/07 (20 September 2007).

of a combined value totalling £116 million.[51] Owing to the admission of guilt and subject to full ongoing cooperation, the fines levied were significantly less than would otherwise have been imposed.

The OFT's finding of price fixing between (non-supermarket) retailers, at both a horizontal and vertical level, was upheld by the Court of Appeal in *Argos/Littlewoods*.[52] The ruling was significant as it was the first appeal to the Court of Appeal rising from an enforcement pursuant to Chapter 1. The Court of Appeal upheld the earlier Competition Appeal Tribunal and OFT decisions that the toy manufacturer, Hasbro, and retailers, Littlewoods and Argos, entered into a number of bilateral and tripartite agreements and concerted practices between 1999 and May 2001 to fix the retail prices for Hasbro toys and games.

The OFT fined Littlewoods £5.37 million and Argos £17.28 million. Hasbro would have been fined £15.59 million, but was granted full leniency as it reported the infringement to the OFT. The Court of Appeal dismissed appeals by Argos and Littlewoods, who challenged the amount of penalty levied on the basis that the OFT wrongly defined the product market. The Court of Appeal stated that in a Chapter 1 enforcement action involving price fixing, a formal analysis of the product market is not required, and that it is sufficient that the OFT be satisfied on a reasonable and properly reasoned basis, that it can identify the relevant product market affected by the infringement.

In *JJB Sports*,[53] the OFT found that a group of ten undertakings had entered price-fixing agreements in breach of Chapter I of the Competition Act 1998 in relation to the sale of replica football kit around the time of the Euro 2000 Championship. Two of these undertakings, JJB Sports plc (JJB) and Allsports Limited (Allsports) appealed the findings of infringement.

The Competition Appeal Tribunal (CAT) found evidence that around the time of Euro 2000, JJB (the largest sportswear retailer) and Allsports had both complained to the manufacturer Umbro in relation to proposed discounting of England replica kit by a third retailer, Sports Soccer. Sports Soccer eventually agreed not to discount on the understanding that JJB and Allsports would not do so either. This amounted to an agreement or concerted practice under the Chapter I prohibition, the object or effect of which was to eliminate discounting in the period around Euro 2000.

[51] OFT, *OFT Welcomes Early Resolution Agreements and Agrees over £116 m Penalties* Press Release 170/07 (7 December 2007).

[52] *Argos Limited and Littlewoods Limited v Office of Fair Trading* [2006] EWCA Civ 1318.

[53] *JJB Sports plc v Office of Fair Trading* [2006] EWCA Civ 1318.

The CAT also found sufficiently strong and compelling evidence that meetings were held between the same retailers discussing pricing prior to the launch of Manchester United replica kit in August 2000. In April 2001, JJB was also found to have received an assurance from Umbro that Sports Soccer would not discount new Manchester United replica kit.

In relation to replica kit sold via the England Direct website, Sportsetail, the retailers, had agreed not to sell below JJB's own retail price. Despite JJB ending its involvement in the arrangement in February 2000, 'price-pegging' continued thereafter with the knowledge of JJB who failed to inform the other parties explicitly that any prices could be charged on the website, which amounted to tacit approval of the unlawful initiative (Aalborg Portland). However, the appeal was allowed as JJB's involvement was prior to 1 March 2000 when the Competition Act 1998 was not in force and there was insufficient evidence to show that JJB has been party to an agreement after that date.

On 25 April 2008, the OFT announced that it had issued a statement of objections alleging that two tobacco manufacturers and eleven retailers, including major supermarkets, had engaged in unlawful practices in relation to retail prices for tobacco products in the UK. Its allegations relate to two practices:

- arrangements between each manufacturer and each retailer to link the retail price of a manufacturer's brand to the retail price of a competing brand of another manufacturer, restricting the ability of each retailer to determine its selling price independently;
- in the case of the manufacturers and certain of the retailers only, the indirect exchange of proposed future retail prices between competitors.

At the end of April 2008 reports emerged that the OFT had conducted on-site inspections of the largest four supermarkets—Asda, Morrisons, Sainsburys, and Tesco—as well as issuing information requests to a large number of suppliers of grocery products investigating:

- co-ordination of retail prices by the supermarkets; and
- facilitation of that coordination by suppliers through the passing of information to retailers.

This investigation may have been triggered as a result of information obtained by the OFT in earlier investigations and from information passed to it by the Competition Commission obtained during the course of its investigation into the groceries market concluded in April 2008.[54]

[54] See further Section B above.

There are a number of other investigations underway into the conduct of suppliers and supermarkets in several other European jurisdictions, including Belgium, France, and Germany.

D. Ex-Post Remedies—Dominance and Economic Dependence

So far as the author is aware, there have been no Article 82 EC cases brought against supermarkets. Indeed the issue is often to establish dominance on the normal basis defined in EU law. It is apparent that the leading supermarket operators are wielding considerably more market power than ever before (at least with regards to their dealings with suppliers), and are consolidating this power.

Within the context of EC merger control, several associated concepts have previously been identified by the Commission which recognize this growing position of supermarket buyer power. This can have beneficial effects. In the *Rewe/Meinl* case[55] the 'spiral effect' described a potential situation where a newly merged (and enlarged) entity might demand larger volume related discounts from upstream suppliers, whilst passing the benefit onto consumers in the form of lower prices, in turn undercutting competitors, leading to a self-perpetuating increase in market share, leading to even larger volume discounts and so on. On the other hand, the case of *Carrefour/Promodes*[56] identified a so-called 'threat' point associated with supplier 'economic dependence' on a retailer. The Commission identified that when a supplier reached a level of 22 per cent of his total revenues originating from just one retailer, the relative bargaining power of the parties changed heavily in favour of the retailer. At that point, there was every likelihood that the supplier would face future insolvency as a result of the disparity in bargaining power.

E. Conclusion

The underpinning feature in the development of competition law at EU (and Member State) level has been to protect competition and not competitors, thereby enhancing consumer protection in terms of price and plurality of choice. The continuing growth of supermarkets across Europe, organically and through acquisitions, together with the commercial advantages inherent in the unique

55 *Rewe/Meinl* (n 16).
56 *Carrefour/Promodes* (n 20).

tri-faceted 'gatekeeper' role, has tested this principle and has exposed the limitations of classic competition law enforcement.

The application of traditional competition law powers pursuant to Article 81, Article 82, and merger control (and equivalent national powers) have been effective in counteracting certain types of anti-competitive practices perpetrated by supermarkets. Such action has been used to rein back supermarket buyer power and address asymmetric bargaining power vis-à-vis suppliers. Typically remedies imposed pursuant to such enforcement action have attempted to stimulate and entrench vigorous competition, particularly at a horizontal level. Such remedies have ranged from outright prohibition, the levying of financial penalties, structural action in the form of divestiture of retail outlets in designated geographic regions, to behavioural commitments in respect of contractual relationships with suppliers.

Although action has been taken under Article 81 against anti-competitive practices between competing supermarkets and upstream suppliers colluding to fix prices and exchange sensitive commercial information, such a stringent approach has not been applied to similar practices committed by supermarkets in their 'gatekeeper' role. The appropriation of commercially sensitive information from suppliers obtained as 'customer', for use to set prices of private label goods as 'competitor' or to auction prominent shelf space as 'supplier' has gone unchallenged. Furthermore, one of the long-standing difficulties under Article 82 in relation to supermarkets has been to establish individual dominance at retail level, with the threshold for establishing collective dominance following the *Airtours* decision high. Merger control can and has been utilized to prevent dominance arising; however, the continuing problem is that supermarkets across Europe exercise market power below the normal dominance thresholds, engaging in conduct that would otherwise be deemed abusive of such market power.

In conjunction with this, arguably, there has been insufficient focus upon other market conditions, namely, supplier welfare. Complaints have been rife of increased supplier economic dependency on retailers, who then engage in commercially unsavoury market practices, adversely affecting the competitiveness of the suppliers. Such practices have been identified as below-cost selling of frequently purchased products, 'price flexing', requiring prospective and retrospective payments from suppliers for prominent shelf positioning, and arbitrary changes to terms of supply, to name but few.

The idea that competition authorities should delve deeper into supermarket conduct arising from their 'gatekeeper' role and extend their evaluation of abusive practices below established levels of dominance has increased calls for an atypical enforcement approach in the supermarket sector. The market investigation powers pursuant to the Enterprise Act 2002 in the UK is perhaps the best example, to date, of such an approach, in trying to address the supermarket sector to make it work more effectively for all actors involved—the retailers, suppliers, and consumers.

The CC's decision on remedies in the groceries investigation indicates a novel position to enhance the protection of competition by, significantly, also protecting competitors. The proposed 'competition assessment' to be applied to the planning regime aims to redress supermarket buyer power, whilst the overhaul of SCOP and institution of a 'Supermarkets Ombudsman' signals a quasi-competition regulatory step to alleviate the pressure being applied to suppliers. The need for a hybrid of competition and quasi-competition remedies to correct the market imbalance between retailers and suppliers and to dilute the competitive advantages intrinsic to the 'gatekeeper' role has been demonstrated; whether the way successfully to achieve this is in the manner that the CC proposes is yet to be seen.

Part VI

PRIVATE LABELS—THE US EXPERIENCE

15

UNITED STATES COMPETITION LAW POLICY—THE PRIVATE LABEL EXPERIENCE

Jeffrey Schmidt and Terry Calvani***

* Director, Bureau of Competition, Federal Trade Commission. The views expressed herein do not necessarily reflect the views of the FTC or any individual Commissioner.

**Of Counsel, Freshfields Bruckhaus Deringer US LLP. The authors wish to thank the staff of the Office of Policy and Coordination of the Federal Trade Commission's Bureau of Competition, and Diane Tuomala of the Washington, DC office of Freshfields Bruckhaus Deringer LLP, for their assistance in the preparation of this chapter.

A. Introduction

Private label[1] issues have been important across the US competition law landscape. For example, the very prominent—and controversial—decision by the Court of Appeals in *LePage's Inc v 3M Co*[2] found that the bundled pricing of branded and private label products by a seller with market power in the branded segment constituted a violation of Section 2 of the Sherman Act.[3] Nevertheless, most of the issues involving private label goods have arisen in the context of market definition incident to merger review and in cases involving alleged price discrimination under the Robinson-Patman Act. This paper focuses on private label issues in the context of both.

B. Private Label Issues in US Merger Review

Introduction

Issues involving private label brands are most likely to arise in the consumer products area. This section will therefore focus on mergers in that sector and consider how the US antitrust agencies and courts treat those issues. The discussion draws heavily on two sources: the Horizontal Merger Guidelines issued by the Antitrust Division of the Department of Justice (DOJ) and the Federal Trade

---

1 Private label brands are products bearing a retail store's own name or a brand name created exclusively by the retailer for its store. According to recent studies private label brands now account for one of every five items sold in US supermarkets, drug chains, and mass merchandise stores and represent more than US$65 billion in retail sales. See website of the Private Label Manufacturers Association <http://plma.com>. The private label merchandise may be produced by large manufacturers of branded merchandise taking advantage of excess capacity, smaller manufacturers that specialize in private label brands, or large retailers that establish their own production facilities dedicated to their private label.

2 324 F 3d 141 (3d Cir 2003) (en banc).

3 15 USC s 2. The plaintiff was the market leader in the sale of private label transparent tape. Confronted with a diminishing market share and falling profits, plaintiff brought suit alleging that the defendant manufacturer of Scotch brand transparent tape, private label transparent tape, and other products that the plaintiff did not produce leveraged its market power in the branded tape business to monopolize the private label business. Specifically, plaintiff alleged that the defendant's bundling practices, under which the rebates became progressively higher when customers purchased across defendant's different product lines and which the plaintiff was unable to match since it did not sell the same diverse array of products, foreclosed the market to it. The court rejected the defendant's argument that its pricing practices could not be exclusionary unless it priced below cost. But see *Cascade Health Solutions (f/k/a McKenzie-Willamette Hospital) v PeaceHealth* 502 F 3d 895 (9th Cir 2007), where the Court of Appeals for the Ninth Circuit reached a different conclusion, holding that there cannot be illegal foreclosure unless the bundled products are sold below cost. This conflict between the courts of appeal may lead the Supreme Court to grant a writ of certiorari in the next case to present these issues.

Commission (FTC or the Commission) in 1992 and last revised in 1997,[4] and the Commentary on those Guidelines issued in 2006.[5] Case law in this area is sparse, but what is available is consistent with agency merger guidance.

When a merger implicates private label brands, the applicable legal principles do not vary. In the most usual case, the evaluation of private label brands will be significant in defining the relevant product market and in determining whether the private label brands can constrain the prices of manufacturer branded products. As will be seen from the discussion of private label in the context of price discrimination, there is some degree of tension between the treatment of private label products in the merger context and their treatment by the courts in Robinson-Patman cases.

An overview of merger analysis

In the merger area, the FTC shares jurisdiction with the Antitrust Division of the Department of Justice for the enforcement of Section 7 of the Clayton Act, which prohibits mergers and acquisitions whose effect 'may be substantially to lessen competition or to tend to create a monopoly' in a relevant line of commerce.[6] Since the passage of the Hart-Scott-Rodino (HSR) Act more than 30 years ago, proposed transactions that meet certain threshold size standards must be reported to the agencies before they are consummated.[7] This reporting gives the agency assigned to review the transaction an opportunity to consider its competitive consequences and seek to halt its consummation if the agency believes that the acquisition would violate Section 7.[8] Even if a merger is not reportable under the

4 US Department of Justice and Federal Trade Commission, '1992 Horizontal Merger Guidelines' (revised April 8, 1997) <http://www.ftc.gov/bc/docs/horizmer.shtm> accessed 8 March 2008, *reprinted in* Trade Reg Rep (CCH) para 13,104 [hereinafter HMG].

5 US Department of Justice and Federal Trade Commission, 'Commentary on the Horizontal Merger Guidelines' (March 2006) <http://www.ftc.gov/os/2006/03/CommentaryontheHorizontalMergerGuidelinesMarch2006.pdf> accessed 8 March 2008 [hereinafter Commentary].

6 15 USC s 18. Mergers may also be challenged under s 1 and 2 of the Sherman Act as unreasonable restraints of trade or as monopolization or attempted monopolization. 15 USC ss 1, 2. Additionally, the FTC may challenge a merger as an unfair method of competition which is prohibited by s 5 of the FTC Act. 15 USC s 45.

7 Hart-Scott-Rodino Antitrust Improvements Act of 1976, 15 USC s 18a. There are two size thresholds in the statute in addition to a commerce test. The size of person test is met if one of the parties has sales or assets of at least US$100 million (as adjusted, currently US$126.2 million) and the other party has sales or assets of at least US$10 million (as adjusted, currently US$12.6 million). The size of transaction test is met if as a result of the transaction the acquiring person will hold an aggregate amount of stock and assets of the acquired person valued at more than US$50 million (as adjusted, currently US$63.1 million). FTC rules governing filing requirements are found at 16 CFR Part 801. Comprehensive information on the HSR pre-merger programme is available on the FTC website <http://ftc.gov/bc/hsr/hsr.shtm> accessed 8 March 2008.

8 Because the agencies share antitrust jurisdiction, there is a protocol for deciding which will investigate a specific transaction. US Department of Justice and Federal Trade Commission,

HSR Act, it may still have anti-competitive effects, and the agencies investigate those mergers as well.[9]

In fiscal year 2006, the agencies received 1,768 merger filings, undertook intensive investigations of 45 transactions, and took enforcement action in 19 cases. In a further 13 cases, the parties withdrew the HSR filings or abandoned the transactions.[10]

The mergers most likely to raise competitive issues related to private labels are those involving consumer products. One 2006 matter reviewed by the FTC was Proctor & Gamble's acquisition of Gillette, which involved toothbrushes, teeth whitening strips, and deodorants.[11] Other mergers and acquisitions that the FTC has examined and sometimes challenged have involved ice cream,[12] tobacco products,[13] liquors,[14] and soft drinks,[15] among others. In recent years, the DOJ has challenged acquisitions in several consumer products including sardines,[16] bread,[17] milk,[18] and consumer paper products.[19]

Clearance Procedures of Investigations (2 December 1993), *reprinted in* Trade Reg Rep (BNA) 746 (9 December 1993). Both agencies apply the analysis of the Horizontal Merger Guidelines. HMG s 0.1, Commentary 1.

9 On relatively rare occasions the agencies learn of a completed merger that originally fell below the reporting threshold but merits investigation because it caused competitive harm. Often they learn of such transactions through post-merger complaints from customers or suppliers of the merged firm. Of course, finding that a consummated merger has 'substantially lessened competition' requires that the agency craft a practical remedy to undo its anti-competitive effects. *Chicago Bridge & Iron Co v FTC* No 05-60192 (5th Cir Jan 25, 2008), *aff'g* 138 FTC 1024 (2004), *as modified* 140 FTC 1161 (2005) (affirming Commission order requiring divestitures); *Re The Hearst Trust* No. 1:01CV02119 (DDC 2001) (consent order) <http://www.ftc.gov/os/2001/12/hearstfinalorder.pdf> accessed 8 March 2008; *United States v EI du Pont de Nemours & Co* 353 US 586, 597 (1957) (the legality of a merger can be determined at any time when the acquisition threatens to ripen into a prohibited effect).

10 Federal Trade Commission and Department of Justice, 'Hart-Scott-Rodino Annual Report' (Fiscal Year 2006) app A <http://www.ftc.gov/os/2007/07/P110014hsrreport.pdf> accessed 8 March 2008.

11 *Re Procter & Gamble and Gillette* 140 FTC 944 (2005).

12 *Re Nestle Holdings Inc, Dreyers Grand Ice Cream Holdings Inc, and Dreyers Grand Ice Cream Inc* 136 FTC 791, 798 (2003) (consent order).

13 *FTC v Swedish Match North America, Inc* 131 F Supp 2d 151 (DDC 2000); FTC File No 041-0017, 'RJ Reynolds Tobacco Holdings, Inc' (22 June 2004) (Closing Statement of the Commission) <http://www.ftc.gov/os/2004/06/040622batrjrstmt.pdf> accessed 8 March 2008.

14 *Re Diageo PLC and Vivendi Universal SA* 133 FTC 156, 167 (2002) (consent order).

15 *Re The Coca-Cola Co* 117 FTC 795, 967 (1994) (consent order).

16 *United States v Connors Bros Income Fund* No 1:04-CV-01494-JDB (DDC 2004).

17 *United States v Interstate Bakeries and Continental Baking Co* 1996-1 Trade Cases (CCH) para 71,271 (ND Ill 1995).

18 *United States v Suiza Foods Corp* 1999-2 Trade Cases (CCH) para 72,645 (ED Ky 1999).

19 *United States v Kimberly Clark Corp* 1996-1 Trade Cases (CCH) para 71,405 (ND Tex 1995).

When the agency reviews mergers, the analysis focuses on whether a specific merger is likely to create or increase market power. Market power is not simply size, or even a large market share. It is defined as the ability profitably to maintain prices above competitive levels for a significant period of time. In simplest terms, the concern is whether a merger will allow the new firm to raise prices and keep them above pre-merger levels over a significant period of time.[20] In some cases, the analysis also considers whether a merger may lessen competition in product quality, service, or innovation.[21]

Typically, to assess whether a merger creates or enhances market power, the reviewing agency examines whether the merger significantly increases concentration in one or more relevant product and geographic markets, as discussed below.[22] A merger is unlikely to create or enhance market power unless it significantly increases the concentration of the firms selling a product within a market, and the agencies do not usually investigate further in those cases where post-merger concentration remains low, or concentration is not significantly increased from pre-merger levels.[23]

Even if the merged firm would obtain a large market share, it might not be able to raise prices and keep them raised.[24] If other market incumbents could readily expand their output rate, or if other firms could quickly enter the market with sufficient capacity, even a monopolist created by merger would not be able profitably to raise and maintain prices above pre-merger levels.[25] For that reason, in instances where the agencies determine that a merger is otherwise anti-competitive, they will consider, before an enforcement decision is made, whether new firms would be likely to enter quickly with sufficient new capacity to counteract the anti-competitive effects of the merger.[26]

---

20 Commentary 2; *United States v Archer Daniels Midland Co* 866 F 2d 242, 246 (8th Cir 1988) (lawfulness of an acquisition turns on the purchaser's potential for creating, enhancing, or facilitating the exercise of market power). Using pre-merger prices as the benchmark in merger analysis acknowledges that some amount of market power may already exist prior to the merger.

21 HMG s 0.1 fn 6.

22 Although we discuss each factor in the merger analysis in turn, the agencies have made it clear that they do not analyse mergers in a step-by-step approach considering each factor only as the analysis of the preceding factor is completed. Rather the agencies use an integrated approach, and consider the competitive totality of each acquisition as a whole. Commentary 2.

23 HMG s 1.0. Mergers that either do not significantly increase concentration or do not result in a concentrated market ordinarily require no further analysis.

24 The HMGs postulate anti-competitive effects from a merger arising either from a single firm's ability to exercise market power or the ability of all post-merger firms to exercise market power in concert. See discussion of Anti-competitive Effects below.

25 HMG s 4.

26 HMG s 3.0. ('A merger is not likely to create or enhance market power or to facilitate its exercise, if entry into the market is so easy that market participants, after the merger, either collectively or unilaterally could not profitably maintain a price increase above premerger levels. Such entry

In some cases, the agencies may inquire into additional areas. For example, parties may claim that the merger will produce efficiencies that would not otherwise be achievable.[27] The agencies will not challenge a transaction if 'cognizable efficiencies likely would be sufficient to reverse the merger's potential to harm consumers in the relevant market, eg, by preventing price increases in that market'.[28] Additionally, if the parties demonstrate that, absent the merger, one party to the transaction faces imminent failure and its assets are likely to exit the market, the agencies may conclude that the competitive effects of the merger are no worse than preventing the merger. In such cases, the agencies will not bring a challenge.[29]

Market definition and concentration

Often, the antitrust analysis of mergers must first define the relevant geographic and product markets. Indeed, the prediction of whether a merger is likely to create or increase market power often turns on the definition of the relevant markets.[30] The major focus in defining a market is consumer choice: if the merged company raises price, what options will consumers have? The investigation begins with an examination of 'overlap' products, those manufactured or sold by both of the merging firms, and asks what would happen if a hypothetical monopolist of that product imposed a 'small but significant and nontransitory' increase in price (SSNIP).[31]

Economics teaches that a rise in price typically leads to some decline in unit sales. The question for analysis becomes whether the reduction in unit sales would be large enough to make the increase in price unprofitable. Would the firm lose more in profits on the lost unit sales than it would gain on the increased profit per item sold? A price increase could be made unprofitable by consumers either withdrawing purchases altogether or switching to substitute products offered by

likely will deter an anticompetitive merger in its incipiency, or deter or counteract the competitive effects of concern.')

[27] HMG s 0.2.

[28] HMG s 4.

[29] HMG s 5. The failing firm defence was first recognized by the Supreme Court in *International Shoe Co v FTC* 280 US 291 (1930), and in *Citizen Publishing Co v United States* 394 US 131 (1969), the court set out the requirements that the company be in imminent danger of failure, that it have no realistic prospect for a successful reorganization, and that there is no viable alternative purchaser that poses less anti-competitive risk (pp 138–139).

[30] Under US case law, the admissibility of direct evidence of post-merger effects to show the legality of a consummated merger depends, inter alia, on whether the evidence is subject to manipulation by the post-merger behaviour of the parties. See e.g. *Chicago Bridge and Iron v FTC* No 05-60192 (5th Cir Jan 25, 2008).

[31] HMG s 1.0.

other firms.[32] If this substitution would make a price increase unprofitable, then the substitute products of other firms are included in the relevant market.[33]

In consumer products cases, the relevant product market is determined by consumers' ability and willingness to substitute one product for another. In the mid-1980s, the Coca-Cola Company proposed to acquire DP Holdings, Inc, the parent of Dr Pepper (a US soft drink). The FTC and the reviewing court found that carbonated soft drinks was the relevant product market in which to assess the merger. Coca-Cola, in contrast, claimed that the market should be 'all . . . beverages including tap water'.[34] Had the broad 'all beverage' market been accepted, the merger of Coca-Cola and Dr Pepper would have had little impact on market concentration.

Although it is true that many liquids, including tap water, can be used to quench thirst, that fact alone did not define the relevant product market. Rather, the SSNIP test was applied in order to find the smallest set of products that would allow a hypothetical monopolist to raise price. The court in the Coca-Cola matter agreed with the FTC that the availability of water and other beverages would not constrain the ability of soft drink manufacturers to raise prices. Therefore, those other beverages were excluded from the relevant market of carbonated soft drinks.[35]

A similar analysis is undertaken to define the relevant geographic market in which the merging firms compete. The agencies ask whether a hypothetical monopolist in any particular region could profitably raise prices. If the hypothetical monopolist could not raise prices because consumers would turn to sellers located outside the region, then the putative relevant geographic market is expanded to include the wider region. This process continues until it is determined that a hypothetical monopolist could raise prices profitably.[36]

---

32 The more elastic the demand for the product, the more a given rise in price will result in fewer sales. *United States v EI du Pont de Nemours & Co* 351 US 377, 400 (1956) (cross-elasticity defined as measuring 'the responsiveness of the sales of one product to price changes of the other'). The standard textbook definition of the price elasticity of demand is the percentage change in quantity demanded that would be induced by a 1% change in price. Cross-elasticity in demand represents the percentage change in the quantity demanded of Good A that is induced by a 1% change in the price of Good B. See e.g.: W L Peterson, *Principles of Economics: Micro* (1917) 42–47; A Marshall, *Principles of Economics* (8th edn, 1920) Book III, ch IV.

33 HMG s 1.1.

34 *FTC v The Coca-Cola Co* 641 F Supp 1128, 1133 (DDC 1986).

35 Ibid, 1133. Of course technology and new products are always changing market conditions. This case was decided before bottled water became a multi-billion dollar industry with multiple products competing on the same shelves with carbonated soft drinks. Today a detailed examination of the competitive interaction between soft drinks and bottled water would be necessary to decide if they are in the same relevant product market.

36 HMG s 1.21.

Once the markets have been properly defined, the next step is to identify the firms that participate. Here the initial focus is on all firms that currently produce or sell in the relevant product market. The analysis then considers firms that, although not currently selling the relevant product, have the capacity and the technical capability to supply the market quickly without incurring significant 'sunk costs', and would have the incentive to supply the market quickly in response to a SSNIP.[37] The agencies count such potential suppliers as market participants up to the point of their capacity to supply the relevant product.[38]

Although it may seem counter-intuitive to include as market participants firms that do not produce or sell in the market, the reasoning is fairly straightforward. A seller must not only take account of its immediate competitors when it makes decisions about what and how much to produce and what prices to charge, but also consider the competitive responses of firms who could quickly become competitors. When there are companies that could supply the market quickly and capture a significant amount of sales, the market power of incumbents is likely to be constrained. Thus, sound merger analysis will account for such supply responses.[39]

Because a merged firm can seldom exercise market power in an unconcentrated market, it is important to evaluate the impact on market concentration from the merger. The Herfindahl-Hirschman Index (HHI) is a measure of market concentration. It is computed by summing the squares of the individual market shares of each market participant. Because the HHI first squares the market shares, it accounts for the size dispersion of the market participants. Under the HMG, a market with an HHI value below 1,000 is considered unconcentrated, 1,000 to 1,800 moderately concentrated, and above 1,800 highly concentrated.[40] Mergers that will leave the market unconcentrated rarely require further investigation. If the merger would raise the HHI level by less than 100 points in a moderately concentrated market, or less than 50 points in a highly concentrated market, the agencies will not presume an anti-competitive effect and may not investigate further unless there are other factors that suggest concern.[41] By contrast, mergers in highly concentrated markets that increase the HHI by 50 points or more raise significant competitive concerns, and the agencies will typically examine those cases closely.

37 HMG s 1.32.
38 Ibid.
39 HMG s 1.0.
40 HMG s 1.51.
41 Ibid.

Anti-competitive effects

The agencies assess the likely competitive effects of mergers under two theories of competitive harm: coordinated interaction and unilateral effects. The concern of coordinated interaction is that a merger will facilitate or enhance the ability of market incumbents to reach a consensus to reduce rivalry on a significant competitive dimension such as price, capacity, or output. Coordinated interaction rests on the idea that accommodation among competitors that reduces competition yields greater total industry profits than vigorous competition.[42] Concern about a merger's impact on coordinated interaction is greatest when market concentration is high and when the market is characterized by firms that produce relatively homogeneous products and sell those products in similar ways to similar sorts of buyers. Effective reduction in competition by dint of coordinated interaction requires that incumbents not only reach consensus, but also are able to detect and punish rivals that deviate from the consensus.[43]

Anti-competitive effects from a merger may also occur when the merged firm is able profitably to reduce output and raise prices unilaterally, i.e. without the accommodation of the other incumbents in the market. The simplest case would be a merger to monopoly, which eliminates all competition in the relevant market.[44] Concerns about anti-competitive unilateral effects often occur when the merger results in a firm with a dominant market position. Unilateral effects concerns are also common when reviewing mergers taking place in differentiated products markets, including mergers in markets where private label brands are significant.

New entry

Even when the agencies initially conclude that a merger could be anti-competitive, the analysis does not end. Entry must be considered. If the entry of new capacity can be expected to take place in a timely fashion after an otherwise anti-competitive merger, if that entry would be profitable at pre-merger prices, and if such entry can be expected to be of sufficient magnitude to restore pre-merger prices, there will be no durable harm to consumers. In other words, effective entry must be 'timely, likely, and sufficient'.[45]

The standard for timeliness is generally two years from initial planning to impact.[46] The likelihood of entry is an objective inquiry: if a firm can expect to

42 HMG s 2.1.
43 HMG s 2.11.
44 Commentary 25.
45 HMG s 3.0.
46 HMG s 3.2.

enter the market and capture enough sales that are profitable at pre-merger prices, entry will be considered 'likely'. Incremental sales from entry must restore prices to the level that prevailed before the merger to be considered 'sufficient' to undo the competitive harm anticipated from the merger.[47] If these conditions are met, the agencies could conclude that a merger does not raise long term antitrust concerns that necessitate an enforcement action.

The role of private label products in merger analysis

When issues surrounding private label products arise in merger analysis, among the key questions is whether those products should be considered within the relevant market. There is no universal answer to this question. The inquiry is highly fact-intensive and must be undertaken in each individual case. Although no court decision has yet addressed precisely this question, the FTC and the DOJ have analysed the impact of private label products when defining markets in several cases. Several factors must be considered, including the strength of consumer brand preferences and the ability of private label owners to reposition their products in response to post-merger profit opportunities.

Differentiated product markets

When defining markets, the antitrust analysis looks to consumers' willingness to substitute one product for another in the face of a price increase.[48] Consumer behaviour may be driven in part by the end use of the product, but the market definition analysis will not necessarily result in markets that include the full range of functional substitutes from which customers can choose.[49] Functionally similar products may be differentiated by branding and manufacturers' efforts to build 'brand equity' and develop consumer loyalty.[50] Thus, markets contain products that are not perfect substitutes for each other, and the different products may vary in their degree of substitutability such that some sellers compete more directly with certain other sellers.[51]

When competing firms in differentiated product markets merge, the merger can have anti-competitive effects if the merging firms' products, brand A and brand B, are also the first and second choices for many consumers.[52] A price increase for

---

47 HMG s 3.4.
48 Commentary 9.
49 Commentary 6. For example, most toothpastes will probably clean teeth satisfactorily, but many consumers may not be indifferent to which brand of toothpaste they purchase and use.
50 HMG s 2.21, Commentary 27 ('Unilateral Effects Relating to the Pricing of Differentiated Products').
51 HMG s 2.21.
52 Ibid.

brand A might have been unprofitable before the merger because too many consumers would have turned to brand B. After the merger, a rise in the price of brand A might cause consumers again to choose brand B, but now those sales would be retained within the newly merged firm.[53] Some sales might be lost to other incumbent firms, either national or private label brands, but if enough consumers prefer either brand A or B, those losses may not be sufficient to make the rise in price unprofitable.[54]

The FTC's review of the merger between Nestle Holdings, Inc, and Dreyer's Grand Ice Cream, Inc, in 2003 illustrates these points.[55] Both companies produced ice cream, as do many companies, and many retailers offered private label ice cream. Ice cream is sold as non-premium, premium, and 'superpremium' brands. In this last category, Nestle sold Haagen-Dazs in competition with the Dreyer's Dreamery, Godiva, and Starbucks brands. Compared to the other categories, superpremium ice cream contains more butterfat, less air, and more costly ingredients, and is typically sold at a substantially higher price. Together, Nestle and Dreyer's accounted for about 55 per cent of superpremium ice cream sales. Unilever, through its Ben & Jerry's brand, had 43 per cent of the superpremium sales, and retailer private label sales accounted for the remaining 2 per cent. Dreyer's had recently increased its efforts in the superpremium space and had expanded its share of sales to more than 20 per cent. This expansion increased competition with incumbent producers in this market.

The proposed merger raised the question of whether superpremium ice cream was sufficiently differentiated from other categories of ice cream that it constituted a separate product market within which the merger would probably permit the merged firm to raise prices unilaterally. FTC staff analysed scanner data and found that a small rise in the price of Haagen-Dazs would induce consumers to switch to other superpremium brands such as Ben & Jerry's or Dreyer's brands, but would not induce them to switch to premium or non-premium ice cream. Moreover, the analysis indicated that a significant proportion of superpremium ice cream consumers viewed Haagen-Dazs and Dreyer's brands as their first and second choices. This finding was corroborated by documentary and testimonial evidence. Thus, the FTC concluded that the relevant market was, in fact, superpremium ice cream, and that within this relevant market, a merger of Nestle and Dreyer's would be likely to result in anti-competitive price increases.

53 Ibid.

54 Ibid; commentary 28.

55 *Nestle Holdings, Inc, Dreyer's Grand Ice Cream Holdings, Inc and Dreyer's Grand Ice Cream, Inc* 68 Fed Reg para 39,564 (2 July 2003), *materials available at* <http://www.ftc.gov/opa/2003/06/nestle.htm> accessed 8 March 2008, discussed in the Commentary at 6, 28–29, 38.

The FTC entered into a consent agreement with the merging firms, requiring divestiture of two superpremium brands and of key distribution assets.

Private label products excluded from the relevant market

Just as consumers' unwillingness to switch from one differentiated brand product to another in response to a change in relative prices can be important evidence in defining a relevant market, strong consumer preferences for manufacturer branded products over private label products may lead to the exclusion of private label products from the relevant market. Exclusion is proper whenever sales of private label products do not constrain the prices of manufacturer branded products.[56] Coca-Cola's proposed acquisition of Dr Pepper provides an example.

In this matter, a district court rejected a putative 'all beverage' market and temporarily enjoined the acquisition.[57] Subsequently, the FTC undertook an administrative proceeding to determine the legality of the transaction, during which it performed a more exacting analysis of the relevant product market.[58] The FTC concluded that the sales of concentrates, and the carbonated soft drinks made from them, were divided into three categories: major national and regional brands, 'warehouse' brands, and private label products.[59] Evidence showed that sodas made from branded concentrate were heavily advertised, widely available in grocery and convenience stores for take-home use, available in the 'cold drink channel' for immediate consumption, and were sold, along with attendant services, to retailers.[60] The private label products, by contrast, were supported by little or no advertising, sold primarily by store chains, rarely available in the cold drink channel, and typically sold at the lowest price.[61]

The FTC found that concentrate manufacturers, soft drink bottlers, and consumers all considered the branded products to be a separate market. Consumers considered branded products to be superior in quality.[62] There was evidence that the pricing decisions of branded producers were unaffected by the prices of non-branded products,[63] and one study indicated that consumers would not

56 Such exclusion illustrates the applicability of general merger analysis principles to instances that implicate private label brands.

57 *FTC v The Coca-Cola Co* 641 F Supp 1128 (DDC 1986).

58 Following the decision of the district court, the original agreement was abandoned by the parties and Dr Pepper was sold to another buyer. The FTC reasoned that if the acquisition would have been illegal, prospective relief was still necessary in case Coca-Cola pursued the purchase at a later date. 117 FTC 795, 905 (1994).

59 Ibid, 930.

60 Ibid.

61 Ibid, 931.

62 Ibid, 932.

63 Ibid, 934.

switch from branded to private label sodas unless the price differential was 80–100 per cent.[64] The pivotal question was whether a small but significant rise in the price of sodas made from branded concentrates would be profitable because of consumers' unwillingness to switch to sodas made from private label concentrates when faced with the price increase. The agency concluded that this was indeed the case. Because the private label products would have had little impact on the post-merger pricing of branded concentrate products, the FTC found that the correct relevant market should be comprised of branded concentrate products and the sodas made therefrom only.[65]

Similarly, the DOJ Antitrust Division determined that private label products would not constrain post-merger price increases in the sale of manufacturer branded white pan bread when it reviewed the proposed acquisition of Continental Baking Co by Interstate Bakeries Corp in 1995.[66] The sale of white pan bread was highly differentiated by branding, and the price for manufacturer branded products was nearly twice that for supermarket private label brands. Scanner data demonstrated significant consumer preferences for manufacturer brands, a high cross-elasticity between the branded products of the merging firms, and little competitive interaction between manufacturer brands and private label products. In five metropolitan areas, the merging firms had either the top-selling brands or two of the three largest-selling brands, and the DOJ concluded that post-merger price increases would be likely in those geographic markets despite the presence of private label products. DOJ's challenge to the proposed merger was settled by a consent decree requiring divestiture of certain brands and related assets in the five metropolitan areas.

In another FTC case, the competitive strength of private label brands, and their ability to constrain post-merger price increases, was found to vary across different geographic regions but was still insufficient to protect consumers from the likely anti-competitive effects of the merger. In particular, General Mills, Inc's proposed purchase of Pillsbury Co[67] raised a potential competitive concern because Pillsbury and General Mills Gold Medal brands were the only two national flour brands, and the merged firm would account for over half of total US retail flour sales. Private label products had close to 25 per cent of national sales, with the balance accounted for by several regional sellers.

---

64 Ibid, 935.

65 Ibid, 940.

66 *United Stated v Interstate Bakeries Corp and Continental Baking Co* 1996-1 Trade Cases (CCH) para 71,271 (ND Ill 1995) (consent decree), discussed in the Commentary at 14, 30, 39.

67 *General Mills, Inc, Diageo plc, and The Pillsbury Co* FTC File No 001 0213 (2001), materials available at <http://www.ftc.gov/opa/2001/10/pillsbury.htm> accessed 8 March 2008, discussed in the Commentary at 14, 29.

In spite of their collective 25 per cent market share, evidence showed that private label flour provided a varying degree of constraint on prices across geographic regions. FTC staff found Gold Medal and Pillsbury flour to be the closest substitutes in some markets, while private label flour brands competed more directly with the manufacturer brands in others. The FTC's econometric analysis indicated that the merged firm could profitably raise prices by 10 per cent even in markets where the competition from private labels was determined to be stronger. The parties resolved the Agency's competitive concerns by selling Pillsbury's product line, and consequently the FTC took no action.

Private label products included in the relevant market

In some cases, the ability of merged firms to raise prices will be constrained by the presence of private label products, and thus the relevant market should include both branded and private label products. For example, in 1996, General Mills, Inc, agreed to acquire the branded ready-to-eat (RTE) cereal and snack mix businesses of Ralcorp Holdings, Inc.[68] At that time, General Mills was the second largest branded producer of RTE cereals, and Ralcorp was the fifth largest producer of branded RTE cereals. Unlike General Mills, Ralcorp also produced RTE cereals for the private labels of national supermarket chains and was the largest manufacturer in the country in that line of business. The acquisition agreement created a new entity, New Ralcorp, to continue the private label business of Ralcorp. New Ralcorp would have the right to produce a private label version of Ralcorp's CHEX line of branded cereals, but, according to the merger agreement, could not exercise that right for 18 months following the acquisition, and could not transfer the right to a third party without General Mills' permission.

The FTC alleged that the relevant market was 'branded and private label RTE cereals', and that the market for the sale of RTE cereals was highly concentrated.[69] Moreover, the post-acquisition HHI in the RTE market would increase by 223 points, from 2,317 to 2,540, based on dollar revenues, and General Mills' post-acquisition market share would be 31 per cent. Timely entry into the relevant markets, it was alleged, would be difficult, and would not be 'sufficient to prevent anticompetitive effects'.[70] The crux of the FTC Complaint was that the acquisition, if consummated, might have the effect of lessening competition in the RTE

[68] The facts of this matter are described in the FTC's Complaint and Agreement Containing Consent order. *Re General Mills Corp* 123 FTC 1380 (1997) (Complaint available at <http://www.ftc.gov/os/1997/05/c3742cmp.pdf> accessed 8 March 2008; Agreement Containing Consent Order available at <http://www.ftc.gov/os/1996/12/genermil.htm> accessed 8 March 2008).

[69] Ibid.

[70] Ibid.

cereal market 'by increasing the likelihood of the unilateral exercise of market power and simultaneously restricting the entry of new private label cereal products into competition with General Mills'.[71] The consent order with the parties allowed the transaction to go forward but required General Mills to forego the restrictions on New Ralcorp on the basis that the possible production of a new private label brand might discipline the market and defeat General Mills' ability to raise price.

Potential impact of private label brands in the relevant market

Once the antitrust analysis concludes that private label products should be included within the relevant market, the analysis must assess the impact of their presence. For example, if a retailer's private label brand is produced by the retailer itself or 'tolled' to an independent firm separate from any manufacturer of branded products,[72] the antitrust agencies will typically treat the private label seller like any other market participant. The private label seller's market share, for instance, would be included in assessing pre- and post-merger concentration.

If the private label product is manufactured by a firm that also produces its own competing branded product, the merger analysis may be more complicated. It may be necessary, for example, to account for the fact that the manufacturer will price its own brand in the context of its pricing for manufacturing the private label. This factor can be important if the manufacturer possesses some degree of market power in the pricing of the latter activity. In this case, the branded manufacturer will have some influence on the downstream pricing of the private label product and potentially can engage in strategic behaviour respecting its rivals' costs that is anti-competitive.[73] There is no clear cut answer as to how this possibility affects the relevant competitive environment in any given merger situation. Each matter must be examined on its specific facts.

Repositioning

Finally, in conducting the antitrust analysis of a merger involving differentiated consumer products, one must consider whether there are profit incentives for private label and other non-party brands to reposition themselves in a way that

---

71 Ibid.

72 In some cases, such private label brands may enjoy a competitive advantage over a manufacturer's brand, particularly if it is the property of an established retailer that possesses a large customer base over a large number of store locations. A large grocery chain that offers private label vegetables, for example, does not need to find independent retailers willing to carry those products, while a branded vegetable cannery must establish relationships with retailers and may need to spend significant sums on advertising and other support of its brand.

73 See: T G Krattenmaker and S Salop, 'Anticompetitive Exclusion: Raising Rivals' Costs to Achieve Power Over Prices' [1986] 96 *Yale Law Journal* 209.

would defeat post-merger attempts to raise prices.[74] Repositioning refers to changing the qualitative attributes of a product such that it competes more closely with the merged firm's products. A successfully repositioned product offers consumers an additional choice to which to turn in response to a change in relative prices after the merger. Thus, repositioning a product entails obtaining consumer acceptance in addition to altering any physical properties.

In merger analysis, consideration of whether repositioning would be likely to prevent durable anti-competitive effects from the merger closely parallels the consideration of new entry.[75] The agencies focus on timeliness, likelihood, and sufficiency.[76] To be an effective constraint, profit incentives must be sufficiently strong such that repositioning can be expected to take place quickly and that expected sales of the repositioned products would be sufficient to defeat an otherwise anti-competitive price increase. As the Commentary on the Merger Guidelines explains, the agencies rarely find evidence that repositioning would be sufficient to prevent or reverse what otherwise would be significant anti-competitive unilateral effects from a differentiated products merger.[77] Altering consumers' perceptions of a product can be difficult, and expensive efforts to do so typically pose a significant risk of failure and thus may not be undertaken.

C. Private Label Issues under the Robinson-Patman Act

The history and organization of the Robinson-Patman Act

Genesis of the legislation[78]

Unlike US competition law generally, which seeks to promote competition, the Robinson-Patman Act was crafted and enacted to protect a specific set of firms from competition. Prior to World War I, a multi-tiered channel of distribution characterized the sale of consumer goods in the US. It was common for a manufacturer to sell to wholesalers, which in turn sold to jobbers, which in turn sold to retailers, which then sold to consumers. After the War, this process was altered by the advent of the 'chain store' which often bought directly from manufacturers and sold directly to consumers. Between 1926 and 1933 this new class of vendors

[74] HMG s 2.212; Commentary 31.
[75] HMG s 2.212 fn 23.
[76] HMG s 3.0. Repositioning is analysed the same as uncommitted or committed entry, depending on the significance of the sunk costs necessary for the repositioning. HMG s 2.212 fn 23.
[77] Commentary 31.
[78] See generally: T Calvani and G Briedenbach, 'An Introduction to the Robinson-Patman Act and Its Enforcement by Government' [1991] 59 *Antitrust Law Journal* 765.

saw its market share in total retail sales increase from 9 per cent to 25 per cent. In grocery sales, 25 per cent of the market had been captured by chain stores by 1929. This development posed a threat to the small independent retailer and to the wholesalers and jobbers that had supplied it.

Those whose interests were injured by this development sought to counter the threat on several fronts. Retailers, with the assistance of their suppliers, sought to organize boycotts of manufacturers that sold directly to chain stores. When this failed to show meaningful results, some independent retailers formed cooperatives in an effort to achieve the scale and perceived 'buyer power' of their chain store rivals. Others sought legislation that might penalize chain stores. Laws that imposed higher taxes on chain stores had been enacted in 27 states by 1939. When these various efforts failed to stem the tide of the chain stores, the independents and their suppliers turned to Congress for a national legislative solution.

In 1933 Congress enacted the National Industrial Recovery Act[79] as part of President Roosevelt's 'New Deal' legislation. Codes of Fair Competition promulgated pursuant to that law sought to preserve traditional methods of distribution by mandating that manufacturers abide by a minimum wholesale discount in some industries and by proscribing discriminatory sales in others. This victory was short-lived when the Supreme Court held the statute unconstitutional as an impermissible delegation of legislative power in *Schecter Poultry Corp v United States*.[80] The independents and their suppliers went in search of another solution.

One of the groups most threatened by the advent of the chain store were the wholesale grocers. The United States Wholesale Grocers' Association drafted new legislation entitled 'The Wholesale Grocers' Protection Act'. It was promptly introduced in Congress. The rationale for the bill was captured by its supporters. Congressman Moritz, for example, stated, 'the chain store should not only be curbed, but . . . should be eliminated'.[81] With the support of the independent grocers and druggists, the bill was enacted and signed into law by President Roosevelt on 19 June 1936. In the interlude between drafting and enactment, it acquired a name change: the Wholesale Grocers' Preservation Act became the Robinson-Patman Act.

Provisions of the Act

The Act prohibits certain forms of price discrimination. It also prohibits certain brokerage payments, certain forms of commercial bribery, discriminatory

79 48 Stat 195 (1933).
80 295 US 495 (1935).
81 80 Cong Rec 8136 (1936).

provision of allowances, discriminatory provision of services, receipt of prohibited discriminatory prices by buyers, and certain predatory pricing. Private label issues generally arise under the price discrimination provisions (and under the prohibition of receiving discriminatory prices). Accordingly, we limit our discussion to the prohibition of the grant and receipt of discriminatory prices.

Section 2(a) of the Act sets forth the price discrimination cause of action.[82]

- Parties subject to the Act must be engaged in interstate commerce. This is true of the US antitrust laws generally. However, the Robinson-Patman Act also requires that the discriminatory sales themselves must be made in the course of such commerce. Thus transactions between a seller and buyers within the same state where the goods themselves do not cross a state line in the course of the sale would not be subject to the Act.
- There must be a discriminatory price, which the courts have interpreted to mean only that there must be a price difference.
- There must be a sale by the same seller to two or more purchasers. Thus leases, licences, and other non-sale transactions are not covered by the Act. Similarly a discriminatory price quotation is insufficient.
- Only sales of 'commodities' are covered. Courts have interpreted this to mean that there must be a sale of a tangible product. Thus services and intangibles are not subject to the Act.
- The goods must be of 'like grade and quality'. We return to this requirement in greater detail, as it is central to the treatment of private label goods.
- Lastly, the Act sets forth a competitive injury requirement. This is complicated by the fact that competitive injury is treated differently depending on whether there is an allegation of primary-line (seller-level) discrimination or secondary-line (buyer-level) discrimination. Primary-line cases are treated like predatory pricing cases under the Sherman Act, and require a conventional demonstration of competitive injury. In secondary-line cases, however, most courts find that persistent price discrimination over time between two competing buyers gives rise to a presumption of injury. Since most private label issues arise in the context of secondary-line cases, a simple difference in price over time is generally sufficient to establish competitive injury.[83]

---

82 The Robinson-Patman Act is codified for the most part as s 2 of the Clayton Act. Therefore most of its provisions are set forth as subsections of that section.

83 In *FTC v Morton Salt Co* 334 US 37 (1948), the Supreme Court held that the existence of substantial price discrimination over time gives rise to an inference of competitive injury. Indeed, some courts have explicitly recognized that the competitive injury requirement may, in secondary-line cases, be satisfied by an injury to a competitor. See e.g.: *JF Feeser, Inc v*

There are three defences to the Act.

- Section 2(b) sets forth a meeting competition defence. To qualify, a seller must show the existence of facts that would lead a reasonable and prudent person to believe that the grant of the lower price would meet the equally low price of a competitor.
- A cost justification defence is contained in Section 2(a) of the Act, and provides that a qualifying defendant must demonstrate that the discriminatory price represents only the savings associated with the cost of manufacture, sale, or delivery resulting from the differing methods or quantities by which the goods are sold or delivered. Note that this does not justify volume discounts unless they are cost justified. Judicial construction of this provision has severely limited the availability of this defence.
- Although not contained in the statute, courts have held that no action lies where the challenged lower price was made available to the allegedly disfavoured buyers. However, the disfavoured buyer must know of this availability, and most buyers must be able realistically to avail themselves of the lower price. Thus, a volume discount that required large purchases that could not be made by most buyers would not qualify.

Buyers too are subject to the Act, which proscribes the knowing receipt of illegal price discrimination. Generally there can be no buyer violation unless there is seller violation. Thus buyer liability is completely derivative.[84] There is no buyer liability unless there is a prima facie case against the seller and the seller has no affirmative defence. Moreover, the plaintiff must also establish that the buyer knew or should have known that the favoured pricing was illegal.

With this background, we turn to issues posed by private labels.

Serv-A-Portion, Inc 909 F 2d 1524, 1534 (3rd Cir 1990); *Alan's of Atlanta, Inc v Minolta Corp* 903 F 2d 1414, 1427 (11th Cir 1990). Under the weight of the case law, injury to a single competitor may be sufficient. ABA Section of Antitrust Law, *Antitrust Law Developments* (6th edn, 2007) 505. Some courts have also held that the presumption is irrebutable. See e.g.: *Chroma Lighting v GTE Prods* 111 F 3d 653 (9th Cir 1997).

84 There is conflict as to whether a buyer's misrepresentation that it had received a competitor's lower offer is an exception to the derivative nature of the cause of action. Compare *Kroger Co v FTC* 438 F 2d 1372 (6th Cir 1971) (finding an exception), with *Orcon Corp v Special's Trading, Inc* No. C-94-0359-DLJ, 1994 US Dist LEXIS 6676 (ND Cal May 13, 1994) (finding none). Moreover, the FTC has held that the inducement and receipt of an illegal favoured discount itself is an unfair method of competition under s 5 of the FTC Act. See: *Re Grand Union Co* 57 FTC 382 (1960), modified, 300 F 2d 92 (2nd Cir 1962).

Private labels under the Robinson-Patman Act

The 'like grade and quality' requirement

Although the case law is not uniform,[85] generally courts in secondary-line cases[86] have taken a physical approach to the determination of whether goods are of like grade and quality. Thus, goods that were physically distinguishable, even with slight differences, have been found not to be of like grade and quality. On the other hand, goods that were physically identical have been treated as being of like grade and quality without regard to differences in branding, marketing, and consumer acceptance.

The decision of the Court of Appeals in *Perma Life Mufflers v International Parts Corp*[87] is instructive. The defendant sold mufflers using two different brands: 'International' and 'Midas'. The trial court found that there was no physical difference between the mufflers,[88] but concluded that they were not of like grade and quality because 'the Midas muffler carried a guarantee good at any Midas muffler dealer wherever located, while the International muffler carried a guarantee good only where purchased'.[89] Notwithstanding obvious differences from a consumer's perspective, since Midas dealers could be found nationwide, the Court of Appeals concluded that the products were of like grade and quality because of their physical makeup.[90]

On the other hand, the case law suggests that even minor differences between products may negate a price discrimination claim. In *Re Champion Spark Plug Co*,[91] the Commission affirmed the dismissal of an aspect of the case finding that 'minute physical distinctions between differently branded' spark plugs negated the required finding of like grade and quality. Similarly, in *Re Universal Rundle Corp*,[92] the manufacturer sold bathtubs to both the plumbing trade and to Sears. Affirming the initial decision of its hearing examiner, the FTC found that the tubs were not of like grade and quality because the Sears tubs were one inch lower in height and had other minor features that distinguished the tubs sold at higher

85 See generally: E W Kintner, *A Robinson-Patman Primer* (1970) 56.

86 Since private label issues principally arise in secondary-line cases, we limit the discussion to such sales. Courts have used a more permissive 'functional equivalence' test in primary-line cases.

87 376 F 2d 692 (7th Cir 1967), *rev'd on other grounds* 392 US 134 (1968).

88 Ibid, 703.

89 Ibid.

90 Ibid.

91 50 FTC 30, 47 (1953). See also the hearing examiner's discussion of this case in *Re Universal Rundle Corp* 65 FTC 924, 942 (1964), which draws on materials not contained in the reported decision.

92 65 FTC 924 (1964), *vacated on other grounds* 352 F 2d 831 (7th Cir 1965) (en banc), *rev'd* 387 US 244 (1967).

prices to the trade. Finding that the differences were not 'merely artificial or fanciful', the hearing examiner concluded that complaint counsel had failed to establish that the differences did not affect the grade and quality of the products.[93] The Commission agreed.[94]

Despite cases to the contrary[95] the test of whether goods are of like grade and quality appears to focus on the physical characteristics of the product.[96] Factors like warranty differences appear irrelevant, notwithstanding the fact that consumers would doubtless value a muffler with a nationwide warranty over one without.

Application of 'like grade and quality' to private label

Notwithstanding the general trend of the case law that physical characteristics of the product alone determined whether the goods were of like grade and quality, there continued to be debate over whether branded goods that enjoyed a customer premium might be separate from private label goods for which there was less customer demand in the marketplace. This debate is reflected in the 1955 Report of the Attorney General's National Committee to Study the Antitrust Laws. Although a majority of the Committee was of the view that economic factors such as a premium associated with a branded product was irrelevant in determining like grade and quality, a vigorous minority disagreed urging that 'business actualities may often contradict the policy . . . of ignoring brands and trade names in determining what goods are "goods of like grade and quality" under the Act'.[97]

---

93 Ibid, 954.

94 Ibid, 955.

95 See: *Re General Foods Corp* 52 FTC 798 (1956), where the Commission found the presence of 'an additional kind of bean' for longer freshness and a distinct coloration and aroma in Maxwell House brand coffee for institutional sales did not negate a finding of like grade and quality with its grocery store product, and *Bruce's Juices v American Can Co* 87 F Supp 985 (SD Fla 1949), *aff'd* 187 F 2d 919 (5th Cir), *modified on rehearing* 190 F 2d 73 (5th Cir 1951), where the court in a suit by a canner against its can supplier found that the size of the products were of like grade and quality notwithstanding that the can size was slightly different. See also: *Re Atalanta Trading Corp* 53 FTC 565 (1956), *rev'd sub nom. Atalanta Trading Corp v FTC*, 258 F 2d 365 (2nd Cir 1958).

96 Differences in packaging are not sufficient to render the products not of like grade and quality. See e.g.: *Re Hansen Inoculator*, 26 FTC 303 (1938), where differences in labelling were found insufficient to negate a finding of like grade and quality where the products were otherwise identical.

97 Report of the Attorney General's National Committee to Study the Antitrust Laws 156–59. Essentially the minority's view was that consumers often valued advertised brands and private label products quite differently. To treat them as being of like grade and quality ignored the reality. The Committee, however, thought that a change to account for consumer preference might 'enmesh the administrators of the statute in complex economic investigations', 'encourage easy evasion of the statute', and be inconsistent with the purposes of the Act (pp 158–159). Nevertheless, the Committee stated that to the extent such differences in price represented only consumer preference, no injury to

This debate was resolved in the Supreme Court's 1966 opinion in *FTC v Borden*,[98] which became the leading case on the issue. The Borden Company processed and marketed evaporated milk under its own nationally advertised brand and various private label brands. It sold the branded milk at a premium price over the private label milk. The milk for all of its brands was identical, and the FTC commenced proceedings alleging that Borden had engaged in impermissible price discrimination. The Commission concluded that Borden had violated the Robinson-Patman Act.

On appeal to the Court of Appeals, Borden argued that the branded milk enjoyed greater consumer appeal and sold at retail for a premium price. The Court of Appeals noted that '[u]nder the construction of the Act adopted here by the Commission the "like grade and quality" determination was based solely on the physical properties of the products without regard to the brand names they bear or the relative public acceptance enjoyed by each'.[99] The court further noted that the branded product commanded a higher price at market.[100] Observing, 'we do not believe that it was the intention of Congress that such clearly demonstrable consumer preferences should simply be ignored',[101] the court agreed finding the branded and private label products not to be of like grade and quality, and reversed the FTC decision.

The Supreme Court granted a writ of certiorari. The court first noted that the statutory language failed to support the view that consumer preference is relevant. Of course, one might also note that the statutory language does not suggest the contrary view either.

Turning to the legislative history, the court concludes that what history exists supports the Commission's interpretation of the statute. Justice White, writing for the court, observed that an effort was made in Congress, by interests concerned that the proposed legislation would eliminate private labelling, to limit actionable price discrimination to cases where the goods were of 'like grade, quality *and brand*'.[102] Justice White noted that Congress rejected the proposed language change. As one commentator has noted: 'Addition of the word "brand" . . . was fruitlessly urged to protect the distribution of privately branded products.'[103]

competition should be found. It did not explain why this solution would not pose the same issues as brand consideration in the context of 'like grade and quality'.

98 383 US 637 (1966).

99 *Borden Co v FTC* 339 F 2d 133, 135 (5th Cir 1964).

100 Ibid.

101 Ibid, 137.

102 *FTC v Borden* (n 98) 641.

103 F M Rowe, 'Price Differentials & Product Differentiation: The Issues Under the Robinson-Patman Act' [1956] 66 *Yale Law Journal* 1. Not surprisingly the Wholesale Grocers' Association

Statements in Congress by Representative Wright Patman, one of the bill's sponsors and namesake, seemed to support this interpretation.

> Mr. TAYLOR of South Carolina. There has grown up a practice on the part of manufacturers of making certain brands of goods for particular chain stores. Is there anything in this bill calculated to remedy that situation?
>
> Mr. PATMAN. . . . I have not time to discuss that feature, but the bill will protect the independents in that way, because they will have to sell to the independents at the same price for the same product where they put the same quality of merchandise in a package, and this will remedy the situation to which the gentleman refers.
>
> Mr. TAYLOR of South Carolina. Irrespective of the brand.
>
> Mr. PATMAN. Yes; so long as it is the same quality . . .[104]

Justice White seemed sympathetic to the view that private label might present an opportunity for sales to large retail vendors to escape the Act's scrutiny if price premium and customer acceptance could be used as an escape hatch:

> We doubt that Congress intended to foreclose these inquiries in situations where a single seller markets the identical product under several different brands, whether his own, his customers' or both. Such transactions are too laden with potential discrimination and adverse competitive effect to be excluded from the reach of § 2 (a) by permitting a difference in grade to be established by the label alone or by the label and its consumer appeal.[105]

Lastly, the court deferred to the Commission in interpreting the Act, and noted that the Commission had taken this view since 1932.[106]

> The Commission's view is that labels do not differentiate products for the purpose of determining grade or quality, even though the one label may have more customer appeal and command a higher price in the marketplace from a substantial segment of the public. That this has been the Commission's long-standing interpretation of the present Act . . . may be gathered from the Commission's decisions dating back to 1936. These views of the agency are entitled to respect . . .[107]

---

opposed the inclusion of 'brand' within the qualifying language of the proposed legislation. Their counsel condemned the idea as 'a specious suggestion that would destroy entirely the efficacy of the bill against large buyers' (p 8).

104 *FTC v Borden* (n 98) 643, quoting 80 Cong Rec 8115.

105 *FTC v Borden* (n 98) 643–644.

106 The court noted that the views of the Commission as expressed in its opinions were entitled to respect, and that the Commission's view on this issue had been 'long standing'. *FTC v Borden* (n 98) 640. See e.g.: *Re United States Rubber Co* 28 FTC 1489 (1939), where the Commission found that nationally advertised and private label, but otherwise identical, tyres were of like grade and quality, and *Re United States Rubber Co* 46 FTC 998 (1950), where the Commission found that nationally advertised and private label, but otherwise identical, shoes were of like grade and quality.

107 *FTC v Borden* (n 98) 640 (citations omitted).

In summary, the test stated by the court is determined by the 'characteristics of the product itself'.[108] Focus on factors other than the product itself is impermissible. Thus, consumer preference, advertising and the like cannot be considered in determining whether goods are of like grade and quality. The determining factor, in the court's view, was that the branded and private label products were 'physically and chemically identical'.[109] Accordingly, they were of like grade and quality.

The opinion provoked a strong dissent by Justice Stewart who was joined by Justice Harlan.

> It is undisputed that the physical attributes and chemical constituents of Borden's premium and private label brands of evaporated milk are identical. It is also undisputed that the premium and private label brands are not competitive at the same price, and that if the private label milk is to be sold at all, it must be sold at prices substantially below the price commanded by Borden's premium brand. This simple market fact no more than reflects the obvious economic reality that consumer preferences can and do create significant commercial distinctions between otherwise similar products. By pursuing product comparison only so far as the result of laboratory analysis, the Court ignores a most relevant aspect of the inquiry into the question of 'like grade and quality' under 2 (a): Whether the products are different in the eyes of the consumer.[110]

Justice Stewart continued, noting that Borden provided a good many services incident to the sale of its branded product that were not provided for private label. In addition to advertising its branded products, Borden personnel inspected the dates and rotated branded product to insure freshness. Borden provided no such service to private label product. Furthermore, for the branded product, the milk was 'tempered' to prevent condensation and resulting rust on the cans.[111]

The dissent's focus on issues such as product rotation and tempering preview the treatment of the case on remand, where the Court of Appeals found the price discrimination between the branded and private label product did not result in competitive injury. Interestingly, however, the Fifth Circuit seemingly interpreted the Act's competitive injury requirement to suggest that there cannot be competitive injury under such facts.[112] This interpretation of secondary-line

---

108 *FTC v Borden* (n 98) 641.

109 *FTC v Borden* (n 98) 638.

110 *FTC v Borden* (n 98) 648.

111 *FTC v Borden* (n 98) 651 fn 6.

112 'We are of the firm view that where a price differential between a premium and nonpremium brand reflects no more than a consumer preference for the premium brand, the price difference creates no competitive advantage to the recipient of the cheaper private brand product on which injury could be predicated. . . The record discloses no evidence tending to show that Borden's price differential exceeds the recognized consumer appeal of the Borden label.' *Borden Co v FTC* 381 F 2d 175, 181

competitive injury seems at worst to be at odds with the case law, which has emasculated the competitive injury requirement in the context of secondary-line price discrimination.[113] At best, the decision is a special exception in premium/private label cases. In the latter case, it is simply a way to ignore the instruction of a superior court. In either event, the decision on remand seems unimportant to the case law development.[114] Although the issue presented to the Supreme Court in *Borden* has not been the subject of much recent litigation,[115] the court did cite *Borden* in its 1990 decision in *Texaco Inc v Hasbrouck* for the proposition that economic factors such as brand should not be considered in determining 'like grade and quality' under the Robinson-Patman Act.[116]

Despite the paucity of cases, a few lower court decisions suggest possible movement. *AA Poultry Farms Inc v Rose Acre Farms Inc*,[117] an important and often cited decision for reasons unrelated to this subject, is one.[118] In this case, Judge Frank Easterbrook considered whether two categories of eggs were of like grade and quality. In *AA Poultry* some suppliers sold off-size eggs as 'breakers' to be used by food processors. Rather than doing so, the defendant sold mixed-size eggs as 'specials' to supermarkets at discount prices. Finding that the eggs were not of like grade and quality, Judge Easterbrook stated:

> Although 'special' eggs as delivered may be physically indistinguishable to the buyer, they are not fundamentally the same good, for the same reason a seat on the

(5th Cir 1967). Frederick Rowe, one of the leading commentators on the Robinson-Patman Act and a critic of the Commission's treatment of this subject, recommended using the competitive injury requirement as a way to avoid liability. Rowe (n 103) 41–45. The 1955 Report of the Attorney General's National Committee to Study the Antitrust Laws took the same position on this issue. See (n 97).

113 See (n 83) and accompanying text.

114 For a discussion of this case and the literature spawned by the series of decisions in *Borden*, see: Note 'Private Label Distribution: Lessening Competition Under the Robinson Patman Act' [1968] 35 *University of Chicago Law Review* 529. There the notewriter argues that private label sales are generally efficient and ought not to be condemned as they increase, rather than decrease, output. Confronted with the Supreme Court's treatment of the discrimination requirement and its embrace of the 'physical identity' approach to 'like grade and quality', the notewriter applauds the treatment of the case on remand by the Fifth Circuit.

115 For similar decisions in several circuits, see *Morning Pioneer, Inc v Bismark Tribune Co* 493 F 2d 383 (8th Cir 1974) (rejecting in dictum the trial court's finding that identical newspapers were not of like grade in quality when sold at a lower price out-of-town than in-town), and *Continental Baking Co v Old Homestead Bread Co* 476 F 2d 97 (10th Cir 1973) (finding private label and branded bread to be of like grade and quality).

116 496 US 543, 556 fn 14 (1990). It should be noted that Texaco did not contest that issue.

117 881 F 2d 1396 (7th Cir 1989).

118 The case is important for two reasons. First, Judge Easterbrook found recoupment to be an important element in a predatory pricing case—foreshadowing the Supreme Court's later decision in *Brooke Group Ltd v Brown & Williamson Tobacco Corp* 509 US 209 (1993). Second, the decision recognized that evidence of 'predatory intent', e.g., 'we'll kill them' type language, is a poor indicator of whether conduct is anti-competitive.

6:00 a.m. flight from Chicago to New York is not the same as a seat on the 5:00 p.m. flight, and a seat on the 5:00 p.m. flight reserved two weeks in advance is not the same as a seat on that flight for which the passenger had to stand by.[119]

Although a primary-line case and although the court could have found the eggs not to be of like grade and quality because of the mixed size of the eggs in the cartons, Judge Easterbrook used a consumer preference, rather than a physical identity, standard for evaluating whether the goods were of like grade and quality.[120] Whether the approach of *AA Poultry* will attract any following remains to be seen.

Pricing of private label products

The judicial construction of the 'like grade and quality' language of the Act effectively makes the sale of private label products more difficult where the manufacturer also sells branded products to competing buyers. While this may seem to ignore the commercial realities of the market place, such observations are irrelevant when considered in light of the statute's underlying purpose.

The avowed purpose of the Act was to handicap the efficiencies garnered by large chain stores, or, as put more poignantly by former Assistant Attorney General Professor William Baxter, 'to put lead in the saddlebags of the fastest riders'.[121] Private label grocery sales were almost exclusively the province of the chain store, and were a potent weapon used against the independents. Accordingly, the court's decision in *Borden* is not an anomaly, but rather a decision that is consistent with the purpose of the statute.

D. Conclusion

Private label products have received quite disparate treatment under US competition laws. Focusing on the merger provisions of the Clayton Act[122] and the price discrimination provisions of the Robinson-Patman Act,[123] the case law seems to

[119] *AA Poultry* (n 117) 1408.

[120] Cf *Flair Zipper Corp v Textron, Inc* 1980-2 Trade Cases (CCH) para 63,555 (SDNY 1980), where the court found that identical branded and non-branded zips were not of like grade and quality because one was guaranteed and the other was not. But see *DeLong Equipment Co v Washington Mills Abrasive Co* 887 F 2d 1499 (11th Cir 1989), where the court found that stock and special media (for metal finishing) were of like grade and quality notwithstanding that the 'special' product was manufactured specially for customers requiring small volumes that might necessitate special dies.

[121] C K Robinson, 'Fitting a Square Peg Into a Round Hole? Competitive Bidding and Price Discrimination' [2006] 7 *Sedona Conference Journal* 57, 61.

[122] 15 USC s 18.

[123] 15 USC s 13(a).

be quite at odds. The current merger case law and enforcement agency practice appears to define the product market in an economically sophisticated way designed to determine whether the transaction under review is anti-competitive. The treatment of the like grade and quality requirement under the Robinson-Patman Act, on the other hand, seems economically primitive with the cases focusing on whether there has been injury to a competitor.

This apparent contradiction, however, is unimportant when one considers the rationale for current merger practice under the Clayton Act and the legislative purpose underlying the Robinson-Patman Act. One protects competition; the other competitors.

Part VII

CONSUMER WELFARE AND ENFORCEMENT STANDARD

16

THE 'CONSUMER WELFARE' STANDARD AS A FORM OF SUBSTANTIVE PROTECTION FOR CONSUMERS UNDER EUROPEAN COMPETITION LAW

*Philip Marsden and Peter Whelan**

* Dr Philip Marsden is the Director and the Senior Research Fellow at the Competition Law Forum (CLF) of the British Institute of International and Comparative Law (BIICL). Peter Whelan is the Research Fellow at the CLF and is a PhD candidate at St John's College, Cambridge. The authors would like to thank Mairead Moore, PhD candidate at Swansea University, for her research assistance. Comments can be sent to the following e-mail addresses: p.marsden@biicl.org; and p.whelan@biicl.org.

A. Introduction

Background

The introduction of the euro and the steady development of the internal market have both led to a growing number of retail sectors operating on a pan-European basis.[1] As retailer consolidation occurs throughout Europe, and as supermarkets and shopping centres continue to replace traditional corner shops and smaller outlets, competition problems may begin to be perceived in these sectors. Consequently, now more than ever, the proper role of competition law in regulating conduct in the retail sector—including the use of private labels by retailers—deserves detailed consideration by legal scholars. Of particular concern is the place of consumers in a given competition law assessment of a retail market. More specifically, the status of a consumer welfare standard under EC competition law needs to be examined. According to the current Director General (DG) for Competition, the primary aim of modern European competition law and policy is to protect the functioning of competition on markets in order to enhance 'consumer welfare'.[2] Consumer welfare, then, apparently represents the standard according to which enforcement of EC competition law should be determined. Given the abundance of official statements to similar effect, it would not be an exaggeration to state that the position of the consumer in European competition law has never been stronger. Some commentators, however, have questioned the accuracy of these claims.[3] One often criticizes the European Commission (the Commission) in this regard for paying insufficient attention to the interests of consumers in its investigations and for producing in its decisions only a cursory note on any potential consumer benefits.[4] The courts too can arguably be criticized on a similar basis. Furthermore, it has also been argued that in any case the decisional practice of the Commission cannot be easily changed to encompass a consumer welfare standard as this would involve either ignoring or contradicting precedents set by the European courts.

[1] A Murray and J Johnstone, 'Consumers and EU Competition Policy' (published by the National Consumer Council, 2005) at 2 <http://www.ncc.org.uk/nccpdf/poldocs/NCC095ft_EU_competition.pdf> accessed 31 May 2008.

[2] P Lowe, 'Consumer Welfare and Efficiency—New Guiding Principles of Competition Policy?' (Speech given at the 13th International Conference on Competition and 14th European Competition Day, Munich, 27 March 2007) <http://ec.europa.eu/comm/competition/speeches/text/sp2007_02_en.pdf> accessed 11 April 2008.

[3] See e.g.: P Marsden and P Whelan, '"Consumer Detriment" and its Application in EC and UK Competition Law' [2006] 27 *European Competition Law Review* 569; and M Hutchings and P Whelan, 'Consumer Interest in Competition Law Cases' [2006] 16 *Consumer Policy Review* 182.

[4] See: Murray and Johnstone (n 1).

Aim and layout

This chapter engages with this on-going debate and in the process offers some observations concerning the current position of the consumer in substantive European competition law. In this regard, it considers the objective of consumer welfare in the context of EC competition law enforcement, and examines to what extent a consumer welfare standard has been followed through in concrete cases.

This chapter is divided into three substantive parts. Section B explains briefly how the maintenance of a competitive market through a consumer welfare standard can bring benefits for consumers. It also details how private labels can affect consumer welfare in a given retail market. Section C considers the objective of maximizing consumer welfare in the context of EC competition law, explaining the 'traditional' objectives of this competition law as well as the recent popularity of consumer-related objectives. Finally, Section D considers the current operation of the consumer welfare standard in practice at EC level.

B. Competition, Private Labels, and the Welfare of Consumers

This part of the chapter explains briefly how maintaining a competitive market through a consumer welfare standard can bring benefits for consumers, as well as what form those benefits can take. It also details how private labels can have negative and positive effects on consumer welfare in a given retail market.

Competition and the welfare of consumers

Modern competition law usually seeks to protect the process of free market competition in order to ensure efficient use of scarce economic resources. It seeks, in other words, to maximize welfare. It is commonly believed that the pursuit of this objective helps to ensure that both allocative and productive efficiency are maximized, and that these efficiencies may ultimately create tangible benefits for consumers, including, *inter alia*: lower costs and prices; improvements in quality, choice, and services; and the introduction of new and innovative products.[5] Indeed, competition between undertakings that vie for the custom of consumers

[5] Whether these benefits accrue to consumers ultimately depends on whether a consumer or total welfare standard is adopted by the authorities. On the difference between these standards, see generally: M Motta, *Competition Policy: Theory and Practice* (2004).

is widely perceived as a good thing in terms of 'consumer welfare'.[6] When rational consumers with limited resources at their disposal are presented with choices in the market they will, by their very nature, attempt to consume those products from which they can derive maximum satisfaction or utility. If this desire to choose wisely is coupled with an ability to switch between competing products (or, if need be, competing retailers), consumers can, by the power of their feet so-to-speak, force competitors to compete vigorously in the market and thus compel them to deliver products which are the most attractive to them in terms of price, quality, range etc. They can exercise, in other words, their right of economic self-determination.[7] Competition, and its protection through anti-trust and merger legislation, can therefore ensure that the economy responds to the demands of consumers rather than to those of individual businesses or indeed of the Government.[8] In short, then, undistorted competition on a given market helps to deliver better results to consumers in that market.[9] This is particularly the case when a consumer—as opposed to a total—welfare standard is adopted by the competition authorities.[10]

These days, it is increasingly difficult to find a recent speech or policy statement that emanates from the DG for Competition that does not mention the important role that competition law can play for the maximization of consumer welfare or that does not highlight the need for a pro-consumer competition policy;[11] in fact, an efficient competition law regime is generally considered to be a necessity if one wishes to maximize consumer welfare: without it a healthy,

[6] See: J Vickers, 'Healthy Competition and its Consumer Wins' [2002] 12 *Consumer Policy Review* 142. By 'consumer welfare', we mean the difference between what a consumer is willing to pay for a good or service and what he or she actually pays for that good or service; see: J Farrell and M L Katz, 'The Economics of Welfare Standards in Antitrust' [2006] 2 *Competition Policy International* 3, 4.

[7] See: J Stuyck, 'European Consumer Law After the Treaty of Amsterdam: Consumer Policy In and Beyond the Internal Market?' [2000] 37 *Common Market Law Review* 367.

[8] See: R H Lande, 'Consumer Choice as the Ultimate Goal of Antitrust' [2001] 62 *University of Pittsburgh Law Review* 503.

[9] E Buttigieg, 'Synergy Between Consumer Policy and Competition Policy' [2006] 33 *Bank of Valletta Review* 1. Cf R W Crandall and C Winston, 'Does Antitrust Policy Improve Consumer Welfare? Assessing the Evidence' [2003] 17 *Journal of Economic Perspectives* 3; and I Haracoglou, 'Competition Law, Consumer Policy and the Retail Sector: The Systems' Relation and the Effects of a Strengthened Consumer Protection Policy on Competition Law' [2007] 3 *Competition Law Review* 175, 180–181.

[10] In fact, pursuing a total welfare standard may sometimes be to the disadvantage of consumers; see e.g.: E Kerber, 'Should Competition Law Promote Efficiency?' in J Drexl, L Idot, and J Moneger (eds), *Economic Theory and Competition Law* (2008).

[11] See e.g.: N Kroes, 'European Competition Policy: Delivering Better Markets and Better Choices', (SPEECH/05/512 given at the European Consumer and Competition Day, London, 15 September 2005) <http://europa.eu/rapid/pressReleasesAction.do?reference=SPEECH/05/512&format=HTML&aged=1&language=EN&guiLanguage=en> accessed 11 April 2008.

competition-driven economy capable of delivering tangible gains to consumers will almost always be undermined by the activities of cartelists and dominant, abusive companies.[12] While it is axiomatic that undistorted competition may bring benefits to consumers, it does not necessarily follow that the objective of a competition law should be to protect competition in order to maximize consumer welfare, even if an efficiency standard is accepted. Other (political and economic) objectives may be pursued. Indeed other objectives have been pursued at EC level, as detailed in Section C below.

Private labels and consumer welfare

In recent years private labels have become increasingly popular in the retail sector, particularly across Europe.[13] They are present in most retail categories and satisfy consumer choice from value goods to those of the premium variety.[14] Indeed, these days virtually every household within the European Union purchases retail own brands and private label products.[15] One of the questions facing competition authorities—when pursuing a consumer welfare standard in relation to the retail sector—should be whether, in developing these private label goods, retailers help facilitate or prevent a restriction of competition in a given market to the detriment of consumers. While a detailed examination of this issue is outside the scope of this chapter, some brief points should nonetheless be made concerning the link between private labels and the welfare of consumers.

Private labels, as vehicles that help distinguish between the goods of different retailers, foster competition between retailers and build store, as opposed to brand, loyalty. This retailer-based competition in turn can help produce the type of consumer benefits that are identified above, in particular those related to price and quality. Furthermore, while private-label goods often start out as cheap products of low quality, with time and investment they can develop into goods which are on par with those of branded manufacturers, and thus are often capable of competing effectively with branded goods.[16] Private goods in this context may

[12] See: P Collins, 'Opening Keynote Speech to BIICL's Conference on Reform of Article 82' (BIICL, London, 24 February 2006), republished in P Marsden, M Hutchings, and P Whelan (eds), *Current Competition Law V* (2007).

[13] See: Planet Retail, *Private Label Trends Worldwide*, 2006, available at: <www.planetretail.net> accessed 1 February 2008.

[14] P Whelan, *Trends in Retail Competition: Private Labels, Brands and Competition Policy* (Report on the Third Annual Symposium on Retail Competition, BIICL: London, May 2007, 1).

[15] See: M Bokkerink and others, 'The Relentless Advance of Private Label: Strategies to Compete' (The Boston Consulting Group, 16 April 2007) <http://www.bcg.com/publications/files/TheRelentlessAdvanceofPrivateLabelStrategiestoCompeteApr07.pdf> assessed 1 June 2008.

[16] See: M Corstjens, 'Private Label Products and their Implications for Consumers', in Whelan (n 14).

bring visible price-related benefits to consumers in that, while of a similar quality to the branded goods, they may be less expensive as they do not incorporate as much 'brand tax' as a branded good.[17] In any case, they may act as a competitive restraint on the branded goods. Indeed according to Steiner, it is when private labels and national brands compete vigorously rather than when either one is dominant that consumer welfare is maximized.[18]

Competition problems can also be attributed to the development of private label goods, a fact that highlights the potential for such products to reduce consumer welfare. Three problems can be readily identified. First, the presence of the private label provides the retailer with greater leverage over manufacturers. Depending on the circumstances, this increase in buyer power has the potential to (i) erode prices to a level where suppliers will lose the incentive to invest or innovate; (ii) eliminate suppliers, wholesalers, and small retailers; and (iii) reduce choice for consumers.[19] Second, private labels may also reduce innovation if retailers introduce their own version of branded goods too quickly.[20] It must be remembered in this context that, for obvious reasons, retailers will often have access to supplier information (far) in advance of the entry of a new product onto the market. Third, retailers may 'free-ride' on the investment undertaken by manufacturers, something that may also in turn reduce both future investment and innovation efforts to the detriment of consumers.[21] It is clear then that, by virtue of *inter alia* these three scenarios, private labels may effect a reduction in consumer welfare in a given retail market. Whether such a reduction in consumer welfare will unleash the antitrust laws depends of course on whether the standard adopted by the competition authorities is one based on consumer welfare, something that is not always the case at European level.

C. Consumer Welfare as an Objective of European Competition Law

This part of the chapter examines the objective of maximizing consumer welfare in the context of EC competition law. It explains the 'traditional' objectives of

---

17 See: Corstjens (n 16).

18 See: R L Steiner, 'The Nature and Benefits of National Brand/Private Label Competition' [2004] 24 *Review of Industrial Organization* 105.

19 See: A Gorrie, 'Private Labels and Powerful Retailers: The Response from Competition Authorities' (Presentation at the Institute of European and Comparative Law, University of Oxford, 9 June 2005) <http://www.competition-law.ox.ac.uk/lawvle/users/ezrachia/Orrick%20Presentation%20-%20Oxford%202005.PPT> accessed 1 June 2008.

20 See: Corstjens (n 16).

21 See: Gorrie (n 19).

this competition law as well as the recent enthusiasm at Commission level for a consumer-orientated competition policy.

'Traditional' objectives of European competition law

The Treaty of Rome, while providing substantive competition rules in the form of Article 81 (ex Article 85) and Article 82 (ex Article 86), did not contain any explicit reference to, or detailed explanation of, the objectives of European competition law. In the very early days of EC law a link was established between the use of competition law and the protection of the functioning of the common market in Europe. The protection of free market integration was in fact considered to be the 'first principle' of EC competition law[22] and a firm understanding of EC competition law is unachievable without knowledge of this underlying objective.[23] Another important objective—particularly in the earlier years of the EC—concerns the protection of economic freedom.

Protection of free market integration

The European Economic Community, established in the late 1950s, attempted to eliminate (public) trade barriers between its Member States, and to create thereby a common market with the objective of promoting, *inter alia*, economic growth and stability and a high standard of living for Europeans. It was widely felt that competition law would be an essential tool to prevent the creation of retaliatory private trade barriers (through restrictive practices) that would undermine these desirable objectives: 'the elimination of tariff barriers would not achieve its objectives if private agreements or economically powerful firms were permitted to be used to manipulate the flow of trade'.[24] In other words, economic integration in Europe could only be achieved by both the free movement provisions of the EC Treaty *and* competition law and policy.[25]

In this vein, the European Court of Justice (ECJ) rendered its judgment in *Consten and Grundig*, a competition case that is often used to highlight the traditional, hard-line attitude towards measures that, by prohibiting parallel trade, effectively compartmentalize the common market: such measures have as their 'object' the distortion of competition in the internal market and therefore are *per se* violations of Article 81(1) EC, irrespective of their impact on

---

[22] B E Hawk, 'Antitrust in the EEC—The First Decade' [1972] *Fordham Law Review* 41, 231. See also: European Commission, *XXIXth Annual Report on Competition Policy* (Brussels, 1999) paras 2–3.

[23] A Jones and B Sufrin, *EC Competition Law* (2007) 42.

[24] D J Gerber, *Law and Competition in Twentieth Century Europe: Protecting Prometheus* (1998) 343.

[25] J B Cruz, *Between Competition and Free Movement: The Economic Constitutional Law of the European Community* (2002).

consumer welfare.[26] The case could be criticized on the basis that, among other things, the court did not consider to an adequate degree the longer-term negative implications for competition that the result in this case would engender due to the free-riding concerns of potential investors. Despite this fact, and although the exact precedent value of *Consten and Grundig* in the 21st century can be questioned, particularly now that a more economics-based approach to competition law appears to be in vogue, the ECJ nonetheless continues to stress the importance of the competition law rules for the achievement of the aim of market integration.[27] Indeed, the new European Reform Treaty, in a protocol, expressly (re)establishes the link between competition policy and single market integration and accordingly challenges the US-inspired trend towards detachment of competition policy from market integration and the adoption of a standard based solely on efficiency considerations.[28] It must be appreciated, however, that the Commission now understands competition and single market integration as instruments that serve the same ends, namely consumer welfare maximization and efficient allocation of resources.[29] It is submitted that this conceptualization of the relationship between consumer welfare and market integration, while perhaps a legal fabrication, is nonetheless useful as it has the potential to reduce possible conflicts between free market and efficiency objectives, and ensures a level of apparent consistency with EC jurisprudence. It is of course an interpretation that requires endorsement from the EC courts, without which its legality can be questioned.

Protection of economic freedom

The protection of economic freedom as an objective of competition law and policy finds its roots in the political and economic philosophy developed by the ordoliberals of the Freiberg school of economic thought.[30] In essence, it holds

[26] Cases 56 and 58/64 *Etablissements Consten SA and Grundig-Verkaufs-GmbH v Commission* [1966] ECR 299.

[27] See e.g.: Case C-126/97 *Eco Swiss China Time Ltd v Bennetton International NV* [1999] ECR I-3055, at para 36. Cf European Commission 'Commission White Paper on Modernization of the Rules Implementing Article 81 and 82 of the EC Treaty' [1999] OJ C132/1, Executive Summary, pt 8.

[28] J L Buendia Sierra, 'Competition Policy and Services of a General Economic Interest' (Presentation King's College, London, 8 February 2008).

[29] See: Communication from the Commission—Notice—Guidelines on the Application of Article 81(3) of the Treaty [2004] OJ C101/97, at para 13. See also: C D Ehlermann, 'The Contribution of EC Competition Policy to the Single Market' [1992] 29 *Common Market Law Review* 257; and J Malinauskaite, 'The Development of "Consumer Welfare" and its Application in the Competition Law of the European Community and Lithuania' [2007] 18 *International Company and Commercial Law Review* 354, 357.

[30] On ordoliberalism, see generally: W Möschel, 'The Proper Scope of Government Viewed from an Ordoliberal Perspective: The Example of Competition Policy' [2001] 157 *Journal of Institutional and Theoretical Economics* 3; and D J Gerber, 'Constitutionalizing the Economy: German

that competition is necessary for the economic-wellbeing of a State and that political freedom can only be achieved if economic freedom exists.[31] Consequently, competition law should exist to protect the conditions of competition; and a structuralist approach maintaining a minimum number of competitors in the market should be adopted in order to ensure a certain degree of rivalry between undertakings.[32] In fact, the goal of competition policy according to ordoliberals is to protect individual economic freedom of action as a value in itself, through the moderation of undue economic power.[33] In contrast to the Chicago school of economic thought, ordoliberalism did not subordinate freedom of action on a market to the pursuit of economic efficiency; rather, although efficiency could be an indirect result of economic freedom, this right exists independently of efficiency concerns and ensures that small and medium-sized competitors are protected regardless of whether or not they are efficient. As Sauter states, 'competition constitutes a value in its own right, which goes well beyond efficiency considerations'.[34]

The drafting of Articles 81 and 82 EC was undoubtedly influenced by these ordoliberal ideas: the German delegation ensured the introduction of the competition laws within this treaty that were based considerably on the German (and therefore ordoliberal-inspired) competition provisions.[35] Likewise, there has been a considerable influence of ordoliberal thinking on the development of European competition law; as the only Member State with a competition law similar to the European model, Germany—and therefore German political/economic thinking—was very influential in this regard for many years.[36] This influence has been particularly evident in the decisional practice and jurisprudence of Article 82 where the protection of the competitive process and not the end result (in terms of either total or consumer welfare) was examined, and conduct that affected the competitive process was prohibited irrespective of its efficiency or welfare implications. In other words, competitors were protected, no rigorous theory of (consumer) harm was advanced, and efficiency arguments were either not considered or ignored. It appears then that economic freedom

Neo-Liberalism, Competition Law and the "New Europe"' [1994] 42 *American Journal of Comparative Law* 25; and W Möschel, 'Competition Policy from an Ordo Point of View' in A Peacock and H Willgerodt (eds), *German Neo-Liberals and the Social Market Economics* (1989).

31 Möschel (1989), ibid 142.

32 A Pera and V Auricchio, 'Consumer Welfare, Standard of Proof and the Objectives of Competition Policy' 9 <http://www.gop.it/documentien/EUcomp.pdf> accessed 11 April 2008.

33 Möschel (2001) (n 30) 4.

34 W Sauter, 'The Economic Constitution of the European Union' [1998] 4 *Columbia Journal of European Law* 27, 47.

35 J Faull and A Nikpay (eds), *Faull & Nikpay: The EC Law of Competition* (2007) 218.

36 A Weitbrecht, 'From Freiburg to Chicago and Beyond—The First 50 Years of European Competition Law' [2008] 29 *European Competition Law Review* 81.

was being pursued as an objective in its own right, and not merely as a means of improving consumer welfare.[37] According to Neelie Kroes, these cases highlight that 'the protection of individual economic freedom—as a value in itself—was regarded as the primary objective of competition policy'.[38] Reports from the European Commission in the 1980s further underline the point that the European authorities believed that competition law should be concerned with the protection of individual economic freedom.[39]

These cases are not just the stuff of European legal history: even recent cases refer to the 'institution' of competition, and are only indirectly concerned with the outcomes of this protection in terms of welfare.[40] Clearly, then, the European courts are still considering the economic freedom of individuals when assessing behaviour under the European competition laws, despite the Commission's recent conversion to a consumer welfare standard. Even the European Commission, in its drive to secure consumer welfare maximization as the ultimate objective of EC competition law, has not completely forgotten that competitors may be allowed to compete in the market, even if they are (currently) inefficient: 'it may sometimes be necessary in the consumers' interest to also protect competitors that are not (yet) as efficient as the dominant firm'.[41] Indeed, according to some, and despite the reduced influence of ordoliberalism as regards EC competition policy, many ordoliberal concepts have been 'hardwired' into the system and are difficult to reconcile with a consumer welfare standard.[42] Consequently, it can be argued that a regime that gives primacy to such an (economics-based) standard cannot be constructed at EC level unless the courts are fully in support of such a project.[43]

---

37 L Lovdahl Gormsen, 'The Conflict Between Economic Freedom and Consumer Welfare in the Modernisation of Article 82' [2007] 3 *European Competition Journal* 329.

38 Lowe (n 2).

39 See e.g.: R Van den Bergh and P Camesasca, *European Competition Law and Economics: A Comparative Perspective* (2006) 62.

40 See e.g.: Case C-95/04 P *British Airways v Commission* [2007] ECR I-2331.

41 European Commission DG Competition 'DG Competition Discussion Paper on the Application of Article 82 of the Treaty to Exclusionary Abuses' (Public consultation, December 2005) para 67 <http://ec.europa.eu/comm/competition/antitrust/art82/discpaper2005.pdf> accessed 11 April 2008 (Discussion Paper on Article 82). It is questionable whether these 'not yet efficient competitors' will actually generate any efficiencies to the benefit of consumer welfare: Lovdahl Gormsen (n 37) 338.

42 C Ahlborn and C Grave, 'Walter Eucken and Ordoliberalism: An Introduction from a Consumer Welfare Perspective' [2006] 2 *Competition Policy International* 197, 206 *et seq*. These concepts include: low thresholds for dominance; the special responsibility of dominant firms; formalistic approaches to types of unilateral behaviour; and the prohibition of exploitative abuses.

43 See: Lovdahl Gormsen (n 37). See also: D Evans and C Grave, 'The Changing Role of Economics in Competition Policy Decisions by the European Commission during the Monti Years' [2005] 1 *Competition Policy International* 133, 133.

The ascendancy of consumer-orientated objectives

The Commission's concern for consumers

Although the Commission remained under the influence of ordoliberal thinking for a number of years, following the enactment of the original European Community Merger Regulation in 1989,[44] it gradually began to adopt its own version of the consumer welfare standard advocated by the Chicago school of economic thought.[45] Consequently, the last 15 years or so have seen dramatic changes in European competition policy, including the injection of economics into competition assessments and the targeting of those activities that are perceived as being most detrimental to consumers, such as 'hard-core' cartels.[46] By the beginning of the 21st century the Commission had begun to reject its hitherto form-based approach to the assessment of allegedly anti-competitive behaviour in favour of one that was concerned with the economic effects of market conduct; it had begun, in other words, its process of 'Modernization'. According to Cseres, it was the Commission's desire to modernize competition enforcement and to introduce more economics-based reasoning in its assessments that fuelled the role of the consumer welfare standard in EC competition law.[47] By placing economic theory at the very heart of EC competition law, the Commission fostered discussion as to the exact efficiency standard (total or consumer welfare) that should guide competition intervention and enforcement. While economists generally prefer a total welfare standard,[48] the Commission appears to pursue a consumer welfare approach, as evidenced by the various policy statements and official speeches that have emanated from the DG for Competition,[49] particularly during the tenure of Mario Monti.[50] Indeed, according to that particular Commissioner for Competition, 'the goal of competition policy, in all its aspects, is to protect consumer welfare by maintaining a high degree of competition in the common market'.[51] Commissioner Kroes has also

---

44 Council Regulation (EEC) 4064/89 of 21 December 1989 on the Control of Concentrations Between Undertakings [1989] OJ L395/1.

45 Weitbrecht (n 36). See also: A Resch, 'Phases of Competition Policy in Europe' [2005] Working Paper AY0504, Institute of European Studies.

46 See: Weitbrecht (n 36).

47 K J Cseres, 'The Controversies of the Consumer Welfare Standard' [2007] 3 *Competition Law Review* 121, 152.

48 See: G Monti, *EC Competition Law* (2007), 84–85.

49 See e.g.: European Commission, *XXVth Report on Competition Policy* (1995) 23.

50 See e.g.: M Monti, 'European Competition Policy for the 21st Century' (SPEECH/00/389, given at the Fordham Corporate Law Institute, New York, 20 October 2000) <http://europa.eu/rapid/pressReleasesAction.do?reference=SPEECH/00/389&format=HTML&aged=0&language=EN&guiLanguage=en> accessed 13 April 2008. See also: Evans and Grave (n 43).

51 M Monti, 'The Future for Competition Policy in the European Union' (SPEECH/01/340, given at London, 9 July 2001) <http://europa.eu/rapid/pressReleasesAction.do?reference=SPEECH/01/340&format =HTML&aged=0&language=EN&guiLanguage=en> accessed 13 April 2008.

pledged her allegiance to this mantra. For her, too, 'an effects-based approach, grounded in solid economics, ensures that citizens enjoy the benefits of a competitive, dynamic market economy', and 'consumer welfare is now well established as the standard the Commission applies when assessing mergers and infringements of the Treaty rules on cartels and monopolies'.[52] Such an approach was reflected in the guidelines and notices that have been adopted by the Commission since the late 1990s.

The Commission's concern with consumer interest has also been reflected in a number of initiatives that aimed to provide consumers with either greater representation (such as the introduction of the Consumer Liaison Officer) or compensation for their welfare losses (such as the encouragement of private damages actions). Twice annually a European Competition day is also organized by the Commission so as to explain the benefits of competition to European consumers.[53] On their face, these initiatives were intended to substantiate the claim that 'the protection of the interests of consumers, and therefore of European citizens, is at the heart of Community competition law'.[54] It appears then that EC competition law is now more consumer-orientated than ever before, something that is obvious from the numerous soft law instruments that have been adopted by the Commission in recent years.[55]

Soft law promotion of consumer welfare

Notices and guidelines issued by the Commission contain very important statements on the role of consumers and consumer welfare in substantive EC competition law.[56] The *European Commission Notice on the Application of Article 81(3) EC* is a good example.[57] First, and most importantly, this notice places consumer welfare at the top of the hierarchy of competition law objectives: 'the aim of the Community competition rules is to protect competition on the market as a means of enhancing consumer welfare and of ensuring an efficient allocation

52 Kroes (n 11).

53 Buttigieg (n 9) 5.

54 This quote is taken from European Commission *XXIXth Annual Report on Competition Policy* (n 22) 5.

55 However, Regulation 1/2003—a hard law measure—does not state that the primary objective of competition law is consumer welfare maximization; rather it ambiguously provides that the competition rules protect 'competition': Council Regulation (EC) 1/2003 of 16 December 2002 on the Implementation of the Rules on Competition Laid Down in Articles 81 and 82 of the Treaty [2003] OJ L1/1, recital 9.

56 Block exemption regulations have also advocated an economics-based approach that aims to maximize consumer welfare; see e.g.: Commission Regulation (EC) 2790/1999 of 22 December 1999 on the application of Article 81(3) of the Treaty to categories of vertical agreements and concerted practices [1999] OJ L336/21.

57 Guidelines on the Application of Article 81(3) of the Treaty (n 29).

of resources'.[58] These guidelines therefore establish the general principle that a reduction of consumer surplus is a necessary precondition for the application of Article 81(1).[59] Indeed, with this notice, the Commission expresses its belief that single market integration, itself an apparent objective of European competition law, should be viewed as a method of ensuring the efficient allocation of resources throughout the Community for the benefit of consumers.[60] The notice also asserts that the more substantial the impact of the agreement on competition, the more likely it is that consumers will suffer in the long run.[61] Furthermore, the greater the restriction of competition found under Article 81(1) the greater the efficiencies and pass-on to consumers must be in order for an exemption to be granted.[62] Finally, and importantly, the entity 'consumer' is given a broad definition: a 'consumer' may not only mean a member of the public who purchases goods for personal use but also those who purchase goods in the course of their trade.[63] Due to this definition of 'consumer', the consumer welfare standard applies not just to conduct directly affecting the retail sector but also to conduct affecting intermediate markets.[64]

The *Horizontal Merger Guidelines* also contain references to the welfare of consumers; they can in fact be easily interpreted as an endorsement of the consumer welfare approach in the context of merger control.[65] According to these guidelines, anti-competitive mergers increase the market power of the merging firms and thereby increase their ability to 'profitably increase prices, reduce output, choice or quality of goods and services, diminish innovation, or otherwise influence parameters of competition'.[66] Anti-competitive mergers, in other words, act to the detriment of consumers. It is possible according to these guidelines that efficiencies brought about by a merger counteract the effects on competition and

[58] Guidelines on the Application of Article 81(3) of the Treaty (n 29) para 33. See also: Guidelines on the Application of Article 81(3) of the Treaty (n 29) para 13. See also: European Commission, Commission Notice—Guidelines on Vertical Restraints [2000] OJ C291/01, paras 7 and 102.

[59] P Lugard and L Hancher, 'Honey, I Shrunk the Article! A Critical Assessment of the Commission's Notice on Article 81(3) of the EC Treaty' [2004] 25 *European Competition Law Review* 410, 411.

[60] Guidelines on the Application of Article 81(3) of the Treaty (n 29) para 13.

[61] Guidelines on the Application of Article 81(3) of the Treaty (n 29) para 92.

[62] Guidelines on the Application of Article 81(3) of the Treaty (n 29) para 90.

[63] Guidelines on the Application of Article 81(3) of the Treaty (n 29) para 84.

[64] Cf Case T-168/01 *GlaxoSmithKline Services Unlimited v Commission* [2006] ECR II-2969, para 118.

[65] Guidelines on the Assessment of Horizontal Mergers Under the Council Regulation on the Control of Concentrations Between Undertakings [2004] OJ C31/5 (*Horizontal Merger Guidelines*).

[66] Ibid, para 8.

in particular the potential harm resulting to consumers.[67] In order for a merger to be cleared in this scenario the efficiencies generated must, however, benefit consumers, as well as be merger-specific and verifiable.[68] To state the obvious then: any alleged efficiencies must cause an increase in consumer welfare to offset the reduction in such welfare effected by the merger.

The public consultation on the reform of Article 82 also highlighted the Commission's preference for the objective of consumer welfare maximization. According to its Discussion Paper, the objective of Article 82 should be 'the protection of competition on the market as a means of enhancing consumer welfare and of ensuring an efficient allocation of resources'.[69] This document advocates the abandonment of an approach that prohibits certain categories or forms of conduct by dominant firms for an approach that is based on evaluating the likely or actual effects a practice has on competition and consumer welfare.[70] Such an approach would ensure benefits for consumers, such as 'low prices, high quality products, a wide selection of goods and services, and innovation'.[71] While the Discussion Paper can be criticized on the grounds that the consumer harm test is not followed through effectively in its analyses,[72] it is clear that, according to the Commission at least, consumer welfare maximization should be the ultimate objective behind the European competition rules concerning exclusionary unilateral conduct. As explained below, however, the European courts have been reticent to abandon its earlier jurisprudence in this particular area, a fact that runs counter to the current agenda of the Commission.

Soft law instruments adopted by the Commission, then, have attempted to establish some clarity as to the objectives of European competition law; more specifically, they have been used to forward the Commission's objective of maximizing consumer welfare. Although such soft law is not, in a technical sense, legally

---

67 Ibid, para 78. Consumers in this context refers to both intermediate and ultimate consumers: ibid fn 105. See also: recital 29 of the Council Regulation (EC) 139/2004 of 20 January 2004 on the Control of Concentrations Between Undertakings (the EC Merger Regulation) [2004] OJ L24/1 (ECMR).

68 *Horizontal Merger Guidelines* (n 65) para 78. Some have questioned whether the requirement of consumer pass-on can be fulfilled in practice by the merging parties; see e.g.: M Kocmut, 'Efficiency Considerations and Merger Control—Quo Vadis, Commission?' [2006] 27 *European Competition Law Review* 19, 24.

69 Discussion Paper on Article 82 (n 41) para 4.

70 Competition Law Forum, 'The Reform of Article 82: Comments on the DG-Competition Discussion Paper on the Application of Article 82 to Exclusionary Abuses' [2006] 2 *European Competition Journal* 169.

71 Discussion Paper on Article 82 (n 41) para 4.

72 See e.g.: para 91 of the Discussion Paper on Article 82 (n 41). Also compare paras 1 and 58 with paras 55, 60 and 162 of the Discussion Paper on Article 82 (n 41). See also: Competition Law Forum (n 70).

binding, or indeed cannot formally change the substance of the European competition law rules, as interpreted by the courts, it is nonetheless an important source of information for businessmen and thus has an enormous influence on their behaviour in the market. However, more important than such soft law is the (legally-binding) jurisprudence of the EC courts; indeed without the support of the EC courts, the Commission's attempts to place consumer welfare at the heart of European competition policy may ultimately fail.

D. The Consumer Welfare Standard in Practice

This part of the chapter considers the operation of the consumer welfare standard in practice at EC level. It explores whether such a standard has been, or will be, followed through in concrete competition cases, and if so what forms of consumer harm have been, or can be, identified therein.

Restrictive agreements

Two recent judgments of the Court of First Instance (CFI) concerning restrictive agreements have identified the objective of European competition law to be the 'wellbeing' or 'welfare' of consumers. In *Österreichische Postsparkasse*, the CFI claimed that 'the ultimate purpose of the rules that seek to ensure that competition is not distorted in the internal market is to increase the well-being of consumers'.[73] In a later judgment the court also stated that 'the objective of the Community competition rules is to prevent undertakings, by restricting competition between themselves or with third parties, from reducing the welfare of the final consumer of the products in question'.[74] This is the first time since 1976[75] that the Community courts have made pronouncements on the precise economic objectives of the EC competition rules.[76] While these judgments held that it is the welfare of the *final* consumer that matters, it may arguably be no more than a reflection of the facts underlying the cases in question;[77] the standard may therefore be read as relating to both intermediate and final consumers.

The impact of the operation of Article 81 in terms of consumer welfare alone can arguably be felt most noticeably in relation to the treatment of cartel activity by

73 Cases T-213/01 and T-214/01 *Österreichische Postsparkasse AG v Commission* and *Bank für Arbeit und Wirtshaft AG v Commission* [2006] ECR II-1601, para 115.

74 Case T-168/01 *GlaxoSmithKline Services Unlimited v Commission* [2006] ECR II-2969, para 118.

75 See: Case 26/76 *Metro v Commission (No 1)* [1977] ECR 1875, para 20 ('workable competition').

76 Jones and Sufrin (n 23) 47.

77 Jones and Sufrin (n 23) 47.

the European Commission and the Community courts. 'Hard-core' cartels, namely those involving price-fixing, output restrictions, market allocation arrangements, or bid-rigging, are simply not tolerated by the European authorities. This is good news for consumer welfare, as the potential effects of such cartels on the welfare of consumers are essentially incontestable: prices rise, output falls, innovation is stifled, and quality and choice are affected to the detriment of consumers.[78] The economics of this is robust and accepted by most if not all economists. In other words, to prohibit cartel activity is to ensure that the welfare of consumers is protected, even in the absence of a vigorous case-by-case analysis of the welfare effects of the activity in question. Even further, a consumer welfare approach mandates zero tolerance of such visibly welfare-reducing activity. Consequently, in the decisions and judgments there is little or no scrutiny of the actual effect in the market of cartel activity,[79] and this is to be expected. Nonetheless, various references are detectable in Community decisions and judgments concerning the negative potential of cartels, particularly as regard consumer welfare.[80] In *PO/Thread*, for example, the Commission stated that price-fixing agreements are 'by their very nature the worst kind of violations of Article 81'.[81] For the Commission, 'by its very nature, the implementation of [a hard-core] cartel automatically generates a serious distortion of competition to the exclusive benefit of the participating producers and does great harm to their customers and, therefore, *the final consumer*'.[82] Such harm, according to the EC authorities, may take the form of, above all, higher prices[83] and reduced output.[84]

Agreements other than those of the hard-core variety may have both efficiency enhancing and/or reducing effects. If a pure consumer welfare approach is taken, then, in contrast to the treatment of such agreements when following equity or free-market-integration objectives, a thorough analysis of the welfare effects of the conduct needs to be undertaken. Traditionally, the ECJ has in fact underlined the necessity of economic analysis in competition cases, even in those cases involving agreements which have as their object, as opposed to their effect, the restriction of competition:

> [i]n considering whether an agreement has as its object the interference with competition within the common market it is necessary first to consider the

78 See e.g.: M L Katz and H S Rosen, *Microeconomics* (3rd edn, 1998); and J M Connor and R H Lande, 'How High Do Cartels Raise Prices? Implications for Optimal Cartel Fines' [2005] 80 *Tulane Law Review* 513.

79 See: *MCAA* (Case No COMP/E-1/.37.773) Commission Decision C(2004)4876 final (19 January 2005), para 284.

80 See: Marsden and Whelan (n 3).

81 *PO/Thread* [2008] OJ C21/10, para 18.

82 *Organic Peroxides* [2005] OJ L110/44, 435 (emphasis added).

83 See e.g.: *Austrian Banks* [2004] OJ L56/1, para 5.

84 See e.g.: *Electrical and Mechanical Carbon and Graphite Products* [2004] OJ L125/45.

> precise purpose of the agreement in the economic context in which it is to be applied.[85]

That said, there has never been a requirement on the authorities, when prohibiting a given conduct, actually to quantify (e.g. in euros) its exact anti-competitive effect in the market. This remains the case even though an objective of consumer welfare maximization is currently being pursued by the authorities. This is not to say, however, that rigorous economic assessments by the Commission are not required under European competition law. In fact, the Commission has recently been rebuked by the Community courts for its lack of economic analysis in a number of Article 81 cases.[86] A single example illustrates this point: *O2 v Commission*,[87] where the Commission's assessment of an agreement between O2 and T-Mobile relating to infrastructure sharing and national roaming for the 3G network on the German market was at issue. In an appeal against the Commission's finding of a breach of Article 81(1), the Court of First Instance partially annulled the decision on the grounds that an insufficient economic analysis was carried out by the Commission. For the CFI, the Commission did not conduct an objective analysis of what the 'competition situation would have been in the absence of an agreement' and its decision did not 'demonstrate, in concrete terms, in the context of the relevant emerging market, that the provisions of the agreement on roaming have restrictive effects on competition, but is confined, in this respect, to a *petitio principii* and to broad and general statements'.[88] Given the current interpretation by the CFI of the objective of EC competition law as expressed in *Österreichische Postsparkasse* and *GlaxoSmithKline*, an assessment of the actual or potential impact of the conduct in question on consumer welfare therefore needs to be undertaken by the Commission in these Article 81 cases; in other words, a solid and realistic theory of harm demonstrating actual or potential detriment to consumers should be established by the Commission before it identifies restrictive agreements under EC law.

It has already been explained that European competition law has been traditionally hostile to agreements that are perceived as having a negative impact on the objective of free market integration, irrespective of efficiency analyses.

---

85 Case 32/65 *Société La Technique Minière v Maschinenbau Ulm* [1966] ECR 389, para 6. See also: Case T-374/94, *European Night Services v Commission* [1998] ECR II-3141.

86 See: Case T-328/03 *O2 (Germany) GmbH & Co. OHG v Commission* [2006] ECR II-1231; and Case T-168/01, *GlaxoSmithKline Services Unlimited v Commission* [2006] ECR II-2969.

87 Case T-328/03 *O2 (Germany) GmbH & Co. OHG v Commission* [2006] ECR II-1231.

88 Ibid, para 116.

Judgments from the Community courts in cases such as *Consten and Grundig*,[89] *Delimitis*,[90] *Pronuptia de Paris*,[91] and *Parker Pen*[92] support this assertion. Indeed, even after the adoption of a consumer welfare approach by the Commission, such hostility is still evident in the treatment of agreements that provide absolute territorial protection to undertakings.[93] In a recent CFI case, however, this traditional hostility was tempered somewhat. In *GlaxoSmithKline Services Unlimited v Commission*,[94] although the agreement in question was found to have as its object the restriction of parallel trade, it was held that according to the particular facts of the case the welfare of final consumers could not be assumed to be adversely affected; the agreement therefore could not be prohibited solely on the grounds of its 'object'. This case, then, on its face at least, seems to be at odds with earlier rulings such as *Consten and Grundig*, where no economic analysis of the welfare effects of agreements restricting parallel trade was conducted or required. It may, however, merely constitute an 'exceptional' case, and one that is confined to the specific characteristics of the pharmaceutical market.[95] Whether that is the case or not remains, for the moment at least, uncertain.

The requirement of a pass-on to consumers in Article 81(3) is obviously important in considering the employment of a consumer welfare approach in Article 81 decisional practice and jurisprudence. According to the text of Article 81(3), consumer benefits include those resulting from improvements in production and distribution of goods or technical or economic progress. On a literal interpretation of this provision improvements in production or distribution only apply to goods and not services; technical or economic progress, however, applies to both goods and services.[96] The ECJ has held that the particular benefits generated by the agreement must outweigh its detrimental effects in order for an agreement to be exempted.[97] Non-price benefits may be considered by the Commission, even when the consumer detriment to be counterbalanced is related to price competition.[98] However, an Article 81(3) exemption will not be appropriate where the resultant limitation of price competition is particularly severe.[99] The Commission

89 Cases 56 and 58/64 *Etablissements Consten SA and Grundig-Verkaufs-GmbH v Commission* [1966] ECR 299.

90 Case C-234/89 *Delimitis v Henninger Bräu* [1991] ECR I-935.

91 Case 161/84 *Pronuptia de Paris GmbH v Pronuptia de Paris Irmgard Schillgallis* [1986] ECR 353.

92 Case T-77/92 *Parker Pen v Commission* [1994] ECR II-549.

93 See: Regulation 2790/1999 (n 56), art 4(b).

94 Case T-168/01 *GlaxoSmithKline Services Unlimited v Commission* [2006] ECR II-2969.

95 Jones and Sufrin (n 23) 231.

96 See: R Whish, *Competition Law* (2003), 151.

97 Cases 56 and 58/64 *Etablissements Consten SA and Grundig-Verkaufs-GmbH v Commission* [1966] ECR 299, 348.

98 See e.g.: Cases 43/82 and 63/82 *VBVB and VBBB v Commission* [1984] ECR 19.

99 Ibid.

has not yet attempted to provide an exact definition of 'fair share' in the context of Article 81(3) EC; indeed it is doubtful if a precise definition could be provided in any case.[100] Although consumers must benefit from the gain, the general expectation has traditionally been that in competitive markets these benefits will inevitably be passed on as part of the competitive process.[101]

That said, there have been cases where the Commission has refused to grant an exemption on the grounds that the agreement in question has not allowed consumers a fair share of its resultant benefits.[102] In *Re VBBB and VBVB Agreement*,[103] for example, the Commission held that resale price maintenance (RPM) in the books market did not provide consumers with a fair share of its alleged benefits, and that as a result of the RPM consumers would in fact be deprived of improved choice and lower prices. Despite this, some commentators have claimed that the Commission's past exemption decisions 'hardly contain any quantification of the benefits under Article 81(3), let alone an elaborate discussion of the magnitude of the identified efficiencies and the reasons why they benefited consumers'.[104] It is clear from the guidelines on Article 81(3), however, that the Commission, in abandoning its exemption monopoly, 'issued a gold-plated blueprint of how it considers Article 81(3) should ideally be applied by national competition agencies and courts';[105] this 'blueprint' highlights that automatic assumption of pass-on should no longer be made and that a structured analysis of pass-on is required.[106] In other words, the criterion of consumer pass-on will now be treated more seriously by the EC authorities, a fact that underlines to a degree the sincerity of its commitment to maximizing consumer welfare. In contrast, however, such a commitment does not appear to be as present in the jurisprudence concerning the unilateral behaviour of dominant undertakings.

Unilateral behaviour

Unlike the situation pertaining to the Treaty provisions on restrictive practices, Article 82 EC, the European law prohibition on abuse of dominance, has not yet been interpreted by the Community authorities as having as its sole or primary object the maximization of consumer welfare. In fact, for over 30 years Article 82

100 Whish (n 96) 156.
101 See: M Furse, *Competition Law of the EC and UK* (4th edn, 2004), 178–179.
102 See e.g.: *Vichy* [1991] OJ L 75/57; and *Screensport/EBU* [1991] OJ L 63/32.
103 *Re VBBB and VBVB Agreement* [1982] OJ L 54/36.
104 Lugard and Hancher (n 59) 419.
105 Lugard and Hancher (n 59) 420.
106 See e.g.: Guidelines on the Application of Article 81(3) of the Treaty (n 29), paras 39, 85, 87, 90, and 94–104.

has been consistently interpreted by the courts as a measure that aims to protect the competitive structure of the market, the so-called 'institution of competition', as a means of upholding the economic freedom of undertakings to enter and compete in a given market irrespective of their efficiency, as is apparent in early competition cases such as *Commercial Solvents*,[107] *Hoffmann-La Roche*,[108] *United Brands*,[109] and *Michelin I*.[110] These cases represent a triumph for ordoliberal ideas in that they are not concerned with the overall impact of unilateral conduct on economic welfare, but rather with the restriction of the individual actions of competitors.[111] These cases, as a result, adopt very formulistic (*per se*) approaches to particular economic activities undertaken by a dominant undertaking, such as the granting of loyalty rebates for example. This remains the current situation despite the fact that the Commission's agenda regarding the adoption of a consumer welfare approach in EC competition law has become increasingly obvious since the mid- to late 1990s.[112] One has only to consider the judgments in *Michelin II*,[113] *IMS Health*,[114] *France Télécom*,[115] and *British Airways*,[116] for example, to see that this is the case. Indeed, even after the publication of the Discussion Paper on Article 82 at the end of 2005—a document that on its face purports to advocate the maximization of consumer welfare as the primary objective of Article 82—the ECJ itself has had the opportunity expressly to adopt and mandate the employment of a consumer welfare approach in the context of unilateral behaviour; it refused to do so.[117]

It is often claimed, however, in the context of Article 82 that once competition, or the competitive process, understood as a process of rivalry between undertakings, is secured there will inevitably be resultant benefits for consumers.[118]

---

[107] Case 6-7/73 *Istituto Chemioterapico Italiano Spa and Commercial Solvents Corporation v Commission* [1974] ECR 223.

[108] Case 85/76 *Hoffmann La Roche v Commission* [1979] ECR 461.

[109] Case 27/76 *United Brands v Commission* [1978] ECR 207.

[110] Case 322/81 *Nederlansche Banden-Industrie Michelin NV v Commission* [1983] 3461.

[111] Cf T Eilmansberger, 'How to Distinguish Good from Bad Competition under Article 82: In Search of Clearer More Coherent Standards for Anticompetitive Abuses' [2005] 42 *Common Market Law Review* 129, 138.

[112] See e.g.: J Kallaugher and B Sher, 'Rebates Revisited: Anti-Competitive Effects and Exclusionary Abuse Under Article 82' [2004] 25 *European Competition Law Review* 263.

[113] Case T-203/01 *Michelin v Commission* [2003] ECR II-4071.

[114] Case C-418/01 *IMS Health GmbH & Co OHG v NHC Health GmbH & Co KG* [2004] ECR I-5039.

[115] Case T-340/03 *France Télécom SA v Commission* [2007] ECR II-107.

[116] Case T-219/99 *British Airways v Commission* [2003] ECR II-5917 (CFI); and Case C-95/04 P *British Airways v Commission* [2007] ECR I-2331 (ECJ).

[117] Case C-95/04 P *British Airways v Commission* [2007] ECR I-2331.

[118] Even in the Discussion Paper on Article 82 the protection of rivalry and the competitive process is given priority over possible pro-competitive efficiency gains in the context of an 'efficiency defence': Discussion Paper on Article 82 (n 41) para 91.

In *British Airways v Commission*, for example, it was stated by the Advocate General that an 'indirect detriment to consumers' can be assumed where 'it is shown that the conduct of a dominant undertaking is likely adversely to affect the structure of competition, unless there is an objective economic justification for it'.[119] To be clear, however, and at the risk of repetition, Article 82 EC does not require demonstration that the conduct in question had any actual or direct effect on consumers: 'competition law concentrates upon protecting the market structure from artificial distortions because by doing so the interests of the consumer in the medium to long term are best protected'.[120] While this remains the situation for the moment, it is submitted that continued pressure will be placed on the Community authorities to interpret Article 82 in terms of (allocative, productive, dynamic) efficiency, if not actually consumer welfare: an effective competition policy, above all one based on efficiency standards, is becoming increasingly necessary in order to guarantee effective economic growth and international competitiveness in the global economy, both of which are explicit objectives of the Community's Lisbon Agenda. For change in this area to occur, however, the lead needs to be taken by the courts. It is arguably, then, immaterial how the Commission intends to define its future competition policy with regard to Article 82: 'even if its administrative practice were to change, the Commission would still have to act within the framework prescribed for it by Article 82 EC as interpreted by the Court of Justice'.[121] An example of where possible conflict could be engendered would be the introduction of an 'efficiency defence' by the Commission, as neither the Commission itself in previous decisions or the courts in its judgments have recognized such a concept.[122] Whether change will indeed occur, and whether any future guidelines adopted by the Commission concerning unilateral behaviour and its impact on consumer welfare will be respected by the courts, remain in the meantime merely subjects for conjecture.

Merger control

In recent years EC merger control has undergone quite radical changes which arguably improve the situation of consumers. These changes show a strong tendency towards the 'significant narrowing of competition law objectives in the direction of a more economics-based analysis, according even greater weight to

---

119 Opinion of A G Kokott in Case C-95/04 P *British Airways v Commission* [2007] ECR I-2331, para 89.

120 Case T-219/99 *British Airways v Commission* [2003] ECR II-5917, para 264.

121 Opinion of AG Kokott (n 119) para 28. See also: Evans and Grave (n 43) 133.

122 C D Ehlermann and L Laudati (eds), *European Competition Law Annual: The Objectives of Competition Policy* (1998) Introduction, ix.

economic efficiency'.[123] Most importantly, in 2004 the substantive test for assessing concentrations with a Community dimension was reformulated so as to avoid any potential 'gap' cases, i.e. situations where anti-competitive mergers would not lead to a position of dominance. The test is now less focused on dominance—itself a rather formulistic concept according to EC jurisprudence—and more on the effects of the merger in the market. Henceforth, the ultimate inquiry of merger control is whether the merger may lead to a 'significant impediment of effective competition' which may, in particular, be caused by the creation or strengthening of a dominant position in the market.[124] The substantive test should in other words be interpreted as 'extending, beyond the concept of dominance, only to the anticompetitive effects of a concentration resulting from the non-coordinated behaviour of undertakings which would not have a dominant position on the market concerned'.[125] According to Monti, this substantive reform reveals how deeply economic thinking now prevails in the Commission, even if it is translated somewhat imperfectly.[126]

A more economics-based approach is also evident in the Commission's *Horizontal Merger Guidelines*, in particular its stance on an efficiency defence in the context of merger control. The welfare of consumers therefore appears to be one of its main concerns, something that is arguably in line with the text of the ECMR itself: 'the Commission shall take into account . . . the interests of the intermediate and ultimate consumers';[127] and '[it is] appropriate to take account of any substantiated and likely efficiencies . . . to counteract . . . in particular the potential harm to consumers'.[128] According to the European Community Merger Regulation, the Commission, in addition to evaluating the anti-competitive effects of a merger, should take into consideration the 'development of technical and economic progress provided that it is to the consumers' advantage and does not form an obstacle to competition'.[129] The guidelines also provide that any efficiency should, among other things, benefit the consumer.[130] Whether benefits will be passed on to consumers depends primarily on the existence of competitive restraints and barriers to market entry.[131] According to Luescher, the consumer

[123] M Dreher and M Adam, 'Abuse of Dominance under Reform—Sound Economics and Established Case Law' [2007] 28 *European Competition Law Review* 278, 279.
[124] Article 2(2) and 2(3) of the ECMR.
[125] Recital 25 of the ECMR.
[126] Monti (n 48) 258.
[127] Art 2(1)(b) of the ECMR.
[128] Recital 29 of the ECMR.
[129] Art 2(1)(b) of the ECMR.
[130] *Horizontal Merger Guidelines* (n 65) para 78.
[131] *Horizontal Merger Guidelines* (n 65) para 84.

welfare standard is therefore what is relevant in appraising efficiencies.[132] While apparent from the wording of the guidelines, such an interpretation has not been expressly confirmed by the Commission.[133] Nonetheless the guidelines are a welcome development in this regard as traditionally merger efficiencies were not acknowledged by the Commission,[134] or indeed by the US authorities,[135] and were sometimes interpreted as evidence of the anti-competitive nature of a proposed concentration.[136] The debate in Europe is now apparently on how to consider efficiencies and not whether to consider them.[137] That said, to date there has been a notable absence of cases where efficiencies have played a decisive role.[138] Indeed, some have even argued that the efficiency defence poses an insurmountable obstacle, particularly due to its requirement of pass-on, an element that is inherent in a consumer welfare approach.[139] If this is the case, efficiencies will consequently only play a minor role in EC merger control.

It should be noted, however, that the protection of failing firms and the development of a European industrial policy are also supported by (hard and soft) law[140] and Commission decisional practice.[141] There is even evidence of cases where an aggressive industrial policy—and one that does not take efficiency considerations into account—has been adopted, although these appear to be fairly rare.[142] For the most part, then, there is a focus on anti-competitive effects and the resultant harm to consumers in the market.[143] Indeed, EC merger review cases reveal that the Commission has considered a wide variety of different types of

132 C Luescher, 'Efficiency Considerations in European Merger Control—Just Another Battle Ground for the European Commission, Economists and Competition Lawyers' [2004] 25 *European Competition Law Review* 72, 81.

133 Kocmut (n 68) 21. Cf J S Venit, 'The Role of Efficiencies in Merger Control' in G Drauz and M Reynolds (eds), *EC Merger Control: A Major Reform in Progress* (2003) 263.

134 Kocmut (n 68) 20.

135 J Kattan, 'Efficiencies and Merger Analysis' [1994] 62 *Antitrust Law Journal* 513, 515; and W J Kolasky and A R Dick, 'The Merger Guidelines and the Integration of Efficiencies into Antitrust Review of Horizontal Mergers' [2003] 71 *Antitrust Law Journal* 207, 209.

136 *AT&T/NCR* (Case IV/M050) [1991] OJ C16/1, 30. It should also be noted in this context that a Williamson trade-off model (where a loss in allocative efficiency can be traded off against the gain in productive efficiency) has been rejected by the Commission: *Danish Crown/Vestjyske Slagterier* [2000] OJ L20/1, para 198. See: Monti (n 48) 292.

137 Kocmut (n 68) 20.

138 Kocmut (n 68) 27.

139 Kocmut (n 68) 24 and 27.

140 See e.g.: *Horizontal Merger Guidelines* (n 65) para 90; European Commission, *XXVIth Report on Competition Policy* (Brussels, 1996), para 8; and recitals 4 and 23 of the ECMR.

141 See e.g.: *BASF/Pantochim/Eurodiol* (Case COMP/M.2314) [2002] OJ L132/45; *Alcatel/Telettra* [1991] OJ L122/48; and *Piaggio/Aprilia* Case COMP/M.3570, 22 April 2004. cf *Volvo/Scania* (Case COMP/M.1672) [2000] OJ L143/74.

142 See e.g.: *Aerospatial-Alenia/de Havilland* (Case M.53) [1991] OJ L334/42.

143 Cf the criticism of the Commission by the US Department of Justice following its decision in the *GE/Honeywell* case: *General Electric/Honeywell* [2004] OJ L48/1.

consumer detriment when assessing a concentration's compatibility with the common market: increased prices,[144] passing-on of costs,[145] the imposition of unfavourable sales conditions on consumers,[146] reductions in innovation,[147] service,[148] and choice[149] have all been alluded to in its merger decisions. More recently in the case of *Ryanair/Aer Lingus*,[150] in prohibiting the merger of the two airlines in question, the Commission was concerned with the reduction of consumer welfare that would be detected through a loss in choice in the market concerned.[151]

The courts too have displayed enthusiasm for an economics-based assessment of the impact of a proposed merger, provided that it meets certain evidentiary requirements. Three cases, decided under the test pertaining before the 2004 merger reform, substantiate this claim: *Airtours*,[152] *Schneider*,[153] and *Tetra Laval*.[154] While the courts in these cases did not expressly state that the sole aim of European merger law is to maximize consumer welfare, they nonetheless provided very important rulings for a Commission that is apparently dedicated to ensuring, through the use of solid economic theory, that consumers get the best available benefits from the operation of the market. In essence, the courts provided that the Commission had provided insufficient economic analyses in its prohibition decisions. The ECJ in *Tetra Laval*, for example, held that the evidence relied upon by the Commission in conducting its economic analysis should be 'factually accurate, reliable and consistent' and it must contain 'all the information which must be taken into account in order to assess a complex situation and whether it is capable of substantiating the conclusions drawn from it'.[155] Furthermore, the courts' powers of review are all the more relevant in the

---

144 See e.g.: *Aerospatiale-Alenia/de Havilland* (Case M.53) [1991] OJ L334/42, para 69.

145 See e.g.: *Kværner/Trafalgar* Case No IV/M.731, para 17.

146 See e.g.: *Courtaulds/SNIA* (Case No IV/M113) Commission Decision, 19 November 1991, para 36.

147 See e.g.: *DSM/Roche Vitamins* (Case No COMP/M.2972) Commission Decision, 23 July 2003, para 67.

148 See e.g.: *Newscorp/Telepiù* (Case No COMP/M.2876) Commission Decision, 2 April 2003, para 190.

149 See e.g.: *Gillette/Duracell* (Case No IV/M.836) [1996] OJ C364/4 para 10.

150 *Ryanair/Aer Lingus* (Case No COMP/M.4439), Commission Decision C(2007) 3104, 27 June 2007.

151 N Kroes, 'Introductory Remarks at Press Conference on *Ryanair/Aer Lingus* Decision' (SPEECH/07/431, Brussels, 27 June 2007) <http://europa.eu/rapid/pressReleasesAction.do?reference=SPEECH/07/431&format=HTML&aged=1&language=EN&guiLanguage=en> accessed 13 April 2008.

152 Case T-342/99 *Airtours v Commission* [2002] ECR II-2585.

153 Case T-310/01 *Schneider Electric v Commission* [2002] ECR II-4071.

154 Case T-5/02 *Tetra Laval BV v Commission* [2002] ECR II-4381 (CFI); and Case C-12/03P *Commission v Tetra Laval* [2005] ECR I-987 (ECJ).

155 Case C-12/03P *Commission v Tetra Laval* [2005] ECR I-987, para 39.

case of a 'prospective analysis' such as that required in examining a conglomerate merger.[156] While ultimately the courts overturned the Commission's prohibition decisions in these cases,[157] it should not be argued that the CFI and ECJ are against an economics-based, consumer welfare approach; rather, the courts have held that the Commission, in following such an approach, had simply failed to reach the standard of proof required.[158] In other words, the judgments do not indicate a divergence in the objectives between the EU and the US, but rather that the Commission needed to reinforce the standard of its legal and economic analyses.[159] The courts, then, take a very serious view of Commission decisions that do not meet the required standard of proof in merger cases: not only are they overturned, but the Commission may have to pay damages for losses incurred due to the unlawful decision.[160]

E. Conclusion

Recently the idea of using the consumer welfare standard as a method of protecting the interests of consumers under the substantive European competition law rules has taken root at EC level. Beginning with restrictive agreements, the Commission and the CFI have both expressly stated that the primary objective of European competition law is consumer welfare maximization. For a prohibition under Article 81 to be upheld, solid economic evidence must establish that the agreement in question will have a negative effect on welfare. Efficiencies are also given their due weight by the Commission, as mandated by the courts. Nonetheless, some formalism does remain: agreements providing absolute territorial protection or involving resale-price maintenance are still treated as *per se* violations of the rules. Merger law has also undergone similar changes. The substantive test, for example, is now less focused on dominance and more on the effects of the merger in the market. And when assessing a merger, the Commission must take into account the interests of the intermediate and final consumers. While a merger with negative effects on competition may be cleared if it ultimately results in the achievements of efficiencies, any alleged efficiencies must cause an increase in consumer welfare to offset the reduction in such welfare effected by the merger.

156 Ibid.

157 On the same grounds, the CFI in a later case overturned a Commission decision *clearing* a merger: Case T-464/04 *Impala v Commission* [2006] ECR II-2289, para 528.

158 See: Pera and Auricchio (n 32) 22.

159 Pera and Auricchio (n 32) 22.

160 Case T-351/03 *Schneider Electric v Commission*, CFI Judgment, 11 July 2007, not yet reported.

One area of competition still needs to be reformed, namely Article 82. The Discussion Paper is a step in the right direction: it advocates the adoption of a consumer welfare approach in relation to the assessment of exclusionary behaviour. While by no means perfect, this document should be welcomed, particularly if one believes that competition law should ultimately protect the interests of consumers. The support of the courts, however, is required if contradictory judicial precedent is to be overcome. So far this has not been forthcoming; the courts appear to envision Article 82 as protecting the 'institution' of competition, a rather formulistic, structural concept that is not primarily concerned with efficiency, or indeed consumer welfare—for the moment in any case. Consequently, the competition rules, at least as applied to unilateral behaviour of dominant firms, are not operating in a manner that maximizes efficiency or the welfare of consumers. This is a worrying situation, not only for European competitiveness, but also for those final consumers who purchase their goods and services at retail level.

17

WELFARE OBJECTIVE AND ENFORCEMENT STANDARD IN COMPETITION LAW

*Renato Nazzini**

* Reader in law, University of Southampton. The views expressed are purely personal.

A. Introduction

The dynamics of consumer goods markets in which own label and branded products compete with each other call into question some of the basic assumptions that underlie the analysis competition authorities and courts carry out when assessing the effects of conduct on competition.

First, when assessing the effect of own label products on competition, the vertical dimension of the competitive relationships becomes as prominent as horizontal competition between branded product manufacturers or retailers. The market power of the retailer on the retailing market is only one piece of the jigsaw. Equally important is the retailer's buyer power[1] or upstream vertical market power.[2] As a result of the exercise of the retailer's buyer power, the manufacturer's profits may be lower and the retailer's profits higher than they would otherwise be. What are the implications for the competitive assessment? Should total surplus of the industry be assessed or should any exercise of buyer power only be relevant if it has an impact on consumer welfare? Should the law focus on economic effects at all or should it rather be concerned with the position of a particular supplier which may be unfairly treated by a powerful buyer?

Second, the retailer combines at least two roles vis-à-vis the branded product manufacturer. The retailer is, at the same time, customer and competitor.[3] A third role also emerges. The retailer is the owner and supplier of shelf space, which some equate to an essential infrastructure in a network industry.[4] This provides the retailer with the incentive and the power to exploit its position

[1] This is discussed in: UK Competition Commission, 'The Supply of Groceries in the UK Market Investigation' (Final Report) (30 April 2008) s 9 <http://www.competition-commission.org.uk/rep_pub/reports/2008/fulltext/538.pdf> accessed 1 June 2008 (Report on *The supply of groceries in the UK market*).

[2] See: R L Steiner, 'Market Power in Consumer Goods Industries', Chapter 4 above herein.

[3] Report on *The supply of groceries in the UK market* (n 1), app 9.10: 'Own-Label Goods', paras 27–30 <http://www.competition-commission.org.uk/rep_pub/reports/2008/fulltext/538_9_10.pdf> accessed 1 June 2008 (Report on *The supply of groceries in the UK market: Appendix 9.10*).

[4] See: P Kuipers, 'Retailer and Private Labels: Asymmetry of Information, In-store Competition, and the Control of Shelf Space', Chapter 9 above herein.

as a powerful customer to gain an advantage as a competitor. How should these market dynamics be assessed? Does it matter that the retailer has an unfair advantage over branded product manufacturers in the sense that the latter cannot replicate that advantage? Or should the focus be on total or rather consumer welfare?

Third, the development of own labels and the marginalization of secondary and tertiary brands has a clear impact on consumer choice. It is unclear, however, how consumer choice and consumer preferences should be assessed within a competition framework. The elimination of secondary and tertiary brands reduces consumer choice. Some consumers may value those particular brands that have been eliminated more than the remaining available brands. However, if the manufacturers of the secondary and tertiary brands have higher costs than the others, their elimination may be beneficial in terms of total and/or consumer welfare. Intervention to protect them may reduce total welfare and, through the creation of a price floor, consumer welfare. At the other end of the spectrum, markets dominated by a leading brand or own label products may be thought to offer too little choice. So how much choice is desirable and what is the level below which intervention is appropriate? And is choice, in itself, relevant at all? Can courts and competition authorities assess how much differentiation is efficient or otherwise desirable on the market?

In light of these challenges, the aim of this chapter is to take a step back to discuss what the objective[5] and the enforcement standard[6] of competition law should be and how they apply to the competitive assessment of the impact of own label products in consumer goods markets.

This chapter is organized as follows. First, it provides an overview of the different objectives of competition law in given jurisdictions and across different jurisdictions. Second, it demonstrates the need for a single objective. Third, it discusses what the objective and the enforcement standard should be. Finally, it draws a general conclusion.

5 The policy objective of competition law does not necessarily coincide with the enforcement standard to be applied by competition authorities and courts. The policy objective is the ultimate goal pursued by competition law or its raison d'être.

6 The enforcement standard is the analytical framework or set of rules or criteria applied to determine which behaviour is prohibited. There may be a number of enforcement standards depending on the type of behaviour under review. This chapter deals with the core enforcement standard, which determines, as a default analytical framework, when behaviour has anti-competitive effects. Object infringements or *per se* prohibitions generally rely on a rebuttable or irrebuttable presumption of anti-competitive effects.

B. Positive Analysis: The *Status Quo* between Fragmentation and Convergence

Overview of possible objectives of competition law

Competition law may be used to pursue different objectives. This is because the concept of 'competition' is open-textured and, therefore, different meanings may be ascribed to it depending on factors such as the political environment, the prevailing market conditions, and the current economic and legal theories.

A 2007 report by the International Competition Network (ICN) identifies ten objectives of unilateral conduct rules.[7] A number of ICN members emphasized that the objectives of unilateral conduct rules are the same as the objectives of competition law more generally.[8] The Report, therefore, may be used as a starting point for a catalogue of the possible objectives of competition law. The ICN report identifies the following objectives: ensuring an effective competitive process, promoting consumer welfare, maximizing efficiency, ensuring economic freedom, ensuring a level playing field for small and medium-sized enterprises, promoting fairness and equality, promoting consumer choice, achieving market integration, facilitating privatization and market liberalization, and promoting competitiveness in international markets. At least one further objective must be added to this list that was not explicitly addressed by the respondents to the ICN questionnaire: maximizing total welfare.

Different objectives of competition law are adopted in different jurisdictions. Furthermore, a single jurisdiction often adopts, in its statutory framework but more often through evolving court jurisprudence and enforcement practice, more than one objective.[9]

The position in the European Union

The European Commission appears to support the view that the Community competition rules serve a number of objectives, interrelated and compatible with each other. The Guidelines on the application of Article 81(3) of the Treaty state

[7] International Competition Network 'Report on the Objectives of Unilateral Conduct Laws, Assessment of Dominance/Substantial Market Power, and State-Created Monopolies' (Presented at the 6th Annual Conference of the ICN, Moscow, May 2007) <http://www.icn-moscow.org/page.php?id=7> accessed 1 June 2008 (ICN Report). The Report is based on questionnaires submitted by 35 ICN members.

[8] ICN Report 6–8.

[9] See Section B below (the discussion on 'The position in the EU', 'The position in the US', and 'The position in other jurisdictions').

that the objective of Article 81 is to protect competition on the market as a means of enhancing consumer welfare and of ensuring an efficient allocation of resources. Competition and market integration both serve the end of promoting allocative efficiency and consumer welfare.[10] The DG Competition discussion paper on the application of Article 82 of the Treaty to exclusionary abuses makes a policy statement along the same lines.[11] The Guidelines on the assessment of horizontal mergers[12] and the Guidelines on the assessment of non-horizontal mergers[13] are less clear in identifying the objective of merger control. Both sets of guidelines, however, point out that effective competition brings benefits to consumers, such as low prices, high quality products, a wide selection of goods and services, and innovation. The objective of merger control is to prevent mergers that would be likely to deprive customers of these benefits by significantly increasing the market power of undertakings.[14] Both sets of guidelines expressly take into account productive and dynamic efficiencies benefiting consumers.[15] This approach appears to be consistent with a consumer welfare objective.

The jurisprudence of the Community courts is less clear in identifying the objective of Community competition law. Different cases seem to suggest different objectives. In particular, it is not clear whether the Community courts are moving towards endorsing a consumer welfare objective or continue to apply the idea that the competitive process is in itself an objective of competition law in an ordoliberal sense.

Two cases are illustrative of this tension. On the one hand, in *GlaxoSmithKline Services Unlimited v Commission*, the Fourth Chamber (extended composition) of the Court of First Instance stated that the objective of Article 81(1) of the EC Treaty is the protection of consumer welfare.[16] On the other hand, in *British*

10 Communication from the Commission: Notice: Guidelines on the application of Article 81(3) of the Treaty [2004] OJ C101/97, para 13 (Article 81(3) Guidelines).

11 European Commission DG Competition, 'DG Competition Discussion Paper on the Application of Article 82 of the Treaty to Exclusionary Abuses' (Public consultation, December 2005) para 4 <http://ec.europa.eu/comm/competition/antitrust/art82/discpaper2005.pdf> (DG Competition discussion paper).

12 Guidelines on the Assessment of Horizontal Mergers Under the Council Regulation on the Control of Concentrations Between Undertakings [2004] OJ C31/5 (Horizontal Merger Guidelines).

13 Commission Notice: Guidelines on the Assessment of Non-horizontal Mergers Under the Council Regulation on the Control of Concentrations Between Undertakings <http://ec.europa.eu/comm/competition/mergers/legislation/nonhorizontalguidelines.pdf> accessed 27 May 2008 (Non-Horizontal Merger Guidelines).

14 Horizontal Merger Guidelines (n 12) para 8 and Non-Horizontal Merger Guidelines (n 13) para 10.

15 Horizontal Merger Guidelines (n 12) paras 12 and 76–88 and Non-Horizontal Merger Guidelines (n 13) para 21.

16 Case T-168/01 *GlaxoSmithKline Services Unlimited v Commission* [2006] ECR II 2969, para 118, where the court stated 'the objective assigned to Article 81(1) EC . . . is to prevent undertakings,

Airways v Commission, Advocate General Kokott stated that Article 82 EC, like the other competition rules of the Treaty, is not designed only or primarily to protect the immediate interests of individual competitors or consumers, but to protect the structure of the market and thus 'competition as an institution'. Since where competition as such is damaged, disadvantages for consumers are also to be feared, in this way, consumers are also indirectly protected.[17] In its judgment, the European Court of Justice did not explicitly endorse the opinion of the Advocate General on this point. However, the court rejected British Airways' plea that the Court of First Instance erred in law by failing to examine whether the conduct in question in the case caused prejudice to consumers as required by Article 82(2)(b) EC. The court pointed out, relying on *Europemballage and Continental Can v Commission*,[18] that Article 82 EC is aimed not only at practices which may cause prejudice to consumers directly, but also at those which are detrimental to them through their impact on an effective competition structure, such as is mentioned in Article 3(1)(g) EC.[19] This may be read as endorsing the objective of the protection of 'competition as an institution'. However, it could also be interpreted as requiring an analysis of market power from which consumer harm may be inferred. This would be consistent with a total or consumer welfare objective because market power, in the short term, is likely to reduce both total and consumer welfare.

The position in the United States

In the US, it is generally accepted that the goal of antitrust policy is to prevent conduct that reduces consumer welfare.[20] However, there is also support for the view that the goal of antitrust policy is to prohibit conduct that reduces total welfare.[21]

---

by restricting competition between themselves or with third parties, from reducing the welfare of the final consumer of the products in question'. The case is under appeal: see *GlaxoSmithKline Services* (Case C-501/06 P) [2007] OJ C42/11.

17 Case C-95/04 P *British Airways plc v Commission* [2007] ECR I-2331, opinion of AG Kokott delivered on 23 February 2006, para 68.

18 Case 6/72 *Europemballage Corporation and Continental Can Company Inc v Commission* [1973] ECR 215, para 26.

19 Case C-95/04 P *British Airways plc v Commission* [2007] ECR I-2331, paras 103–108.

20 R H Lande, 'Wealth Transfers as the Original and Primary Concern of Antitrust: The Efficiency Interpretation Challenged' [1982] 34 *Hastings Law Journal* 65; R H Lande, 'Proving the Obvious: The Antitrust Laws Were Passed to Protect Consumers (not Just to Increase Efficiency)' [1999] 50 *Hastings Law Journal* 959; S C Salop, 'Question: What is the Real and Proper Antitrust Welfare Standard? Answer: The True Consumer Welfare Standard' (Statement before the Antitrust Modernization Commission, 4 November 2005) <http://govinfo.library.unt.edu/amc/public_studies_fr28902/exclus_conduct_pdf/051104_Salop_Mergers.pdf> accessed 2 June 2008.

21 R H Bork, 'Legislative Intent and the Policy of the Sherman Act' [1966] 9 *Journal of Law and Economics* 7.

The Department of Justice and the Federal Trade Commission apply a consumer welfare test in merger control. The Joint Horizontal Merger Guidelines state that mergers should not be permitted to create or enhance market power or to facilitate its exercise. Market power to a seller is defined as the ability profitably to maintain prices above competitive levels for a significant period of time. The result of the exercise of market power is a transfer of wealth from buyers to sellers or a misallocation of resources.[22] As regards efficiencies, the Guidelines state that the Agencies consider whether cognizable efficiencies are likely to be sufficient to reverse the merger's potential to harm consumers in the relevant market, for instance by preventing price increases in that market.[23]

As regards collusive behaviour assessed under Section 1 of the Sherman Act, the US case law tends to focus on whether the behaviour under review increases prices and lowers output. In *Business Electronics Corp v Sharp Electronics Corp*, the US Supreme Court held that the *per se* prohibition applies to agreement that would always or almost always tend to restrict competition and decrease output.[24] In *Leegin Creative Leather Products, Inc v PSKS, Inc*, the Supreme Court explained that the rule of reason distinguishes between restraints with anti-competitive effect that are harmful to the consumer and restraints stimulating competition that are in the consumer's best interest.[25]

As regards the analysis under Section 2 of the Sherman Act, the case law is also leaning towards a consumer welfare standard. In *Brooke Group Ltd v Brown and Williamson Tobacco Corp*, the Supreme Court held that a dangerous probability of recoupment is a prerequisite for a finding of liability under Section 2 of the Act. Without recoupment, predatory pricing produces lower aggregate prices in the market and consumer welfare is enhanced.[26] Under a total welfare standard, below cost pricing may be prohibited regardless of whether recoupment is probable as it is inefficient and may result in lower total welfare.[27]

In *United States v Microsoft Corp*, the US Circuit Court of Appeals for the DC Circuit held that, to be condemned as exclusionary, a monopolist's act must have an 'anticompetitive effect'. Anti-competitive effect means harm to the competitive process and, thereby, harm to consumers. In contrast, harm to one or more

22 US Department of Justice and Federal Trade Commission, 'Horizontal Merger Guidelines' [Revised 1997], reprinted in 4 Trade Reg Rep (CCH) § 13, 104 (8 April 1997), § 0.1.

23 Ibid, § 4.

24 *Business Electronics Corp v Sharp Electronics Corp*, 485 US 717, 723 (1988).

25 *Leegin Creative Leather Products, Inc v PSKS, Inc* 551 US (2007).

26 *Brooke Group Ltd v Brown and Williamson Tobacco Corp*, 509 US 209, 224 (1993).

27 Salop (n 20) 6.

competitors will not suffice.[28] The court went on to say that if the plaintiff successfully establishes a prima facie case under Section 2 of the Sherman Act by demonstrating anti-competitive effect, then the monopolist may proffer a 'procompetitive justification' for its conduct, for instance greater efficiency or enhanced consumer appeal. If the justification is not rebutted, the plaintiff must show that the anti-competitive effect outweighs the pro-competitive justification. The court in the *Microsoft* case did not explicitly and clearly address how this balancing exercise is to be performed. However, it said that, for the conduct to be prohibited, the anti-competitive harm resulting from it must outweigh its pro-competitive benefit and that the focus must be on whether the monopolist's conduct on balance harms competition. Because the court defined anti-competitive effect and harm to competition as harm to consumers, it may be inferred that the weighing-up of anti-competitive and pro-competitive effects aims at establishing whether, on balance, consumers are harmed.[29]

The position in other jurisdictions

A number of other jurisdictions adopt other goals which are often said to be compatible with the promotion of consumer welfare and economic efficiency. In Germany and France, for instance, the protection of the competitive process would appear to be a goal in itself, in line with Advocate General Kokott's opinion in the *British Airways* case. In these jurisdictions, the protection of economic freedom also plays an important role as an objective of competition law.[30] Furthermore, Germany regards the protection of small and medium-sized enterprises as a goal of unilateral conduct laws.[31]

Australia, New Zealand, and the Russian Federation regard market integration as an objective of their respective competition laws.[32] In the EU, market integration has also been regarded as an objective of competition law in its own right. However, the Commission appears now to have taken the view that market integration is only relevant insofar as it enhances consumer welfare and promotes an efficient allocation of resources.[33] Some judicial pronouncements, however,

[28] *United States v Microsoft Corp*, 253 F 3d 34, 58–59 (DC Cir 2001).

[29] Ibid.

[30] ICN Report (n 7), Annex A: 'Objectives of Unilateral Conduct Laws Identified in Agency Responses' (ICN Report: Annex A). The Response by the Bundeskartellamt to the ICN Unilateral Conduct Working Group Questionnaire, 2006, suggests that the objective of unilateral conduct rules is the same as the objectives of German competition law more generally (see, in particular, 2). So does the French Response to the ICN Unilateral Conduct Working Group Questionnaire, 2006 (see, in particular, 3 and 4).

[31] ICN Report: Annex A (n 30).

[32] ICN Report: Annex A (n 30).

[33] Article 81(3) Guidelines (n 10), para 13 and DG Competition discussion paper (n 11), para 4.

suggest that market integration is still to be considered an objective in and of itself.[34]

C. The Need for a Unifying Principle

The problem

The review of the objectives of competition law carried out in the previous section shows that often more than one objective is ascribed to competition law in any given jurisdiction. Furthermore, there is no consensus internationally on the main or primary objective of competition law.

The argument is often made that certain objectives of competition law are not incompatible with each other. Therefore, it is entirely legitimate to say that the objective of competition law is to protect the market mechanism in the form of a competitive process. This, in turn, would increase consumer welfare, ensure the efficient allocation of resources, and foster technological progress and innovation.[35] However, the better view appears to be that the protection of the competitive process, total welfare, and consumer welfare may not be always be reconciled or pursued at the same time.

The protection of the 'competitive process'

An objective often assigned to competition law is the protection of the competitive process 'as an institution'.[36]

The protection of the competitive process 'as an institution' raises a preliminary definitional problem because this objective appears to be indeterminate. It is not possible to define what 'competitive process' means in a market context without reference to a further objective.

The 'competitive process' may be defined as a process of rivalry among firms on a given market. However, this definition does not provide a standard for distinguishing between anti-competitive and non-anti-competitive behaviour. Even those who argue that competition law has the objective of protecting the 'competitive process' would agree that it is necessary to introduce a further normative standard in order to establish whether any conduct is anti-competitive.

---

[34] Case C-295/04 *Vincenzo Manfredi v Lloyd Adriatico Assicurazioni SpA* [2006] ECR I-6619, para 38.

[35] ICN Report (n 7), 21–22.

[36] This section discusses whether protection of the 'competitive process' is or should be the objective of competition law. A different point is that the competitive process is the subject matter of the assessment of collusive or unilateral conduct under competition law.

Such a normative standard cannot be the 'competitive process' itself, because this would not take the analysis any further. Therefore, some other objective must be identified, such as the protection of competitors or a total or consumer welfare objective.

In practice, often the protection of the 'competitive process' results in the protection of competitors. Let us assume that a major retailer has confidential information provided to it by a leading branded product supplier and uses it to plan the launch of its own label product.[37] It could be argued that the competitive process has been affected because the retailer exploits an 'unfair advantage'. However, if the retailer is challenging an incumbent monopolist, the result may be increased total and consumer welfare. The decision to prevent the retailer to exploit its advantage, therefore, results in the protection of the branded product supplier. The protection of the competitive process 'as an institution' becomes, essentially, protection of competitors.[38] The protection of competitors is incompatible with a total or consumer welfare objective.

Consumer choice

Another competition law objective that is sometimes cited alongside others is consumer choice. Consumer choice is generally discussed in the context of the consumer welfare objective. However, while generally effective competition enhances consumer welfare, it is difficult to determine how much choice maximizes consumer surplus, all other things being equal. Excessive product differentiation may increase transaction costs for consumers and raise costs for firms trying to gain market share through inefficient advertising and other wasteful strategies. Even if a consumer welfare objective is preferred, the better approach would be to focus on price and output only rather than on 'choice'. An emphasis on choice may lead to competition authorities and courts making qualitative judgments as to how many different products should be on the market. This would almost inevitably lead to very high risk of enforcement errors.[39]

---

37 On this particular concern, see: Report on *The supply of groceries in the UK market: Appendix 9.10* (n 3), para 40.

38 The same analysis applies to concepts such as the protection of 'fair competition' or the protection of 'economic freedom'. Such concepts must be defined in relation to a further standard and are generally used to disguise the protection of competitors.

39 This analysis applies to consumer choice as an objective of competition law in its own right. This chapter attempts to show that the ultimate objective of competition law is maximization of total welfare in the long term. In order to achieve this objective, an enforcement standard that focuses on long term consumer harm is proposed (see: Section E below, 'Total welfare, effective competition and consumer harm as the founded modes of the enforcement standard'). In certain markets where price is not the main driver of competition, it is appropriate to assess the impact of the conduct under review on consumer choice or the rate of innovation rather than on price and output.

More generally, there is no proven correlation between the number and size of the firms on a market and total or consumer welfare.[40]

The idea of consumer choice may also be a disguised form of competitor protection if a competitor is protected because it offers a differentiated product without more. The introduction of own label products may lead to the marginalization and even the elimination of secondary and tertiary brands and, ultimately, to a market where a leading brand competes with retailers' own brands. In such a market there may be less choice in terms of number of available brands but total surplus or consumer surplus (or both) may be larger than in a market with a leading brand and a number of secondary and tertiary brands. Intervention to protect consumer 'choice' could result in the protection of the suppliers of secondary and tertiary brands to the detriment of total or consumer welfare.

Consumer choice is, however, an important element of the consumer welfare assessment in that effective competition that lowers price and output can be expected to deliver the optimal level of product differentiation that consumers value and firms are willing to supply efficiently. Conversely, lack of choice in the form of unmet consumer demand may be evidence of lack of effective competition on the market.

Total or consumer welfare

Economists and, increasingly, a number of competition authorities around the world support a welfare objective as the goal of competition law. On balance, economists appear to prefer a total welfare objective, which gives equal weight to the surplus of producers and consumers in a given industry.[41] Some economists[42] and a majority of competition authorities around the world[43] appear to support a consumer welfare objective, which takes into account only the surplus of consumers.

It is often not clear whether competition authorities adopt a total welfare or a consumer welfare objective in their investigations. In its Report on *The supply of groceries in the UK*, the Competition Commission considered whether the retailers' buyer power prevented, distorted, or restricted competition in relation to the supply of groceries in the UK. The Commission found that, overall, grocery

However, this should be seen as an element of the long term consumer harm standard rather than as an objective of competition law.

40 M Motta, *Competition Policy: Theory and Practice* (2004) 22 and 23.
41 Ibid, 17–22.
42 Salop (n 20).
43 ICN Report (n 7).

retailers' buyer power is of benefit to consumers since part of the lower purchase prices will be passed on to consumers in the form of lower retail prices. The financial viability of food and drink manufacturers was not under threat as a result of the exercise of buyer power by grocery retailers. However, the Commission went on to say that when grocery retailers transfer excessive risks or unexpected costs to their suppliers, this is likely to lessen suppliers' incentives to invest in new capacity, products, and production processes. The Commission concluded that, if unchecked, these practices will ultimately have a detrimental effect on consumers.[44]

In carrying out this assessment, the Commission appears to adopt an overall consumer welfare standard. It is particularly interesting to note that suppliers' decreased profits are only taken into account to the extent that they result in lack of innovation to the detriment of consumers. A total welfare standard could lead to a different conclusion. If, because of the retailer's buyer power, the profits of the suppliers decrease more than the profits of the retailer increase, all other things being equal, this would amount to a restriction of competition. However, the Commission introduces an element of total welfare analysis by looking at the financial viability of suppliers. This assessment suggests that if the price paid to the suppliers is not below the cost of production, total welfare is not affected because any reduced profits of the suppliers simply result in increased profits of the retailers and increased consumer surplus. In other words, the transfer is welfare neutral. Furthermore, by using the adverb 'ultimately', the Commission may be introducing a different time frame in the analysis. Reduced suppliers' profits may be welfare neutral in the short term but, if they result in lack of innovation, they may affect innovation in the long term. Even in the long term, however, the ultimate focus of the analysis is on whether there is likely to be any consumer detriment. As explained below, this approach may be consistent with a total welfare objective even if it applies a consumer harm standard.

D. Normative Analysis

Preliminary conclusions and premises of the further inquiry

The previous section demonstrates that:

(a) it is necessary to identify a primary objective of competition law. Once a primary objective has been identified, other socially desirable goals may also

[44] Report on *The supply of groceries in the UK market* (n 1), para 9.83.

be achieved through competition law but only insofar as they are consistent with the primary objective;

(b) the protection of the competitive process 'as an institution', without more, results in the protection of competitors. This approach may lead to loss of total or consumer welfare;

(c) consumer choice cannot be an objective of competition law in and of itself. However, the choice of products available to the consumers may be part of the evidence of effective competition on the market or lack thereof;

(d) the two strongest candidates for the primary objective of competition law are total and consumer welfare;

(e) the choice between these two objectives is not straightforward. It is unclear why consumer surplus should be valued more than producer surplus. However, competition authorities, including the Competition Commission in its Report on *The supply of groceries in the UK*, seem to focus on consumer detriment although they do not completely disregard producer surplus in the appropriate cases.

This section discusses law from a normative viewpoint, whether the objective of competition law should be total or consumer welfare.

Total welfare

The prevailing view among economists is that competition law should have the objective of preventing conduct that has a negative effect on total welfare. Total welfare may be defined as the sum of consumer surplus plus producer surplus. In conditions of perfect competition, total welfare is maximized. Furthermore, production and consumption are efficient. No possible rearrangement of resources can increase output of one product without reducing the output of at least another product. Buyers place on consuming the product a value equal to its marginal cost of production, and no rearrangement of products among consumers can benefit a consumer without harming at least one other consumer. Unless a clear case is made for attaching more weight to the surplus of some members of the society (for instance, consumers relative to producers), there appears to be a strong argument that competition law should prohibit conduct that reduces total welfare. In this way, firms are spurred towards an outcome that maximizes the welfare of the society as a whole.[45]

[45] The objective of competition law should be total welfare and not allocative efficiency in itself. An allocative efficiency objective would require competition agencies and courts to focus their analysis on whether firms are producing products that are most valued by consumers, whether they are doing so at the lowest possible cost of production, and whether prices tend towards marginal cost.

The total welfare objective, however, if applied as an enforcement standard in a short-term, static framework, may lead to inefficiency and welfare loss in the medium or long term.

A simple example can illustrate this point. Let us assume that the market comprises a leading branded product and strong own label products. Secondary and tertiary brands have been already eliminated or marginalized, so that they do not exercise any effective competitive constraint on the leading branded product supplier and on the own label products. At this stage, major retailers selling own label products may have an incentive to marginalize the leading brand further through unfavourable allocation of shelf space or an unattractive price structure. This behaviour may increase total welfare if the extra sales captured by the own label brands produce higher profits than the sales lost to the leading brand, for instance because the leading brand supplier has higher advertising costs. However, the marginalization or elimination of the leading brand may result in lower total welfare in the long term if the retailers, free from competitive constraints exercised by the leading brand, have lower long-term incentives to reduce their costs and prices further and invest in innovation.

The problem with allowing behaviour that increases market power and total welfare in a market with high entry barriers is that such an approach does not take into account the medium- and long-term benefits of competitive pressure for economic growth. It is necessary, therefore, to introduce a temporal element in the analysis. If a firm is not subject to effective competitive pressure, a short-term increase in total welfare is likely to be outweighed by long-term inefficiency. This is because rent seeking and X-inefficiencies, including lack of innovation, are likely to characterize a monopoly that does not face any credible competitive pressure in the medium or long term.

Consumer welfare

Definition of the consumer welfare objective

As an alternative to total welfare, many commentators argue that the objective of competition law should be to prohibit behaviour that reduces consumer welfare. Firms' behaviour that results in higher prices or lower output reduces consumer surplus. It also brings about allocative inefficiency as, *ceteris paribus*, the decreased consumer surplus is generally greater than the increased profits due to the deadweight loss of market power.

This would be a complex exercise two steps removed from the firms' behaviour on the market. A better approach is to focus on the impact of firms' behaviour on consumer surplus (measured based on price and output on the market). Competition rules that tend to maximize total welfare also bring about allocative efficiency. The latter is, however, an indirect objective in the sense that it is not immediately reflected in the legal tests to be applied by competition authorities and courts.

There are two problems with this approach. The first is that there appears to be no obvious justification for treating the surplus of the consumer of a product differently from the surplus of all other members of the society. The second is that short-term profits may result in long-term investment that increases consumer surplus. This means that to ignore profits in the short term may lead to inefficiency in the long term.

Both points outlined above can be exemplified by looking at a retail market shared by three competing retailers. The retailers all stock the leading branded product and their own label product. There is some weak inter-store own label competition. One retailer decides to delist the leading branded product in order to sell only its own brand. The leading brand supplier will not be able to recapture the lost sales through the other two retailers. Its profits are lower. The increased profits of the delisting retailer are not enough to offset the leading brand supplier's losses. As some, albeit weak, inter-store own label competition takes place, the delisting retailer keeps prices at the previous level in order not to risk losing customers in the short term. Consumer welfare is unaffected. In such a situation, total welfare decreases but consumer welfare is unchanged. Should the delisting be prohibited? If not, what is the justification to disregard the loss of producer surplus? Furthermore, let us assume that the branded product supplier was an innovator and the own label products followed its lead. Let us assume further that the lower profits resulting from the delisting mean that the branded product supplier will not be able to invest in innovation any longer. The incentives to innovate of the retailers are also negatively affected due to lack of effective competitive pressure from the branded product supplier. This is likely to lead to lack of innovation and higher prices in the long term.

The example above shows that, even if consumer welfare is adopted as an objective, it would appear necessary to focus on long-term consumer welfare rather than on a static, short-term analysis that would completely overlook dynamic efficiencies. However, this proposition still does not answer the question whether it is justified to adopt consumer welfare as the objective of competition law.

Income redistribution

The clearest argument favouring consumer welfare instead of total welfare is based on the desirability of redistribution of wealth. While a total welfare objective assumes that wealth transfers are neutral, some argue that wealth transfers should not be seen as welfare neutral but as regressive.[46] Because, the argument

---

46 R Pittman, 'Consumer Surplus as the Appropriate Standard for Antitrust Enforcement' [2007] 3 *Competition Policy International* 205, 207–215.

goes, the income of owners of firms is on average higher than the income of the consumers, a consumer welfare objective would mean that competition law would, on average, bring about a transfer of wealth from higher income individuals with a lower marginal utility of income to lower income individuals with a higher marginal utility of income.[47] This approach generalizes some limited observations relating to the ownership of firms and the burden of market power on consumers to arrive at the determination of the appropriate objective of competition law. It is far from clear that a consumer welfare objective would prevent regressive wealth transfers from lower income consumers to higher income firm owners. To achieve such an objective, competition authorities and courts would have to determine the levels of income of firm owners and consumers in individual cases and make a judgment on the distributional effects of the transfer. This would lead to outcomes that have little to do with competition law as we understand it.

It is true that the proponents of the redistributive consumer welfare standard do not argue that distributional issues should be considered on a case-by-case basis. They argue that redistribution is the rationale for choosing consumer welfare as the objective of competition law.[48] Once the objective has been determined, the case-by-case assessment of firms' conduct will be carried out against a consumer welfare standard without consideration of redistributive issues. This line of reasoning appears to be contradictory because it posits as the rationale for the consumer welfare standard an objective that the consumer welfare standard cannot achieve. If competition authorities and courts are not required to have regard to redistributive issues in individual cases but only to determine whether the conduct under review reduces consumer surplus, all that can be said is that a transfer from consumers to owners of firms is prohibited. It is impossible to say whether the redistribution achieved by applying this standard is from higher income firm owners to lower income consumers or vice versa, or indeed from a certain group of consumers to another group of consumers.

Even if the redistributive objective were a legitimate one, the focus on consumer welfare would be misconceived since consumers often own interests in firms, directly or indirectly, and increased profits result in higher equity yields.[49] The intended distributional outcome would depend on the structure of company ownership. For premium products supplied or sold by firms regularly

47 Ibid, 208.

48 Ibid, 209–210.

49 This argument is discussed and rejected by J Farrell and M L Katz, 'The Economics of Welfare Standards in Antitrust' [2006] Paper CPC06-061, Institute of Business and Economic Research, Competition Policy Center (University of California, Berkeley), 12.

distributing high dividends and owned by low income investors, a producer surplus rather than a consumer surplus standard would be appropriate to achieve distributional goals.

Assuming that redistribution of wealth is a desirable objective, there appears to be a strong argument for pursuing this objective across society in a principled way and not through competition law. Other policy frameworks such as taxation or social policy may take into account and weigh up the factors that are relevant to redistributive objectives more efficiently than competition law may do.[50]

Imperfections in corporate governance

Another argument in favour of consumer welfare over total welfare is that, because of imperfections in corporate governance, part of the profits of the firms is dissipated by management in their own interests.[51] This argument carries some weight but cannot be generalized. Even in the presence of dissipation of profits, it is highly likely that part of the profits will also be distributed to shareholders or reinvested. In order to account for managerial dissipation of profits, competition authorities and courts would have to undertake a case-by-case analysis of the managerial performance of the firms under investigation. Otherwise, a competition policy that weighed consumer surplus more than producer surplus because of managerial dissipation of profits would penalize efficient corporate governance structures and effective shareholder supervision. Arguably, the problem of managerial dissipation of profits is best addressed at the level of the company by designing an appropriate framework for corporate governance and supervision of managers. Corporate governance rules rather than competition law are the appropriate tool for addressing imperfections in corporate governance.

Enforcement efficiency and institutional capability arguments

It is also argued that a consumer welfare standard is easier to administer and allows for simpler monitoring of the outcomes achieved through competition law intervention.[52] A variant of this argument is based on the need for a standard that competition authorities and courts are capable of applying (an institutional capability argument). The short-term impact on price and output is easier to assess, both ex ante and ex post, than the impact on total welfare or on consumer welfare in the medium or long term.

50 Social policy makers, whether the legislature or public officials, would be able to consider the specific features of the distributional issue to be addressed and tailor the policy to the need in question, which may change over time, even quite rapidly. Distributional choices, furthermore, require political judgments that competition authorities and courts should not be required to make.

51 Farrell and Katz (n 49) 12.

52 Salop (n 20) 22–23.

To the extent that it attempts to answer the question of objective of competition law, this argument addresses the problem from the wrong end. What is required is to identify the appropriate objective of competition law and then, based on such an objective, design an enforcement standard that is administrable. It would be absurd to identify an administrable enforcement standard first and then elevate it to the objective of competition law because it is an administrable standard. Arguments based on the need for an administrable standard that competition authorities and courts are capable of applying relate to the enforcement standard and not to the objective of competition law.

E. Consumer Harm as Effective Standard to Achieve a Total Welfare Objective

From the objective to the enforcement standard

The previous analysis suggests that the appropriate objective of competition law is the maximization of total welfare in the long term. None of the arguments in favour of consumer welfare as an objective in itself are compelling. In particular, competition law should disregard distributional concerns.

The identification of maximization of the long-term welfare of society as the objective of competition law does not automatically mean that the enforcement standard competition authorities and courts should apply is a total welfare standard. It may be that a focus on long-term consumer harm may provide a workable enforcement standard that ensures that total welfare is maximized in the long term. This would be consistent with the approach of a number of competition authorities around the world that focus on the effect of behaviour on price and output but do not disregard increased profits insofar as they are passed on to consumers at some point. As discussed above, this approach was adopted by the Competition Commission in the Report on *The supply of groceries in the UK*, where the Commission focused on the effect that retailers' market power and own label products have on the price of groceries to consumers[53] but also examined the impact of retailers' practices on innovation.[54]

53 See, for instance: Report on *The supply of groceries in the UK market* (n 1), paras 9.1–9.5. At para 9.3, the Commission says: 'While we do not need to identify specific harm to the interests of customers in order to find an AEC, we will be more confident of an AEC finding where the feature, or combination of features, adversely affects the interests of present or future customers.'

54 Report on *The supply of groceries in the UK market investigation: Appendix 9.10* (n 3), paras 38–44.

This section discusses the justifications for choosing long-term consumer harm as the enforcement standard both from a political economy and from an incentives analysis viewpoint.

Self-selection, information asymmetry, and lobbying

Optimal objective and optimal standard

The debate about the appropriate economic welfare standard in competition law has focused on the merits of attaching more weight to consumer surplus than to producer surplus as a means of maximizing total welfare. Arguments cited in favour of a consumer welfare standard are self-selection, information asymmetry, biases in the decision-making process, and lobbying by firms. These arguments do not rely on redistribution in order to set consumer surplus as the objective of competition law. Rather, under these models, it is accepted that total welfare should be the ultimate objective of competition law. However, certain political economy models suggest that consumer surplus may be a better standard to achieve the intended outcome of preventing conduct that reduces total welfare in the long term. The economic literature focuses mainly on mergers. However, it provides insights into the relative merit of different standards more generally.

Self-selection

Lyons argues that a total welfare standard for individual mergers is unlikely to maximize total welfare.[55] Competition authorities can only assess mergers that are proposed by firms. Firms propose the most profitable private merger that would be approved. Under a total welfare standard, firms would propose less socially desirable mergers than under a consumer welfare standard. The basic assumption on which the argument relies is that the economic conditions and market structures are such that there is a sufficient range of merger opportunities that allow comparable efficiencies to be realized with different market power outcomes. Under a consumer welfare standard, firms will propose mergers that allow comparable efficiencies to be realized but with a lower market power increase. As a result, the merger proposed is socially better than the merger that would be proposed under a total welfare standard.

By way of a critique of Lyons' argument, Farrell and Katz show that a consumer surplus standard may also lead to lower total surplus than a total welfare

55 B Lyons, 'Could Politicians Be More Rights than Economists? A Theory of Merger Standards' [2002] Revised CCR Working Paper CCR 02-1, Centre for Competition and Regulation (University of East Anglia, Norwich).

standard.[56] This is intuitive in circumstances in which the firms face a set of opportunities that increase market power but realize significant productive efficiencies that are unlikely to be passed on to consumers in full. A consumer surplus standard may force firms to choose a sub-optimal course of conduct.

The insight provided by this model is that competition law is concerned with the assessment of the conduct of firms and not with the design of first best solutions. It can be assumed that firms will choose a course of conduct which is profitable. It makes sense, therefore, to impose on them the obligation to choose the course of conduct that, while still profitable (otherwise firms will simply do nothing), is the least harmful to consumer welfare or, to put it another way, results in the least increase in market power. On average, it may be that such a policy is likely to perform better in maximizing total welfare in the long term than a policy requiring a total welfare assessment in individual cases.

Asymmetric information

Besanko and Spulber propose a model showing that, under asymmetric information, expected social welfare is maximized when the decision maker applies a standard that is tougher than the social welfare standard.[57] A welfare standard that gives relatively more weight to consumer surplus moves the equilibrium enforcement outcome closer to the first-best solution.

Under this model, a total welfare standard gives the competition authority the incentive to clear all mergers. In other words, the competition authority strongly prefers avoiding false positive errors. A standard that gives more weight to consumer surplus introduces a bias in favour of false positive errors that counterbalances the bias in favour of non-intervention that is inherent in the adoption of a total welfare standard.[58]

This model has been criticized for assuming that the decision maker cannot commit to a given enforcement standard.[59] Furthermore, in this model the merger reduces marginal cost but the effect of increased market power is ignored.[60] However, this was one of the earliest studies demonstrating that, at least in certain circumstances, there may be biases in the decision-making process that can be counterbalanced by adopting a consumer surplus standard.

---

56 Farrell and Katz (n 49) 18.

57 D Besanko and D F Spulber, 'Contested Mergers and Equilibrium in Antitrust Policy' [1993] 9 *The Journal of Law, Economics, and Organisations* 1.

58 Ibid, 16–19.

59 Farrell and Katz (n 49) 22.

60 Farrell and Katz (n 49) 22.

System-level models

Other models have focused on the biases inherent in the institutional structure. Farrell and Katz discuss a system-level perspective that gives weight to biases arising in the decision-making process leading to a merger prohibition.[61] If in any stage of the decision-making process there is a bias towards producer surplus, then it makes sense to introduce a bias towards consumer surplus in another stage so as to move the ultimate outcome closer to the first-best. Pittman reaches a similar conclusion by analysing the structure of the Antitrust Division of the US Department of Justice. He identifies a bias against enforcement action which could be counterbalanced by a tougher enforcement standard, which the author argues should be the consumer surplus standard.[62]

Lobbying

Neven and Röller discuss the optimal standard in merger review in a model in which merging firms and competitors engage in lobbying but consumers do not.[63] They find that neither a consumer welfare nor a total welfare standard performs better in all or even in most circumstances. However, their model tends to suggest that lobbying by firms introduces a potential bias in the decision-making process. If the decision maker is subject to perfect monitoring, this eliminates the bias, and the best standard would appear to be total welfare. If, however, monitoring is not perfect, the function of the decision maker is more likely to lead to the first best if a consumer surplus bias is introduced. The size of mergers also plays a role as firms are willing to invest more in lobbying for larger mergers. Therefore, if the average size of mergers is large, a consumer welfare standard may perform better.[64]

Consumer welfare as optimal standard to achieve total welfare maximization?

None of the models discussed above is capable of providing conclusive proof that a consumer welfare standard is optimal in achieving a total welfare objective in all or most circumstances. Nor have these models been applied to competition between branded consumer products and own label products. However, the fundamental idea that the optimal standard to be applied by the decision maker may not be the same as the ultimate objective of the law is correct. Furthermore, the observation that there are biases in the system induced by the firms' advantage in self-selecting the behaviour to be reviewed by competition authorities and

61 Farrell and Katz (n 49) 22.

62 Pittman (n 46) 219–223.

63 D J Neven and L-H Röller, 'Consumer Surplus vs. Welfare Standard in a Political Economy Model of Merger Control' [2005] 23 *International Journal of Industrial Organization* 829.

64 Ibid, 846–847.

courts, asymmetric information, and lobbying is empirically and intuitively correct. The models analysed in this section, while not conclusive, provide support for an enforcement standard biased towards consumer surplus.

Total welfare, effective competition, and consumer harm as the founded modes of the enforcement standard

The key elements of the standard

The preceding analysis supports the following three propositions that may be adopted as founded modes of the competition enforcement standard:

1. Maximizing total welfare in the long term is the objective of competition law.
2. There are many policies that contribute to achieving this objective, including taxation, industrial policy, and employment policy. Competition law aims at maximizing total welfare in the long term by prohibiting firms from acting strategically to eliminate (or reduce) the competitive pressure that other firms exert on them.
3. In order to determine whether total welfare is likely to be reduced in the long term as a result of elimination of competition, it may be appropriate to focus on the short-, medium-, or long-term impact of the conduct under review on price, output, or innovation.

Proposition 1 has been demonstrated in the previous sections. Proposition 2 is intuitive and expresses the specificity of competition law as a set of principles and rules concerned with the competitive process as the spur for societal welfare maximization. It is necessary to expand on proposition 3.

The focus on price, output, and innovation

It follows from proposition 2 that long-term total welfare is maximized if firms are subject to effective competitive pressure. Competitive pressure gives firms the incentives to lower price, expand output, and innovate. A short-term total welfare test that disregarded the incentives to behave efficiently would risk jeopardizing maximizing societal welfare in the long term.

It follows from propositions 1 and 2 that the constitutive elements of the test must be the elimination of effective competitive pressure and the reduction of total welfare in the long term.

The first constitutive element of the test is the elimination of effective competitive pressure. In order to determine whether the conduct under review eliminates effective competitive pressure, it is appropriate to focus on the effect of the conduct on price, output, and innovation. If, as a result of the conduct under review, price and output are unaffected (or increase), there is a strong presumption that firms continue to be subject to effective competitive pressure that forces them to pass to their customers any increased profits resulting from harm to competitors. The focus on price, output, and innovation distinguishes between harm to competitors and harm to competition.

The second constitutive element of the test is the reduction of total welfare in the long term. Total welfare analysis requires that the profits of the industry be taken into account and be given the same weight as consumer surplus. However, increased profits may be the result of efficient competition and lead to productive and dynamic efficiencies, or may be a market power rent and lead to reduced total welfare through higher prices, X-inefficiencies, and lack of innovation. In the same way, reduced profits may reflect inferior market performance or may be the result of strategic behaviour by other firms that reduces total welfare in the long term. A static, total welfare analysis would simply require aggregating all the profits and consumer surplus in the industry under review before and after the conduct. However, this approach would disregard the analysis of the firms' incentives to compete and their long-term welfare implications. In order to determine whether increased or decreased profits result in a long-term total welfare reduction, it is appropriate to focus on the impact of increased or reduced profits on price, output, and innovation. If price, output, or innovation is not likely to be affected in the long term, any increased profits of certain firms or reduced profits of other firms are likely to be simply the result of healthy competitive market dynamics. If, however, price, output, or innovation is likely to be negatively affected in the long term, increased profits are likely to be an inefficient market power rent and reduced profits are likely to be the result of strategic elimination of competition that reduces total welfare in the long term.

In conclusion, the competition enforcement standard proposed prohibits conduct that reduces or eliminates effective competitive pressure and, as a result, is likely to cause appreciable consumer harm in the long term. This standard adopts a consumer harm focus principally because this allows for a robust analysis of the firms' incentives to compete in the long term and not on political economy grounds. However, this approach is also consistent with the political economy literature discussed in Section E above (the discussion on 'Self-selection, information asymmetry, and lobbying') and with the enforcement efficiency and institutional capability critique discussed in Section D above (the discussion on 'Enforcement efficiency and institutional capability arguments').

Two potential objections to the proposed standard

Before providing some examples of the application of the proposed standard to scenarios of competition between branded products and own label products, it may be helpful briefly to address two potential objections to the standard in question.

The first objection could be that a long-term analysis is too complex, burdensome, and speculative. It is likely to lead to errors and inconsistencies. Competition authorities and courts should (and generally do) focus on a short-term analysis, typically two years maximum. We have already discussed throughout this chapter why a short-term analysis is unsatisfactory. It is worth stressing here that the proposed standard does not require competition authorities and courts to calculate, or speculate on, the levels of producer and consumer surplus in the medium and long term. The long-term effects of the conduct under review are captured by the analysis of its impact on the firms' incentives to compete. Let us assume that the profits of the leading brand supplier are being eroded by retailers concerned about strengthening their own label products through their in-store shelving and pricing strategies. It is generally possible to infer based on past and current market data:

(a) whether the main effective competitive pressure on own label products is exercised by the leading brand supplier or there are other effective competitive constraints on own label products (e.g. competition between retailers);
(b) whether innovation is driven by the leading brand supplier or by own label products;
(c) whether, given past history of expenditure on R & D, current market trends, and experience in comparable industries, the decreasing profits of the leading brand supplier will lead to less innovation on its part;
(d) whether barriers to entry are high.

The evaluation of these factors allows a competition authority or court to assess whether the conduct under review is likely to have an appreciable negative effect on price, output, or innovation in the long term. This assessment is likely to be carried out in two stages. First, the focus is on the short-term impact of the conduct. Second, if appropriate, the medium- and long-term impact of the conduct is taken into account based on the analysis of the firms' incentives to behave efficiently given the competitive pressure they are likely to face. Furthermore, not all cases require a long-term analysis. Given the characteristics of the industry and the evidence available, competition authorities and courts will define the appropriate analytical timeframe bearing in mind that, ultimately, what counts is long-term total welfare maximization. Finally, the longer the timeframe of the analysis, the higher the evidential standard required of the authority or party bearing the legal burden of proof.

The second objection to the proposed standard could be that it reintroduces an element of competitor protection because it requires that the decreased profits of competitors be taken into account. However, the reduced profits of competitors are only relevant if they result in a negative effect on price, output, and innovation in an appropriately defined timeframe (short, medium, or long term). The focus is, therefore, on ensuring that firms do not behave strategically to harm competitors that provide effective competitive pressure, thus increasing total welfare in the long term. The focus on consumer harm also ensures, from a political economy viewpoint, that a counter-bias is introduced to guard against the risk of regulatory capture and competitor protection.

F. Application of the Proposed Standard to the Assessment of the Competitive Effects of Own Label Products

The proposed standard can be usefully applied to assess the impact on competition of the introduction and growth of own label products. The increased commercial power that own label products confer on retailers vis-à-vis branded product suppliers is assessed based on the impact on downstream prices, output, and innovation. Own label products may challenge the dominant position of a leading brand. This is likely to result in increased consumer surplus in the short term. Therefore, there is a strong presumption that the conduct under review does not eliminate or reduce effective competitive pressure. On the contrary, the increase in consumer surplus shows that competition in the industry becomes more effective as a result of the introduction or growth of own label products. The long-term incentives to compete and innovate are also likely to be enhanced. The behaviour under review is not likely to cause appreciable long-term consumer harm.

If own label products significantly increase a retailer's buyer power vis-à-vis branded product suppliers with no or lower market power, the competition analysis becomes more complex. Under the proposed standard, the focus is on short-, medium-, and long-term consumer harm. The focus on consumer harm discriminates between benign negotiation of lower purchase prices and welfare-reducing exercise of buyer power. *Ceteris paribus*, if the exercise of buyer power does not induce output reductions, lower purchase prices are unlikely to reduce total welfare in the long term. The Competition Commission in its Report on *The supply of groceries in the UK market* appears to address the question of output reduction when it considers whether the financial viability of suppliers is threatened.[65] The Commission applies a test of financial viability of the supplier. It may be argued that this test is appropriate because if a supplier continues to sell on the

[65] Report on *The supply of groceries in the UK market* (n 1) 9.23–9.27, dealing with buyer power generally.

market, the price it charges is still above its production costs. Any exercise of buyer power, therefore, is not likely to be welfare-reducing. It is worth noting that, even on a total welfare analysis, the focus on price and output downstream is appropriate because any upstream output reduction is likely to result in lower output and higher prices downstream. Suppliers may exit the market because they are inefficient or because they are forced to exit by sub-competitive purchase prices. The focus on downstream price and output discriminates between these two situations because if downstream price and output are unaffected, it means that other suppliers have found it profitable either to expand output or to enter the market.

The exercise of buyer power may be detrimental to total welfare not only if it leads to an output reduction but also if it leads to lack of innovation in the long term. If the suppliers' incentives to innovate are negatively affected, they will be exercising a less effective competitive constraint on retailers' own label products. Retailers may in turn have lower incentives to innovate. This would depend on the intensity of competition among retailers themselves. The Competition Commission in its Report on *The supply of groceries in the UK market* discussed the levels of innovation in the industry and found that there was no evidence of declining levels of expenditure in R & D.[66] This approach is consistent with a long-term total welfare objective. However, the assessment focused on consumer harm because industry profits are not considered relevant in themselves but only insofar as they result in innovation that benefits consumers.

The position of the retailer as a customer, the owner and provider of shelf space, and competitor may also lead to distortions of competition that cause long-term consumer harm and, thus, are likely to lower total welfare in the long term. Own label copycat products, control on allocation of shelf space and in-store prices, and buyer power may have a negative impact on the suppliers' incentives to innovate in the long term. If this is the case, long-term consumer surplus may be appreciably reduced and intervention may be justified. This is particularly true if the leading brand supplier was the main driver of competition and innovation on the market, there is no effective competition between retailers' own label products, and barriers to entry are high.

66 Report on *The supply of groceries in the UK market* (n 1) paras 9.72–9.77, dealing specifically with own label products. See also: Report on *The supply of groceries in the UK market: Appendix 9.10* (n 3) paras 38–44.

G. Conclusion

The dynamics of competition between branded products and own label products call for a re-examination of the objective and the standard of competition law. This chapter questioned the view that competition law should seek to protect the 'competitive process' or competition 'as an institution'. It also questioned the view that the maximization of consumer welfare should be the objective of competition law. There is no convincing argument for valuing the surplus of the consumer any higher than the surplus of any other member of the society.

The objective of competition law is the maximization of total welfare in the long term. In order to ensure that this is achieved, competition law relies on the assumption, which attracts considerable consensus as a general proposition, that effective competitive pressure spurs firms to behave efficiently and innovate. In order to achieve the maximization of long-term total welfare, competition law relies on an enforcement standard that focuses on whether firms' behaviour causes appreciable consumer harm in the long term. The profits of the firms in a given industry are relevant insofar as they are passed on to the consumers, at least in part and in the long term. The 'passing on' element of the standard ensures that the standard only prohibits behaviour that eliminates effective competitive pressure and that, if efficiencies are realised at the expense of increased market power, effective competitive pressure continues to provide the firms with the incentive to behave efficiently and innovate in the long term. The elimination of effective competitive pressure is likely to lead to X-inefficiencies, rent seeking, and lack of innovation that harm total welfare and productivity in the long term even if on a static, short-term analysis total welfare increases at the expense of consumer surplus.

More research is needed to explore the normative implications of the proposed standard and its application to different types of conduct and within given positive legal frameworks. These questions are beyond the scope of his chapter. However, Section F above discussed how the proposed standard may be applied to scenarios of competition between branded products and own label products. The Competition Commission in its Report on *The supply of groceries in the UK* has given own label products a clean bill of health. The Commission's assessment is consistent with the analytical framework proposed in this chapter, although it fails to articulate it clearly. The Commission's conclusion, however, depends on the persisting strength of branded product suppliers and on healthy competition among retailers. In the future, retailers' behaviour having the effect of marginalizing or eliminating leading brand suppliers and collusion among retailers are likely to give rise to significant competition concerns.

INDEX